I0890860

Transforming Corporate Governance and Developing Models for Board Effectiveness

Qaiser Rafique Yasser
Centre for Rural Economy, Pakistan

Abdullah Al-Mamun
University of Wollongong, Australia

A volume in the Advances in Logistics, Operations, and Management Science (ALOMS) Book Series

IGI Global
PUBLISHER of TIMELY KNOWLEDGE

Published in the United States of America by
IGI Global
Business Science Reference (an imprint of IGI Global)
701 E. Chocolate Avenue
Hershey PA, USA 17033
Tel: 717-533-8845
Fax: 717-533-8661
E-mail: cust@igi-global.com
Web site: http://www.igi-global.com

Copyright © 2021 by IGI Global. All rights reserved. No part of this publication may be reproduced, stored or distributed in any form or by any means, electronic or mechanical, including photocopying, without written permission from the publisher.
Product or company names used in this set are for identification purposes only. Inclusion of the names of the products or companies does not indicate a claim of ownership by IGI Global of the trademark or registered trademark.

Library of Congress Cataloging-in-Publication Data

Names: Yasser, Qaiser Rafique, 1983- editor. | Al-Manum, Abdullah, 1984- editor.
Title: Transforming corporate governance and developing models for board effectiveness / Qaiser Rafique Yasser and Abdullah Al-Manum, editors.
Description: Hershey, PA : Business Science Reference, [2021] | Includes bibliographical references and index. | Summary: "With corporate governance as the system by which companies are directed and controlled, this book discusses different theories for boards of directors that are responsible for the governance of their companies and their practices around the globe"-- Provided by publisher.
Identifiers: LCCN 2020026781 (print) | LCCN 2020026782 (ebook) | ISBN 9781799866695 (hardcover) | ISBN 9781799866701 (paperback) | ISBN 9781799866718 (ebook)
Subjects: LCSH: Corporate governance. | Boards of directors.
Classification: LCC HD2741 .T6695 2021 (print) | LCC HD2741 (ebook) | DDC 658.4/22--dc23
LC record available at https://lccn.loc.gov/2020026781
LC ebook record available at https://lccn.loc.gov/2020026782

This book is published in the IGI Global book series Advances in Logistics, Operations, and Management Science (ALOMS) (ISSN: 2327-350X; eISSN: 2327-3518)

British Cataloguing in Publication Data
A Cataloguing in Publication record for this book is available from the British Library.

All work contributed to this book is new, previously-unpublished material.
The views expressed in this book are those of the authors, but not necessarily of the publisher.

For electronic access to this publication, please contact: eresources@igi-global.com.

Advances in Logistics, Operations, and Management Science (ALOMS) Book Series

ISSN:2327-350X
EISSN:2327-3518

Editor-in-Chief: John Wang, Montclair State University, USA

MISSION

Operations research and management science continue to influence business processes, administration, and management information systems, particularly in covering the application methods for decision-making processes. New case studies and applications on management science, operations management, social sciences, and other behavioral sciences have been incorporated into business and organizations real-world objectives.

The **Advances in Logistics, Operations, and Management Science** (ALOMS) Book Series provides a collection of reference publications on the current trends, applications, theories, and practices in the management science field. Providing relevant and current research, this series and its individual publications would be useful for academics, researchers, scholars, and practitioners interested in improving decision making models and business functions.

COVERAGE

- Networks
- Finance
- Computing and information technologies
- Information Management
- Decision analysis and decision support
- Marketing engineering
- Production Management
- Operations Management
- Risk Management
- Political Science

IGI Global is currently accepting manuscripts for publication within this series. To submit a proposal for a volume in this series, please contact our Acquisition Editors at Acquisitions@igi-global.com or visit: http://www.igi-global.com/publish/.

The Advances in Logistics, Operations, and Management Science (ALOMS) Book Series (ISSN 2327-350X) is published by IGI Global, 701 E. Chocolate Avenue, Hershey, PA 17033-1240, USA, www.igi-global.com. This series is composed of titles available for purchase individually; each title is edited to be contextually exclusive from any other title within the series. For pricing and ordering information please visit http://www.igi-global.com/book-series/advances-logistics-operations-management-science/37170. Postmaster: Send all address changes to above address. Copyright © 2021 IGI Global. All rights, including translation in other languages reserved by the publisher. No part of this series may be reproduced or used in any form or by any means – graphics, electronic, or mechanical, including photocopying, recording, taping, or information and retrieval systems – without written permission from the publisher, except for non commercial, educational use, including classroom teaching purposes. The views expressed in this series are those of the authors, but not necessarily of IGI Global.

Titles in this Series

For a list of additional titles in this series, please visit:
http://www.igi-global.com/book-series/advances-logistics-operations-management-science/37170

Encyclopedia of Organizational Knowledge, Administration, and Technology
Mehdi Khosrow-Pour D.B.A. (Information Resources Management Association, USA)
Business Science Reference • © 2021 • 2734pp • H/C (ISBN: 9781799834731) • US $3,950.00

Corporate Leadership and Its Role in Shaping Organizational Culture and Performance
Azza Bejaoui (High Institute of Management of Tunis, Tunisia)
Business Science Reference • © 2021 • 350pp • H/C (ISBN: 9781522582663) • US $195.00

Demand Forecasting and Order Planning in Supply Chains and Humanitarian Logistics
Atour Taghipour (Normandy University, France)
Business Science Reference • © 2021 • 313pp • H/C (ISBN: 9781799838050) • US $195.00

Interdisciplinary Perspectives on Operations Management and Service Evaluation
Panagiotis Manolitzas (Ionian University, Greece) Constantin Zopounidis (Technical University of Crete, Greece) Michael Talias (Open University of Cyprus, Cyprus) Evangelos Grigoroudis (Technical University of Crete, Greece) and Nikolaos Matsatsinis (Technical University of Crete, Greece)
Business Science Reference • © 2021 • 401pp • H/C (ISBN: 9781799854425) • US $195.00

Agile Leadership Methods for Industry 4.0
Bülent Akkaya (Manisa Celal Bayar University, Turkey)
Business Science Reference • © 2021 • 300pp • H/C (ISBN: 9781799842941) • US $195.00

Relating Information Culture to Information Policies and Management Strategies
Denise A.D. Bedford (Georgetown University, USA) and Wioleta Kucharska (Gdańsk University of Technology, Poland)
Business Science Reference • © 2021 • 314pp • H/C (ISBN: 9781799843153) • US $175.00

For an entire list of titles in this series, please visit:
http://www.igi-global.com/book-series/advances-logistics-operations-management-science/37170

IGI Global
PUBLISHER of TIMELY KNOWLEDGE

701 East Chocolate Avenue, Hershey, PA 17033, USA
Tel: 717-533-8845 x100 • Fax: 717-533-8661
E-Mail: cust@igi-global.com • www.igi-global.com

Table of Contents

Detailed Table of Contents

The structure and composition of the board are determined by the characteristics of an organisation, its environment, and its information needs. If the role of the board is to advise and supervise, this then talks to the relationships that account for its composition so that it may carry out these duties. Boards of directors are now faced with a change in the priority of the functions that must be undertaken by them, with supervision and monitoring being more important than the usual function of administration. The chapter discusses the literature on board diversity, corporate governance, role of the boards of public entities, effectiveness of boards, role of board committees, strategic leadership theory, and the impact of board diversity on board effectiveness. In terms of practical implications, the chapter makes a unique and significant contribution to the functionality of board members in South Africa. The analysis may encourage board nomination committees to seek board diversity beyond the gender and ethnic characteristics of directors.

Corporate governance is a significant tool to build strong and long relationships among various stakeholders in kinds of business organizations. Family businesses are not an exception to this. Like any other businesses, family businesses also need to have governance in place and practice to achieve the business strategies and to have long-term succession. Family-owned businesses are the backbone of many countries' economies in the world contributing substantial portion of GDP. Considering these, it is important to know the best practices of governance in family owned business

is because of a better understating by the family in having a strategic approach to risk management. Therefore, all the more important to have the right governance conditions in place which reflects the positive aspects of family ownership. The author further states that in order achieve the said perspectives, there emanates a need for a design structure of governance to have a balance between family and business. Hence, it becomes all the more vital to define family values and have the involvement of each and every family member. The author further elucidates on the fact that it becomes imperative to improvise capital and ensure a proper leadership succession planning so that business continuity does not suffer.

This chapter looks at the concept of corporate social responsibility (CSR), specifically in terms of the diverse definitions and perspectives of it that currently exist within emerging economies. This is explored from its foundation and the interaction between business and society across different emerging economies. This discourse is linked to the interplay between corporate governance and corporate social responsibility across emerging economies. This is hinged on the influences of both the academia and industry, as the definitions of the former does contribute to the practical application of the concept by practitioners and vice versa. The chapter is divided into three sections, which are definitions, perspectives, and case studies, with each of these focusing on the issues as they affect the theme of the chapter.

Gender diversity is a new and challenging issue of research in business. Women on boards are a heavily discussed topic in developed countries, though this issue has recently appeared to gain the attention of researchers in developing economies as well. However, research on gender diversity in Malaysia is limited. This study aims to examine whether female directors on boards can affect firm performance based on selected public listed companies in Malaysia. In examining the effect of gender diversity on firm performance, Pearson correlation coefficient and regression analysis tests are employed using economic value added (EVA) as a measurement tool. This study found no relationship between gender diversity and firm performance. Given this, future studies should try to consider other aspects of corporate governance.

This chapter analyzes the connection between CEO hubris and corporate governance contingencies, including a case study of an Italian bank for which the state of financial distress shall be linkable also to bad governance. The main objective is to verify whether, in presence of hubristic CEO, the internal control mechanisms, set to ensure the board vigilance and limit the overconfidence of the leader, are implemented, and if so, whether such mechanisms, even when formally respected, may be not so appropriate to guarantee a good governance. Particularly, the existence of a CEO hubris could neutralize their positive expected balancing effects on the power dynamics between CEO and board, such as to give prevalence to substance over form. Therefore, it may occur that some governance mechanisms (e.g., independence, non-duality), even if formally implemented, are unable to stem the managerial entrenchment of the CEO, who succeeds in enhancing immoderately his substantial power in the decision-making process.

The last few decades have witnessed serious sustainability challenges such as economic uncertainty, depletion ozone layer, increase in pollution, urban decay, overpopulation, degradation, and shortage of natural resources, etc. The increasing pace of change and rising competition has posed unknown challenges and unparalleled pressure on the corporates not only to prosper, but also to sustain in future. With customers, investors, and other stakeholders becoming increasing aware and critical about sustainable practices, the companies are forced to think past short term monetary gains. As there exists an interdependence, integration, and co-creation among the three basic tenets of sustainability-people, planet, and profits. There is a global call on companies to pursue socially responsible conduct and adopt innovative practices which create value for people, planet, as well as economy.

The concept of governance is as old as human civilization. However, recently the usage of this term has increased multifarious. A broader concept of corporate governance involves a set of relationships amongst the organization's stakeholders. A stakeholder is any person, organization, social group, or society at large that has a stake in the business. Recognizing the importance of corporate governance, most of the countries in the world have developed their own corporate governance mechanism known as corporate governance models. The mechanism of corporate governance depends upon various indigenous factors such as legal framework, regulatory framework, the pattern of shareholding, breadth, and depth of financial markets.

In the wake of corporate scandals in major companies like Enron, Tyco, and East Asian crisis have emphasized the need of sufficient number of independent directors on the board for proper oversight and functioning of the company. Code of corporate governance recommends the presence of independent directors for better performance of the company. As board independence ensured good corporate governance practices, it is considered that having independent directors on the board is not for better performance but for better governance. In seeking reasonable answer for these arguments, the purpose of this study is to review some of the literature of board independence with respect to corporate governance theories specifically agency theory, stewardship, and resource dependency theory. All these theories have provided mixed evidences in different studies about the impact and importance of board independence and reason behind these mixed evidences might be the institutional context of different organizations in different countries.

Diverse boards have been seen as providing impetus for initiating change. This study focuses on the relationship between female representation on boards of directors and its effect on firm performance, based on evidence from the Thailand. The authors use empirical data on SET 100 Index firms observed in 2015 to 2019. The result indicate that at least one female director in the board is associated with the firm financial performance, while the female CEO/Chairman or higher percentage of females in board having no firm performance association.

For a sample of listed Portuguese and Spanish firms from 2010 to 2018, this study draws on audit pricing, substitution, signaling, and complementary theories to evaluate the impact of conservatism accounting on audit fees. Using fixed effects technique, the author finds a positive relationship between conservatism accounting and audit fees. The results suggest that firms with more conservative accounting (with strong internal corporate governance) could be more likely to demand high-quality audit to strengthen investor confidence in financial information and, thus pay higher audit fees. Therefore, this study supports signaling and complementary theories. The results also suggest that Big 4, growth, firm size, and leverage are positively related with audit fees. To Spain, audit risk and ROA are also positively related with audit fees.

Corporate governance, the soul of every corporate body, is indispensable for the survival, growth, and development of any kind of organization. It has significant impact and influence in attaining the confidence of stakeholder. Good governance leads to instill the confidence of stakeholder. The significance of corporate governance has increased globally in past decades due to financial crises, technology advancement, liberalizations, emergence of financial markets, and liberalization of trade and capital mobilization. Corporate boards, academicians, legislators, and in all businesses, corporate governance are believed to be a mainstream concern in corporate structure.

Preface

Good corporate governance contributes to sustainable economic development by enhancing the performance of companies and increasing their access to outside capital as well. In emerging markets good corporate governance serves a number of public policy objectives. It eases vulnerability of the financial crises, reinforcement property rights; reduces transaction cost and cost of capital and leads to capital market development. Corporate governance concerns the relationship among the management, board of directors, controlling shareholders, minority shareholders and other stakeholders. To operate successfully, a firm needs a competent corporate governance structure. Over time, if a firm finds its existing corporate governance mechanisms insufficient to guarantee good performance, it will develop an intention to improve it.

Various aspects of potential conflict of interest between corporate governance managers and dispersed shareholders when managers do not have an ownership interest in the firm. There is an incentive for the manager to adopt that investment and financing policies that benefit him, but reduce the payoff to outside stockholders. An offset cost is that with larger shareholders the manager may become entrenched, and immune to other forms of discipline. A particular form of entrenchment that might be important in emerging markets is that the manger could become resistant to monitoring by a large outside shareholder.

Previous studies consider board of directors' decision-making as vital to the organization, especially because they meet only few times in the year to discuss for important decisions. They argue that it is difficult to describe generic characteristics of effective board because there are many contingency factors which influence board process. Thus, the complement of many elements from different levels of analysis and factors could reflect board process of creating outcomes.

Chapter 1
Board Diversity and Its Effects on the Functionality of Boards in South Africa

Thokozani Ian Nzimakwe
University of KwaZulu-Natal, South Africa

ABSTRACT

The structure and composition of the board are determined by the characteristics of an organisation, its environment, and its information needs. If the role of the board is to advise and supervise, this then talks to the relationships that account for its composition so that it may carry out these duties. Boards of directors are now faced with a change in the priority of the functions that must be undertaken by them, with supervision and monitoring being more important than the usual function of administration. The chapter discusses the literature on board diversity, corporate governance, role of the boards of public entities, effectiveness of boards, role of board committees, strategic leadership theory, and the impact of board diversity on board effectiveness. In terms of practical implications, the chapter makes a unique and significant contribution to the functionality of board members in South Africa. The analysis may encourage board nomination committees to seek board diversity beyond the gender and ethnic characteristics of directors.

DOI: 10.4018/978-1-7998-6669-5.ch001

Copyright © 2021, IGI Global. Copying or distributing in print or electronic forms without written permission of IGI Global is prohibited.

INTRODUCTION

Corporate governance is a process that aims to allocate corporate resources in a manner that maximises value for all stakeholders – shareholders, investors, employees, customers, suppliers, environment and the community at large. It holds those at the helms to account by evaluating their decisions on transparency, inclusivity, equity and responsibility. A board of directors is considered to be the key decision-making body in an organisation and is responsible for approving important strategic operational and financial decisions. Corporate governance is the set of processes, customs, policies, laws, and institutions affecting the way a corporation (or company) is directed, administered or controlled. Corporate governance also includes the relationships among the many stakeholders involved and the goals for which an organisation is governed. In contemporary business corporations, the main external stakeholder groups are shareholders, debt holders, trade creditors, suppliers, customers and communities affected by the corporation's activities. Internal stakeholders are the board of directors, executives, and the employees.

Diversity in the boardroom has been a hot topic in recent years. The questions then are: Does the traditional boardroom of a fairly uniform group of individuals really produce the most effective decisions and strategy for a company? Does such a boardroom have exposure to a wide enough range of perspectives to facilitate robust discussions of issues that arise? Good corporate governance calls for a solid theoretical framework which recognises and manages risks in an organisation. This chapter discusses the concept of corporate governance, principles of corporate governance, functions of the board of directors, parties to corporate governance, board composition and board committees, board diversity, board independence, the role of stakeholders and shareholders in corporate governance. The chapter further analyses the impact of board diversity on board effectiveness and organisational performance, corporate governance and corporate financial performance, recommendations, and areas for future research.

WHAT IS CORPORATE GOVERNANCE?

Corporate governance in simple words means the extent to which organisations are run in an open and honest manner. It is a broad term that defines the methods, structure and the processes of an organisation in which the business and affairs of an organisation are managed, controlled and directed (Gill, 2008). Corporate governance also enhances the long term shareholder value by the process of accountability of managers and by enhancing the firm's performance (Khan, 2011).

Corporate governance is the way a corporation monitors and regulates itself. In short, it is a method of governing an organisation like a sovereign state, instating its own customs, policies and laws to its employees from the highest to the lowest levels (Sun, 2020). It is intended to increase the accountability of an organisation and to avoid massive disasters before they occur. Corporate governance is a cornerstone in improving economic efficiency and growth in order to attract investors and gain their confidence. In order for corporate governance to function efficiently, several dimensions might be taken into consideration including role and responsibilities of the board, board composition, management processes, relationship between board members, and duality of the chief executive officer and chairman (Zerban, Abdullah, Abdullateef, 2017).

The King IV Report on Corporate Governance for South Africa 2016 was released in November 2016 and advocates an outcomes based approach and defines corporate governance as the exercise of ethical and effective leadership towards the achievement of the following governance outcomes; namely ethical culture, good performance, effective control, and legitimacy (King IV Report on Corporate Governance for South Africa, 2016). Well-executed corporate governance means that an organisation can hold meetings with internal members, such as shareholders and debtholders, as well as suppliers, customers and community leaders, to address the requests and needs of the affected parties. Corporate governance is the set of policies that are created for deciding an organisation's performance and direction. It is an overview of rules and regulations for the people in-charge of an incorporated firm. They are the ones who agree to take responsibility towards the shareholders (Kulkani and Maniam, 2014). The main function of corporate governance is to make agreements that describe the privileges and tasks of shareholders and the organisation.

Corporate governance is viewed as a moral duty in the corporate world these days. The essence of the corporate world lies in promoting transparency and accountability and in fulfilling the fair expectations of all the stakeholders. Corporate governance is one such tool to achieve this goal and to safeguard the interests of various stakeholder groups. It involves promoting the compliance of law in letter and spirit, and demonstrating ethical conduct. The framework of corporate governance encourages efficient use of resources and also requires accountability for the stewardship of those resources (Aggarwal, 2013).

Corporate governance broadly refers to the mechanisms, relations, and processes by which a corporation is controlled and is directed; involving balancing the many interests of the stakeholders of an organisation. It is a framework of rules and practices by which a board of directors ensures accountability, fairness, and transparency in a company's relationship with its all stakeholders (financiers, customers, management, employees, government, and the community). The corporate governance framework consists of (a) explicit and implicit contracts between the company and the stakeholders for distribution of responsibilities, rights, and rewards, (b) procedures for reconciling the sometimes conflicting interests of stakeholders in accordance with their duties, privileges, and roles, and (c) procedures for proper supervision, control, and information-flows to serve as a system of checks-and-balances (Chen, 2020; Sun, 2020).

PRINCIPLES OF CORPORATE GOVERNANCE

Corporate governance principles and codes have been developed in different countries and issued from stock exchanges, corporations, institutional investors, or associations (institutes) of directors and managers with the support of governments and international organisations. As a rule, compliance with these governance recommendations is not mandated by law, although the codes linked to stock exchange listing requirements may have a coercive effect (Raut, 2018). One of the most influential guidelines has been the 1999 Organisation for Economic Cooperation and Development (OECD) Principles of Corporate Governance. This was revised in 2004. The OECD guidelines are often referenced by countries developing local codes or guidelines.

The Principles of Corporate Governance Include the Following (Sun, 2020)

- **Shareholder Recognition:** This is key to maintaining an organisation's stock price. More often than not, however, small shareholders with little impact on the stock price are brushed aside to make way for the interests of majority shareholders and the executive board. Good corporate governance seeks to make sure that all shareholders get a voice at general meetings and are allowed to participate.
- **Stakeholder Interests:** This should also be recognised by corporate governance. In particular, taking the time to address non-shareholder stakeholders can help an organisation to establish a positive relationship with the community and the press.
- **Board Responsibilities:** These must be clearly outlined to majority shareholders. All board members must be on the same page and share a similar vision for the future of the organisation.
- **Ethical Behaviour:** The violations in favour of higher profits can cause massive civil and legal problems down the road. Underpaying and abusing outsourced employees or avoidance around lax environmental regulations can come back and bite an organisation hard if ignored. A code of conduct

regarding ethical decisions should be established for all members of the board.

- **Business Transparency:** This is the key to promoting shareholder trust. Financial records, earnings reports and forward guidance should all be clearly stated without exaggeration or 'creative' accounting.

Raut (2018) further states that besides the above, the following are popularly espoused principles of corporate governance:

Rights and Equitable Treatment of Shareholders: Organisations should respect the rights of shareholders and assist shareholders to exercise those rights. They can help shareholders exercise their rights by effectively communicating information that is understandable and accessible and encouraging shareholders to participate in general meetings.

Interests of Other Stakeholders: Organisations should recognise that they have legal and other obligations to all legitimate stakeholders.

Role and Responsibilities of the Board: The board needs a range of skills and understanding to be able to deal with various business issues and have the ability to review and challenge management performance. It needs to be of sufficient size and have an appropriate level of commitment to fulfil its responsibilities and duties. There are issues about the appropriate mix of executive and non-executive directors.

Integrity and Ethical Behaviour: Ethical and responsible decision making is not only important for public relations, but it is also a necessary element in risk management and avoiding lawsuits. Organisations should develop a code of conduct for their directors and executives that promotes ethical and responsible decision-making. It is important to understand, though, that reliance by an organisation on the integrity and ethics of individuals is bound to eventual failure. Because of this, many organisations establish Compliance and Ethics programmes to minimise the risk that an organisation steps outside of ethical and legal boundaries.

Disclosure and Transparency: Organisations should clarify and make publicly known the roles and responsibilities of board and management to provide shareholders with a level of accountability. They should also implement procedures to independently verify and safeguard the integrity of the company's financial reporting. Disclosure of material matters concerning the organisation should be timely and balanced to ensure that all investors have access to clear and factual information.

Importance of Corporate Governance

Corporate governance importance arises in modern corporations due to the separation of management and ownership control in the organisations. Khan (2011) contends that the interests of shareholders are conflicting with the interests of managers.

The principal agent problem is reflected in the management and direction related challenges due to the differential interests of firm's stakeholders. The corporate governance structure specifies the distribution of rights and responsibilities among different participants in the corporation, such as the board, managers, shareholders and other stakeholders, and clarifies the rules and procedures for making decisions on corporate affairs. By doing this, it also provides the structures through which the organisation objectives are set, and the means of attaining those objectives and monitoring performance (Khan, 2011).

Corporate governance affects organisations as well as countries in different ways such as firm's access to outside financing increases, which leads to more investment, better growth opportunities and that causes the job market to flourish (Kulkani and Maniam, 2014). Fraudulent behaviour of companies has caused countries to go through financial crises. Corporate governance hence became a critical issue for all the countries around the world. Understanding corporate governance standards and issues is also significant to executives of foreign multinationals planning to do business with other countries.

The basic purpose of corporate governance is to hold those in power to account. Therefore, accountability is the key to corporate governance. There are six principles that have to be satisfied to ensure accountability. Raut (2018) contends that these are **6 Ds** namely: **Diversity** in composition of the board and differentiating the gene pool and gender; encouragement of **Dialogue** as opposed to monologue; valuing **Dissent**, **Dispersion** of authority (separation of chairman and CEO is one example), **Disruption** of status quo; and fostering a culture of full **Disclosure** to build trust.

Corporate governance highlights the important principles of oversight and control over the executive management's performance and strategic directions; and their accountability to the shareholders. A code of ethics, which clarifies and stipulates adherence to some of more abstract ideals of trust and accountability, is essential for good corporate governance. The board and management should endeavour to uphold and encourage accountability, transparency, fairness, and integrity in all aspects of an organisation's operations (Zerban, Abdullah, Abdullateef, 2017).

Governance, Risk Management, and Compliance Issues

Governance, Risk Management, and Compliance (GRC) is the authoritative term covering an organisation's approach across these three areas. Being closely related concerns, governance, risk and compliance activities are increasingly being integrated and aligned to some extent in order to avoid conflicts, wasteful overlaps and gaps. While interpreted differently in various organisations, GRC typically encompasses activities such as corporate governance, enterprise risk management (ERM) and corporate compliance with applicable laws and regulations (Raut, 2018):

Governance describes the overall management approach through which senior executives direct and control the entire organisation, using a combination of management information and hierarchical management control structures. Governance activities ensure that critical management information reaching the executive team is sufficiently complete, accurate and timely to enable appropriate management decision making. It also affords the control mechanisms to ensure that strategies, directions and instructions from management are carried out systematically and effectively.

Risk management is a set of processes through which management identifies, analyses, and where necessary responds appropriately to risks that might adversely affect realisation of the organisation's business objectives. The response to risks typically depends on their perceived gravity, and involves controlling, avoiding, accepting or transferring them to a third party. Whereas organisations routinely manage a wide range of risks (e.g. technological risks, commercial/financial risks, and information security risks), external legal and regulatory compliance risks are arguably the key concern in GRC.

Compliance means conforming to specified requirements. At an organisational level, it is achieved through management processes which identify the applicable requirements (defined for example in laws, regulations, contracts, strategies and policies), assess the state of compliance, evaluate the risks and potential costs of non-compliance against the projected expenses to achieve compliance, and hence prioritise, fund and initiate any corrective actions deemed necessary (Raut, 2018).

CORPORATE GOVERNANCE FUNCTIONS OF THE BOARD OF DIRECTORS

Corporate governance is of utmost importance to an organisation and is almost as important as its primary business plan. When implemented effectively, it can prevent corporate scandals, fraud and the civil and criminal liability of an organisation. It also enhances an organisation's image in the public eye as a self-policing organisation that is responsible and worthy of shareholder and debtholder capital. It dictates the shared philosophy, practices and culture of an organisation and its employees. An organisation without a system of corporate governance is often regarded as a body without a soul or conscience. Corporate governance keeps an organisation honest and out of trouble. If this shared philosophy breaks down, then corners will be cut, products will be defective and management will grow complacent and corrupt. The end result is a fall that will occur when significance, in the form of audited financial reports, criminal investigations and compliance probes, finally catches up, bankrupting an organisation overnight. Dishonest and unethical dealings can cause shareholders to desert an organisation because of fear, distrust and disgust (Sun, 2020).

A board member is an elected member on the board of directors of an organisation or the supervisory committee of an organisation. The board of directors of an organisation is defined as the governing body that is tasked with decisions pertaining to the future direction of an organisation (MyAccountingCourse, 2020). Board members are elected by the shareholders of an organisation and are responsible to set an organisation's vision and appoint senior management to carry out that vision. Each member of the board participates in board meetings wherein the discussions of performance, critical decisions, turnaround strategy, and future strategy take place. In other words, they are responsible for the global direction of the company.

The existence of the board of directors, as a crucial axis in the governance structure of an organisation, has become the prominent model around the world. Molano-León (2011) states that the board of directors is considered a universal characteristic of large organisations regardless of whether they have a large shareholder or a disperse group of shareholders. The roles and responsibilities of a board of directors are different, depending on the nature and type of organisation and the laws applied in a certain country. Similarly, the establishment of different committees is a means to channel the functions of a board into expertise groups of directors that focus on specific issues in an organisation. The role of the board is critical for the success of organisations (Zerban, Abdullah, Abdullateef, 2017).

The board of directors applies corporate governance over all employees of an organisation, including the CEO, and can dismiss any of them at any time. Corporate governance as a broad term describes the processes, customs, policies, laws and institutions that directs the organisations and corporations in the way they act, administer and control their operations. It works to achieve the goal of the organisation and manages the relationship among the stakeholders including the board of directors and the shareholders (Khan, 2011).

Some of the activities which should be performed by the board of directors includes the following tasks (Molano-León, 2011):

- Reviewing and monitoring performance of an organisation's business and its operating, financial and other corporate plans, strategies and objectives, and changing plans and strategies as appropriate;
- Adopting policies of ethical conduct and monitoring compliance with those policies and with applicable laws and regulations;
- Understanding the risk profile of an organisation and reviewing and overseeing risk management programmes;
- Understanding an organisation's financial statements and monitoring the appropriateness of its financial and other internal controls as well as its disclosure control and procedures;

- Choosing, setting goals for, regularly evaluating and establishing the compensation of the chief executive officer and the most senior executives, and making changes in senior management when appropriate;
- Developing, approving and implementing succession plans for the chief executive officer and the most senior executives;
- Reviewing the process for providing adequate and timely financial and operational information to an organisation's decision makers (including directors) and shareholders;
- Evaluating the procedures, operation and overall effectiveness of the board and its committees; and
- Establishing the composition of the board and its committees, including choosing director nominees who will bring appropriate expertise and perspectives to the board, recognising the important role of independent directors.

Parties to Corporate Governance

The three key constituents of corporate governance are the shareholders, board of directors and management. Aggarwal (2013) states that the components of corporate governance include: board size, independence of board from management, separation of chief executive officer and chairman, financial expertise of directors, number of board meetings, role of external auditors, and committees of the board. The most influential parties involved in corporate governance include government agencies and authorities, stock exchanges, management (including the board of directors and its chair, the chief executive officer or the equivalent, other executives and line management, shareholders and auditors). Other influential stakeholders may include lenders, suppliers, employees, creditors, customers and the community at large (Raut, 2018).

The literature written from a stakeholder theoretical viewpoint draws on its origins in management theory, politics and law to explain what it perceives the role of the governing board to be. Indeed, it views the board as having a coordinating role, whereby it balances the interests of the organisation's various stakeholders. According to L'Huillier (2014), stakeholder theorists see the board, as a collective group, being there to support and endorse the right of all stakeholders to have their say about decisions and actions taken by the organisation.

A board of directors is expected to play a key role in corporate governance. The board has the responsibility of endorsing the organisation's strategy, developing directional policy, appointing, supervising and remunerating senior executives, and ensuring accountability of the organisation to its investors and authorities (Martín & Herrero, 2018).

Raut (2018) further states that all parties to corporate governance have an interest, whether direct or indirect, in the financial performance of an organisation. Directors, workers and management receive salaries, benefits and reputation, while investors expect to receive financial returns. For lenders, it is specified interest payments while returns to equity investors arise from dividend distributions or capital gains on their stock. Customers are concerned with the certainty of the provision of goods and services of an appropriate quality; suppliers are concerned with compensation for their goods or services, and possible continued trading relationships. These parties provide value to an organisation in the form of financial, physical, human and other forms of capital. Many parties may also be concerned with corporate social performance.

A key factor in a party's decision to participate in or engage with an organisation is their confidence that the organisation will deliver the party's expected outcomes. When categories of parties (stakeholders) do not have sufficient confidence that an organisation is being controlled and directed in a manner consistent with their desired outcomes, they are less likely to engage with the organisation. When this becomes a prevalent system feature, the loss of confidence and participation in markets may affect many other stakeholders, and increases the likelihood of political action. Board of directors should play different roles in organisations in order to maintain their sustainability. They have to plan strategic direction, advising, active monitoring and disciplining roles (Zerban, Abdullah and Abdullateef, 2017).

BOARD COMPOSITION AND BOARD COMMITTEES

The board, expectedly, will be a grouping of distinguished individuals from diverse backgrounds. There is no contradicting the fact that effective corporate governance is a long-term factor which enables an organisation to evolve business excellence. It is capable of enhancing board competence and teamwork which will result in much improved benefits to the shareholders. The board has to be structured in such a way that it can achieve three ends which are stated thus: (a) proper understanding of, and capability to contend with, the matters of an organisation; (b) effective review and appraisal of the output of management; and (c) exercise of incisive and unbiased judgment. A majority of the directors should have independent status and minds. They should be independent of management and free of all business and other relationships which could materially interfere with or be perceived to materially interfere with the exercise of independent judgment. Directors who are considered as independent by the board should be so acknowledged in the statutory annual report under the subject-matter of 'corporate governance' (Chen, 2020; Mudashiru, Bakare, Babatunde and Ishmael, 2014).

Many argue that achieving the right balance of independent directors is crucial to a well-functioning board. The European Confederation of Directors' Associations (ECoDA) principles view the involvement of independent non-executive directors on the board as a key step in the governance evolution of an organisation (Deloitte Centre for Corporate Governance, 2017).

Boards have experienced some modifications in their structure, composition and practices. One of the most important issues in corporate governance is related to boards' structure by creating specialised board committees. Committees are the product of delegation by the board of directors in defined areas. Nevertheless, it has to be understood that committees serve for decision-shaping and decision taking but the board remains collectively responsible for its role. Board audit committees are intended to implement and support the boards' manager-monitoring functions by periodically reviewing the corporations' processes for compiling financial data, their internal controls, and the independence of the corporations' external auditors (Molano-León, 2011).

Committees of the Board

Committees of the Board have become part of a standard corporate governance structure. Board committees add to effectiveness of the board by exercising better control over management decisions. According to Aggarwal (2013), these include:

Audit Committee: High-profile corporate scams have heightened the need for an effective audit committee. Frequent meetings and independence of audit committee can ensure credibility of corporate reports.

Remuneration Committee: A board remuneration committee helps in deciding the suitable amount of remuneration for the top level executives like the CEO.

Nomination Committee: The nomination committee evaluates the skills, knowledge, and expertise needed to become a director and identifies the suitable candidates.

Some corporates in South Africa have committees like Social and Ethics Committee. Committees enhance board effectiveness by permitting directors to use and develop expertise in specialised areas and to focus their energies on a subset of issues confronting the organisation. Some organisations have established the corporate governance committee and its main goal is to review corporate governance processes (Molano-León, 2011).

BOARD DIVERSITY AND BOARD INDEPENDENCE IN CORPORATE GOVERNANCE

Board diversity refers to the distribution of different attributes and characteristics among directors, which impact attitudes and opinions, and variations in the way boards are composed (Goyal, Kakabadse and Kakabadse, 2019). A board of directors is considered to be the key decision-making body in an organisation and is responsible for approving important strategic operational and financial decisions. The board also forms a fundamental element of the organisation's corporate governance system. In South Africa, the second and third King Reports on Corporate Governance recommend that the majority of the board should consist of non-executive directors (Institute of Directors in Southern Africa, 2009; 2002). Non-executive means that the board member is not involved in the day-to-day running of the firm.

Organisations must be satisfied that the balance of knowledge, skills, experience, and diversity on the board is sufficient (King IV Report, 2016). Several authors have illustrated that the diversity of an organisation's board of directors aids creativity and innovation, which can translate into improved financial performance. Diversity goes beyond the observable demographic features of an individual, by also including non-observable (cognitive) features such as leadership ability and communication skills (Mans-Kemp and Viviers, 2015).

Diversity takes various forms in a boardroom and can be broadly categorised into the following elements (Deloitte Centre for Corporate Governance, 2017):

Skills, Expertise and Experience: Having the optimal mix of skills, expertise and experience is paramount to ensure that the board as a collective is equipped to guide the business and strategy of an organisation. Business unit heads, regional leaders, academics, entrepreneurs, government leaders, and other non-executives can create a wider, more diverse pool with some very talented individuals that could bring interesting and insightful perspectives into the boardroom. Directors are usually selected for their leadership qualities. They often have experience with generalised management or leadership experience rather than narrow expertise or technical acumen.

Gender: This element is one of the more emphasised forms of diversity in the boardroom. Females are increasingly sitting shoulder to shoulder with their male counterparts in the boardroom, bringing with them a unique style of management and differing perspectives.

Ethnicity: Ethnic diversity pertains to having a mix of individuals from various racial, cultural and religious backgrounds. The ethnic mix of a board should ideally represent the area in which the company operates. In South Africa, legislation such as the Broad-Based Black Economic Empowerment Act promotes ethnic diversity in the workplace.

Age: Age diversity is sometimes an overlooked element in the boardroom. Board members tend to be older, as many boards equate age with experience. There is some marginal evidence of generational diversity in boardrooms, with so-called 'younger' directors being in their fifties. While older directors do provide a wealth of knowledge, having younger directors introduces a fresh perspective to the boardroom which should not be underestimated.

Geography: Geographic diversity refers to having a mix of individuals from various geographic locations on the board.

Independence: Independent directors bring a balanced perspective to the boardroom as they assess matters in a more objective fashion. The board should determine if a director is independent in character and judgement after considering all relevant factors. These factors may include having regard to the relationship of the individual or his/her close family ties with an organisation, board and shareholders. In South Africa, approximately 60% of non-executive directors of listed companies are deemed to be independent. This is largely due to the regulatory requirements in terms of the Companies Act, King IV Report on Corporate Governance and the Johannesburg Stock Exchange Listing Requirements to have such individuals on the board.

A diverse board thus consists of a group of non-homogeneous individuals. Mans-Kemp and Viviers, (2015) claim that board diversity can increase board independence. They argue that individuals with different gender, race, ethnicity and/or professional backgrounds tend to ask questions that are not usually addressed by directors who have a more 'traditional' background. Increased questioning could lead to higher-order problem solving and ultimately to a stronger competitive advantage.

The principal argument in favour of a diverse board is the wide range of perspectives that each individual would bring to the boardroom table. A diverse board better understands its customer base and the environment that the business operates in. As a result of this enhanced understanding, the board is better placed to find and seize opportunities for innovation, which ultimately creates value for the business. A spectrum of diverse perspectives in the boardroom, specifically with regard to skills and expertise, also aids to counteract 'silo thinking' when the board is faced with a challenge. A board that is equipped to consider an issue from many angles (e.g. financial, economic, legal, generational, and geographic) is far more effective at assessing the risk of such an issue than one that adopts a one-dimensional approach. Incorporating independence into the boardroom also has its own specific advantages. Independent directors bring an unbiased view distinct from that of shareholders and management which provides reassurance to external parties that the company is being run in an effective manner. Governance is positively related to the percentage of independent board members (Deschênes, Rojas, Boubacar, Prud'homme and Ouedraogo, 2015).

The King IV Report on Corporate Governance for South Africa 2016 (King IV) emphasises the need for the board to comprise the appropriate balance of knowledge, skill, experience, diversity and independence for it to discharge its governance role and responsibilities objectively and effectively (Deloitte Centre for Corporate Governance, 2017). The skills, expertise and experience of individuals should be the single largest consideration for the ideal board. Once the appropriate skills, expertise and experience have been identified, other elements of diversity should then be woven into the framework to allow for effective and robust decision-making and discussion in the boardroom.

The findings on a study conducted by Scholtz and Kieviet (2018), indicate that the proportion of female directors, the proportion of directors with a business qualification and the size of a board are significantly positively related to an organisation's performance. Literature confirms that a diverse board in terms of gender as well as directors with a business qualification and the size of a board contribute to the performance of South African organisations.

Directors' contribution to an organisation's ethnic diversity has a significantly negative effect on an organisation's performance in South Africa. The negative relationship between company performance and directors of ethnic diversity can be attributed to the shortage of qualified directors of ethnic diversity. These directors are likely to receive multiple appointments and thus become too busy to contribute a positive effect on company performance. Board diversity is about building a board that accurately reflects the make-up of the population and stakeholders of the society where an organisation operates. Goyal, Kakabadse and Kakabadse (2019) emphasise that the aim of board diversity is to promote a broad range of attributes and perspectives that reflect real-world demographics as boards need to continue to earn their 'licence to operate in society' as organisations have a responsibility to multiple constituents and stakeholders, including the community and the wider society within which they exist.

There are arguments that indicate that female representation on a board as well as directors with a business qualification improve company performance, whilst directors of ethnic diversity may be too busy, resulting in a negative effect on an organisation's performance. A study by Scholtz and Kieviet (2018) contributes to literature by adding that a positive relationship exists between the proportion of female directors on a board and company performance in South Africa. This can be attributed to the finding that female representation on a board can bring a greater knowledge base, more creativity and a higher competitive advantage. Governance is positively related to the female presence on the board of directors (Deschênes, Rojas, Boubacar, Prud'homme and Ouedraogo, 2015).

Board diversity (excluding ethnic diversity) has a positive relationship with company performance could provide support for the Employment Equity and Broad-based Economic Empowerment Acts and the Women Empowerment and Gender Equality Bill. There is a positive relationship between the proportion of directors with a business qualification on a board and company performance in South Africa. Due to South Africa's history of discrimination, diverse board members often do not have the necessary skills, but acquire them only in the process of their board membership. The Institute of Directors South Africa (IoDSA) thus undertakes effort to develop, mentor, coach and teach directors. In the second King Report, organisations are urged to extend their mentoring programmes for inexperienced directors, since guidance by an experienced director can clarify the board's dynamics for new and inexperienced board members. Business Unity South Africa also suggests that organisations develop and implement (more) measures to overcome under-representation by females and blacks on corporate boards (Mans-Kemp and Viviers, 2015).

THE ROLE OF STAKEHOLDERS AND SHAREHOLDERS IN CORPORATE GOVERNANCE

The question to whom the board of directors is responsible in the fulfilment of its functions could be considered very important from the corporate governance perspective. A general answer to this question it is that the board owes its duties to the organisation. Molano-León (2011) argues that there are other groups which are related to the economic interest of an organisation like shareholders and other stakeholders like employees, creditors, customers, general public or even the community related to the business activity.

In business, a stakeholder is usually an investor in an organisation whose actions determine the outcome of the business decisions. According to Sun (2020), stakeholders do not have to be equity shareholders. They can also be employees, who have a stake in an organisation's success and incentive for the products to succeed. They can be business partners, who rely on the success to keep the supply chain going. Every business takes a different approach to stakeholders. The roles of stakeholders differ between businesses, dependent on the rules and responsibilities laid out at the founding of an organisation or as the business evolved over the years. The most common definition of a stakeholder, however, is a large investor that has the influence to hold a viable 'stake' in an organisation.

For shareholders to determine the effectiveness of the board they must be provided with appropriate financial and non-financial information in determining a fair and balanced assessment of an organisation's position and its prospects. The directors are tasked with providing information to give shareholders a clear and broad view of solvency and liquidity, an organisation's risk management approach and the long term viability of the business. The chairman is expected to report in the annual statements on the role and the effectiveness of the board. It is a requirement of the chairman to ensure that the views of shareholders are communicated to the board. The chairman should discuss key issues on governance and strategy with major shareholders and non-executive directors should have an opportunity to attend these meetings with the major shareholders. The board needs to protect minority shareholders against majority shareholders (Kelly, 2019; Davies, 2000).

Corporate social responsibility (CSR) affects a wide range of stakeholders, unlike financial performance, which is more focused on shareholders. Regulatory bodies should be sensitive to the fact that the effects of the characteristics of boards of directors on the CSR have an impact on a larger number of stakeholders than simple financial performance (Deschênes, Rojas, Boubacar, Prud'homme and Ouedraogo, 2015). Corporate governance practices should be planned in such a way that it will encourage a suitable atmosphere for corporate social responsibility, reliability, and ethics.

Corporate governance acts as a bridge between shareholders, stakeholders, and board of directors. It should be able to restore the trust and confidence of management and an organisation to the shareholders in the organisation. Corporate directors have fiduciary duty towards the shareholders. Board members are the eyes and ears for the shareholders. Zerban, Abdullah and Abdullateef (2017) contend that in many countries shareholders have a dominant role in appointing the board of directors. Shareholders believe that appointed board and senior managers will act in their interests. Senior managers are responsible for directing, planning and controlling work and take corrective actions where necessary. They should manage risk, have appropriate control systems, provide accurate information and act ethically. Shareholders place their trust in board's decisions in supervising senior manager's actions and proficiency.

Governance structures in form of a corporate governance code should identify the distribution of rights and responsibilities among the corporation's different stakeholders such as the supervisory board, management board, shareholders, creditors, auditors, regulators, and others and should include rules and procedures for decision-making in corporate affairs. Furthermore, corporate governance includes the processes through which the corporation's objectives are defined and pursued in the context of the social, regulatory and market environment (Michelberger, 2016).

THE IMPACT OF BOARD DIVERSITY ON BOARD EFFECTIVENESS AND ORGANISATION PERFORMANCE

A board of directors forms one of the pillars of a robust corporate governance framework. Recent academic literature suggests that one of the ways to enhance corporate governance, arguably, is to diversify the board of directors. Le Quang, Kwang Soo and Yu (2014) argue that studies that used the independence of the board of directors as a measure of corporate governance found that increasing independence of the board of directors is strongly associated with better firm performance.

Board diversity can offer both challenges and opportunities for an organisation. In South Africa the issue of board diversity and the influence on an organisation's performance is an important question in view of the history of the country. Board diversity or more independent board composition can result in enhanced decision making through increased information flows, although this may entail a cost (Muchemwa, Padia and Callaghan, 2016).

Diversity in educational and functional backgrounds should increase the breadth of an organisation's cognitive perspectives. The reason for this is that individuals from different cognitive backgrounds provide a diversity of knowledge, experience and information-processing behaviours, which leads to more alternatives, more accurate prediction of environmental changes and better evaluation of strategic options (Scholtz and Kieviet, 2018).

Organisations with a more educated board of directors perform better. Mori (2014) furthermore proved that the level of directors' education has a positive effect on the performance of their roles as directors. Based on the studies conducted on this topic, there is an expectation that an organisation's performance will be higher for organisations where a board of directors has a higher proportion of business and diverse qualifications.

A diverse board better understands its customer base and the environment that the business operates in. As a result of this enhanced understanding, the board is better placed to find and seize opportunities for innovation, which ultimately creates value for the business. Incorporating independence into the boardroom also has its own specific advantages. Independent directors bring an unbiased view distinct from that of shareholders and management which provides reassurance to external parties that an organisation is being run in an effective manner. The view by Goyal, Kakabadse and Kakabadse (2019) is that boards presently are considered the most critical component in improving corporate governance. Board diversity is increasingly being recommended as a tool for enhancing firm performance.

A further benefit of having a diverse board is the external perception that may be created. An organisation that embraces diversity in the upper levels of the organisation may be perceived by outsiders to adopt a top-down approach to being a good corporate citizen. Such a view may inspire investor confidence in the organisation which ultimately creates value for the organisation. Board members consider diverse boards to be critical for the effective performance in a range of their roles and in dealing with dynamic governance environment of today. Since the collapse of apartheid in 1994, certain corporate governance and legislative reforms were introduced to improve the diversity of South African boards. Corporate governance reforms, including the King Reports on Corporate Governance (issued in 1994, 2002, 2009 and 2016), recommend that a board of directors be as diverse as possible.

Figure 1. Strategic leadership theory, board diversity and board effectiveness
Source: Goyal, Kakabadse and Kakabadse (2019)

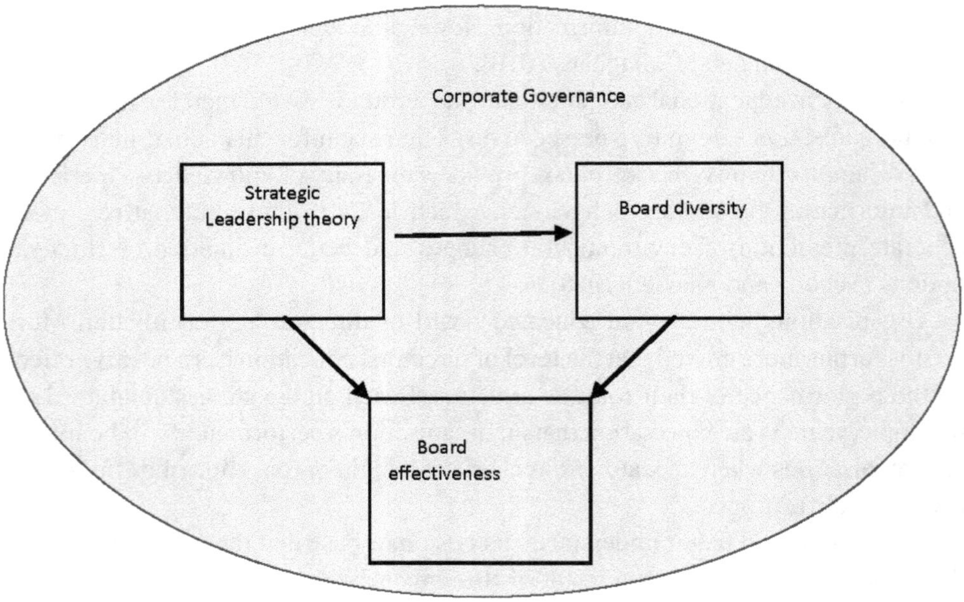

As shown in Figure 1 above, the discussion/research explores the impact of board diversity on board effectiveness for enhancing corporate governance, while defining board diversity through the lens of strategic leadership theory (Goyal, Kakabadse and Kakabadse, 2019). Seeing the positive impact of having a diverse board as mentioned above, in itself creates an incentive for organisations to continue incorporating diversity in the boardroom. Boards that strive for effectiveness and embrace diversity as a mechanism to deliver that effectiveness are likely to perform better than boards who incorporate diversity with compliance in mind. Functional diversity on boards can be obtained by nominating people with diverse educational, industry/sector-specific and role-specific experiences, which leads to an improved intellectual capital on boards.

Corporate Governance and Corporate Financial Performance

Corporate governance and corporate financial performance are correlated and governance rating of an organisation has significant positive impact on its financial performance. Aggarwal (2013) argues that research supports decisions of organisations to improve their governance structures. Organisations should strive to improve their performance along indicators of good governance, namely leadership ethics, board composition and independence, executive compensation, transparency and reporting, stakeholder engagement, and compliance with law in true letter and spirit. Further, organisations should understand that improving governance and sustainability performance is as important as improving the financial performance. Corporate governance eliminate the conflict of ownership and control by separately defining the interest of shareholders and managers (Khan, 2011).

RECOMMENDATIONS

Board of directors is the foundation in effective corporate governance. Efficient roles and responsibilities for the board with commitment to comply with rules and regulation can aid in creating value and protect interests of stakeholders. Sustainable accountability of senior management nowadays is necessary, especially with the recent collapses of organisations which appeared massive and efficient while actually they were delicate. It is recommended that organisations design a system of governance, in which it will be easy for the board of directors to monitor and ensure managers are fulfilling their responsibilities. Also, the board of directors should control the process of appointing executives and assessing their actions.

Corporate governance measures implemented after 1994 in South Africa enhanced corporate governance. Research indicates that the legislation reforms that have been implemented have resulted in at least some diversity. Organisations should strive to improve their performance along indicators of good governance, namely leadership ethics, board composition and independence, executive compensation, transparency and reporting, stakeholder engagement, and compliance with law in true letter and spirit. Organisations should understand that improving governance and sustainability performance is as important as improving the financial performance.

It is recommended that more attention should be given to the development and mentoring of diverse board candidates. The adoption of good corporate governance practices enhances transparency of an organisation's operations, ensures accountability and improves a firm's profitability. It also helps to protect the interest of the shareholders by aligning their interest with that of the managers. The results show that generally corporate governance has a positive impact on all the performance indicators of an organisation.

FUTURE RESEARCH

The usage of other performance measures could lead to different results. The only board diversity factors that were considered included the proportion of female directors, and the proportion of directors with business and diverse qualifications. However, findings indicate that female representation on a board as well as directors with business and diverse qualifications improve an organisation's performance. This research finding may support decisions of organisations to improve their governance structure. Further research is required into the nature of the relationship between board diversity and market-based performance measures on the stock exchanges. Attention could also be given to variables such as the size of the board, the age of directors and board tenure in future studies. Board leadership and the role of black female directors could also be investigated in more depth.

It is suggested that future research could use alternative organisation performance measures such as market value added, shareholding returns, return on equity or headline earnings per share. Additional corporate governance characteristics could be tested against company performance. Future research could provide a valuable input by investigating whether a relationship between board composition and company performance exists over a period of time. Another interesting approach would also be to test the extent to which the composition of a board changes and to compare this aspect to the market value of companies. To study this topic further, in future more research can be done to see how organisations from countries like South Africa affect the corporate governance of other countries as they develop new relations abroad.

CONCLUSION

This chapter has presented the fact that a board of directors forms one of the pillars of a robust corporate governance framework. Board diversity can offer both challenges and opportunities for an organisation. Boards continually need to monitor and improve their performance. This can be achieved through board evaluation, which provides a powerful and valuable feedback mechanism for improving board effectiveness, maximising strengths and highlighting areas for further development. When appointing non-executive directors, more careful consideration may need to be given to the benefits they may bring, be this in terms of independent expert business knowledge and experience, or other sources of advantage to boards, and the organisations they manage.

The discussion in this chapter of corporate governance and board diversity has important implications for policy makers, governments and regulatory authorities. To remain relevant in an increasingly competitive world, directors cannot ignore the crucial role that diversity plays in governance, particularly in the boardroom. Organisations that fail to tap into the ever-deepening talent pool of diverse, well-educated and ambitious individuals, run the risk of limiting value creation, compromising sustainability and undermining their long-term competitiveness.

REFERENCES

Aggarwal, P. (2013). Impact of Corporate Governance on Corporate Financial Performance. *Journal of Business and Management, 13*(3), 1–5.

Chen, J. (2020). Corporate Governance Definition. Investopedia. Retrieved 12 April 2020, from https://www.investopedia.com/terms/c/corporategovernance.asp

Davies, P. L. (2000). *The Board of Directors: Composition, Structure, Duties and Powers*. Company Law Reform in OECD Countries A Comparative Outlook of Current Trends.

Deloitte Centre for Corporate Governance. (2017). Diversity in the boardroom. Available online at: Retrieved 14 April 2020, from https://www2.deloitte.com/za/en/services/centre-for-corporate-governance.html

Deschênes, S., Rojas, M., Boubacar, H., Prud'homme, B., & Ouedraogo, A. (2015). The impact of board traits on the social performance of Canadian firms. Corporate Governance International Journal of Business in Society., 15(3), 293–305. doi:10.1108/CG-08-2014-0097

Gill, A. (2008). Corporate Governance as Social Responsibility: A Research Agenda. *Berkeley Journal of International Law, 26*(2), 452–478.

Goyal, R., Kakabadse, N., & Kakabadse, A. (2019). Improving Corporate Governance with Functional Diversity on FTSE 350 Boards: Directors' Perspective. *Journal of Capital Markets Studies., 3*(2), 113–136. doi:10.1108/JCMS-09-2019-0044

Institute of Directors in Southern Africa (IoDSA). (2009). King Report on Corporate Governance in South Africa. Retrieved 16 April 2020, from https://www.iodsa.co.za/page/kingIII

Institute of Directors in Southern Africa (IoDSA). (2016). King IV Report on Corporate Governance for South Africa 2016. Retrieved 20 April 2020, from https://www.adams.africa/wp-content/uploads/2016/11/King-IV-Report.pdf

Johannesburg Stock Exchange Listing Requirements. Service Issue 14. April 2011. Second edition. Johannesburg, South Africa.

Kelly, M. (2019). The Role of the Board of Directors in Corporate Governance. CPA Ireland. Retrieved 14 April 2020, from https://www.cpaireland.ie/CPAIreland/media/EducationTraining/Study%20Support%20Resources/P1%20Corp%20Laws%20and%20Governance/Relevant%20Articles/p1-corp-governance-the-role-of-the-board-of-directors.pdf

Khan, H. (2011). A Literature Review of Corporate Governance. In International Conference on E-business, Management and Economics. IPEDR. IACSIT Press.

Kulkani, R., & Maniam, B. (2014). Corporate Governance: Indian Perspective. International Journal of Trade. *Economics and Finance.*, *5*(4), 364–368.

L'Huillier, B. M. (2014). What does "corporate governance" actually mean? Corporate Governance International Journal of Business in Society., 14(3), 300–319. doi:10.1108/CG-10-2012-0073

Le Quang, C., Kwang Soo, K., & Yu, Y. (2014). Effects of Corporate Governance on the Performance of Private Economic Groups in Vietnam. Muyeog Yeon'gu, 10(6), 39–56. doi:10.16980/jitc.10.6.201412.39

Mans-Kemp, N., & Viviers, S. (2015). Investigating Board Diversity in South Africa. *Journal of Economic and Financial Sciences.*, *8*(2), 392–414. doi:10.4102/jef.v8i2.100

Martín, C. J. G., & Herrero, B. (2018). Boards of directors: Composition and effects on the performance of the firm. Economic Research-Ekonomska Istraživanja., 31(1), 1015–1041. doi:10.1080/1331677X.2018.1436454

Michelberger, K. (2016). Corporate Governance Effects on Firm Performance: A Literature Review. Regional Formation and Development Studies., 3(20), 84–95. doi:10.15181/rfds.v20i3.1346

Molano-León, R. (2011). The roles of the board of directors: The unresolved riddle. *Vniversitas.*, *122*, 541–602.

Mori, N. (2014). Directors' diversity and board performance: Evidence from East African microfinance institutions. *Journal of African Business*, *15*(2), 100–113. doi:10.1080/15228916.2014.920654

Muchemwa, M. R., Padia, N., & Callaghan, C. W. (2016). Board Composition, Board Size and Financial Performance of Johannesburg Stock Exchange Companies. *Suid-Afrikaanse Tydskrif vir Ekonomiese en Bestuurswetenskappe*, *19*(4), 497–513. doi:10.4102/sajems.v19i4.1342

Mudashiru, A., Bakare, I. A. O., Babatunde, Y., & Ishmael, O. (2014). Good Corporate Governance and Organisational Performance: An Empirical Analysis. *International Journal of Humanities and Social Science*, *4*(7), 170–178.

MyAccountingCourse. (2020). What is a Board Member? Retrieved 02 April 2020, from https://www.myaccountingcourse.com/accounting-dictionary/board-member

Organisation for Economic Cooperation and Development (OECD). (1999). *Principles of Corporate Governance*. OECD.

Raut, S. (2018). *Corporate Governance: Concepts and Issues*. Research Scholar with Institute of Directors.

Republic of South Africa. (2003). *The Broad-Based Black Economic Empowerment Act No 53 of 2003*. Government Printers.

Republic of South Africa. (2008). *The Companies Act No 71 of 2008*. Government Printers.

Scholtz, H., & Kieviet, S. (2018). The Influence of Board Diversity on Company Performance of South African Companies. *Journal of African Business*, *19*(1), 105–123. doi:10.1080/15228916.2017.1356065

Sun, L. (2020). Why is Corporate Governance Important? BusinessDictionary. Retrieved 20 April 2020, from http://www.businessdictionary.com/article/618/why-is-corporate-governance-important/

Zerban, A. M., Abdullah, M., & Abdullateef, M. (2017). Corporate Governance and Board of Directors Responsibilities: The Case of Saudi Arabia. *International Journal of Accounting Research.*, *5*(2), 1–5. doi:10.4172/2472-114X.1000171

Chapter 2
Family Business Governance

Reena Agrawal
Jaipuria Institute of Management, Lucknow, India

Ganga Bhavani
Amity University, India

ABSTRACT

Corporate governance is a significant tool to build strong and long relationships among various stakeholders in kinds of business organizations. Family businesses are not an exception to this. Like any other businesses, family businesses also need to have governance in place and practice to achieve the business strategies and to have long-term succession. Family-owned businesses are the backbone of many countries' economies in the world contributing substantial portion of GDP. Considering these, it is important to know the best practices of governance in family owned business organizations and the role played by governance to improve the strengths of these businesses. The chapter throws light on family business governance and explores various important practices highlighting their advantages and disadvantages in detail.

INTRODUCTION

Family business have unique capacities to fuel economic growth and these businesses have always nurtured entrepreneurial talent across generations to have long-term strategic commitment and independence. Family businesses contribute in social and environmental development, incessantly create new jobs, and provide better quality of life for citizens. Family businesses are the most long lived business entities and they are agile and resilient.

DOI: 10.4018/978-1-7998-6669-5.ch002

Copyright © 2021, IGI Global. Copying or distributing in print or electronic forms without written permission of IGI Global is prohibited.

Family Business- Definitions

"A company is considered as family business when it has been closely identified with at least two generations of a family and when this link has had a mutual influence on company policy and on the interests and objectives of the family". Donnelley (1964)

"Family businesses are those where policy and direction are subject to significant influence by one or more family units. This influence is exercised through ownership and sometime through the participation of family members in management. It is the interaction between two sets of organizations, family and business that establishes the basic character of the family business and define its uniqueness". Davis (1983)

"Family business is a business governed and/or managed with the intention to shape and pursue the vision of the business held by a dominant coalition controlled by members of the same family or a small number of families in a manner that is potentially sustainable across generations of the family or families." Chua et. al. (1999)

"Family business includes any business in which the bulk of the ownership or control lies in a family, and in which two or more family members are involved directly". Brockhaus, (2004).

"Family business is an enterprise which is built on the family's needs and abilities; is owned, managed, and controlled by the family; exists for perpetuating family values and unity; the business policies and decisions are significantly influenced by the family; the family members are deputed on key positions and the succession of the business passes down from one generation to the other". Rastogi and Agrawal (2010)

"Family business is a business governed and/or managed in order to form and follow the vision of the business held by a dominant coalition controlled by members of the same family or a small number of families that is potentially sustainable in all generations of the family or families." Alderson (2011)

"Family businesses is group of people with family ties that promote the adoption of "best practices" and the development of competitive advantages in business they own, based on the assumption that these firms were or are source of generating value for themselves". Zapatero *et* al., (2012)

According to Poza and Daugherty (2013) a business can be considered as a family business when: ownership rights (fifteen percent or more) are with two or more members of a family; family members serve in management, as board member or advisors, and thus influence strategic decisions; relationships are given importance and there is dream of continuity across generations; there is overlap of family, ownership and management, and absence of growth plan may make it vulnerable during succession; and has unique competitive advantage derived from the family.

BACKGROUND

Significance of Family Business

Throughout history family businesses have being acknowledged for their noteworthy economic presence (Alderson, J. K. (2011), Comi & Eppler, 2014; (Tirdasari & Dhewanto, 2012; De Massis *et al.*, 2018). Family businesses are among longest-lived institutions and regarded as backbone of many economies round the world (Duh et al 2009; Astrachan, 2010). It is estimated that annually 70% to 90% of global GDP is produced by family businesses (Rexhepi, 2015). Family business are successful in creating 50% to 80% of employment worldwide. Family enterprises have emerged as central force driving economies across world (EFB, 2009).

Surveys suggest that world's Top 500 family businesses constitute 68% of the total global turnover, they employ twenty one million people and contribute USD 6.5 trillion to global GDP (University of Vermont, 2014; Bain, 2015; Stiftung Familienunternehmen, 2016). Many of world's largest multinational companies (MNCs) are family owned, and are globally recognized for their strategies (Forbes Insights. (2012). Examples include Ford Motor, Wal-Mart, Acer Computers, Arcelor Mittal, Matthew Algie, BMW, SC Johnson, L'Oréal, Ikea, Tetra Pak, Anheuser-Busch, Vanee Foods Company, DuPont, Cadbury, Kosh Industries, Samsung, Hyundai, LG, Tata, Birla, Godrej, and Mahindra ...etc.

Family businesses make noteworthy contribution to economies in United States (Caspar, Dias, & Elstrodt, 2010), Europe (Berghe & Carchon, 2002), Australia (Dana, L., & Smyrnios, K. 2010 b), Asia (Credit Suisse, 2011; Forbes Insights, 2012) and the African region. In United States, eighty percent of businesses are family owned. One third of Standard and Poor 500 firms are owned-controlled-managed by founding family. In United States family businesses account for eighty nine percent of total tax returns, sixty four percent of GDP, and employ sixty two percent of total workforce (Family Firm Institute, 2017). In Canada, eighty percent of companies listed on Toronto Stock Exchange are closely held by families (Gulzar & Wang, 2010).

Across European countries, family businesses constitute 55% to 90% of all businesses companies, and they are existing in all sizes (PWC, 2009). In Europe over 14 million family businesses make available over 60 million jobs. 93% to 95% percent of all German companies are family-controlled and they generated sales revenue of 2.9 trillion euros (Haunschild &Wolter, 2010). 250 largest companies in France and Germany are family-owned (Bernard, 2015). In United Kingdom 3 million family businesses represent 66% of private businesses. In United Kingdom it is estimated that family business have given employment to 9.2 million people and this constituted 41% of total employment created by private businesses (Institute for

Family Business, 2011). In Belgium family businesses amounts to 70% and represent 55% of Gross National Product. In Spain, 85% of private businesses are owned and managed by business families These family businesses constitute 70% of Spain`s GDP and they create 70% of employment in the country (Venter & Farrington, 2009; Finnigan, 2014; Fernández-Olmos *et al.*, 2016). Family businesses consist of above 85% of all businesses in OECD countries (OCED, 2005). They also significantly contribute to the growth of economies in Latin America, and Africa (Tharawat Magazine, 2014.

Beyond West (Botero *et al.*, 2015), Asia-Pacific regions stand with more than half of family businesses represent (Tharawat Magazine, 2014; Fernández-Aráoz, Iqbal, & Ritter, 2015). In India family businesses account for 90 percent of India's industrial output 79% of organized private sector employment. Some of India`s largest conglomerates are still family controlled (CII, 2011; KPMG, 2013, PwC, 2019). In Thailand family businesses account for 80% of GDP (PwC, 2019), Singapore, Hong Kong and China have similar story (Accenture Strategy, 2019). In the Middle East over 95% of businesses are family owned and they employ 70% of people outside of government and especially in Saudi Arabia of all companies 95% are family owned (PwC, 2012, PwC, 2019).

MAIN FOCUS

Uniqueness of Family Business

A family business derives its essence from its unique features: presence of family; interplay of family-ownership-management; special competitive edge; overlap of family, ownership management; strategic influence of family values and goals. In centre of family businesses is the family, which directly or indirectly influences business; their key goals are both financial and non-financial such as sustainability and satisfaction of internal as well as external stakeholders (clients and local community); their management style is value-driven and emotional, goal aligned, they thrive on quality, reputation, long-term relationships, etc. Contrary to this, in centre of non-family businesses are shareholders and managers; their sole goal is maximum profits and growth; their aim is to satisfy the shareholders; their management style is driven by data rather than emotions, use and rationale of agency theory. Some of the unique features are mentioned below-

- **Family Relation:** There is respect and mutual trust amongst family members. Workforce is committed and loyal. There is common values, ideologies and belief system. Family essence, family reputation, family dreams influence the mission/vision of the business. Family, relatives and extended family have strong sense of faithfulness towards family that unsurprisingly translates into loyalty towards business.

- **Culture:** Usually the culture is informal. Such businesses are agile, flexible and adaptable. They share common language so the communication is very efficient.
- **Family Role:** Family often plays multiple roles and decision making is quick.
- **Leadership:** Family businesses are entrepreneurial and ambitious. There is informal authority.
- **Survival:** The single minded devotion safeguard family business`s survival through harshest times.
- **Time:** It has long-term viewpoint, loyalty; committed; deeper ties; patient capital; trust built up over time.
- **Complexity:** Can easily foster creativity; rich interchange of goals and roles.
- Governance: There is integration of strengths of family and business. Family business is closely held and clearly defined principles and philosophy leads to smooth governance. There are less agency problems.
- **Succession:** In family business training begins early. Mentoring is long term process. Incumbent can choose when to leave. There is stability in leadership thus promising long-term direction.
- **Capital:** There is committed capital owners may also sacrifice return if need be. Family's reputation attract investors.
- **Authority:** There is greater independence. People place family interest before business interest.
- **Decision Process:** The decision making is quick. Co-ownership in family leads to better strategies.
- **Business Skill:** Family members have wide-ranging knowledge of business fundamentals and strategies.
- **General:** In family business gap of knowledge, skill, expertise is filled by appointment of professionals.

Governance Challenges in Family Business

Corporate governance is defined as "Procedures and processes according to which an organization is directed and controlled". The corporate governance structure specifies the distribution of rights and responsibilities among the different participants in the organization–such as the board, managers, shareholders and other stakeholders and lays down the rules and procedures for decision-making. Corporate governance essentially involves four components - regulatory governance, market governance, stakeholder governance, and internal (shareholder) governance. Regulatory governance refers to the public control and order through government policies, laws, regulations. Market governance refers to application of numerous market factors such as demand and supply, competition, price, market norms etc. to discipline and control company`s action and behaviour. Stakeholder governance refers to direct and indirect influence and control over company`s business, behaviour and decision-making by the key stakeholders. Classically stakeholders may include customers, investors, suppliers, local communities, employees, government and media. Internal corporate governance refers to the official plan of checks and balances amongst shareholder through board of directors', general meeting and management within the company, suggested by corporate laws.

Governance challenges in family business arise from interlinking of the family and business. Classically in family is primarily concerned about well-being of family members (driven by love, bitterness, attachment, promises and expectations etc.), while business is concerned about results-oriented behaviours (driven by wisdom, decision-making, adapting change etc.). In order to have efficient governance system that enables the two institutions (family and business) interact positively and professionally in spite of their dissimilar values, aims, and formal structures, attention should be focused on both simultaneously. Reconciliation of family concerns with those of business and mutuality of influences of both institutions certainly impact the composition and structure of governance. Governance structures should aim to separate family issues from business issues but many of them overlap. There are various challenges by faced by family businesses governance includes the below:

Heterogeneity of Family Businesses

Family businesses are more heterogeneous in comparison to publicly owned companies. They vary in size, objectives, ownership and management. There can be family businesses whether ownership is in few hand or dispersed, total family control or not; and where control is dominated by family insiders or shared with non-family member. Varied patterns of ownership give rise to conflicts between executive and non-executive members. Other features that influences governance is cross-generation intentions. Family businesses change over time, and governance structures that work for one generation may need review and modification of existing system. Therefore corporate governance codes used for public companies are not relevant for private family businesses. Country cultures contexts and legal frameworks also differ. Governance recommendations in UK and USA lean towards market-based models, while in Asia, Latin America, and portions of Europe, governance is control based. Thus, it is essential not to generalize and not to assume that one model will all. Instead, governance model for family businesses should consider nature of business, specific context, sector, size, stage of growth etc.

Formal or Informal Governance

Governance can be formal or informal, i.e. contractual or relational. Where there is strong solidity, collective outlook and alignment of individual interests, governance may be interpersonal, with fewer formal structures. In some places formal contracts and structures and may go against the local norm and culture. Most North American and European nations have strong official frameworks where contracts and formal structures are standard. In developing nations, legal set-up to enforce contracts relatively are less prevalent, and thus informal governance predominates. Many endorsements of 'good governance' are founded on premise of agency theory which disregards relationships and social forces. Some argue that strong relationships and emotional ties are more effective than formal governance methods. Formal governance structures intend to create put procedures, guidelines and structures before any crisis arises, to avoid hasty decisions.

Complexity of Family Relationships

Family can create positive impact in business, by promoting commitment, network, loyalty, long-term views, expertise and good relations within and outside. Family provides an unequalled learning experience for next generation. Families in business are innovative, creative and they drive growth and excellence. Many are unselfish, dependable and are known for creating positive influence in community. On contrary family can become locus of conflict, entangled in former damages and engrained enmities made eviler by favoritism, malicious personal-interest and free riding. If such behaviours is tolerated the consequences can be devastating. The un-conditional love can result in free riding and avoidance. Family members avoid to tackle bad behaviours of members in the family it can lead to bitterness and anger in family. Rivalries can blow up and destroy business.

Increasing Complexity of Multiple Generations

As family business moves generations family issues are likely to have bigger implications. With addition of new generation the total number of family owners expand: some family have hundreds of members an intricate range of uncles, aunts, cousins, parents, siblings and grandparents. Family members who are detached may have less emotions and attachment for business and are likely to pay attention on personal-interest and monetary gains, rather than long-term strategic goals of business. An expanding group of shareholders can result in divisions developing - for instance, between diverse divisions of family, amid decision-making and non-employed family members etc. Multiple owners, their conflicting executive identities and their desire for influence and control further affects governance.

Power and Dominance

Family businesses are usually established by dynamic persons with strong personality sets. The energy and supremacy that give them victory in initial days can at times become a limitation as business grows. Senior family members might hold controlling position, rule decision making and limit the involvement of others. Many cultures consider it improper to challenge or question senior member in family. Supremacy by senior members can obstruct business growth and create resentment or conflict. There is danger of creation cross generation divisions. Younger members may lose interest and leave family business. Innovation gets hampered due to lack of diverse ideas and viewpoints. Ownership concentration is linked to weak corporate governance, inefficient investment, excessive risk taking and excessive diversification. Pyramidal ownership structures are always criticized.

Understanding Rights and Responsibilities

The interweaving of family and business can lead to confusion around privileges and duties. Family members may try interfere in domains and decisions beyond their territory. Younger members in family may receive shares directly without understanding their duties and right. Member with small ownerships expect big role and control in business. Family members may try to have access to company's assets in inappropriate manner.

Work Family Conflict

The level of conflict, attribute and direction of conflict (family-to-work or work-to-family) differ in family and non-family businesses due to variety of changing role and responsibilities in the two spheres. In family businesses conflicts that result in work pressures and are anticipated to originate in family domain whereas in non-family business work is frequently the root cause of the conflict. Since the conflicts and tensions affect relationships and performance in the family and in the business, a challenge for any governance mechanism is to endeavor to eradicate root cause of the conflict and provide redressal when they do occur.

Leadership Transition

Nothing affects family business above the departure of founding member and transfer of authority to his/her successors. This can create loss of vision and purpose as the inheritors may have contradictory views on way business should be operated and developed. The deficiency of clear line of power may result in the decline of the business after the retirement or death of the incumbent. The challenge for family business is to prepare for transition in leadership to provide family and business atmosphere where the successors' requisite for self-determination and self-fulfillment are properly obtained.

Best Practices of Corporate Governance in Family Businesses

Increase in globalization has created new challenges for family businesses. As family business expands, the relationships among its stakeholders becomes more complicated. Corporate governance provides an organizational structure that clarifies roles and responsibility. It also demarcates between owners and managers and lays down policy direction for day-to-day operation. Unlike corporate governance family governance is totally voluntary and typically aims at governing and strengthening relations between family and the business. Family governance mechanisms can be customized to suit specific business family's conditions, values and interests.

Family Constitution

Family constitution, also called family charter is an arrangement by family members that states family's duties and obligation towards each other and the ideologies and principles with which they will manage their relation with business. This is established collectively and prepared by way of document and is re-examined at consistently. The family constitution is specific to family so it can include aspects that family thinks are relevant, it also states functioning of family council. Some possible features of a family constitution can be: definition of family (who is considered to be part of family and who is not); family values, aspirations and strategic goals; roles, duties, values, engagement of family in business; education, rights and engagement of next generation; how family is symbolized; relation amongst family members, structure of family council; board of directors; compensation, expense, budget; process to revise constitution and item that family considers proper and significant.

Family constitution is a platform where family members can raise queries and discuss matters that are relevant for family and business, before they become sensitive and nasty. But it but it does eliminate differences and conflicts. Family constitution allows family members to question and cross examine time old customs and practices. A family constitution turn out to be more pertinent as complication surges. Added age group may get new outlooks, with increase in numbers of members with ownership rights are liable to create larger difference of interests and incentives. Wisely drafted principles and processes to govern relationship will provide greater clarity and stability for long-term existence.

Family Meetings

Family meetings are most suitable for small family businesses with very simple structures. Some families depend on ad hoc meetings for purposes, such as succession planning or to deal with a crisis; other conduct planned meeting at regular intervals. Involvement is open to people (above certain age), precise to groups of family. For family meetings to work efficiently, it is essential that family sets clear goals, duties and decision-making. Family meetings are good way of adding new family members in business, increases communication and engagement between family and business, builds business learning, improves communiqué and develops decision-making abilities in family members.

Family meeting are very popular among first generation family businesses, which usually includes the entrepreneur, the spouse and their children. Generally meetings take place when family members are taking meals and/or in pleasant conditions. The subject of meetings depends on the stage of life cycle and growth of family business. Initial meetings center on sharing of domestic tasks. In subsequent meetings business owners try to shape the business activities, deliberate about rights and duties of owners as well as managers, set expectations and goals to be achieved in family business, debate about the ambitions and goals alignment of family and future growth of family business.

Family Assembly

A family assembly is an inclusive forum for all family members. Family can decide who should to be incorporated in family assembly. Larger families may hold retreats with well-thought-out program of events and meetings suitable to diverse groups such as children, elderly members, shareholders. The objective of family assembly can be education, communiqué, building relations with distant family members, contribution to business growth and governance. Family assemblies include social events and activities. Through social activities and interactions detached family members can build solid associations help decreases conflict and increases acceptance of varied viewpoints.

The family assembly of siblings and cousins' consortium, usually they are the people who are responsible for leadership, control and governance of family business.

Nevertheless, this is not mandatory. A sensitive issue is benchmarks (age, voting rights etc.) used to select participates. Family assembly is governed by family charter which lays down: who will be the head of assembly; frequency at which meeting are held; principles to vote; and other relevant matters. Generally issues deliberated in family assembly are election of the board; dividend policy; review of performance of executive members and future goals.

Family Council

Formal family councils are suitable for larger and more complicated family businesses. Family councils usually comprise of representatives from different groups in business family. Families influence business in numerous ways. Family councils are also useful for non-family executives, they provide family platform to share views without including non-family executive in family matters, and they decrease family`s interference in daily operations.

Family councils lessen possibility of fights, align diverse beliefs, facilitate planning of transition of power and allow specific preferences of members to be incorporated in transmissible goals, thus supporting commitment to decisions and decision-making. Main topics in family council meetings usually are: plan for leadership transition, investment strategy, philanthropy, dividend policy, and integration board of directors.

Family Council work with following purposes:

1. Family mission and meaning (shared values, appreciate family history
2. Steward of all the family business, share philanthropy)
3. Understanding business (review strategy, vision, performance, openings and challenges); communication and mutual understanding (strengthen relations, exchange information)
4. Problem solving (address issues and grievances)
5. Family knowledge (understand rights
6. Duties and effects of ownership
7. Improve interactive skills, family dynamics)
8. Leadership transition (review family constitution, train younger generation)

Family Office

Family office includes extensive variety of facility centers and wealth administration functions. Family office is adopted very large family setups explicitly either for their personal benefit or in alliance with others. The main function of family office is to manage family wealth centrally, but many also offer services like insurance financial advisory, legal advice, tax consultancy and asset management. In adding, family office can organize events and activities like education and mentoring of youngsters, family newsletter, physical security, philanthropic services and custodian services for family members.

Family offices can be of three groups: (a) not-for-profit family office controlled by one or more families, offering services only those families; (b) for-profit family office controlled by family owners, offering services to other clients and also family; (c) for profit family office owned by professionals and consultants, who offer wealth management and several other services to numerous families. The decision on type of family office depends on quantity of wealth, readiness and capability of family members to handle roles and responsibilities in family office as well as trust and faith amongst sets of family owners and experts. Family offices can also organize distinct company with paid managers and board of directors.

Other Practices

The family business that have over the period grow in size of a conglomerate have greater accountability and responsibilities not only towards internal stakeholders but more importantly towards external stakeholders such as local community, society government and environment, business competitors etc. Thus it is necessary that they adopt some additional governance practices as discussed below:

Separation of Ownership and Management

One of the crucial aspect that results destruction of owners' value in family business are splits in family. Splits only does not upsets business atmosphere and admin process, but it also corrode net worth and growth potentials. Family businesses are affected by psycho-dynamic aspects such as rivalry among siblings, desire of children to separate from parents, nuptial disharmony, identity issues and ownership allocations amid family members. Hence is it desirable that there is separation of ownership and management to minimize the detrimental impact of family rivalries. This involves placing the management of business under the supervision of professionals who do not have the ownership right in family business. This separation allows accomplished experts to manage the complicated issues business in unbiased manner.

Board of Directors

The board should balance executive and non-executive directors including independent directors to provide efficient board management. The number of directors should be decided on the basis of age, size, nature of operations and prospective growth plan of the organization. Non-executive directors should be selected by family council and elected by shareholders. The board of directors should appreciate role of employees, particularly key management, in success of business and should ensure that employees are treated with equity and fairness. The business should recognize rights and responsibilities of its stakeholders, both through mutual agreement and established laws and should inspire active collaboration to attain financial and operational sustainability.

Ethics, Disclosure, and Transparency

Disclosing the financial statements always enhances the confidence among various stakeholders of the company, but transparency is the biggest block in corporate governance worldwide. The business organizations should have a strong ethical practice of true and fair presentation of financial statements and effective answerability mechanisms. In family businesses, there are certain systems of financial and non-financial perks, reward systems brings transparency which is an essential tool to improve justice to stake holders.

Professional Management

Family members, who control and manage businesses need to be desirably qualified and are expected to behave in professional. In today's challenging times of economic uncertainty, technological disruptions, ever-changing business norms and environment, it is implausible that family members alone can steer growth in family business. Stewardship theory also reasons that the rationalization of control and management amid owners to professional managers can be a positive move towards managing intricacies of modern day business. Lack of professional management may damage competitiveness and destroy shareholder value. Family need to appreciate that there are countless opportunities are present in liberalized and globalized markets.

Succession Planning

Leadership transition is very crucial for continuity of family businesses. Succession Planning is important because at the heart of leadership transition is the talent identification, training and grooming of potential successor. There should be system in place that identifies key roles and map out ways to ensure family business has right people with the right expertise, abilities, and experiences, in the right place at the right time.

Individual family can choose the format of governance based their size, scale of operations, ownership style, concerns of the family, therefore governance structure and mechanism may vary. Sound corporate governance framework facilitates the below:

1. Succession planning and helps in leadership transition
2. Separates ownership from management
3. Reduces conflicts of interest amid family members
4. Improves management processes
5. Fosters cooperation between family and businesses
6. Enhancing the positive impact on economy
7. Introduces better recruitment and promotion policies in business
8. Promotes democracy
9. Ensures transparency of roles and responsibilities
10. Protect all stakeholders interests thus leads to growth and sustainability

CONCLUSION

Increasing globalization has posed new challenges for family businesses. Many of these challenges were might be tackled by adopting sound corporate governance structures. By adopting good corporate governance measures at both family and business levels, reduce problems associated with information asymmetry and makes family business less risky. Finally, applying good governance principles adds strategic outlook through external independent directors, enhances corporate entrepreneurship, creates new value, improves competitiveness, mitigate agency risks and ensure long-term sustainability of family business.

REFERENCES

Accenture Strategy. (2019). *Family Businesses in Asia. Accenture Strategy, 2019.* Retreived from https://www.accenture.com/_acnmedia/thought-leadership-assets/pdf/accenture-family-businesses-in-asia-deepening-the-roots-of-trust.pdf

Alderson, J. K. (2011). *Understanding the family business.* Business Expert Press. doi:10.4128/9781606491706

Astrachan, J. (2010). Strategy in family business: Toward a multidimensional research agenda. *Journal of Family Business Strategy*, *1*(1), 6–14. doi:10.1016/j.jfbs.2010.02.001

Bain, D. (2015). *The top 500 family businesses in the world*. Retrieved from https://familybusiness.ey-vx.com/pdfs/182-187.pdf

Berghe, L., & Carchon, S. (2002). Family business research: Corporate governance practices in Flemish family businesses. *Corporate Governance*, *10*(3), 225–245. doi:10.1111/1467-8683.00286

Bernard, C. (2015). *European Family Business Trends*. KPMG Enterprise.

Botero, I., Cruz, C., De Massis, A., & Nordqvist, M. (2015). Family business research in the European context. *European Journal of International Management*, *9*(2), 139–159. doi:10.1504/EJIM.2015.067858

Caspar, C., Dias, A., & Elstrodt, H. (2010). Organizational practice: The five attributes of enduring family businesses. *The McKinsey Quarterly*, *1*, 1–10.

Chua, J. H., Chrisman, J. J., & Sharma, P. (1999). Defining the family business by behavior. *Entrepreneurship Theory and Practice*, *23*(4), 19–39. doi:10.1177/104225879902300402

CII. (2011). *Indian IT/ITeS Industry: Evolving business models for sustained growth*. Confederation of Indian Industry Report.

Comi, A., & Eppler, M. J. (2014). Diagnosing capabilities in family firms: An overview of visual research methods and suggestions for future applications. *Journal of Family Business Strategy*, *5*(1), 41–51. doi:10.1016/j.jfbs.2014.01.009

Credit Suisse. (2011). *Asian Family Businesses Report*. Zurich, Switzerland: Emerging market research institute. Retrieved from http://www.efiko.org/material/Asian%20Family%20%20Report%20by%20Credit%20Suisse.pdf

Dana, L., & Smyrnios, K., (2010). *The MGI Australian Family and Private Business Survey: 2010*. Academic Press.

Davis, P. (1983). Realizing the potential of the family business. *Organizational Dynamics*, *12*(1), 47–56. doi:10.1016/0090-2616(83)90026-8

De Massis, A., Audretsch, D., Uhlaner, L., & Kammerlander, N. (2018). Innovation with limited resources: management lessons from the German Mittelstand. *Journal of Product of Innovation Management, 35*(1), 125-146. Doi:10.1111/jpim.12373

Donnelley, R. G., (1964). The family business. *Harvard Business Review, 42*(4), 93-105.

Duh, M., Tominc, P., & Rebernik, M. (2009). The Importance of Family Enterprises in Transition Economies: Is It Overestimated? *Eastern European Economics*, *47*(6), 22–42. doi:10.2753/EEE0012-8775470602

EFB. (2012). *Family Business Statistics. European Family Businesses 2009*. Retrieved from http://www.europeanfamilybusinesses.eu/uploads/Modules/Publications/pp---family-business-statisticsv2.pdf

Family Firm Institute. (2017). *Global Data Points*. Retrieved from the FFI website on o November 27, 2017: https://www.ffi.org/page/globaldatapoints

Fernandez-Araoz, C., Iqbal, S., & Ritter, J. (2015). Why family firms in East Asia struggle with succession. *Harvard Business Review*. Retrieved from https://hbr.org/2015/03/why-family-firms-in-east-asia-struggle-with-succession

Fernández-Olmos, M., Gargallo-Castel, A., & Giner-Bagües, E. (2016). Internationalization and performance in Spanish family SMES: The W-curve. *BRQ Business Research Quarterly*, *19*(2), 122–136. doi:10.1016/j.brq.2015.07.001

Finnigan, M. (2014). *Infographic: Spanish family businesses | Campden FB*. Campdenfb.com. Retrieved 8 January 2016, from http://www.campdenfb.com/article/infographic-spanish-family-businesses

Forbes Insights. (2012). Global wealth and family ties. A worldwide study of how fortunes are founded managed and passed on. New York: Author.

Gulzar, M. A., & Wang, Z. J. (2010). Corporate Governance and Non-Listed Family Owned Businesses: Evidence from Pakistan. *International Journal of Innovation, Management and Technology*, *1*(2), 124–129.

Haunschild, L., & Wolter, H. (2010). *The economic importance of family and women's enterprises*. Institute for SME Research.

Institute for Family Business. (2011). *The UK Family Business Sector*. Oxford Economics.

KPMG. (2013). *CII's Family Business Network (India chapter)*. Retrieved from http://www.kpmgfamilybusiness.com/family-owned-businesses-backbone-indias-economy

OCED. (2005). *Organization for Economic Cooperation and Development, OECD (2005) Glossary of Statistical Terms*. Retrieved from https://stats.oecd.org/glossary/detail.asp?ID=6778

Poza, E. J., & Daugherty, M. S. (2013). *Family business* (4th ed.). Cengage Learning.

PwC. (2009). *Family Business Survey 2007-2008, Price Water House Coopers, 2009*. Retrieved from https://www.pwc.com/extweb/home.nsf/docid/1FB68AE4ADAFB42E85257395004EEC89

PwC. (2019a). *Thailand Family Business Survey 2019*. Price Waterhouse Cooper (PwC) Thailand. Retrieved from https://www.pwc.com/th/en/services/epb/thailand-Family-Business-survey-2019.html

PwC. (2019b). *India Family Business Survey*. Price Waterhouse Cooper (PwC). Retrieved from https://www.pwc.in/assets/pdfs/research-insights/fbs/2019/pwc-india-family-business-survey-2019.pdf

PwC. (2019c). *PwC Middle East Family Business Survey*. Price Waterhouse Cooper (PwC). Retrieved from https://www.pwc.com/m1/en/publications/documents/family-business-survey-2019.pdf

PwC Family Business Survey. (2012). *The family firm: Central to the success pf the Middle East*. Retrieved from https://www.pwc.com/m1/en/publications/documents/family-firm-english.pdf

Rastogi S. & Agrawal, R., (2010). Intention of offspring to join the family enterprise: a study of Indian businesses. *Annals of Innovation & Entrepreneurship 2010, 1*, 5603. Doi:10.3402/aie.v1i1.5603

Rexhepi, B. (2015). *Small family business: guarantor of economic and social development (PhD)*. University of Pristina.

Stiftung für Familienunternehmen. (2014). *Informationsmaterial Familienunternehmen*. https://www.familienunternehmen.de/media/public/pdf/daten-zahlen-fakten/sfudaten-zahlen-fakten_de.pdf

Tharawat Magazine. (2014). *The Economic Impact of Family Business*. Author.

Tirdasari, N., & Dhewanto, W. (2012). Family business succession in Indonesia: A study of hospitality industry. *Social and Behavioral Sciences*, *57*, 69–74. doi:10.1016/j.sbspro.2012.09.1159

University of Vermont. (2014). *Family Business Facts*. Available on line at: https://www.uvm.edu/business/vfbi/?Page=facts.html

Venter, E., & Farrington, S. (2009). *The nature of family businesses and their importance for economic development*. Nelson Mandela Metropolitan University.

Zapatero, M., Rodriguez, J. M., & Rodriguez Alcaide, J. (2012). El consejero en la empresa familiar: Teoria y praxis. *Revista de Empresa Familiar*, *2*(1), 45–54.

Chapter 3
Corporate Social Performance and Governance Quality Across the BRICS Countries

Sinem Ates
Department of Business Administration, Yalova University, Turkey

ABSTRACT

This chapter seeks to examine the level of corporate social performance of the BRICS companies and investigate the effect of the country's governance quality on the environmental, social, and governance (ESG) performance of the companies. Analysis of the BRICS companies' ESG scores for 2009 - 2018 indicated that the level of ESG performance in the BRICS countries differs from each other considerably. Overall, results of fixed effects regression analysis revealed that governance quality of countries has a positive effect on ESG scores of companies. Based on these findings, it was suggested to improve governance quality thereby encouraging companies to fulfill their social responsibilities.

INTRODUCTION

Before joining South Africa to the group in 2010, Brazil, Russia, India, and China were called the BRIC countries by economist Jim O'Neill suggesting that they would play an active role in the economic growth of the world (O'Neill, 2001). In a following report published in 2003, highly positive projections were made about the economic development of the BRIC countries. The prediction that the BRIC countries would have a larger economy than the United States within less than 40 years is just one of them. However, as also stated in the report, the main assumption underlying

DOI: 10.4018/978-1-7998-6669-5.ch003

Copyright © 2021, IGI Global. Copying or distributing in print or electronic forms without written permission of IGI Global is prohibited.

these positive projections is growth-supportive policy settings implemented by the BRIC countries. More precisely, the authors indicated macroeconomic stability, institutional capacity, openness, and education as the crucial factors that may affect economic growth (Wilson and Purushothaman, 2003).

Governance quality of countries has been discussed for several decades as one of those institutional factors which have a correlation with the economic growth of countries (e.g. Hall and Jones, 1999; Kurtz and Schrank, 2007; Wilson, 2016). Governance mechanisms at country-level shape also governance attributes at firm-level (Aggarwal et al., 2008). Traditionally, the main concern of corporate governance was shareholders, thereby to protect the interests of shareholders was at the heart of corporate governance rules. However, this traditional model of corporate governance has been criticized for not having a long-term perspective due to its merely focus on short-term profit maximization. Recently, there has been a shift from a short-term financial oriented stance to an objective of long-term sustainable development (Fenwick et al., 2019).

It is hard to give a generally accepted definition of sustainable development. One of the early definitions of sustainable development appeared in the Brundtland Report of the World Commission on Environment and Development (WCED) as: "development that meets the needs of the present without compromising the ability of future generations to meet their own needs" (WCED, 1987). The responsibility mentioned in the definition is valid for all types of organizations such as governments, companies, individuals, and so forth.

In order to achieve the objective of sustainable development at the corporate level, companies should concentrate on the interests of all other stakeholders such as employees, customers, governments, and even the general public, as well as shareholders. All the mentioned stakeholders have different requirements and expectations from companies. While employees may expect safe working conditions and fair wages, governments may care about the payment of a fair share of tax. Customers are satisfied when the quality and the price of the products and/or services meet their expectations. On the other hand, the general public may be interested in the environmental effect of business activities. It is possible to list many more examples regarding both the types of stakeholders and the different requirements of them. In summary, the underlying principle towards an attempt to be sustainable should be the awareness of the requirements of all stakeholders and developing a business strategy in accordance with these requirements. Whether and to what extent companies fulfill this obligation represents their corporate social performance (CSP, henceforth) and is measured by various indicators in various studies. Membership of a sustainability index (Lourenço et al., 2012) publication of sustainability report (Cardamone et al., 2012), GRI-based sustainability reporting (Miralles-Quirós et al., 2017) are just a few examples of CSP measurement tools used in academic studies.

However, in order to be able to assess the sustainability performance on different dimensions separately, it is more efficacious to utilize the environmental, social and governance (ESG, henceforth) scores of rating agencies such as ESG scores of Thomson Reuters, MSCI ESG KLD STATS, Bloomberg's ESG Disclosure Scores.

Through this study, in the first stage, the CSP of the BRICS companies was analyzed using The Thomson Reuters ESG scores for 2009-2018. As the second stage of this study, utilizing World Bank Worldwide Governance Indicators Database, governance quality of the BRICS countries were identified and the relationship between governance quality of the BRICS countries and CSP of the BRICS companies was examined with panel data methods.

The contribution of this study is twofold: First, identifying the ESG performance of the BRICS companies over 10 years would provide evidence to determine whether the anticipated economic growth potential of BRICS countries would be sustainable. Second, identification of governance quality dimensions having a positive relationship with CSP would prompt policymakers to focus on and try to improve those governance quality dimensions.

Background

Corporate Social Performance in the BRICS Countries

Signitzer and Prexl (2007) use the term "corporate sustainability" to define sustainable development at the firm-level and indicate that it can be considered as a hypernym for all other terms referring to the role of business in society, such as corporate social responsibility (CSR), corporate social performance (CSP), social accountability. While CSR covers the environmental, social, and economic issues addressed by the companies besides their routine business activities, CSP is the assessment of the level of active engagement with CSR activities (Conway, 2018).

Due to the positive projections regarding the economic growth of BRICS countries, the potential sustainability of this anticipated economic growth has come under question. However, since there has not been a common method to measure the level of corporate social responsibility disclosure or activities of companies, differential conclusions have been made in various studies utilizing different tools to measure corporate social responsibility and/or performance.

Examining ESG scores of BRICS companies over the period 2010-2012, Garcia et al. (2019) reported that while Brazil and Russia showed an increase in ESG scores, India and South Africa had a decreasing trend. For the period under consideration, the highest ESG scores belonged to South Africa, whilst China had the lowest environmental and social scores. Peterson and Bishop (2015) compared

BRICS countries with each other and also with other country groups in terms of sustainability performance utilizing the Sustainability Society Index. When compared with developed countries, the only sustainability dimension which had a statistically significant difference was the human well-being dimension. More precisely, BRICS countries had a lower human well-being score than developed countries but did not differ on the other sustainability dimensions. The authors also revealed that Brazil had the highest sustainability score while the score of South Africa was the worst among the BRICS countries.

A similar comparison with those of Peterson and Bishop (2015) was done by Bhatia and Tuli (2018) for the BRIC and Bhatia and Makkar (2019) for the BRICS countries but this time the benchmarking criterion was sustainability reporting practices instead of sustainability performance. Using their self-created CSR disclosure index, Bhatia and Makkar (2019) compared the level of CSR disclosures of the companies from the BRICS countries and the USA and the UK. The content analysis of the websites and annual reports of the companies revealed that developed countries had a higher level of CSR disclosure than BRICS companies. On the other hand, when the BRIC companies were compared with the companies from the USA and the UK as per the GRI-based reporting practices, BRIC companies were found to report on GRI performance indicators more than the companies in developed countries. As a result of the content analysis of sustainability reports, India took place on the top and Brazil was the second of the list showing the GRI-based sustainability disclosure scores of the BRIC countries (Bhatia and Tuli, 2018). This finding is similar to those of Arrive and Feng (2018) who found that Brazil and India had a higher CSR disclosure than the other BRICS countries. The authors attributed this finding to the fact that whilst reporting on CSR practices was mandatory in Brazil and India, it was voluntary in other BRICS countries. In some other studies, Brazil was found to have the highest percentage of companies with transparent CSR reporting (Miras-Rodríguez et al., 2019) and the strongest intensity of CSR communications through channels such as annual reports, websites, CSR reports (Li et al., 2010). The BRICS companies were also compared in terms of compliance with their sustainability reporting practices with GRI guidelines. The content analysis of the relevant reports of the companies revealed that Indian companies had the highest coverage level of GRI indicators. On the contrary, the Russian companies had the lowest coverage score of GRI indicators. This research has an additional finding, which is in line with those of Bhatia and Tuli (2018), indicating economy and environment categories as the most and least reported categories, respectively for all BRICS countries (Kumar and Das, 2018).

Using a quite different methodology from the mentioned studies, Ali et al. (2018) examined the adoption level of the United Nations' Sustainable Development Goals (UN SDGs) in the BRICS countries. To this end, the authors analyzed the vision and mission statements of multinational companies via content analysis. China was determined as the country which had the highest adoption level of UN SDGs. On the other hand, South Africa took place at the bottom of the list.

Based on the mentioned studies, it is possible to comment that the finding indicating a significant difference between CSP performances and/or disclosure levels of the BRICS companies and the companies from developed countries is not surprising. However, these studies also provide insights into the significant variation in the levels of CSP within BRICS countries. This variation has been explained by the different institutional contexts of BRICS countries.

Institutional Context and CSP

The BRICS countries represent 42% of the world's total population. With a total GDP of $20,2 trillion in 2018, BRICS countries cover 24% of the world's total GDP. It seems that Goldman Sach's prediction that BRIC countries could be worth more than 50% of the G6 countries by 2025 has already been realized. As of 2018, the combined GDP of BRIC(S) countries accounts for 53% (54%) of the G6 countries in US dollar terms (World Bank, 2018).

The BRICS countries have been predicted to have significant economic growth over the next years. However, it was also noted in the Goldman Sach's report that some assumptions should be satisfied to realize these positive projections. The main underlying assumption is that macroeconomic stability, institutional capacity, openness, and education would all support the economic growth of the countries.

Although economic growth potential is common for all the BRICS countries, they have environmental differences which Luo et al. (2011) elaborated on. Luo et al. (2011) addressed these differences for the BRIC countries in terms of economic, institutional, social-cultural, and industrial environments. Under the economic environment heading, the authors discussed the differences in natural resources, literacy levels, and some economic indicators of the BRIC countries. While examining the social-cultural environment, a comparison was made between the BRIC countries based on cultural values, Human Development Index, and some World Bank indicators such as income distribution and poverty. Since the BRIC countries have a competitive advantage in different industries, the strategic management decisions of the countries based on the industrial parameters are expected to differ from each other. Finally, utilizing World Bank Worldwide Governance Indicators, the authors emphasized the strengths and weaknesses of the institutional environment of the BRIC countries.

Based on these arguments, the institutional context may be claimed as one of the factors which shape the strategic management decisions of the countries and thereby the companies incorporated in those countries. Since the corporate social responsibility strategy is also a specific type of strategic management decision, it is expected to change based on the institutional context of countries. It is possible to support these theoretical assertions with the empirical research conducted on this issue. Thus, along with the increasing importance of sustainable development, the relationship between governance quality of the countries and social performance of the corporations has been tested empirically.

In a recent study of Coluccia et al. (2018), regulatory quality, rule of law, and voice and accountability were found to be positively correlated with ESG scores of companies listed in Eurostoxx 50 index. Gómez and Garcia (2020) developed a governance quality index based on the Worldwide Governance Indicators and examined the impact of the governance quality of the Latin American countries on the CSR disclosures of the companies determined by the content analysis of annual and CSR reports. Empirical analyses showed that while the governance quality had a positive effect upon the information disclosure related to customers and products and human rights and ethics, it had no significant effect on the other disclosure indices, i.e. employees, environment, and community. Based on a sample of 14,174 firm-year observations from 26 countries, Baldini et al. (2018) investigated country and firm-level determinants of ESG disclosure. Among the country-level factors, the level of corruption was found to influence all disclosure scores negatively, whilst the unemployment rate had a positive effect on the combined ESG score and its three pillars. The authors got mixed results for the remaining country-level variables including the legal framework, labor protection, and cultural values.

The nexus between governance quality and CSR in the BRICS countries has been examined in a limited number of studies. Through these studies, the corporate social responsibility strategies of the companies in the BRICS countries have been discovered to change based on the institutional governance characteristics (Li et al., 2010; Miras-Rodríguez et al., 2019).

Using the rule and relation-based classification of Li and Filer (2007), Li et al. (2010) concluded that rule-based governance structure fosters the CSR disclosure of firms. Likewise, Miras-Rodríguez et al. (2019) classified the BRICS countries as the rule, family, and relation-based and labeled this classification as an institutional-level corporate governance mechanism. Using additional firm and group-level corporate governance indicators as independent variables, the authors concluded that determinants of CSR reporting practices change based on the institutional-level governance mechanisms. The high CSR disclosure levels in the countries with laws and regulations regarding CSR practices (Arrive and Feng, 2018) provide additional evidence for the impact of institutional settings on CSR activities of the companies. A cross-sectional survey of business professionals and undergraduate business students from the BRIC countries showed that the countries with self-expression values and more control of corruption attach more importance to social and environmental corporate responsibility issues (Ralston et al.,2015).

The economic growth potential of BRICS countries and their different institutional governance characteristics create a need to explore whether these countries could achieve sustainable development through their CSR activities and their governance indicators would support this sustainable development or not. This study aims to fulfill this need by investigating the ESG performance of the BRICS companies and the link between governance quality and ESG performance.

RESEARCH

Sample and Measurement of Variables

In this study, the Datastream database was used to collect the financial and ESG data of the BRICS companies. Hence, the initial sample consisted of all the BRICS firms having data in the Datastream for 2009-2018. From these, the firm-year observations with missing values were excluded. After this elimination, the final sample is composed of 3,727 firm-year observations, most of which belong to firms from China and South Africa. The percentage distribution of the firm-year observations by countries is as follows: China (28), South Africa (25), Brazil (20), India (19), and Russia (8).

Sustainability Performance of the BRICS Companies

In this study, to measure corporate social performance, ESG scores of the BRICS companies were collected from the Thomson Reuters Datastream ASSET4 Database. The Thomson Reuters ESG scores have been used by various academic studies to measure the sustainability performance of the companies (e.g. Miralles-Quirós et al., 2018; Coluccia et al., 2018; Rajesh, 2020). Having a bottom-up calculation methodology, the ESG score calculation of Thomson Reuters begins with data points gathered from publicly available information and used to calculate indicator values. Then, calculated indicator values are grouped into ten categories which are finally rolled up into three pillar scores, namely environmental, social, and governance. The environmental pillar score is calculated on the basis of three categories: resource use, emissions, and environmental innovation. The social pillar score is composed of category scores regarding workforce, human rights, community, and product responsibility. Finally, the category scores of management, shareholders, and CSR strategy constitute the government pillar score. The overall ESG score is an aggregated measure of ten categories which constitute the three pillar scores (Refinitiv, 2020).

Governance Quality of BRICS Countries

In the extant literature, there have been various ways of specifying the governance characteristics of countries. Some studies classified the sample countries as rule, relation (Li et al., 2010) and, also family-based (Miras-Rodríguez et al., 2019) and made an overall assessment of governance characteristics of the sample countries. On the other hand, some studies have addressed the governance characteristics of countries separately, utilizing some specific indexes developed for this purpose (Coluccia et al., 2018).

In this study, the assessment of governance quality of the BRICS countries is based on the Worldwide Governance Indicators (WGI) of the World Bank. WGI covers the following six dimensions related to governance quality (Kaufmann et al., 2011):

- ***Control of Corruption:*** *Capturing perceptions of the extent to which public power is exercised for private gain, including both petty and grand forms of corruption, as well as 'capture' of the state by elites and private interests.*
- ***Government Effectiveness:*** *Capturing perceptions of the quality of public services, the quality of the civil service and the degree of its independence from political pressures, the quality of policy formulation and implementation, and the credibility of the government's commitment to such policies.*
- ***Political Stability and Absence of Violence/Terrorism:*** *Capturing perceptions of the likelihood that the government will be destabilized or overthrown by unconstitutional or violent means, including politically-motivated violence and terrorism.*
- ***Regulatory Quality:*** *Capturing perceptions of the ability of the government to formulate and implement sound policies and regulations that permit and promote private sector development.*
- ***Rule of Law:*** *Capturing perceptions of the extent to which agents have confidence in and abide by the rules of society, and in particular the quality of contract enforcement, property rights, the police, and the courts, as well as the likelihood of crime and violence.*
- ***Voice and Accountability:*** *Capturing perceptions of the extent to which a country's citizens are able to participate in selecting their government, as well as freedom of expression, freedom of association, and a free media.*

Control Variables

Several country and firm-level indicators were included as control variables in the research models which were developed to examine the link between ESG performance of the companies and governance quality of the countries in which those companies are incorporated.

Size, financial leverage, and return on assets (ROA) were determined as firm-level control variables. While ROA was gathered directly from Datastream, size and financial leverage were calculated by the natural logarithm of the assets and ratio of total liabilities to total assets, respectively.

Gross Domestic Product (GDP) per capita and development level of the capital market were the country-level control variables. GDP per capita of the BRICS countries was derived from the World Development Indicators Database of the World Bank. The development level of the capital market is an author-created index utilizing several indicators related to capital markets, namely "market capitalization of listed domestic companies (% of GDP)", "stocks traded, total value (% of GDP)", "stocks traded, turnover ratio of domestic shares (%)", and "listed domestic companies per capita". First of all, all countries were ranked according to each of these four indicators for every year of the sample period. Then, the yearly averages of each countries' rank on these indicators were calculated and used as the proxy for the countries' level of capital market development in that specific year.

Empirical Model

In order to investigate whether the governance quality of countries has an effect on the ESG performance of the companies located in those countries, the following regression model was developed:

$$CSP_{it} = \beta_0 + \beta_1 GQ_{it} + \beta_2 X_{it} + a_i + u_{it} \tag{1}$$

where *CSP* represents the corporate social performance of the company and was proxied by overall ESG score or each of the pillar scores (*ENV, SOC, GOV*) of the company. *GQ* stands for the governance quality of the country and proxied by Control of Corruption (*CC*), Government Effectiveness (*GE*), Political Stability and Absence of Violence/Terrorism (*PV*), Regulatory Quality (*RQ*), Rule of Law (*RL*), and Voice and Accountability (*VA*) in separate models. X_{it} covers both firm-level (*SIZE, LEV, ROA*) and country-level (*GDP* per capita, development level of capital *MARKET*) control variables. β_0 represents the constant term. $(a_i + u_{it})$ is the composite error term. Finally, *i* and *t* denote for the company and year, respectively.

RESULTS

ESG Performance of the BRICS Companies

Table 1 provides the mean and standard deviation figures of environmental, social, governance, and overall ESG scores for each BRICS country over the sample period: 2009-2018. From Table 1 it can be seen that South Africa had the highest mean values of overall ESG scores for the period of concern. South Africa was followed by Brazil, India, Russia, and finally China having the lowest overall ESG score. South Africa also had the highest social and governance scores. China had the lowest overall ESG score since it had the lowest environmental and social scores. When it comes to the pillar scores of ESG, the best score among the three pillars was the social score for Brazil, India, and South Africa, while it was the governance score for Russia and China.

Table 1. ESG Statistics for 2009 – 2018

COUNTRY	Firm-Years	Environmental		Social		Governance		Overall ESG	
		Mean	S.D.	Mean	S.D.	Mean	S.D.	Mean	S.D.
BRAZIL	732	53.78	20.41	58.07	21.63	50.29	20.75	54.24	16.96
RUSSIA	296	45.69	19.42	46.96	20.89	49.93	20.17	47.43	15.47
INDIA	703	52.52	21.88	54.31	20.31	50.51	20.40	52.54	16.24
CHINA	1,048	41.41	21.15	35.36	17.37	50.47	20.37	42.03	15.14
S. AFRICA	948	52.71	20.04	59.55	17.69	50.97	21.01	54.61	15.52
BRICS	3,727	49.15	21.38	50.47	21.65	50.53	20.59	50.04	16.71

However, Table 1 does not provide insight into the annual comparison of the ESG performances of the BRICS countries. It is possible to see this comparison in Figures 1-4 for environmental, social, governance, and overall ESG scores, respectively.

Figure 1 shows the comparison of the environmental scores of the BRICS countries over 2009-2018. At the beginning of the sample period, the ranking among the BRICS countries was as follows: while South Africa took place on the top, Brazil and India followed it relatively closely. However, Russia in the 4th place and China in the last place had considerably lower environmental scores compared to other countries. During the period of concern, each country had a quite different pattern for the environmental score, hence, the ranking at the end of the sample period was a little bit different than in 2009. The top 3 countries according to their environmental scores were Brazil, India, and South Africa, respectively. Although the ranking of Russia and China was the same as at the beginning of the period, their environmental performance at the end of the period was relatively closer to other countries.

Figure 1. Environmental scores of the BRICS countries

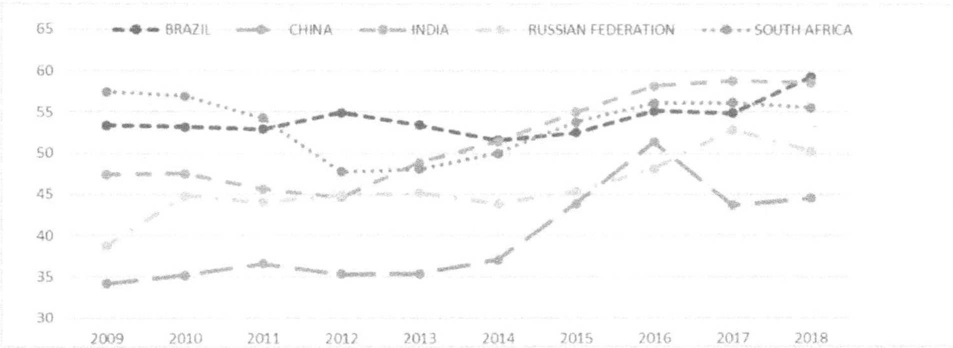

The comparison of social scores of the BRICS countries is given in Figure 2. Similar to the picture in the environmental score, according to the social scores, China and Russia were again on the last two ranks both at the beginning and end of the period. However, unlike Figure 1, Figure 2 reveals that China had very low social scores not only at the beginning but also at the end of the sample period compared to other countries. At the end of 2018, the country with the highest social score

Figure 2. Social scores of the BRICS countries

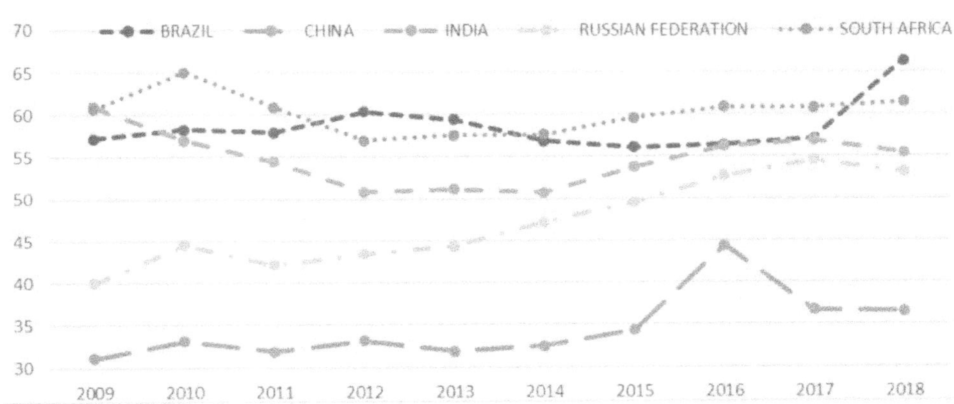

was Brazil due to the sharp increase in 2018 and it was followed by South Africa and India, respectively.

Figure 3. Governance scores of the BRICS countries

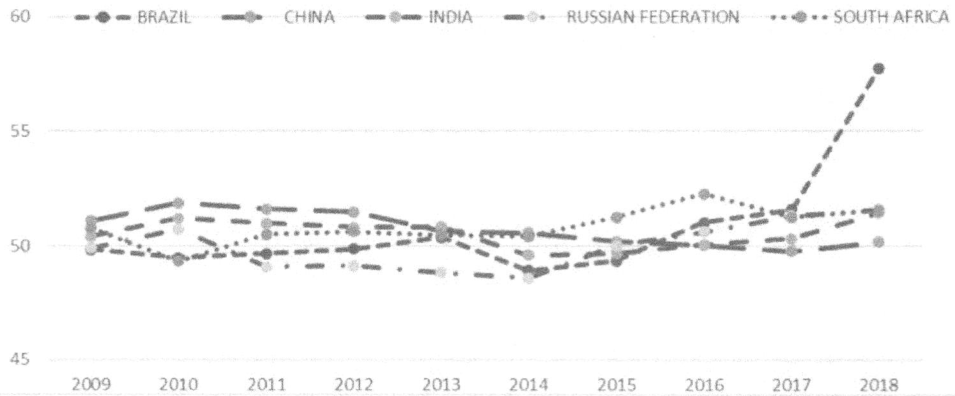

Figure 3 presents the governance scores of the BRICS countries from 2009 to 2018. As can be seen from the figure, the dispersion of the governance scores across the BRICS countries between 2009-2017 was considerably smaller compared to the environmental and social scores. However, as is the case for environmental and social scores, Brazil hit the peak of governance scores in 2018 and reached up to number one.

Figure 4. Overall ESG scores of the BRICS countries

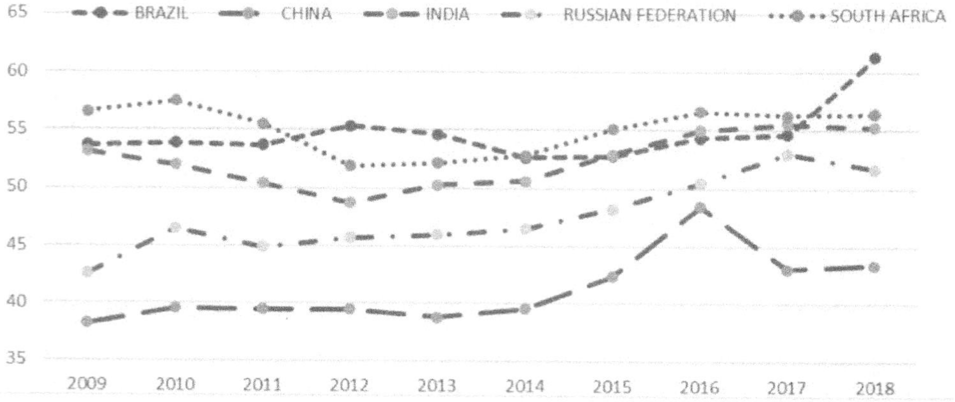

Finally, the overall ESG scores of the BRICS countries are presented in Figure 4. Although each country's ESG score fluctuated throughout the period, the ranking at the end of the period was not much different from the ranking at the beginning of the period. The only exception was Brazil which reached a peak in 2018 and became the top of the list.

Besides the comparison between the ESG performance of the BRICS countries, focusing on the change in countries' individual environmental, social, and governance performances over the years would provide additional insight. Thus, the tendency of the mean values of each ESG scores during 2009 - 2018 is given through Figure 5-9 for Brazil, Russia, India, China, and South Africa, respectively.

Figure 5 shows the trends of the three pillars of ESG and overall ESG scores of Brazilian companies for the sample period. The ranking of pillar scores did not change during 2009-2018, i.e. Brazilian companies had always higher social scores than environmental and governance scores, respectively. The scores of all pillars were relatively stable over 2009 – 2011. Although there was a slight increase in 2012 for all pillar scores, they experienced a decrease from 2013 to 2015. The slight increase which began in 2015 continued steadily until 2018 and it turned a sharp increase in 2018. Brazilian companies have achieved the highest ESG scores in 2018.

Figure 5. ESG performance of Brazil

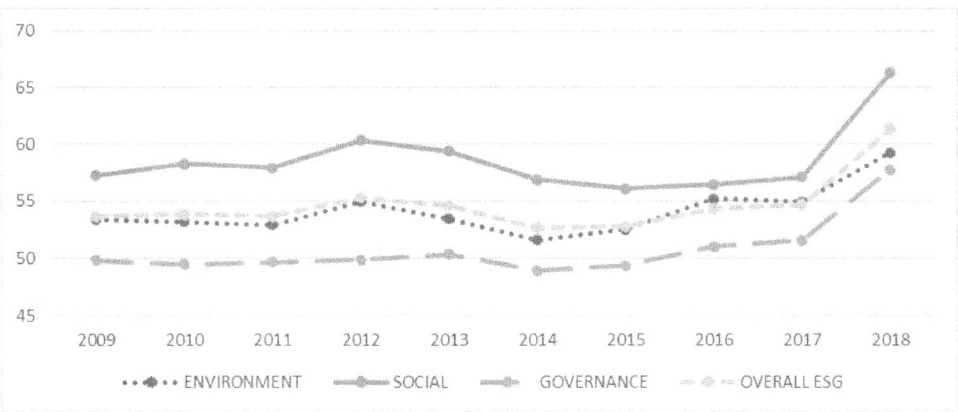

Figure 6 illustrates the change in ESG scores of Russian companies between 2009 – 2018. The governance pillar score showed a gradual decrease from 2009 to the end of 2014 with the exception of a slight increase in 2010. The increase that started in 2015 continued steadily until the end of 2018. On the other hand, the starting point of the environmental and social scores was very close to each other,

Figure 6. ESG performance of Russia

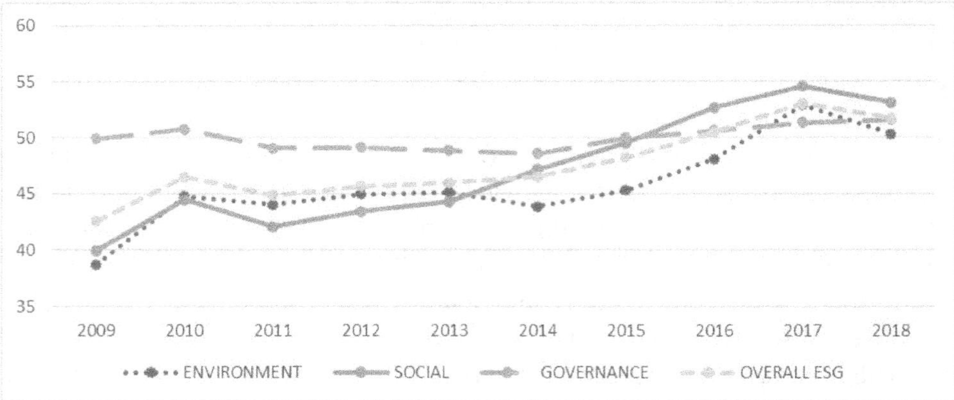

both scores reached almost the same level showing a significant increase in 2010. However, the decrease in social score in 2011 left it behind the environmental score until 2014. In 2014, the social score increased sharply, and this increase continued steadily until 2018. Although it showed a slight decline in 2018, the social score had the highest value among all scores at the end of 2018. The environmental score had a similar pattern with the social score between 2015 and 2018.

Figure 7 gives information about the ESG performance of Indian companies. During the period covered by the figure, the governance score remained almost steady. On the other hand, both environmental and social scores experienced significant fluctuations. During 2010, while the environmental score was stable, the social score decreased steeply. This sharp decrease in social score continued

Figure 7. ESG performance of India

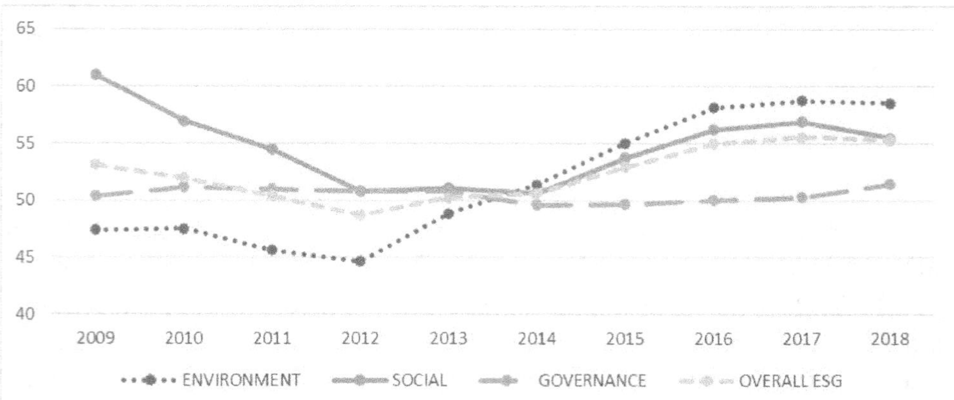

during 2011 and 2012 and made the social score equivalent to the governance score in 2012. The social score, which remained stable until 2015, became higher than the governance score at the end of 2018 thanks to the significant increases recorded in 2015 and 2016. Finally, the environment score with a decreasing trend between 2011 and 2012 showed a rapid increase during 2013-2016 and a slow increase in 2017. Although it decreased slightly in 2018, it was the highest score among the three pillars of ESG at the end of the period of concern.

Figure 8 shows the ESG scores of Chinese companies from 2009 to 2018. Governance scores had always higher than the environmental (except 2016) and social scores, respectively and maintained almost the same level during 2009-2018. The environmental score experienced slight fluctuations until 2015, but sharp increases in 2015 and 2016. However, with the huge decline in 2017, the environmental score fell back to its level in 2015 and maintained that level in 2018 as well. Finally, the social score varied slowly until 2016, with a sudden increase in 2016 it reached its peak. However, it dropped dramatically in 2017 and finished 2018 at a little higher level than in 2015.

Figure 8. ESG performance of China

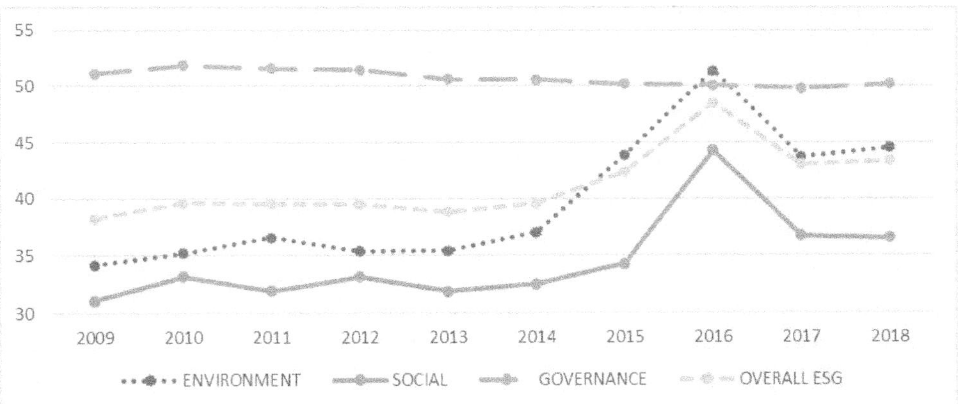

Figure 9 provides data about the ESG performance of the firms in South Africa between 2009 and 2018. It is apparent from this figure that South African firms had the best scores in the social pillar of ESG in every year of the sample period. The environmental scores were higher than the governance scores except from 2012 to 2014. While the governance scores remained relatively stable, the environmental score decreased gradually between 2009-2011 and it showed a steep decrease in 2012. An uptrend in the environmental score began in 2013 and continued gradually

Figure 9. ESG performance of South Africa

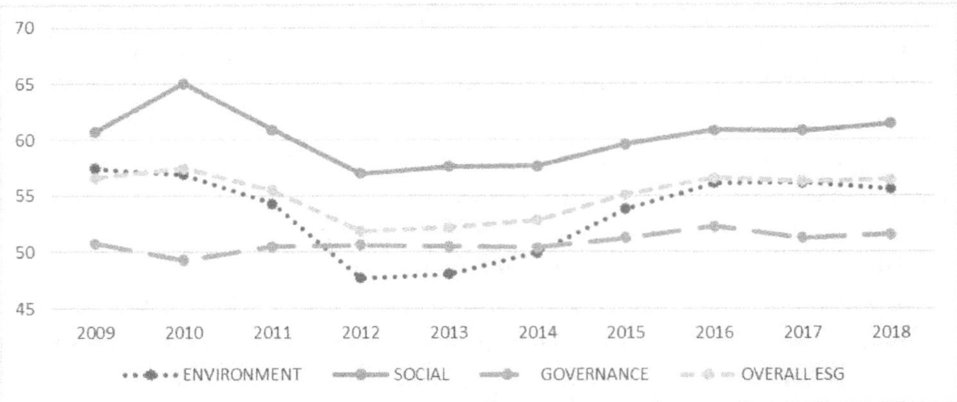

until 2018. Despite this uptrend over 5 years, the environmental score could not climb back to the level of 2009 even at the end of 2018.

Governance Quality of the BRICS Countries

Table 2 presents the average percentile ranks of the BRICS countries in the six dimensions of governance between 2009 and 2018. The percentile rank reported by the World Bank indicates how well the company performs in terms of governance indicators in comparison to countries worldwide. The percentile rank ranges between 0 (for the lowest rank) to 100 (for the highest rank).

Table 2 reveals that, among the BRICS countries, South Africa was the country with the highest level of percentile ranks in all six governance dimensions for the sample period. South Africa was followed by Brazil for four governance dimensions: control of corruption, political stability and absence of violence/terrorism, regulatory quality, and voice and accountability. China and India had the second-best performance in the dimensions of government effectiveness and rule of law, respectively. On the other hand, Russia had the lowest percentile ranks in the majority of governance dimensions, namely control of corruption, government effectiveness, regulatory quality, and rule of law. The worst performance on political stability and absence of violence/terrorism belonged to India and China seemed to perform quite poorly in voice and accountability.

The Link Between ESG Performance and Governance Quality

Table 2. WGI Statistics for 2009 – 2018

COUNTRY	CC		GE		PV		RQ		RL		VA	
	Mean	S.D.	Mean	S.D.	Mean	S.D.	Mean	S.D.	Mean	S.D.	Mean	S.D.
BRAZIL	50.64	9.08	48.38	4.03	39.15	6.34	51.99	3.94	51.90	4.24	62.47	1.45
RUSSIA	15.93	2.71	44.83	3.96	19.05	4.37	37.47	3.46	24.75	2.26	20.62	2.24
INDIA	42.70	5.18	54.33	5.49-	13.93	2.55	39.72	3.83	53.91	1.16	60.59	0.68
CHINA	44.19	4.33	64.72	5.12	32.05	5.25	46.15	2.03	42.70	3.82	6.71	1.64
S. AFRICA	57.49	2.21	65.64	0.84	40.83	3.94	62.91	0.87	57.97	3.92	68.29	1.62
BRICS	46.31	11.87	58.20	8.93	31.23	11.25	49.66	9.37	49.08	9.84	44.60	26.56

CC: Control of Corruption; GE: Government Effectiveness; PV: Political Stability and Absence of Violence/ Terrorism; RQ: Regulatory Quality; RL: Rule of Law; VA: Voice and Accountability

In order to examine the link between six governance dimensions and three pillar scores of ESG as well as overall ESG score, Equation (1) was estimated twenty-four times in total for each combination of governance dimensions and ESG score. Ordinary least squares (OLS), random effects and fixed effects estimators were used to estimate Equation (1). Random effects was preferred to OLS and then fixed effects was preferred to random effects due to the significant test statistics of the Breusch-Pagan LM test and robust Hausman test, respectively. Accordingly, the regression results estimated with fixed effects and Driscoll Kraay standard errors that are robust to heteroskedasticity, serial correlation, and cross-sectional dependence were reported in Table 3-6.

Table 3 provides the estimation results of Equation (1) including the overall ESG score as the dependent variable. The results in Table 3 indicate that there was a significant positive correlation between overall ESG score of the company and all governance dimensions of the country except control of corruption (CC) and government effectiveness (GE). This means that the higher the country's performance in political stability, regulatory quality, rule of law, and voice and accountability, the higher the overall ESG performance of the companies located in those countries. GDP per capita and the level of capital market development of the country, which are the country-level control variables, had a positive and significant effect on the overall ESG performance of the companies except for the model including rule of law as the governance dimension. When it comes to company-level control variables, while the overall ESG score was found to be positively correlated with the company size (SIZE) and profitability (ROA-except PV model), there was no

Table 3. Indicators of ESG Performance

	CC Model	GE Model	PV Model	RQ Model	RL Model	VA Model
CC	0.002					
	(0.044)					
GE		0.076				
		(0.067)				
PV			0.229***			
			(0.047)			
RQ				0.256**		
				(0.093)		
RL					0.576***	
					(0.028)	
VA						0.353*
						(0.160)
GDP	0.001**	0.001*	0.001**	0.001*	0.000	0.001***
	(0.000)	(0.000)	(0.000)	(0.000)	(0.000)	(0.000)
MARKET	2.467**	2.242**	1.034*	2.588**	0.531	2.935***
	(0.816)	(0.905)	(0.519)	(0.797)	(0.472)	(0.683)
SIZE	2.684***	2.661***	2.233***	2.472***	2.302***	2.627***
	(0.571)	(0.563)	(0.601)	(0.604)	(0.488)	(0.671)
LEV	-3.351	-3.413	-3.064	-2.719	-2.607	-2.989
	(2.180)	(2.214)	(1.993)	(2.013)	(2.020)	(1.950)
ROA	0.053***	0.052***	0.032	0.059***	0.042**	0.059***
	(0.015)	(0.014)	(0.018)	(0.015)	(0.014)	(0.012)
Constant	-10.023	-12.336	-3.757	-19.114*	-22.413**	-26.161*
	(12.754)	(12.525)	(12.500)	(10.085)	(9.033)	(12.689)
YEAR	YES	YES	YES	YES	YES	YES
N	3,727	3,727	3,727	3,727	3,727	3,727
R2	0.244	0.245	0.253	0.249	0.271	0.247

CC: Control of Corruption; GE: Government Effectiveness; PV: Political Stability and Absence of Violence/ Terrorism; RQ: Regulatory Quality; RL: Rule of Law; VA: Voice and Accountability. YEAR represents the dummy variables created for each sample-year. Driscoll Kraay standard errors which are robust to autocorrelation, heteroskedasticity, and cross-sectional dependence are in parenthesis. * $p<0.10$, ** $p<0.05$, *** $p<0.01$

Table 4. Indicators of environmental performance

	CC Model	GE Model	PV Model	RQ Model	RL Model	VA Model
CC	0.107***					
	(0.032)					
GE		0.110				
		(0.088)				
PV			0.351***			
			(0.017)			
RQ				0.419***		
				(0.104)		
RL					0.700***	
					(0.033)	
VA						0.514**
						(0.204)
GDP	0.002**	0.002***	0.001**	0.001**	0.001**	0.002***
	(0.001)	(0.000)	(0.000)	(0.001)	(0.000)	(0.000)
MARKET	3.051**	2.415*	0.546	2.942**	0.390	3.424***
	(1.170)	(1.176)	(0.927)	(1.257)	(0.782)	(1.045)
SIZE	3.657***	3.886***	3.227***	3.571***	3.456***	3.836***
	(0.705)	(0.615)	(0.798)	(0.648)	(0.556)	(0.773)
LEV	-8.528***	-8.759***	-8.229***	-7.634***	-7.766***	-8.141***
	(2.386)	(2.428)	(2.121)	(2.235)	(2.207)	(2.013)
ROA	0.104***	0.108***	0.079**	0.121***	0.097**	0.119***
	(0.031)	(0.029)	(0.034)	(0.032)	(0.031)	(0.025)
Constant	-35.790**	-38.999**	-26.018	-50.503***	-50.666***	-59.119***
	(15.117)	(15.316)	(15.266)	(11.852)	(10.080)	(11.420)
YEAR	YES	YES	YES	YES	YES	YES
N	3,727	3,727	3,727	3,727	3,727	3,727
R2	0.303	0.302	0.312	0.308	0.321	0.304

CC: Control of Corruption; GE: Government Effectiveness; PV: Political Stability and Absence of Violence/ Terrorism; RQ: Regulatory Quality; RL: Rule of Law; VA: Voice and Accountability. Driscoll Kraay standard errors which are robust to autocorrelation, heteroskedasticity, and cross-sectional dependence are in parenthesis. YEAR represents the dummy variables created for each sample-year. * $p<0.10$, ** $p<0.05$, *** $p<0.01$

Table 5. Indicators of social performance

	CC Model	GE Model	PV Model	RQ Model	RL Model	VA Model
CC	0.033					
	(0.079)					
GE		0.136				
		(0.110)				
PV			0.221**			
			(0.083)			
RQ				0.146		
				(0.150)		
RL					0.485***	
					(0.079)	
VA						0.138
						(0.183)
GDP	0.001***	0.001*	0.001***	0.001**	0.001**	0.002***
	(0.000)	(0.001)	(0.000)	(0.000)	(0.000)	(0.000)
MARKET	3.015**	2.524*	1.540**	2.989***	1.292*	3.102**
	(1.044)	(1.138)	(0.573)	(0.913)	(0.643)	1.063)
SIZE	2.446**	2.479**	2.089*	2.405**	2.203**	2.504**
	(0.933)	(0.991)	(0.962)	(1.018)	(0.992)	(1.035)
LEV	-3.214	-3.365	-2.980	-2.896	-2.631	-3.116
	(2.146)	(2.252)	(1.988)	(1.961)	(2.046)	(2.094)
ROA	0.052*	0.052*	0.035	0.058*	0.045	0.057*
	(0.025)	(0.026)	(0.030)	(0.028)	(0.027)	(0.027)
Constant	-10.512	-14.621	-4.417	-15.657	-20.893	-16.780
	(18.236)	(17.622)	(16.648)	(16.848)	(15.460)	(21.242)
YEAR	YES	YES	YES	YES	YES	YES
N	3,727	3,727	3,727	3,727	3,727	3,727
R2	0.151	0.152	0.156	0.151	0.162	0.151

CC: Control of Corruption; GE: Government Effectiveness; PV: Political Stability and Absence of Violence/ Terrorism; RQ: Regulatory Quality; RL: Rule of Law; VA: Voice and Accountability. Driscoll Kraay standard errors which are robust to autocorrelation, heteroskedasticity, and cross-sectional dependence are in parenthesis. YEAR represents the dummy variables created for each sample-year. * $p<0.10$, ** $p<0.05$, *** $p<0.01$

significant relationship between the overall ESG score and the financial situation of the company (LEV).

The results of the regression model developed to investigate the effect of governance dimensions on the environmental performance of the companies are given in Table 4. From Table 4, it can be seen that all governance dimensions other than government effectiveness affected environmental score significantly. Among the country-level control variables, GDP per capita had a positive and significant correlation with the environmental score for all models. However, the level of capital market development did not have a significant effect in the models including political stability and rule of law as governance dimensions. While there was a significant negative correlation between environmental score and financial leverage of the company, SIZE and ROA were found to have a significant positive effect on the environmental score.

Equation (1) was also estimated to test whether the governance quality affects the social performance of the companies and the results of this estimation were given in Table 5. According to the results, only two of six governance dimensions, namely political stability and rule of law, had a significant positive impact on social performance. There was no significant relationship between the other governance dimensions and social score. All the country-level control variables (GDP, MARKET) were found to be positively correlated with social performance. Among the company-level control variables, while SIZE and ROA (except for the models including the governance dimensions of political stability and rule of law) had a significant positive correlation with social performance, the financial leverage (LEV) was found to have an insignificant effect on social score of the companies.

Finally, Table 6 presents the estimated parameters of the regression model developed to investigate the relationship between the governance quality of the countries and governance performance of the companies in those countries. The correlation between governance score of the companies and the governance dimensions of regulatory quality, rule of law, and voice and accountability was significant and positive. On the other hand, there was no significant relationship between governance score and governance dimensions of government effectiveness and political stability. The most surprising correlation was with the control of corruption. It was found to have a significant negative effect on the governance performance of the companies. While GDP per capita had a significant negative effect only in the rule of law model, MARKET had a significant positive effect in all the models other than political stability and rule of law model. Among the company-level variables, SIZE was the only variable that had a significant effect on the governance performance of the companies.

Table 6. Indicators of governance performance

	CC Model	GE Model	PV Model	RQ Model	RL Model	VA Model
CC	-0.151***					
	(0.041)					
GE		-0.033				
		(0.062)				
PV			0.102			
			(0.069)			
RQ				0.202**		
				(0.078)		
RL					0.545***	
					(0.091)	
VA						0.424**
						(0.161)
GDP	0.000	-0.000	-0.000	-0.000	-0.001***	-0.000
	(0.001)	(0.001)	(0.000)	(0.000)	(0.000)	(0.000)
MARKET	1.178*	1.722*	0.989	1.727*	-0.198	2.195***
	(0.551)	(0.853)	(1.052)	(0.787)	(0.999)	(0.591)
SIZE	1.876***	1.508***	1.293**	1.325**	1.131**	1.422**
	(0.430)	(0.421)	(0.411)	(0.453)	(0.450)	(0.499)
LEV	2.259	2.489	2.592	2.964	3.169	2.901
	(2.428)	(2.398)	(2.340)	(2.233)	(2.215)	(2.145)
ROA	-0.003	-0.012	-0.022	-0.008	-0.023	-0.006
	(0.029)	(0.027)	(0.026)	(0.027)	(0.024)	(0.028)
Constant	19.277**	20.045*	21.833**	11.859	7.322	-0.336
	(7.678)	(9.701)	(9.355)	(7.280)	(6.630)	(9.488)
YEAR	YES	YES	YES	YES	YES	YES
N	3,727	3,727	3,727	3,727	3,727	3,727
R2	0.030	0.027	0.028	0.029	0.039	0.029

CC: Control of Corruption; GE: Government Effectiveness; PV: Political Stability and Absence of Violence/Terrorism; RQ: Regulatory Quality; RL: Rule of Law; VA: Voice and Accountability. Driscoll Kraay standard errors which are robust to autocorrelation, heteroskedasticity, and cross-sectional dependence are in parenthesis. YEAR represents the dummy variables created for each sample-year. * $p<0.10$, ** $p<0.05$, *** $p<0.01$

DISCUSSION

An initial objective of this study was to assess the ESG performance of the BRICS countries throughout 2009 – 2018. As a result of the analysis on this purpose, China stood out with its lowest ESG scores among the BRICS countries, especially in the environmental and social pillars. Further analysis shows that the low environmental score of China stems from the fact that it had considerably lower emissions and resource use scores in comparison to other BRICS countries. While the average of emissions score for the BRICS countries was 48.07 for the sample period, China had an average of 38.61. A similar comparison applied to resource use score with an overall average of 51.54 for BRICS group and 39.96 for China. This means that China was the country having the worst performance in reducing environmental emissions in its operational and production processes and usage of resources effectively and efficiently. China's environmental score experienced sharp increases in 2015 and 2016 and reached a peak in 2016 most probably due to enforcement of New Environmental Law in 2015 (Qin et al, 2019). However, it is obvious that China still needs improvement on this issue. Similarly, China had remarkably lower scores for workforce, human rights, community, and product responsibility which constitute the social pillar score. The average values of workforce, human rights, community, and product responsibility were 44.65, 35.67, 15.01, and 37.20 for China while they were 55.84, 51.26, 41.05, and 48.47 for BRICS, respectively.

Russia was determined as the second country with the worst environmental and social scores after China. Although Russia had improvement in social and environmental scores throughout the sample period, it had still lower scores at the end of 2018 in comparison to Brazil, India, and South Africa. Russia also had the poorest performance in most of the governance dimensions. Lower scores of Russia in terms of both ESG and governance quality support the finding of this study which revealed that the higher the governance quality of the countries the higher the corporate social performance of the companies in those countries.

The best evidence of the mentioned finding above is South Africa which had the highest performance in both corporate social performance proxied by ESG scores and governance quality measured by WGI. South Africa and Brazil were found to be similar to developed countries with regard to the level of development of legal regulations on corporate social responsibility issues (Yamahaki and Frynas, 2016). The empirical analyses of this study revealed that, until 2018, the corporate social performance in South Africa, India, and Brazil were relatively closer to each other when compared to China and Russia. However, Brazil outscored in all pillar scores of ESG since it experienced a sharp increase in 2018. A possible explanation for this sharp increase may be the "comply or explain" model brought by the Brazilian Securities and Exchange Commission (CVM) Instruction 586. This new instruction, which was published in June 2017, mainly requires companies to disclose information regarding their application of the practices outlined in the Brazilian Code of Corporate Governance (Barbosa et al., 2019).

After analyzing the ESG performance of the companies in the BRICS countries, this study examined whether the governance quality of the BRICS countries affects the ESG performance of the companies incorporated in those countries. Although the governance dimensions that had an impact on ESG performance varied depending on the ESG pillar, overall results indicated a positive correlation between governance dimensions and ESG performance. The only exception was the negative correlation between control of corruption and the governance pillar score of ESG. Further analysis showed that this surprising result was mainly due to the data of Russia. Although Russia had considerably lower scores in control of corruption in comparison to other BRICS countries, the Russian companies had relatively similar governance pillar scores to those in other BRICS countries.

CONCLUSION

This study set out to analyze the ESG performance of the BRICS companies and determine whether the governance quality of the countries affects the level of ESG performance of these companies. For this purpose, WGI of the World Bank was used to collect the governance indicators of the BRICS countries and ESG data was derived from the Thomson Reuters Datastream ASSET4 Database for 2009-2018. The relationship between governance quality and ESG performance was analyzed by the regression model estimated with fixed effects method.

Analysis of ESG data of the BRICS countries revealed that Brazil, South Africa, and India had similar performances in ESG scores showing a significant gap with the performances of Russia and China. Despite the increase in ESG scores of China and Russia throughout the sample period, they had still by far the worst ESG scores compared to other BRICS countries. This finding suggests that Chinese and Russian companies need to do more to improve their ESG performances.

Regression analysis conducted to test the relationship between ESG performances of the companies and governance quality of the countries generally revealed that the governance dimensions have a positive effect on the ESG performance. Thus, a governance structure with effective governance dimensions such as regulatory quality, political stability, rule of law, and so on, is expected to prompt companies' compliance with ESG issues.

Taken together, these results suggest that although all BRICS countries have a significant potential of economic growth, they are not in the same position both in terms of ESG performance and governance quality. In order to turn this potential of economic growth into realized sustainable development, BRICS countries should give importance to ESG issues at both corporate and government level and provide supportive governance settings.

Based on the findings of this study, it would be interesting to assess the effect of specific improvements in governance dimensions on the ESG scores of companies via event analysis. Additionally, further studies could compare the ESG performances of the BRICS countries with their emerging market peers and developed countries, as well.

ACKNOWLEDGMENT

This research received no specific grant from any funding agency in the public, commercial, or not-for-profit sectors.

REFERENCES

Aggarwal, R., Erel, I., Stulz, R., & Williamson, R. (2009). Differences in governance practices between US and foreign firms: Measurement, causes, and consequences. *Review of Financial Studies*, *22*(8), 3131–3169. doi:10.1093/rfs/hhn107

Ali, S., Hussain, T., Zhang, G., Nurunnabi, M., & Li, B. (2018). The implementation of sustainable development goals in "BRICS" countries. *Sustainability*, *10*(7), 2513. doi:10.3390u10072513

Arrive, J. T., & Feng, M. (2018). Corporate social responsibility disclosure: Evidence from BRICS nations. *Corporate Social Responsibility and Environmental Management*, *25*(5), 920–927. doi:10.1002/csr.1508

Baldini, M., Dal Maso, L., Liberatore, G., Mazzi, F., & Terzani, S. (2018). Role of country-and firm-level determinants in environmental, social, and governance disclosure. *Journal of Business Ethics*, *150*(1), 79–98. doi:10.100710551-016-3139-1

Barbosa, C. D., Francato, A. L., & Barbosa, P. S. (2019). Towards Brazilian Corporations Better Stock Price Valuation and Operational Performance with Corporate Social Responsibility and Environmental Socio Responsibility. In C. Stehr, N. Dziatzko, & F. Struve (Eds.), *Corporate Social Responsibility in Brazil* (pp. 129–146). Springer. doi:10.1007/978-3-319-90605-8_6

Bhatia, A., & Makkar, B. (2019). CSR disclosure in developing and developed countries: A comparative study. *Journal of Global Responsibility*, *11*(1), 1–26. doi:10.1108/JGR-04-2019-0043

Bhatia, A., & Tuli, S. (2018). Sustainability reporting: An empirical evaluation of emerging and developed economies. *Journal of Global Responsibility*, *9*(2), 207–234. doi:10.1108/JGR-01-2018-0003

Cardamone, P., Carnevale, C., & Giunta, F. (2012). The value relevance of social reporting: Evidence from listed Italian companies. *Journal of Applied Accounting Research*, *13*(3), 255–269. doi:10.1108/09675421211281326

Coluccia, D., Fontana, S., & Solimene, S. (2018). Does institutional context affect CSR disclosure? A study on Eurostoxx 50. *Sustainability*, *10*(8), 2823. doi:10.3390u10082823

Conway, E. (2018). Sustainability, the Triple Bottom Line and Corporate Social Responsibility. In E. Conway & D. Byrne (Eds.), *Contemporary Issues in Accounting* (pp. 15–35). Palgrave Macmillan. doi:10.1007/978-3-319-91113-7_2

Fenwick, M., McCahery, J. A., & Vermeulen, E. P. (2019). The end of 'corporate' governance: Hello 'platform' governance. *European Business Organization Law Review*, *20*(1), 171–199. doi:10.100740804-019-00137-z

Garcia, A. S., Mendes-Da-Silva, W., & Orsato, R. J. (2019). Corporate Sustainability, Capital Markets, and ESG Performance. In W. Mendes-Da-Silva (Ed.), *Individual Behaviors and Technologies for Financial Innovations* (pp. 287–309). Springer. doi:10.1007/978-3-319-91911-9_13

Gómez, N. A., & García, S. M. (2020). Governance and Type of Industry as Determinants of Corporate Social Responsibility Disclosures in Latin America. *Latin American Business Review*, *21*(1), 1–35. doi:10.1080/10978526.2019.1697185

Hall, R. E., & Jones, C. I. (1999). Why do some countries produce so much more output per worker than others? *The Quarterly Journal of Economics*, *114*(1), 83–116. doi:10.1162/003355399555954

Kaufmann, D., Kraay, A., & Mastruzzi, M. (2011). The worldwide governance indicators: Methodology and analytical issues. *Hague Journal on the Rule of Law*, *3*(2), 220–246. doi:10.1017/S1876404511200046

Kumar, A., & Das, N. (2018). Sustainability Reporting Practices in Emerging Economies: A Cross-Country Study of BRICS Nations. *Problemy Ekorozwoju*, *13*(2), 17–25.

Kurtz, M. J., & Schrank, A. (2007). Growth and governance: Models, measures, and mechanisms. *The Journal of Politics*, *69*(2), 538–554. doi:10.1111/j.1468-2508.2007.00549.x

Li, S., Fetscherin, M., Alon, I., Lattemann, C., & Yeh, K. (2010). Corporate social responsibility in emerging markets. *Management International Review*, *50*(5), 635–654. doi:10.100711575-010-0049-9

Li, S., & Filer, L. (2007). The effects of the governance environment on the choice of investment mode and the strategic implications. *Journal of World Business*, *42*(1), 80–98. doi:10.1016/j.jwb.2006.11.006

Lourenço, I. C., Branco, M. C., Curto, J. D., & Eugénio, T. (2012). How does the market value corporate sustainability performance? *Journal of Business Ethics*, *108*(4), 417–428. doi:10.100710551-011-1102-8

Luo, Y., Sun, J., & Wang, S. L. (2011). Comparative strategic management: An emergent field in international management. *Journal of International Management*, *17*(3), 190–200. doi:10.1016/j.intman.2011.05.002

Miralles-Quirós, M., Miralles-Quirós, J., & Valente Gonçalves, L. (2018). The value relevance of environmental, social, and governance performance: The Brazilian case. *Sustainability*, *10*(3), 574. doi:10.3390u10030574

Miralles-Quirós, M. D. M., Miralles-Quirós, J. L., & Arraiano, I. G. (2017). Are firms that contribute to sustainable development valued by investors? *Corporate Social Responsibility and Environmental Management*, *24*(1), 71–84. doi:10.1002/csr.1392

Miras-Rodríguez, M. D. M., Martínez-Martínez, D., & Escobar-Pérez, B. (2019). Which corporate governance mechanisms drive CSR disclosure practices in emerging countries? *Sustainability*, *11*(1), 61–81. doi:10.3390u11010061

O'Neill, J. (2001). *Building Better Global Economic BRICs*. Goldman Sachs Global Economics Paper, 66.

Peterson, M., & Bishop, M. (2015). Sustainability in the BRICS and beyond: an examination of the Sustainability Society Index. In B. L. Kedia & K. Aceto (Eds.), *Emerging Markets and the Future of the BRIC Nations* (pp. 41–64). Edward Elgar Publishing. doi:10.4337/9781783479764.00010

Qin, Y., Harrison, J., & Chen, L. (2019). A framework for the practice of corporate environmental responsibility in China. *Journal of Cleaner Production*, *235*, 426–452. doi:10.1016/j.jclepro.2019.06.245

Rajesh, R. (2020). Exploring the sustainability performances of firms using environmental, social, and governance scores. *Journal of Cleaner Production*, *247*, 119600. doi:10.1016/j.jclepro.2019.119600

Ralston, D. A., Egri, C. P., Karam, C. M., Naoumova, I., Srinivasan, N., Casado, T., Li, Y., & Alas, R. (2015). The triple-bottom-line of corporate responsibility: Assessing the attitudes of present and future business professionals across the BRICs. *Asia Pacific Journal of Management*, *32*(1), 145–179. doi:10.100710490-014-9376-x

Refinitiv. (2020). *Environmental, Social and Governance (ESG) Scores from Refinitiv*. Retrieved from https://www.refinitiv.com/content/dam/marketing/en_us/documents/methodology/esg-scores-methodology.pdf

Signitzer, B., & Prexl, A. (2007). Corporate sustainability communications: Aspects of theory and professionalization. *Journal of Public Relations Research*, *20*(1), 1–19. doi:10.1080/10627260701726996

WCED. (1987). *Report of the World Commission on Environment and Development: Our Common Future*. Retrieved from http://www.un-documents.net/wced-ocf.htm

Wilson, D., & Purushothaman, R. (2003). *Dreaming with BRICs: The path to 2050*. Goldman Sachs Global Economics Paper, 99.

Wilson, R. (2016). Does governance cause growth? Evidence from China. *World Development*, *79*, 138–151. doi:10.1016/j.worlddev.2015.11.015

World Bank. (2018). *World Development Indicators*. Retrieved from https://databank.worldbank.org/source/world-development-indicators

Yamahaki, C., & Frynas, J. G. (2016). Institutional determinants of private shareholder engagement in Brazil and South Africa: The role of regulation. *Corporate Governance*, *24*(5), 509–527. doi:10.1111/corg.12166

ADDITIONAL READING

Ali, W., Frynas, J. G., & Mahmood, Z. (2017). Determinants of corporate social responsibility (CSR) disclosure in developed and developing countries: A literature review. *Corporate Social Responsibility and Environmental Management*, *24*(4), 273–294. doi:10.1002/csr.1410

De Bakker, F. G., Groenewegen, P., & Den Hond, F. (2005). A bibliometric analysis of 30 years of research and theory on corporate social responsibility and corporate social performance. *Business & Society*, *44*(3), 283–317. doi:10.1177/0007650305278086

De Villiers, C., & Marques, A. (2016). Corporate social responsibility, country-level predispositions, and the consequences of choosing a level of disclosure. *Accounting and Business Research*, *46*(2), 167–195. doi:10.1080/00014788.2015.1039476

Dorfleitner, G., Halbritter, G., & Nguyen, M. (2015). Measuring the level and risk of corporate responsibility–An empirical comparison of different ESG rating approaches. *Journal of Asset Management*, *16*(7), 450–466. doi:10.1057/jam.2015.31

Jamali, D., & Karam, C. (2018). Corporate social responsibility in developing countries as an emerging field of study. *International Journal of Management Reviews*, *20*(1), 32–61. doi:10.1111/ijmr.12112

Lélé, S. M. (1991). Sustainable development: A critical review. *World Development*, *19*(6), 607–621. doi:10.1016/0305-750X(91)90197-P

Santana, N. B., Aparecida do Nascimento Rebelatto, D., Périco, A. E., & Mariano, E. B. (2014). Sustainable development in the BRICS countries: An efficiency analysis by data envelopment. *International Journal of Sustainable Development and World Ecology*, *21*(3), 259–272. doi:10.1080/13504509.2014.900831

Wood, D. J. (2010). Measuring corporate social performance: A review. *International Journal of Management Reviews*, *12*(1), 50–84. doi:10.1111/j.1468-2370.2009.00274.x

KEY TERMS AND DEFINITIONS

Corporate Social Performance: An organization's performance in fulfilling its responsibilities to its stakeholders.

Corporate Social Responsibility: An organization's responsibilities to its stakeholders other than its business activities

ESG Performance: An organization's performance in fulfilling its responsibilities regarding environmental, social, and governance issues.

Governance Quality: The measurement of how well an organization performs at governance dimensions, namely control of corruption, government effectiveness, political stability and absence of violence/terrorism, regulatory quality, rule of law, and voice and accountability.

Institutional Context: The set of institutional characteristics such as rules, regulations, policies, cultural factors and so on.

Sustainability: The ability to continue its existence for a long time with activities that are in harmony with environmental, social and governance concerns.

Sustainable Development: The development that achieved without ignoring the needs of all type of stakeholders.

Chapter 4
Corporate Social Responsibility:
Way Forward for Sustainable Growth

Ganga Bhavani
Amity University, India

Reena Agrawal
Jaipuria Institute of Management, Lucknow, India

ABSTRACT

In recent years, many organizations have incorporated corporate social responsibility (CSR) as part of their vision and mission statements. There are many evidences demonstrates the positive results after implementation of CSR. Now, the question is, what are the contributions of CSR towards sustainable development of society and growth? The current study shows the association between CSR and sustainable growth. Real-time analysis of relevant studies of organizations who initiated CSR strategies towards sustainable development and growth are incorporated in the present chapter.

INTRODUCTION

The twentieth century will find its place in history for its exemplary technological disruptions and growth in living standards, but also for rise in sustainability issues related to society and environment. The main objective of this chapter is to explore the contributions of CSR towards sustainable development of society and growth. The current study shows the association between CSR and Sustainable development.

DOI: 10.4018/978-1-7998-6669-5.ch004

Copyright © 2021, IGI Global. Copying or distributing in print or electronic forms without written permission of IGI Global is prohibited.

It is implicit that industrial capitalism, multinational corporations and globalization are main players in this story. Today as societies across the globe combat intricate issues such as increasing social inequality, enormous unemployment, depletion of natural resources, climate change, waste creation, rising pollution levels, scarcity of clean drinking water and big refugee groups, outbreak of deadly Covid-19 etc., the need is to retrospect and redefine perception of growth and well-being. As these problems are too multifaceted, intricate and dire to find solutions in governments alone, need also is for corporate participation.

The ground-breaking UNO-Brundtland Report of 1987 (WCED, 1987) stating "meeting the needs of the present generation without comprising the ability for future generations to meet their own needs" emphasized that businesses and organizations should operate in socially responsible manner. The report created consciousness about balancing profits with its implications for people and planet. It said that maximizing short-term profits would not result in sustainable growth of enterprises, considering external factors was the only way to achieve long-term equilibrium. Growing awareness about conservation of environment, corporate governance and social wellbeing among the stakeholders, is creating mounting pressure on companies to carry out their functions in socially and environmentally responsible manner. Corporate Social Responsibility (CSR) thus has become crucial component of modern corporate culture. Therefore, it is significant to explore the impact of CSR on sustainable development and growth.

BACKGROUND

Corporate Social Responsibility: Origin and Evolution

The neoclassical viewpoint was that goal of business is to maximize shareholder wealth and money spent on moral stakes is loss for shareholders. It is believed that ethical behavior and profit are not mutually exclusive, as investing in moral area may be an opportunity to minimize future risks and construct strong brand. The concept of CSR first emerged in 1950s and its development over ever since is described below:

1950s -1960s

1. **Bowen (1953):** Obligations of people doing business to make policies, decisions and action in a manner which are desirable in terms aims and principles of society.
2. **Davis (1960):** Socially responsible business decisions that warrant long-term economic gain of firm, thus paying back for socially responsible behavior.

3. **Frederick (1960):** Contribution to society's human and economic resources and readiness of business to ensure that resources were used for wider social goals.

1970s

1. **Johnson (1971):** Instead of ensuring only bigger returns to shareholders, responsible enterprise should cater to interests of suppliers, employees, local societies, dealers, and country as whole.
2. **CED (1971):** Businesses should have broader duties to society taking into account the varying social bond between business and community (or nation) in common.
3. **Carroll (1979):** CSR is three-dimensional construct comprising of corporate accountabilities (i.e., legal, ethical, economic, charitable), social issues of business (e.g., human rights, labour standards, anti-corruption, environment conservation) and corporate actions (e.g., proactive, defensive, reactive, accommodative).

1980s-1990s

1. **Jones (1980):** CSR is not bunch of consequences rather a developing process (e.g. debate, analysis, and modification) controlled by officially embedded policies and principles.
2. **Wartick and Cochran (1985):** CSR is an integration of doctrines of corporate responsibility, rules to manage social issues and process of action into a progressing system.
3. **Wood (1991):** CSR comprises of three principles of corporate conducts and outcomes- rightfulness, public accountability and executive discretion.

2000s

1. **Schwartz and Carroll (2003):** Three domains of corporate responsibilities: legal, economic, and ethical.
2. **International Labour Organization (2007):** Enterprises deliberate impact of their activities on society and CSR principles are incorporated in organizations` in-house procedures and communications with stakeholders on voluntary basis.
3. **European Commission (2011):** Process to integrate social, ethical, environmental, human rights and consumer worries in core strategy and business operations in close alliance with stakeholders.

As businesses face grave challenges, comprising rapid globalization, increasing environmental concerns and rising pro-poor needs, there is mounting need for adopting result-based CSR management and rigorous assessment of CSR performance. The concept of all-encompassing business or pro-poor business is also gaining consideration. CSR should be achieved within core business activities and add value to corporate success.

CORPORATE SOCIAL RESPONSIBILITY: RELEVANT THEORIES

First School of Thought

Secchi (2007) came up with a group of theories based on a criterion what role the theories confer to the corporation and society. The theories are as follows: 1) The utilitarian theory, 2) The managerial theory, and 3) The relational theory:

Utilitarian Theory: in this, businesses are considered as part of economic system in which they work for profit maximization. Idea of CSR emerged from consciousness that there is requirement for an economics of accountability, rooted in business ethics of enterprises. Hence, the ideology of *laissez faire* business crumbled and made way for determinism, from individualist to collective approach, and from individual responsibility to public responsibility. The utilitarian theory is further divided into two subsets:

Social Cost Theory: This theory states that businesses non-economic forces influence socio-economic system in community. It suggests that businesses need to accept societal responsibilities and privileges to partake in social co-operation. CSR regarded as means to end, which states that social power of business is materialized specially in its political affiliation with society.

Functionalist Theory: Businesses are viewed as investment, which should generate profit for investors and stakeholders. CSR can be used as defense tactic from external attacks because it necessitates equilibrium amid profit creation and social goals for bringing equilibrium in economic system.

In utilitarian theories businesses are seen as device for wealth creation, and the social actions are means to achieve financial results. The utilitarian theories are associated to strategies for competitive advantages and altruistic activities.

Managerial Theory: This stresses upon the need to adopt CSR as inherent part of business management. Here CSR is considered as variable to measure businesses` socio-economic performance, and as linkage of social accountability ideology to business strategy. Managerial theory has been divided into three sub-groups:

Corporate Social Performance: This aims to assess contribution made by social variable to financial performance. It`s basic premise is that businesses depends on society for its growth and sustainability. Corporate Social Performance has been further sub-divided into five parts:

Centricity: Evaluates whether CSR is attuned with core mission;

Specificity: Meters the benefits CSR brings to business;

Pro-Activity: Gauges degree of response to outside demands;

Voluntaries: Explains discretion used by business in effecting CSR; and

Visibility: Refers to manner in which responsible behavior is observed by stakeholders community.

Social Accountability, Auditing and Reporting: Firms are involved in social accountability, auditing and reporting activities for communiqué, and better involvement with stakeholder and discloser. However, these activities appear distinct but are interconnected to each other. All these activities measure the social impact created by business and thus contribute to socially responsible behavior. By doing so, businesses synchronize their activities with core goals while remaining accountable to pertinent community.

Social Responsibility for Multinationals: This aspect of came because of challenges faced by multinational corporations to survive in foreign countries. MNCs should go beyond profit expansion while making decisions in firms. The rationale was derived from events like protests, strikes boycotts and other such undesirable actions against employers. This called for formulation and adoption of 'code of conduct' by MNCs, the success of which, however, depends on hope of client, repute of company, approval, level of trust, support shown by workers and group of stakeholders.

Managerial theories emphasized that social responsibilities arise because of social power possessed by corporation and engagement in community. Public responsibility lays emphasis on public policy and law for social performance, while corporate social performance searches for social legitimacy relevant to social issues.

Relational Theory: These roots from intricate business environment relationship. As the term suggests, inter-relationship amid society and business are focus of scrutiny. Relational theory is further divided into four sub-groups:

Business and Society: In this CSR emerges as substance of interaction between the two entities that is business and society. One measure of CSR is to create financial values in society and other is responsibility is to deliberate effects of its decision and deed on social system as whole. Businesses need to consider social power they possess.

Stakeholder Approach: It regards business as interlocked web of dissimilar interests where self-development and community development happens inter-relatedly. This considers fiduciary duties towards stakeholders and emphasizes on balance among interests of various stakeholders.

Corporate Citizenship: It is about bond that businesses develop with its stakeholders, and thus, former has to constantly search for engagement and commitment with latter. It is a path that businesses may take to behave responsibly.

Social Contract: This refers to vital matter of justifying ethics of economic undertakings in order to theoretically analyze social relationships amid business and society. It is derived from moral legality businesses achieve in society and accepts that CSR is limited ti validation of social actions that legalize behavior of business.

The relational theories are based on associations that businesses build with individuals, community and systems as whole and legitimacy with which they use their social power to attain the economic goals.

Second School of Thought

On the other hand, Garriga and Mele's (2004) analysis maps CSR into four types of territories. They are: 1) Instrumental theories, 2) Political theories, 3) Integrative theories, and 4) Ethical theories:

Instrumental Theory: This is based on elementary idea that says CSR are merely means to an end. In this, businesses are seen as instrument for wealth creation and their social activities only as means to achieve economic results.

Political Theory: This is based on ideology, which says that businesses are social institutions and they must use power conscientiously. It is also says that businesses` choice of adoption of CSR initiatives are influenced by political structures present in local market. It also found link among pressure created by globalization, domestic political structures and CSR policies.

Integrative Theory: This considers fiduciary duties of businesses towards its stakeholders. It emphasizes the need for the integration of social demands in business goals and strategies.

Ethical Theory: As businesses get the legitimacy to operate from the society they should adopts practices that are acceptable and ethical towards it various stakeholders such as employee, customers, business collaborates, society, systems and environment etc.

Though there exists some similarities in both school of thoughts the major distinction comes from the discussions will be based on approaches and emphases.

Corporate Social Responsibility: Definitions

A well-aware society does not subscribe to Friedman's principle that business of business is to do business. It keeps keen watch on socially responsible deeds of businesses, thus, literally compelling enterprises to include their numerous stakeholders in order to succeed and sustain it in today`s era of high competition. The increasing yearning of mindful society for socially responsible initiatives demands that organizations be more responsible to the environment they operate in. Corporate Social Responsibility (CSR) is widely employed notion.

1. **European Commission (2011):** "A concept whereby companies integrate social and environmental concerns in their business operations and in their interaction with their stakeholders on a voluntary basis".
2. **World Business Council for Sustainable Development (1998):** "Corporate social responsibility is the commitment of business to contribute to sustainable economic development, working with employees, their families, the local community and society at large to improve their quality of life".
3. **Kotler and Lee (2005):** Corporate social responsibility is a "commitment to improve community well-being through discretionary, business practices and contribution of corporate resources. Corporate social initiatives are major activities undertaken by a corporation to support social causes and to fulfill commitments to corporate social responsibility".
4. **CGA-Canada (2005):** "A company's commitment to operating in an economically, socially, and environmentally sustainable manner, while recognizing the interests of its stakeholders, including investors, customers, employees, business partners, local communities, the environment, and society at large".
5. ICAEW (2004). "Corporate Responsibility is about ensuring that organizations manage their businesses to make a positive impact on society and the environment whilst maximizing value for their shareholders".

CSR is thoughtful insertion of community interest in business policymaking, and revering triple bottom line: people, planet, profit. Corporate social responsibility (CSR) is about how businesses bring into line their values and conduct with expectations and necessities of stakeholders – not just investors and customers, but also regulators, employees, communities, special interest groups, suppliers, environment and society. CSR describes a company's commitment to be accountable to its stakeholders. CSR demands that businesses manage the economic, social and environmental impacts of their operations to maximize the benefits and minimize the downsides.

To sum CSR comprises of four elements: moral duty- obligation|| to act responsibly as good corporate citizen; sustainability, meeting the needs of present without damaging ability of future generations to meet their own needs; legitimate, inherent or explicit sanction from administration, communities and stakeholders; and repute, where firms aim to improve imageries, build up brands and enhance values.

CORPORATE SOCIAL RESPONSIBILITY: MULTIFACETED FEATURES

CSR: Strategy for Sustainable Growth

The concept of sustainable development has steadily extended its application from society to organizations. According to International Institute for Sustainable Development, corporate sustainability is applying business strategies to meet the present requirements of enterprises and stakeholders, also protecting resources for future needs. Globally business sustainability objectives have increasingly become more vital for companies, but also for stakeholders. More and more organizations are expected must give equal importance to human resources, societal balance society, and the environment and realizing the importance of building sustainable business. The need exists to blend the triple bottom line of people, planet, and profits to achieve sustainability.

Literature highlighted significance of corporate social responsibility in business strategy. It stressed the need for corporate social responsibility to be internalized and integrated with core businesses strategy in order to derive benefits such as enhanced reputation, improved confidence of customers, increased employee motivation and larger market share. Inclusion of social responsibility objectives in business strategy to be prompted not simply by wish to shape positive image, thru operative efficacy or prospective competitive edge, but as intent enjoy sustainable growth.

Corporate social responsibility offer opportunities to businesses to align it goals, values and principles with sustainable development. Incorporation of social responsibility as strategy for sustainable business is based on level of business operations, and can have the following categories: societal strategies, ecological strategies, supply chain strategies, strategies for corporate image, strategies for creating competitive advantage and strategies for value creation. Based on approach of business towards sustainability values and degree of execution businesses can choose to use any of the following- passive (defensive) approach, reactive approach, proactive approach or aggressive approach. Business, which are proactive, can differentiate themselves by identifying social responsibilities, engaging actively, initiating voluntary actions to minimize the negative impact people and planet and meet stakeholder need.

Many businesses use strategy of benchmarking to compete in their particular industries in corporate social responsibility policy, execution, and efficacy. Benchmarking involves appraising competitor corporate social responsibility initiatives, and evaluating and estimating the impact that those policies have on society and environment, and how customers perceive competitor corporate social responsibility strategy.

CSR: Creating Shared Value

Figure 1.
(Google, 2019)

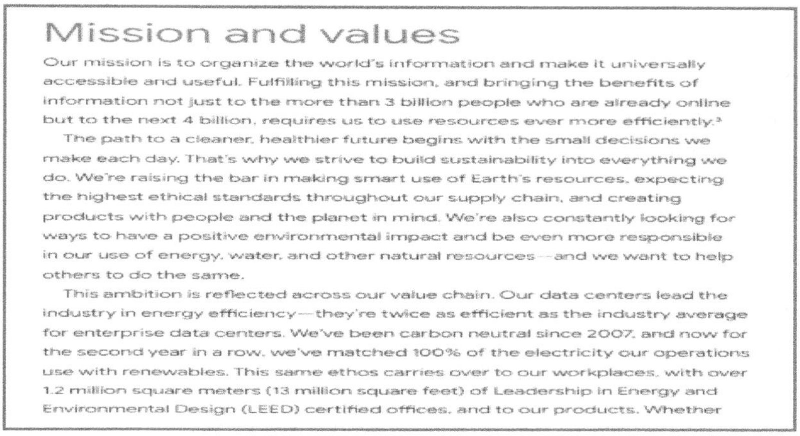

Mission and values

Our mission is to organize the world's information and make it universally accessible and useful. Fulfilling this mission, and bringing the benefits of information not just to the more than 3 billion people who are already online but to the next 4 billion, requires us to use resources ever more efficiently.[3]

The path to a cleaner, healthier future begins with the small decisions we make each day. That's why we strive to build sustainability into everything we do. We're raising the bar in making smart use of Earth's resources, expecting the highest ethical standards throughout our supply chain, and creating products with people and the planet in mind. We're also constantly looking for ways to have a positive environmental impact and be even more responsible in our use of energy, water, and other natural resources—and we want to help others to do the same.

This ambition is reflected across our value chain. Our data centers lead the industry in energy efficiency—they're twice as efficient as the industry average for enterprise data centers. We've been carbon neutral since 2007, and now for the second year in a row, we've matched 100% of the electricity our operations use with renewables. This same ethos carries over to our workplaces, with over 1.2 million square meters (13 million square feet) of Leadership in Energy and Environmental Design (LEED) certified offices, and to our products. Whether

The shared value model is based on idea that business success and social welfare are inter-dependent. Businesses need proficient government, educated and healthy workforce, sustainable resources to compete efficiently. So that societies can thrive, businesses must be profitable and able to create wealth, income, tax revenues and prospects for charity. Some corporate social responsibility put businesses against society, highlighting costs, compliance of environmental and social standards. Creating shared value recognizes trade-offs between short-term gain and social as

Figure 2.
(Apple, 2019)

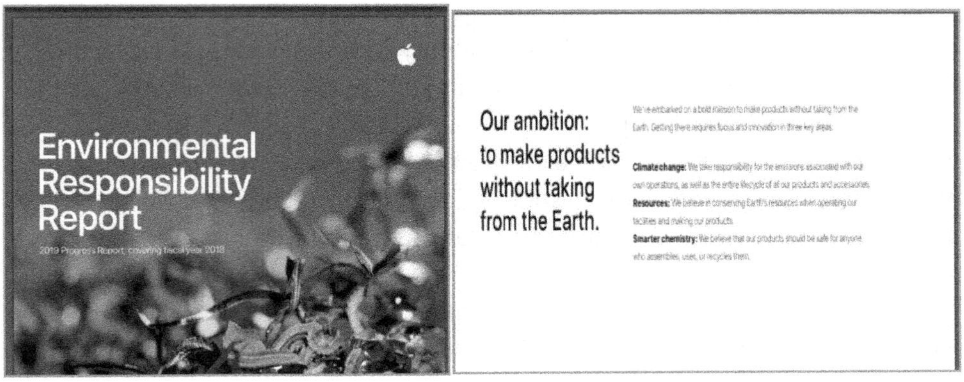

well as ecological goals, but attentions more on prospects for competitive advantage by integrating social value proposition in core business strategy.

Engagement with various stakeholders can help business in changing cold relationships to emotional ones and can augment competitive edge. Building relationships with stakeholders indicates that business is not self-centered and the resulting moral capital can be valuable in case some adverse event occur such as issues related to product safety or environment preservation. However, the moral capital might not advance profits, but it can render insurance like benefits. Positive stakeholder relations not only helps in gaining competitive advantage, sustain benefit over long term, builds trust and facilitates growth.

CSR: Tool for Risk Management

Figure 3.
(Tata Steel, 2004)

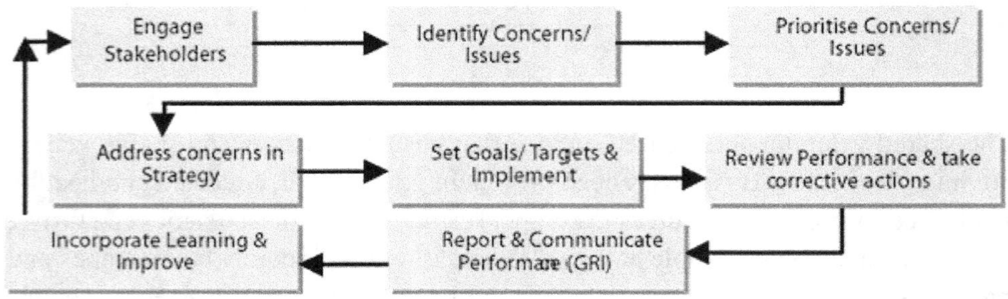

Managing risk is essential part of corporate strategies. Reputes that may take ages to build up can be destroyed within seconds due to undesirable occurrences such as scandals, corruption, legal glitches and environmental mishaps. These can attract uninvited attention from policy maker, regulator, media and courts. Building genuine culture of *doing right things* within businesses can counterbalance these risks.

Experts say that corporate social responsibility is instrument to manage reputation risk, financial risk, supply chain risk and environmental risk. Businesses that are socially responsible present positive image to customers and enhanced customer satisfactions results in higher financial gains. Studies have also found that good customer relations can decrease elasticity of demand and therefore make sales more resilient in down turn. Good relations with stakeholder improve company's resilience during adverse economic conditions.

Choosing appropriate social responsibility strategy influences business by decreasing costs and risk, maximizing competitive edge and profits, increasing

Figure 4.
(Emirates, 2016)

dnata4good

dnata4good is an employee-led initiative that rallies the philanthropic efforts of dnata's 38,000 employees. Staff are encouraged to participate as little or as much as they like, through fundraising, donations, and even front-line volunteering.

In December 2015, total fundraising by our employees in support of dnata4good crossed the AED 1 million mark – a sum also matched by dnata.

During the year dnata4good funded the building of five schools and dnata volunteers helped build three of those, in remote areas of Senegal, Malawi and Nepal.

South Africa-based Rhino Revolution, an organisation also supported by dnata4good, took in four orphaned rhino calves during the year. These young rhinos will be under expert care for the next three years, before being released back into the wild.

Importantly, dnata4good is driven by our passionate, global workforce and their volunteering and fundraising initiatives. From baking cakes to building schools, their efforts are delivering real change.

legitimacy and reputation and constructing synergistic value. By creating business strategy to align social, economic, and environmental performance to long-term business values, corporate social responsibility becomes part of business itself and adds long-term value for both business and society and can help reduce business

Figure 5.
(Apple, 2019)

Educating partners.

We share our learnings with our supplier partners and help them plot their transition to renewable energy. In 2017, Apple developed the Clean Energy Portal, an online platform to help suppliers identify commercially viable renewable energy solutions in regions around the world. We continue to add new content, including policy guidance and financial analysis tools, intended to make adoption of clean energy in key markets even easier. Over 100 suppliers have registered for the site.

Advocating for strong policy.

Clean energy technology offers tremendous benefits to our suppliers, to electricity grids, and to countries. So we actively support policies that create cost-effective renewable energy markets, and we work closely with suppliers to engage local, regional, and national governments. This encourages the development of policies that support scalable renewable energy solutions.

"The Supplier Clean Energy Program is at the center of Apple's commitment to making world-class products with greener manufacturing. Our suppliers are taking significant actions to join us in this work, and we look forward to seeing more bold pledges as we continue to address our environmental impact."

Jeff Williams
Apple's Chief Operating Officer

risks. Engagement with primary and secondary stakeholders helps in creating moral capital that in effect reduces firm-specific risk.

CSR: Value Creation for Stakeholders

Businesses who invest in social programs can create 'insurance-like' benefits. Reducing waste, avoiding ecological disasters, prevents financial proceedings, consumer rejections and reduce cost in the end. Corporate social responsibility benefits are broad: increase in reputation and brand value, higher motivation amid employees, customer attraction and retention, bigger financial return.

Figure 6.
(Apple, 2019)

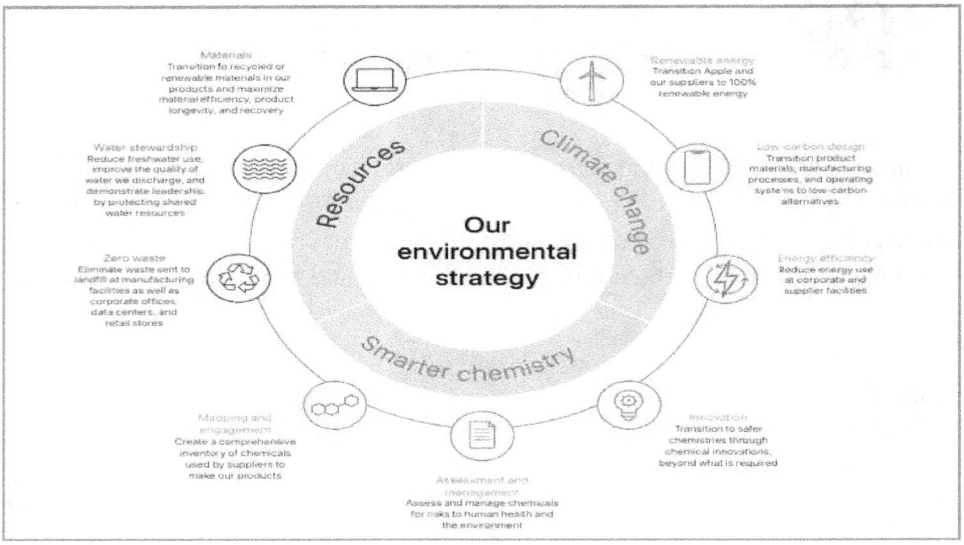

CSR and Customer Satisfaction

Customer satisfaction is a prime goal and has special focus in business strategy. CSR is positively linked to customer satisfaction. The fundamental hypothesis is that firm which is socially responsible could present positive image to customers and enhanced customer satisfactions generates added financial gains. CSR can play a vital role in building customer loyalty based on distinctive ethical values. Often consumers look for companies who embraced CSR strategies and integrated them in principal values and strategies. There also exists positive relationship between perceptions of CSR and intent to purchase. CSR strategically linked company`s image, reputation and brand and is source of potential growth, competitive advantage and financial returns.

CSR and Employee Satisfaction

Companies realize that employees are their most valuable asset and company's capability to retain employees is symbol of sustainable performance. Indeed, capacity to retain employees not only signals it is valued place to work, but it is also employee retention has positive consequences for firms' financial performance and productivity. Of particular concern to firms then, are the mechanisms and activities that can enable them to lower employee turnover. It is suggested that CSR is one such activity. CSR activities civilize company in unique way and is thus source of competitive edge. The salaries alone cannot keep employees emotionally associated with their jobs, CSR helps them to emotionally connect with their work. Growing sum of employees prefer to work for establishments with good reputes and positively supposed CSR. Company`s social performance impacts employees image about organization, which in turn affects employees' productivity levels.

CSR activities have suggestively larger influence on employees' identity with enterprise and their creative work when they believe that firm work in ethical manner. When employees observe that management has compassionate attitude to them, they reciprocate the same. Employees quickly adapt changes; when they work in an environment that is sensitive and empathetic they develop positive attitude. CSR requires alliance and teamwork between management and employees, employees derive sense of belongingness and pride towards organization. CSR policies can facilitate in retaining best talent which eventually improves goodwill and performance.

CSR and Investors Perception

Some investors value corporate social responsibility, even if ethical behaviour is not financially rewarding. Ethical fad cause good companies to be overrated in comparison to their counterparts. Therefore, doing well translates into ethical goodwill or market premium. Corporate social responsibility rating agencies hugely influence performance of companies and their stakeholders, and CSR rating declarations have substantial affirmative effect on stock returns, suggestive of that CSR initiatives help to modify investors' views and firms' valuations. So there exists a positive relationship between eco-efficiency and market value and.

CSR and Financial Performance

Over the last decade, numerous researches have been conducted to examine the relationship between Corporate Social Responsibility initiatives taken by companies and the impact on company's financial performance. Some authors have used accounting-based variables based on firm's historical performance such as return on sales (ROS), return on assets (ROA), return on equity (ROE), earnings before interest, taxes, depreciation, and amortization (EBITDA), operating cash flows and earning per share (EPS). While other authors have used market based variables such as market capitalization, price earning (P/E ratio) which reflect investors' evaluation and expectation of firms. It has been found that corporate social responsibility has positive correlation with corporate financial performance. Return on assets (ROA), operating cash flows and profit before taxation are higher in case of companies engaged in corporate social responsibility practices in contrast to those with no or lower CSR initiatives. CSR awareness among the public also has positive effect on firm value.

CSR: Community Development

Systems thinking theory emphasizes need to comprehend inter-relation of constituents within any systems. Because society and business are interdependent and interrelated, only harmonizing their respective needs can create meaningful system. Lack of sustainability initiatives by corporates will continue deteriorating the environment, which can result in shortening survival of humankind.

Besides generating profits, organizations should work for the betterment of society and preservation of environment. They should enhance wellbeing in local communities. They need to collaborate with local communities to preserve non-renewable natural resources and train them to adopt health lifestyle. Companies should harnesses innovation for public welfare and ecological preservation, keep people and planet at center-stage, spread economic opportunity, and pursue purpose beyond profit. Because only when communities would continue to exist will the enterprises be able to generate profits.

CONCLUSION

Corporate Social Responsibility has moved beyond the borders of philanthropy, compliance and public relations to be an inherent component of corporate governance, strategy, and risk and reputation management. Thus, it is inevitable that company` business model displays socially and environmentally responsible constructs.

Figure 7.
(Tata Steel, 2017)

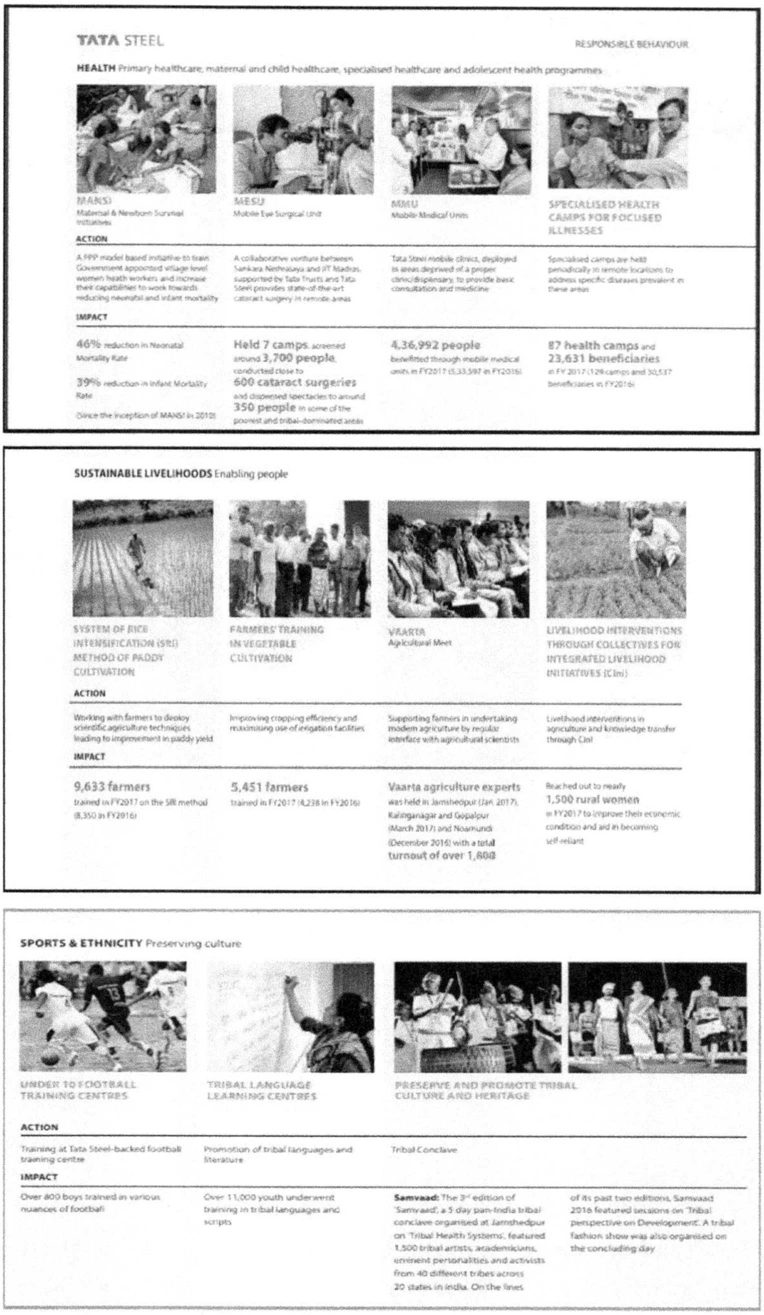
TATA STEEL

RESPONSIBLE BEHAVIOUR

HEALTH Primary healthcare, maternal and child healthcare, specialised healthcare and adolescent health programmes

MANSI
Maternal & Newborn Survival Initiatives

MESU
Mobile Eye Surgical Unit

MMU
Mobile Medical Units

SPECIALISED HEALTH CAMPS FOR FOCUSED ILLNESSES

ACTION

A PPP model based initiative to train Government appointed village level women heath workers and increase their capabilities to work towards reducing neonatal and infant mortality

A collaborative venture between Sankara Nethralaya and IIT Madras, supported by Tata Trusts and Tata Steel provides state-of-the-art cataract surgery in remote areas

Tata Steel mobile clinics, deployed in areas deprived of a proper clinic/dispensary, to provide basic consultation and medicine

Specialised camps are held periodically in remote locations to address specific diseases prevalent in these areas

IMPACT

46% reduction in Neonatal Mortality Rate

39% reduction in Infant Mortality Rate

(Since the inception of MANSI in 2010)

Held 7 camps, screened around 3,700 people, conducted close to 600 cataract surgeries and dispensed spectacles to around 350 people in some of the poorest and tribal-dominated areas

4,36,992 people benefitted through mobile medical units in FY2017 (5,33,597 in FY2016)

87 health camps and 23,631 beneficiaries in FY 2017 (129 camps and 30,537 beneficiaries in FY2016)

SUSTAINABLE LIVELIHOODS Enabling people

SYSTEM OF RICE INTENSIFICATION (SRI) METHOD OF PADDY CULTIVATION

FARMERS' TRAINING IN VEGETABLE CULTIVATION

VAARTA
Agricultural Meet

LIVELIHOOD INTERVENTIONS THROUGH COLLECTIVES FOR INTEGRATED LIVELIHOOD INITIATIVES (CInI)

ACTION

Working with farmers to deploy scientific agriculture techniques leading to improvement in paddy yield

Improving cropping efficiency and maximising use of irrigation facilities

Supporting farmers in undertaking modern agriculture by regular interface with agricultural scientists

Livelihood interventions in agriculture and knowledge transfer through CInI

IMPACT

9,633 farmers trained in FY2017 on the SRI method (8,350 in FY2016)

5,451 farmers trained in FY2017 (4,238 in FY2016)

Vaarta agriculture experts was held in Jamshedpur (Jan. 2017), Kalinganagar and Gopalpur (March 2017) and Noamundi (December 2016) with a total turnout of over 1,800

Reached out to nearly 1,500 rural women in FY2017 to improve their economic condition and aid in becoming self-reliant

SPORTS & ETHNICITY Preserving culture

UNDER 10 FOOTBALL TRAINING CENTRES

TRIBAL LANGUAGE LEARNING CENTRES

PRESERVE AND PROMOTE TRIBAL CULTURE AND HERITAGE

ACTION

Training at Tata Steel-backed football training centre

Promotion of tribal languages and literature

Tribal Conclave

IMPACT

Over 800 boys trained in various nuances of football

Over 11,000 youth underwent training in tribal languages and scripts

Samvaad: The 3rd edition of 'Samvaad', a 5 day pan-India tribal conclave organised at Jamshedpur on 'Tribal Health Systems', featured 1,500 tribal artists, academicians, eminent personalities and activists from 40 different tribes across 20 states in India. On the lines of its past two editions, Samvaad 2016 featured sessions on 'Tribal perspective on Development'. A tribal fashion show was also organised on the concluding day

Figure 8.
(Emirates, 2017)

Corporate Social Responsibility plays a significant role in influencing the sustainable development and growth.

REFERENCES

Apple. (2019). *Environmental Responsibility Report 2019*. Apple Inc. Retrieved from https://www.apple.com/environment/pdf/Apple_Environmental_Responsibility_Report_2019.pdf

Bowen, H. R. (1953). *Social Responsibilities of the Businessman*. Harper & Row.

Carroll, A. B. (1979). A three-dimensional conceptual model of corporate performance. *Academy of Management Review*, *4*(4), 497–505. doi:10.5465/amr.1979.4498296

CED. (1971). *Social Responsibilities of Business Corporations*. Committee for Economic Development.

CGA-Canada. (2005). *Measuring Up: A Study on Corporate Sustainability Reporting in Canada*. Certified General Accountants' Association of Canada Burnaby, BC. Retrieved from https://books.scholarsportal.info/viewdoc.html?id=358907

Davis, K. (1960). Can business afford to ignore social responsibilities? *California Management Review*, *2*(3), 70–76. doi:10.2307/41166246

Emirates. (2016). *Environment Report 2015-16*. Emirates Group. Retrieved from https://cdn.ek.aero/downloads/ek/pdfs/environment/ENV_REPORT-2015_2016.pdf

Emirates. (2017). *Environment Report 2016-17*. Emirates Group. Retrieved from https://cdn.ek.aero/ae/english/images/environment-report-2016-17_tcm277-4662773.pdf

European Commission. (2011). *Communication from the Commission to the European Parliament, the Council, the European Economic and Social Committee and the Committee of the Regions – A renewed EU strategy 2011-14 for Corporate Social Responsibility*. Available from https://eurlex.europa.eu/LexUriServ/LexUriServ.do?uri=COM:2011:0681:FIN:EN:PDF

Frederick, W. C. (1960). The growing concern over business responsibility. *California Management Review*, *2*(4), 54–61. doi:10.2307/41165405

Garriga, E., & Mele, D. (2004). Corporate social responsibility theories: Mapping and territory. *Journal of Business Ethics*, *53*(1/2), 51–74. doi:10.1023/B:BUSI.0000039399.90587.34

Google. (2019). Google. *Environment Reporter, 2019*. https://services.google.com/fh/files/misc/google_2019-environmental-report.pdf

ICAEW (2004). *Sustainability: The Role of Accountants*. The Institute of Chartered Accountants in England & Wales.

International Labour Organization. (2007). *International Instruments and Corporate Social Responsibility: A Booklet to Accompany Training – The Labour Dimension of CSR: from Principles to Practice*. Available from http://www.ilo.org/wcmsp5/groups/public/@ed_emp/@emp_ent/@multi/documents/instr uctionalmaterial/wcms_101247.pdf

Johnson, H. L. (1971). Business in Contemporary Society: Framework and Issues. Belmont, CA: Wadsworth.

Jones, T.M., (1980, Spring). Corporate social responsibility revisited, redefined. *California Management Review*, 59-67.

Kotler, P., & Lee, N. (2005). Corporate Social Responsibility: Doing the most good for your business. John Wiley & Sons, Inc.

Schwartz, M. S., & Carroll, A. B. (2003). Corporate social responsibility: A three-domain approach. *Business Ethics Quarterly*, *13*(October), 503–530. doi:10.5840/beq200313435

Secchi, D. (2007). Utilitarian, managerial and relational theories of corporate social responsibility. *International Journal of Management Reviews*, *9*(4), 347–373. doi:10.1111/j.1468-2370.2007.00215.x

Steel, T. (2017). *Towards a Sustainable Future. Integrated Report and Annual accounts 201-6-17, Tata Steel*. Retrieved from https://www.tatasteel.com/media/4852/csr-2016-17.pdf

Steels, T. (2004). *Corporate Sustainability Report (2003-04) Tata Steels*. Retrieved from https://www.tatasteel.com/files/csr-2003-04/management_sys/ms_07.htm

Wartick, S. L., & Cochran, P. L. (1985). The evolution of the corporate social performance mode. *Academy of Management Review*, *10*(4), 758–769. doi:10.5465/amr.1985.4279099

WCED. (1987). *Our Common Future, World Commission on Environment and Development*. Oxford University Press.

Wood, D. J. (1991). Corporate social performance revisited. *Academy of Management Review*, *16*(4), 691–718. doi:10.5465/amr.1991.4279616

World Business Council for Sustainable Development. (1998). *Meeting Changing Expectations*. Corporate. www.wbcsd.org/work-program/business-role/previous-work/corporate-social-responsibility.aspx

Chapter 5
Governance Structure Theories for Family Business

Ashok Chopra
Amity University, Dubai, UAE

Satish Menon
Amity University, Dubai, UAE

ABSTRACT

It is perceived by the authors that family ownership may be seen as an opportunity or a threat based on various factors. Ownership and commitment to business would definitely be able to address the concerns of the investor community. This is because of a better understating by the family in having a strategic approach to risk management. Therefore, all the more important to have the right governance conditions in place which reflects the positive aspects of family ownership. The author further states that in order achieve the said perspectives, there emanates a need for a design structure of governance to have a balance between family and business. Hence, it becomes all the more vital to define family values and have the involvement of each and every family member. The author further elucidates on the fact that it becomes imperative to improvise capital and ensure a proper leadership succession planning so that business continuity does not suffer.

DEFINING FAMILY BUSINESS GOVERNANCE

Family businesses have been there for many centuries and as such each family entity shares a sense of identity and collectiveness in terms of mutual interests. Every family business had its own unique proposition from a business dynamics point of

DOI: 10.4018/978-1-7998-6669-5.ch005

Copyright © 2021, IGI Global. Copying or distributing in print or electronic forms without written permission of IGI Global is prohibited.

view, but as time passed, structures that facilitated a better business approach started taking prominence. This slowly gave rise to family business governance.

Family governance is a way to facilitate communication and help educate family members through a constructive process. It provides a platform that empowers family members to collectively contribute to business decisions and problem resolutions. In other words, it should encourage ownership discussions and provide for continuous feedback. This ensures peaceful business continuity and helps the family realize its business goals that are shared by all members.

Family business governance is also a mechanism through which family members especially in large family entities, can be educated about the various aspects of the business, the transitional challenge that needs to be considered, and also its genesis. This paves a way for family members to support each other and get alignment with the shared vision and goals of the business.

Effective governance, whilst creating value is also a significant contributor to the success of the family business, especially from a long-term perspective. There are lot of forces at play and crucial in the long-term success of families in business. Good governance mechanisms can help create a seamless structure - one that brings more clarity into relationships and the respective rights and responsibilities of various family members to ensure that businesses are managed professionally, whether the ones managing are family members or non-family members.

A fallout of poor governance could result in destroying the value system that has been put in place. Therefore, there is even more need for sound principles that will underpin the need for good and effective governance.

It is here that one needs to consider investing in family governance tools that would enhance the sense of family member's identification with the firm. There needs to be a comprehensive approach to identifying the governance too, one that would be fit for the purpose (Gersick & Feliu,2014) This drives entrepreneurial orientation into the ensuing generations and helps drive productivity, efficiency, and profitability of the family business.

EVOLUTION OF FAMILY BUSINESS GOVERNANCE

Family businesses are common around the world and their survival is crucial to fueling and funneling economic growth both locally and at a global level. Interestingly many well-known and successful organizations started out as family businesses, including some of the Fortune 500 companies. Not only do these companies play a very vital role but they open windows of opportunities for newer investments which are secure and provide a more stable outlook. Many business models have been societal oriented ones, both at a local and at a regional level.

From an evolutionary point of view most of the family business saw their birth as being entrepreneurial. This has slowly, but surely gone through many changes due to various external forces at play and this has brought about a much-diversified thought process amongst the families. In that, business diversifications were seen to emerge that gave rise to big and profitable conglomerates. Over the years we have seen the family business go through generational transitions which paved the way for other business opportunities to be explored.

Given this pace of change, the need for a structured governance mechanism became more imperative. To explain the evolution more elaborately, we need to rewind to the era of 80's. This period saw the three-circle family system model which was put forth by The Harvard Business School.

The three-component model has interdependent yet an overlapping system within a family enterprise. It is basically Family, Ownership, and Business. For seamless functioning, it is important to know the dependence of one system on the other and how they interact and provide a support mechanism for other systems. This

Figure 1. The three circle model of family business system by Renato Tagiuri and John Davis

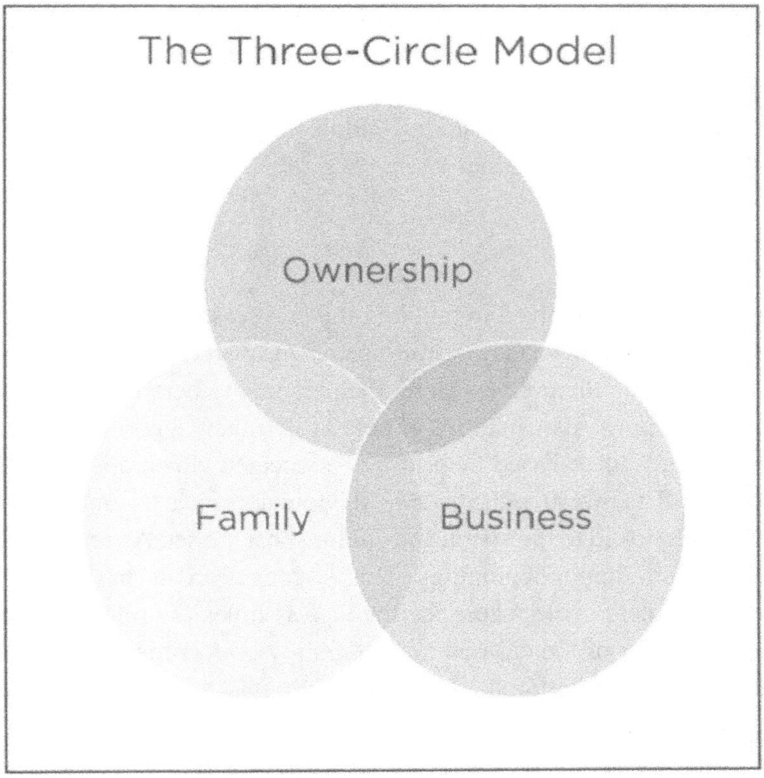

system gives a certain autonomy to individual family members and let them know the extent of empowerment given to each of them. A combination of the above is the essence of Governance.

In this evolutionary process, it is even more critical to have guidelines and regulatory mechanisms governing the business considering the sensitive nature of these transitions and the varying views of the family members. All these will help put into place a robust structure for Family, Business, and Ownership practices which will help enhance both business and family relationships.

This was further enhanced by a new model introduced by Gersick. It was called the developmental model which incorporated aspects of the development of Ownership, Family and Business. This model was a stage wise transition from inception to maturity. In this model, the family expands its business across generations who participate and contribute at various levels of management. As such evolutionary transitions came about which encompassed the following - the controlling owner -stage to sibling partnership, and further to cousin consortium. In effect, the tangible outcome form this was the concept of Succession Planning, which warranted transfer of managerial responsibilities coupled with experience. This effectively brings into play the transfer of business ownership which is about control over the Company and a change in the equation within the family dynamics.

When we talk about evolution, we focus on the decision making and the board of directors which is typical of a family governance structure. With passage of time, we have seen the development of different stages in a family business. Given the complexities of the family governance evolution, it is best to understand the different stages and its respective transitions.

Stage 1

The generation first is involved in building the business. At this stage most of the businesses are informal in terms of governance. During this stage, the decisions are taken by the founders themselves. Here, the personality perspective of individual owners come into play. Also, in terms of board roles many theories such as agency, stewardship and resource-based theories are advocated which does talk about the board attributes. The investments made by the founders have an emotional element attached which is linked to the vision and cultures that are set. As such, the business evolves from such simple beginnings. This is considered to be the initial stage of the family business cycle where the founder assumes the role of CEO as well chairman in majority of the cases, since the family prefers the higher echelons of the business to be from within the family itself. In this stage, succession planning also starts to take importance as this is factor that needs addressing by the founder to ensure business continuity.

Stage 2

This is the middle stage of the business cycle, also referred as sibling partnerships. In this phase we see the transfer of ownership to the children of the founders. When this transition happens, we see that there is an increase in the formal power of the CEO, and in terms of ownership there is an equal stake that could come into existence. In all this, what dominates are aspects of family belongingness and a sustainable and a stable family ownership structure. This stage warrants the need to develop family employment policy with set policies and procedures that are controlled. It could range from family rights to stipulated conditions for entry and exit to defining family vs non-family member treatment at different levels within the business.

In this stage, the board may be quite small as it may contain of only the owner and few other family members. Therefore, it has a bearing on the selection criteria of the board members. Often, we see increasing family membership on the board. The overall contribution to the business strategy by the board may be limited but this can change when there are further transitions to the family business structure.

Stage 3

This in effect is the transition from the second to the third generation, also called the advanced stage. Here, we see the modern market dynamics comes into play wherein takeovers and specific legal protection mechanisms now take the center stage. At the onset of this phase we see succeeding generations coming into the forefront and play an important role in the wealth and employment creation of the business entity. Since there is an enhancement in the number of family members, this transition is also termed as the cousin confederates.

Wealth preservation takes prominence as it becomes crucial to sustain and maintain their standing in the market. Therefore, this requires well-written governance policies that is communicated to the family and the business. As compared to other stages, we also witness an enhanced participation by the board. Given new task dimensions involved, a business in this stage could require people with new skills, relevant knowledge, and abilities. This stage warrants and emphasizes expertise rather than family ties. In other words, the policy document becomes the family constitution. All aspects relating to corporate capital, dividends, debt, profit levels, shareholder liquidity, conflict resolution, family participation and role gets defined in the constitution very clearly.

In summary, the continuance of family business depends on how every component of the family business is managed during the various phases of its evolution. Learning to do so with well laid down structures will reap the necessary dividends in the long run.

CHALLENGES OF GOVERNANCE IN FAMILY OWNED BUSINESS

Major forces of change like globalization, technology and sustainability brought along many challenges to family businesses. Hence, the need increases for practicing good governance which helps prepare family firms for the future and helps anticipate and manage challenges to it. Accountability and transparency are the key.

The main challenge for family business is the potential mix-up of family and business issues and interests thereof. Governance challenges for families in business arise from the intertwining of family and business issues. Challenges could take the form of emotional attachments and expectations of various family members and when not met could ruin the very fabric of the family business structure. It becomes even more challenging when multiple family members are involved is the aspect of succession and inheritance.

The family is often structured by multiple generations and family trees. Over a period, newer generations are added, which results in limited interaction amongst family members and as a result, a generation gap is formed. This makes it crucial for measures to be taken to hold all the family members accountable but also preserve and maintain family values, traditions, and culture.

One of the key challenges to family business governance is with respect to multiple relationships the owning/controlling member brings to the business. From a stakeholder point of view there are many complexities amongst the family members during the first two generations where business is managed by the initial family members. Working together intensifies family interactions and can lead to more family problems, such as rivalry amongst siblings which in turn can create unhealthy competition for further generations. Conflicts, if remain unresolved can derail the operations of the business and can harbor mistrust amongst the family members which in turn will have a negative impact on the business side.

In such a scenario, Talent acquisition becomes a challenge as well. Especially, in terms of sustaining and retaining talented and highly qualified professionals which makes it even more important to find talent that are not just fit for the job, but also for the organization. This leads to managing external stakeholder expectations from the business point of view as well since they hold a significant stake in giving directions to shape the governance of a family business. In an age of globalization, new governance patterns emerge all the time and they vary across geographies and industries. Moreover, there is no one rule that governs all – every family business is unique, deriving its personality from generations of family and business heritage.

Other Key Challenges

Most family business must manage growth expectations and one of the biggest expectations that need to be taken care of is funding. Funding can be sourced in term of equity or debt, which leads to the dilemma that many family-controlled businesses face in terms of diluting their stake. With this, comes new ways to run the business. This, often, reduces the leverage the family members have on the business. In other words, it is essential to balance the demands of the business and the family. To compound these, there is a psychological dimension in having family members to work as a cohesive unit as many external forces can change the dynamics of the business operations. These things become more and more prominent where there were no well-defined company and family relationships created at the set-up stage of the business itself (Shleifer & Vishny, 1997)

When most governance policies are of an informal nature, another challenge that stems from this is asset ownership and use as it becomes a challenge to figure out company-owned assets from the ones that can be used by the family members. Each is not independent of the other from a statutory point of view. So, does this concept pertain to the financial matters of the business as well? Key man dependency is massive as there is no regulated structure in place. This is particularly true with respect to financial relations and accounts — the company's and family's assets are not legally separated. Uncertainty brews within both internal (non–family employees) and external stakeholders as the control environment is customized to the needs of the family members.

This becomes an issue, as the business expands, and the controls do not. A significant gap is thus prevalent and can result in governance challenges for the future generations of the business.

Leadership Transition Challenge

This is a significant challenge for family businesses globally. Transition from one generation to next is something that is not planned out in advance, as the existing leaders tend to carry on well beyond their retirement age which comes from the fear of ceding control. This part of disengagement is very demanding as it has implications from the point of view of tasks, relationships, and processes to be in continuance. In an ongoing battle, we see conflict avoidance is common and issues remain unresolved for a long period. This influences the way junior members of the family are inducted into the business.

Beyond these, the other aspects family businesses need to consider is crisis management, cash flow and partner management. Not to forget liquidity, and merger and acquisition scenarios. There are many psychological challenges related to these as well which results in slow decision making and missing out on alignment within the team creating potential problems for execution.

It is therefore important for the leader of the family business to understand that the organization is larger than one person and the best way forward would be to leave a legacy to the next generation which revolves around values that possess a societal bearing and need for commitment in desire and obligations. This also paves a path for continuous commitment either in terms of cost or dependency. So, succession planning is vital to the continuing success of the business (Suess -Reyes, 2017)

Risk Radar for the Family Business Governance

To understand this concept, it is important to understand the risk culture of a business. This goes back to the three aspects - Business, Ownership and Family. Often biases, more specifically optimism bias, seem to creep in which prevents an objective assessment of risk. Studies further show that from a gender point of view, men are more likely than women to be predisposed to taking risks becoming a premise for the broad stereotype. In effect, it is vital to have an enterprise approach to risk which calls for an understanding of the risk appetite of the family members and assess how advisors could influence the family business leader towards taking those calculated risks.

Relevance of Risk to Family Business Governance

From a family business governance perspective, it is especially important to consider the strategic aspects of risk. Whilst a mechanism of risk may be in place, it is even more imperative for the family firm to not only be able to identify but also be able to assess risk. In today's world, it is always a risk-based approach to doing business. Hence, it is important to map the risks early on and manage any consequence arising out of it. The question to be asked is "what is the risk of doing it and what is the risk of not doing it?" The levels of risk must be clearly defined as the long-term survival of the business depends on it. Having said all this, let us explore the topic of risk appetite and risk tolerance perspectives.

Risk Appetite

Is the total exposure and types of risk an Organization is willing to undertake based on the return tradeoffs for one or more desired outcomes?

- Aggregate at the "top of the house".
- Defined typically at the Board Level in the form of a "Risk appetite Statement"

- Usually details activities and businesses that are unacceptable
- Should be closely aligned to Strategic Objectives with mentions of risk metrics.

Risk Tolerance

- Defines the variance of risk an organization is willing to accept in a particular risk category.
- Is usually defined in a quantitative form as a metric and is more granular.
- Acts as a checkpoint and helps management with decisions and escalations.

Therefore, family business owners must ask key questions from a self-assessment perspective.

Some examples of these questions are: -

- Has a proper assessment of the risk appetite been done?
- Is there a current and future assessment of risk mechanism put in place?
- Does the assessment of business continuity risk consider all the external factors?
- Are their mitigations in place for identified risks?

That said the risks to family business can classified as given in the risk radar below.

As per the report, risk is defined as the outcome of the probability and the loss exposure of the occurrence. The outcome or potential loss expectancy is highest with strategic and operational risks and lowest with hazard and financial risks.

However there some incredibly unique situations of risk that could add on to the already long list. It is important to understand that not all risks can be eliminated or have mitigants to it.

It could be on account of,

- A non-family member influencing the owners in a negative manner due to certain self-interests.
- Failure by the first-generation family members to recognize formal structures that can cause elements of risk interfering within the system. Businesses are evolving continuously as organizations are leaning towards being learning organizations. Due to a lack of comprehension by the first generation, an absence of formal structures can cause many issues in terms of risk management. This can lead to an ignorance in differentiating between profit and revenue, which eventually results in negating the built value for the various stakeholders to the business.

Figure 2.
Source: Wartsilla Annual Report 2011

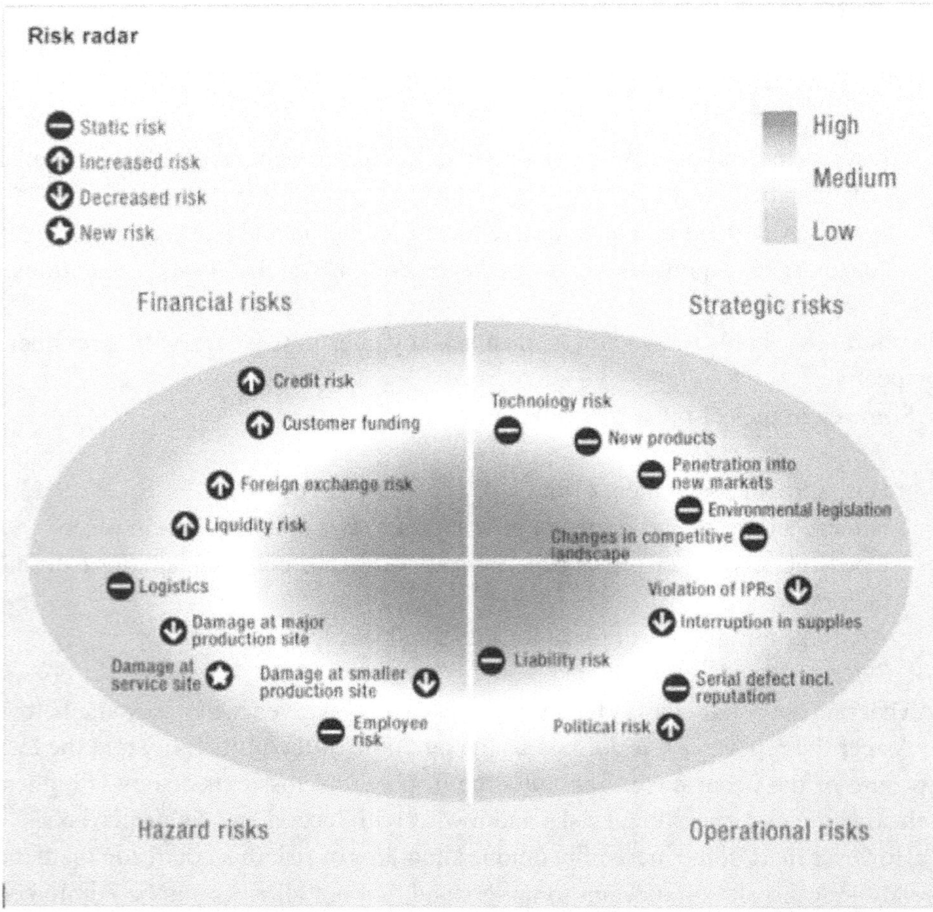

To possibly tackle these issues, there needs to be an integrated approach to managing risk at each level and communicating it to each level. As per figure, a need for proactive flow of information is required. This is driven from the risk Radar framework that is put in place.

Figure 3.
Source SU Report Risk 2002

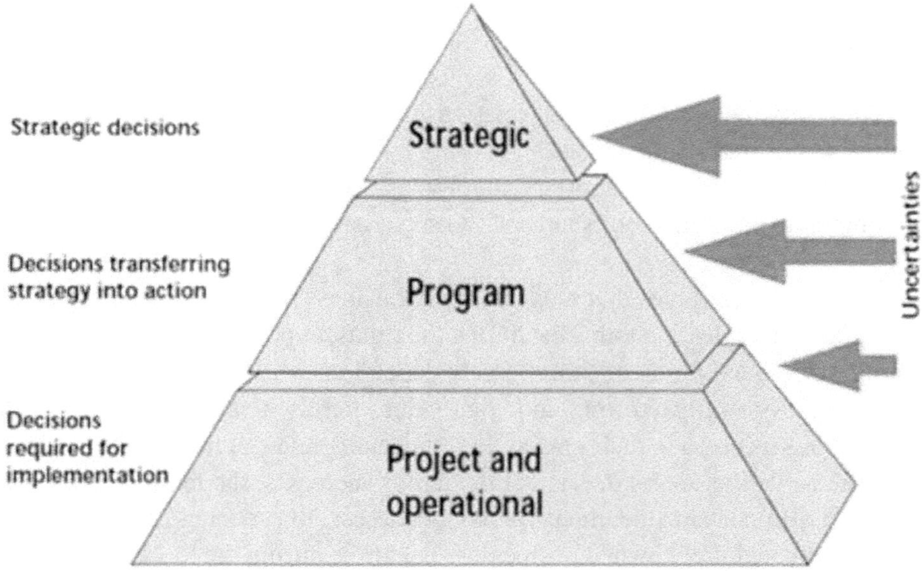

FAMILY BUSINESS CONSTITUTION

Family Constitution

Definition: The family constitution can be referred to as a statement outlining family promise and obligation of commitment to core values including vision and mission of the business. Thus, many times, the family constitution is alternatively termed as "Statement of Family Principles", "Family Rules", "Family Values", "Family Doctrine", "Family Protocol", "Family Faith", and "Family Beliefs". A Family Constitution includes defining areas like composition, roles, power of key governance bodies, family shareholders/members, and board of directors. It also clearly spells out how members of family can participate in meaningful ways and govern the business (Almeida & Wolfenzon, 2006)

The family constitution is thus ever evolving and keeps getting updated as family business evolve. So, regular updates and effecting changes are basic characteristics of family constitutions where important attributes of its form and content differ from one family business to another family business depending on size, degree of involvement, and stage of development of family business.

However, a typical family constitution will cover the following components:

- Family values, vision, and mission statement.
- Family institutions, including the family assembly, the family council, the education committee, the family office, etc.
- Board of directors
- Senior management.
- Authority, responsibility, and relationship among the family, the board, and the senior management.
- Policies regarding important family issues such as family members' employment, transfer of shares, CEO succession, etc.

It is normally observed that most of family business have an informal unwritten set of rules, principles, customs that define the rights, expectations, and obligations of family members. Some of these largely depend on which part of the world the family business originated from and what values family members involved in the business have received in their upbringing, especially relevant in the eastern part of the world. Nevertheless, as the size of the family increases, the family constitution becomes an important document. It has been seen that during the Covid - 19 Pandemic, many family owned businesses spent time during the lockdown to make family constitution an important exercise in their life.

Family Member Employment Policies

One of the most important aspects of family constitution is defining employment policies of family members. If employment policies for family members are not clear, then businesses may employ more than required family members disturbing their employee - family members' equilibrium which is critical to any family business' success. It is seen that some these employees might not even be suitable for the jobs they are given within the business. Even worse, these family members further acquire businesses which may have no synergy or compatibility with the original business. Sometimes, such moves are precedent just to ensure that everybody in the family gets a job.

It is suggested that one family member, who has knowledge about Human Resources, should formalize family member employment policies in consultation with other senior members. This would solicit setting up rules, and terms and conditions of family employment within business. These rules would include clarity regarding a family member's entry, stay, and exit from business.

Normally, content and structure of employment policies differs from one family business to another. Practically, there is no one set of rules that a family business must follow. It is observed that different family businesses deal with this differently. There are some family businesses who forbid any of their family members from being employees, and on the other hand, there are family businesses who set clear rules, education background, prior work experience and age limits. While developing rules, focus should be in attracting best talent for the family enterprise - be it from within or outside the family. It is important to set policies in a manner that do not differentiate and discriminate between family and outside employees. Such action leads to motivation and helps establish an atmosphere of fairness for all employees of family business.

Finally, when developed and agreed upon by family, the written employment policy document should be circulated and made available to all family members. This would set the right tone and expectations about family employment among all family members.

Family Member Shareholding Policies

It is of paramount importance to define shareholding policy for family businesses at the initial stage of its existence. This sets the right tone and expectations among family members' shareholder's ownership rights. Policy should clearly define ownership rights to be given to in-laws and other family members with maximum cap applicable (if any), mechanism to sell or prefer cash instead. It is normally seen as the pool of share - holders grows larger, majority holders end up receiving lower number of dividends. Often, situation can get frustrating when lower receiving dividend members compare themselves to salary receiving family members. Making a provision to allow liquidation usually helps avoid conflict. It is seen that many family-owned companies create share redemption fund to buy back shares that members would like to liquidate. The normal practice for doing so is through creation of fund that is financed by contributing a small percentage of profit every year.

Family Governance Institutions

In family businesses, a practice of having an informal institution with organized structure, where members can participate, be part of discussions/deliberations, and make decisions, strengthens the harmony, and brings cohesiveness. It improves communication link and provides solid foundation for taking joint decisions in the best interest of the organization and its shareholders. In the Gulf region, it is known as Majlis (an Arabic and Persian term meaning "council"). Such meetings can also be formalized by serving an agenda in advance to focus on purpose and objectives. It is important for family members to differentiate such meetings with other formal meeting like the one with board of directors or meetings with other governing bodies. A written communication to this effect can improve such an institution role.

Such institutions are not binding for any organization but do play an important role. Thus, the degree of involvement from family members to such institutions largely depends on culture and practices prevalent in various parts of the world. Below are descriptions of family governance intuitions which may be present.

Family Forum (aka Family Assembly)

Definition: Usually a formal format of meeting that involves discussion with all family members regarding business and family issues related to business. At the founding stage, such meetings are more common and informal, thus the name Family Meeting is also prevalent. In these meetings, founder(s) normally communicate values of the family, discussion of readiness of next line of leaders within family, and new ideas. As the time passes, family businesses become more complex involving cousins, siblings, and others, making the need of having a family forum more crucial and essential part of business.

Objective: To remove communication and ego barriers among family members, bring members together as a single team and cohesive unit, a Family Forum keeps members informed about business issues, challenges, and gives an opportunity to seek advice from all. Such forums help avoid potential conflict if any. The usual frequency can range from quarterly to twice a year. Issues normally handled and taken up in such a forum may include -

- Endorsement on family values and vision as envisaged by founder.
- Education, rights, and responsibilities of family member.
- Discussion and seeking approval on employment and compensation of family members.
- Election/selection of family council (if exists)
- Nomination, selection, and election of other family committees and members

Membership: Normally, in family businesses, membership is open to all primary and secondary (if permitted) members. However, in some families, there can be restrictions on minimum age, voting rights, and involvement of in-laws. Such forums are normally headed and called by the head of the family. However, in larger families, this task is usually given to the family council.

Family Supervisory Board

Definition: "Family Supervisory Board" is also known as "Family Council", and "Family Executive Committee". The Family Supervisory Board is a principal working body that is elected by members of Family Forum to deliberate day to day working issues of the business. The supervisory council is enacted once family reaches critical size i.e. thirty members and onwards. The sheer size of the family makes it difficult to have meaningful discussion and make right business decisions. The supervisory council established is entrusted with responsibilities of smooth running of business affairs and coordinating the interest of family members in their business.

Objective: The configuration, composition and functioning of family supervisory board may differ from family to family but broad duties include:

- To serve as a vital link between board, family, and senior management.
- To play a pivotal and central role in helping family members arrive consensus regarding issues where the owners' wishes matter most.
- Advise on candidates for the board.
- Update the vision, mission, values, and strategy to be adapted by the family business.
- Update policies and procedures regarding employment, compensation, and shareholding position as and when required
- Take care of any other important matters that are critical to the family business
- Provide a systematic way for family members to achieve core business objectives
- Initiate policies that can help balancing the family business
- Evaluate and articulate fundamental values and communication across board as guiding principles
- Engage non-participating family members formally or informally about strategic challenges faced by family business.

Membership: Like any other effectively managed and functioning committees, the supervisory council should also have the right sized, manageable team of five to ten members. The selection/election of these members would be primarily driven by their qualification, experience, drive, trust, and ability to perform day to day functioning of the family business. There is also a practice of imposing certain restrictions like age, experience, and other deemed suitable attributes when defining the main selection criteria for such membership. Among many, one ideal practice is to set limited terms for the supervisory board and have a policy of fairness and equal opportunities for entire family.

Family Supervisory Board Evolution

In a family owned business, governance is perpetual, thus a Family Supervisory Board should be looked at as a journey too rather than a destination. Normally, governance challenges tend be complicated as family grows generation after generation making professional handling the key to success. Sometimes governance or lack thereof can give rise to legal battles if a generation did not plan succession properly. It is also not justified that Family Supervisory Board would be able to operate on an auto pilot mode on its own. Thus, regular, and timely reviews with foresight and planning of family supervisory board is recommended to be fit for purpose. Research has shown that as children grow mature, informal meetings practiced by family business owners are replaced by Family Supervisory Board consisting of both parents and children providing a more formal platform for discussion of business issues. The issues which normally dominate such formal forum discussions include career, skill development, succession planning, diversifications, and technology upgradation matters. At this stage, it becomes important for parents/older generation to encourage and nurture an atmosphere of free and open discussion, highlight accomplishments of the younger generation and take pride in their achievements, and lay a foundation for value- based vision definition, which reinforces family involvement. As business transitions, leadership and succession topics should also be introduced as agenda items. Aspects of member involvement in day to day matters of the company with clear responsibilities and portfolio allocation can be next facets tackled by a Family Supervisory Board. As the journey progresses, topics of how to involve siblings can also be discussed and prioritized. It has been seen that involvement of family member's spouses is already a contentious issue in most forums. During such times, it is the Family Supervisory Board that should organize social events to build cohesiveness among all members. Slowly, issues like leadership and succession can move in agenda upwards, along with sibling partnership issues. Combination of such issues can give birth to business ownership changes which many times leads to changed management roles (Bettinelli, 2011).

The tertiary generation of family consists of cousin syndicate level in which majority of members are mainly from extended family who usually have weaker relationships or hardly any connection with the business. At this stage, it is expected that family governance through Family Forum (Broad institution consisting of shareholders and immediate family members) would have delegated executive function to newly appointed Family Supervisory Board to which membership has been restricted through the process of nomination. The focus of Family Supervisory Board would be in managing complexities of an enlarged family, strengthening an emotional connection (also known as "psychological ownership), and nurturing sense of family commitment and identity. At this stage, normally, outside managers are appointed which includes trained, professional directors and executives who run the family business in a more professional way while family members focus shifts to dividend issues and shares trading/transfer which can offer exit route if required.

Table 1 on Family Supervisory Board Functions

Family Supervisory Board Functions: · Objective and Meaning, · Think and introspect why are in business together as single family/unit, · Inception and communication of family values, culture and vision through family and business, · Nurturing family next generation inclusivity, · Enunciating and improving long term plan of the family, · Rejoicing family's culture, tradition, success, achievements, and dynasty, · Encouraging social bonding among members, · Carrying on family benevolence. **Learning and Improvement:** Ø Learning all about detailing of family business areas, issues, freedom, ownership, compulsions, and responsibilities, Ø Enabling and helping in attaining required qualification for employment, Ø Extending support on scholarships and venture funds, Ø Developing and promoting leadership, Ø Promoting and supporting relationship building, Ø Promoting and enabling improved intra family communication, Ø Team Building, mediating relation building and differences. **Building Rapport within Business:** · Defining and involving degree of family participation, · Drafting, preparing and regular updating of family constitution, · Relationship with the business, · Defining and Protecting personal and family business issues, · Defining and working of unified voice of family, · Defining and promoting merit-based employment policies, · Working on management succession plan. **Leadership and Decision-Making Development:** · Providing critical relationship between management board and family, · Communicating family perspective of strategic plan to board, · Managing Family Supervisory Board committees, · Developing and Reviewing Code of Conduct of Family Supervisory Board, · Managing and coordinating other family boards. **Issues of Family ownership:** · Overseeing Share Ownership policies, · Looking after estate and its ownership issues, · Managing and reviewing policies related to inactive shareholders in the family, · Management of assets, · Defining of exit routes, · Defining and managing of rights to income of shareholders, · Developing and defining communication policies, · Working and defining business growth targets and reviewing them

Family Office

Definition: The Family office is an advisory and investment center/wing managed by the Family Forum. Such kind of advisory is common among wealthier families in business, whose members seek expert advice on accounting, banking, personal finance, taxation, and other related issues.

Objective: To advice on estate planning, taxation matters, personal finance, investment tools, career counseling, and any other matters which are more personal in nature.

Membership: It is a separate operation away from day to day business activities, but few members of family could play an integral part to this office. The office usually consists of professional managers who oversee investments, advisory, financial planning, intra family transactions, taxations, insurance, stocks, and estate matters.

Table 2 outlines the major differences between the Family Meeting, Family Forum, and Family Supervisory Board

Table 2.

	Family	Family Forum	Family Supervisory Board
Stage	Founder (s)	Sibling Partnership/ Cousin Confederation	Sibling Partnership/ Cousin Confederation
Status	Usually informal	Formal	Formal
Membership	Normally open to all family members. Criteria may be defined for additional by founder (s)	Normally open to all family members. Criteria may be defined for additional by founder (s)	Family members elected by Family Supervisory Board Selection criteria defined by the family.
Size	Small size since family still at founder(s) stage. Usually 6- 12 family members.	Depends on the size of the family and membership selection criteria.	Depends on criteria set up for the membership. Ideally 5-10 members.
Number of Meetings	Depends on the stage of the business development. When the business is growing fast, can be as frequent as once a week.	1-2 times a year.	2-6 times a year
Main Activities	• Communication of family values and vision and mission. • Discussion and generation of new business ideas. • Preparation of the next business leader(s).	Discussion and communication of ideas, disagreements, and vision. • Approval of major family related policies & procedures. • Education of family members on business issues. • Election of family Forum and other committees' members	• Conflict resolution. • Development of the major family related policies & procedures. • Planning. • Education. • Coordination of the work with the management and the board and balancing the business and the family.

Other Family Institutions

Many businesses might like to develop other types of institutions that might be of huge interest to them. These institutions can be helpful in joint governance of business and allied care of family interests.

Education Committee: This type of committee is normally responsible for taking care and nurturing of human capital of the family, which eventually might help in organizing number of seminars where family members can participate to learn various aspects of handling and managing business, reading balance sheets and financial statements etc.

Portfolio Management and Shares Redemption Committee: Many family members would want to liquidate their shares at a fair price to pursue different management of their portfolio. This committee is overseen by the Family Supervisory Board.

Career Development Committee: This committee looks after entry and overseeing policies and procedure for family members who are interested in joining the family business. Committee also looks after career planning, development, and mentoring family members. It also provides status updates to shareholders and family supervisory board. This committee also provides counselling and advising to family members, who are not interested in joining the family business and want to pursue a different career outside.

Family Recreational & Reunion Committee: The main objective of this team is to bring the family together by organizing fun family reunion events and recreational activities. The relationship nurturing among family is achieved through organizing events best suited for providing an opportunity for the family members to come together and understand each other.

The Art of Agreeing

In early forming stage of the Family Supervisory Board, when sensitive matters and topics like agreeing on how to agree on important issues are up front and center, it is appropriate to consider having a trusted, matured, and impartial person from outside (independent) be trusted as a skilled facilitator. This person can not only help sort many issues in a systematic and impartial manner but also help in drafting future policies by benchmarking them with other established, similar, family-owned businesses which may already be industry leaders. Such a facilitator can also ensure taking proper notes and jotting down all relevant issues that are brought up, considering "selective amnesia" is common in family owned businesses.

Normally, a starting point for such upcoming family supervisory board comes from residential retreats, away from daily routine and rut with quiet environment.

The important point in art of agreeing is not to have too much too soon at such forums. First few sessions should be devoted as warming up sessions with focus on core values, main governance procedures, and building trust among so called extended family. The main task of facilitator would be to drive agreement between family members on how to agree on topics that hold importance to the business.

Another crucial area is the inclusion of family members in the membership of supervisory board. Striking a critical balance between active and non-active members is crucial in the initial stage of family business. Research has shown inclusion of both active and non-active members is critical to the success of a family business enterprise. Among many, best practice is participation from all family members who were directly or indirectly involved from the beginning.

Overall importance of Family Supervisory Board can be seen from two aspects - from family as a single unit and consensus driven entity, and overall business effectiveness and performance. The key to success of above lies in separating day to day family and business affairs which helps bring out a positive perspective of family relationships, success, and smooth operations. Family Supervisory Board also strikes a critical balance in looking at problem areas and selecting the right path which works for both, the family, and the business (Almeida et al., 2011) It also provides mechanisms for interacting positively as members and bringing higher motivation levels to help members focus on providing a competitive edge to family business.

Planning and Designing Governance Structural Design

When we discuss principles of planning and designing a governance structure or its design, then it is important to know that being flexible is the key to success. There are no set formulas, equations, tools, or principles which can be used to have an ideal structure. The diagram below may be best termed as a probable scheme/ structure that is representative of a governance scheme for a multigenerational family owned business.

In this, the Family Supervisory Board is the fulcrum on which structure design of governance is standing. This fulcrum beautifully maintains critical balance between family and business as mutually exclusive yet independent entities. One can think of many variations e.g. families with large/ huge ownership, normally term their Family Supervisory Board as "ownership supervisory board" whose objective is focus on strategic matters and ownership concern, and Family Supervisory Board focuses on educational development and social agenda matters.

Sometimes, family members feel that the Family Supervisory Board is ambiguous in nature so the term "family council" is opted for as the alternative nomenclature. Important is comprehensiveness of governance process and clear definition of roles and responsibilities bestowed upon members.

By the time stage for cousin consortium comes, the structural design should be robust and clear enough to manage complexity and maintain relationship tracks. In fact, many multigenerational companies are now global conglomerates so structural design of a governance structure is also multi-continental and consists of multi-culturally diverse perspectives.

Figure 4. Family business model

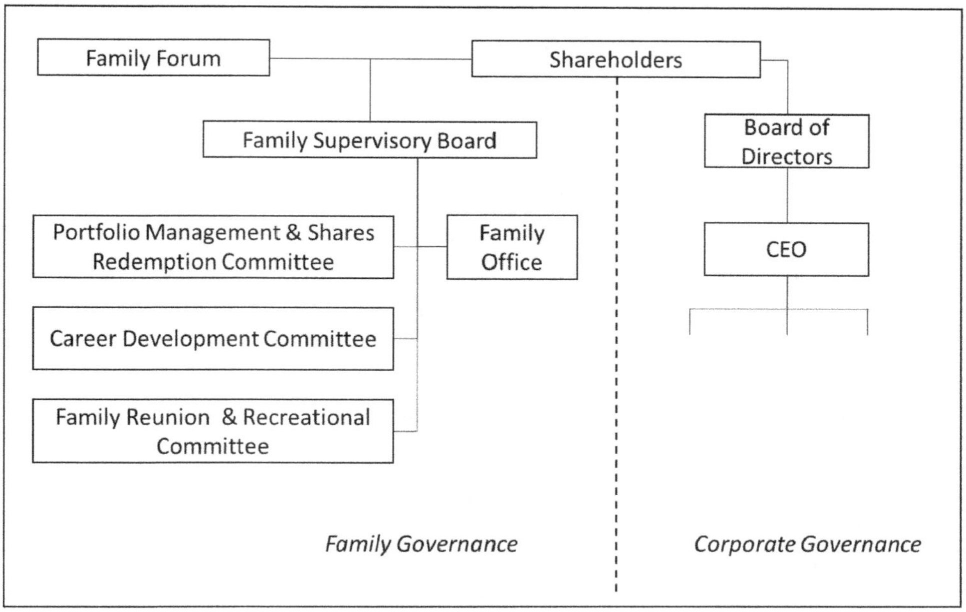

FAMILY BUSINESS CHARTER

Family Charter is a dynamic living document whose contents are not limited to vision and mission statements but also include definitions, roles, responsibilities, mutual and independent relationships, power, composition, configuration, and structure of key bodies. Although content of the family charter is dependent on size and development of organization/company, a charter should contain something resting on the following pillar base at a minimum:

- Vision, Mission, and family values
- Board of directors

- Advisory board if it exits
- Senior management team members
- Family institution which may include family assembly
- The board, senior management, and family in respect to authority, responsibilities, and relationship
- All critical details which are originating and are part of Family Forum and Family Supervisory Board.
- Any other detail is deemed fit as written rather than verbally in nature.

BEST GROWTH COMMANDMENTS FOR A FAMILY OWNED BUSINESS

Looking at Owners as the Enablers of Growth in Family Owned Business Means

- Crafting and implementing tested and everlasting set of tools
- Having unequal and strong leadership structure
- Holding high your belief values and convictions unparalleled to none,
- Holding yourself as onus of your family's assets and being amenable to innovation and an entrepreneurial spirit

Ten Commandments for a Family Owned Business

1. Focus in understanding through Hawk eyes on development within your sector of business,
2. Craft innovative yet flexible organization,
3. Have leadership succession planning,
4. Constantly improvise your capital,
5. Continuously Capitalize and build USP of family owned and managed business,
6. Throughout look for best external managers and bind them to business,
7. Define vision, mission, strategy, and family goal and communicate to all family members,
8. Define and adhere to your family values,
9. Ensure involving each member of your family,
10. Draft owner's led business principles to lead long term in business and industry.

Figure 5. Ten commandments for a family owned business

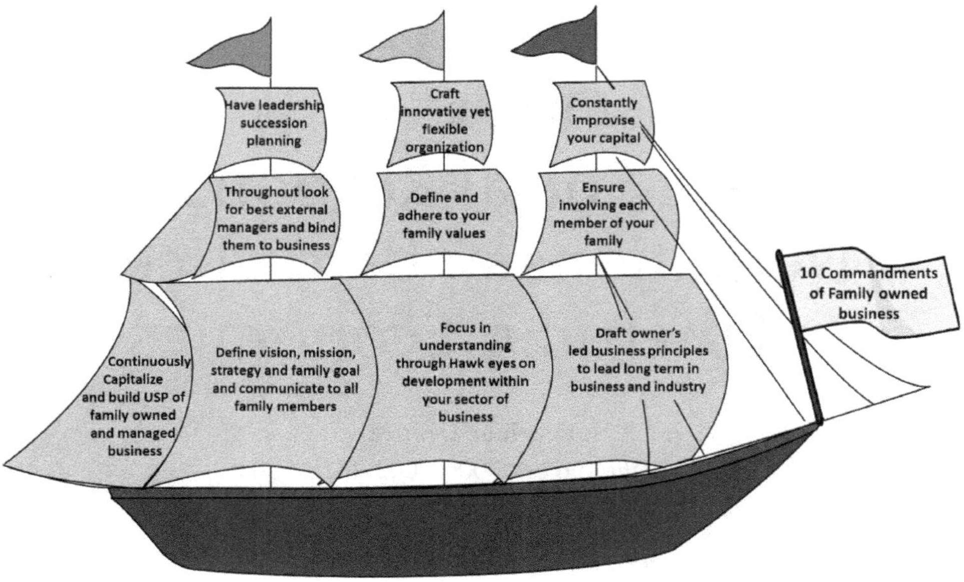

REFERENCES

Almeida, H., Park, S., Subrahmanyam, M., & Wolfenzon, D. (2011). The Structure and Formation of Business Groups: Evidence from Korean Chaebols. *Journal of Financial Economics*, *99*(2), 447–475. doi:10.1016/j.jfineco.2010.08.017

Almeida, H., & Wolfenzon, D. (2006). A Theory of Pyramidal Ownership and Family Business Groups. *The Journal of Finance*, *61*(6), 2637–2680. doi:10.1111/j.1540-6261.2006.01001.x

Bettinelli, C. (2011). Board of Directors in Family Firms: An Exploratory Study of Structure and Group Process. *Family Business Review*, *24*(2), 151–169. doi:10.1177/0894486511402196

Gersick, K. E., & Feliu, N. (2014). Governing the family enterprise: Practices, performance, and research. The Sage Handbook of Family Business, 196-225.

Shleifer, A., & Vishny, R. (1997). A Survey of Corporate Governance. *The Journal of Finance*, *52*(2), 737–783. doi:10.1111/j.1540-6261.1997.tb04820.x

Suess-Reyes, J. (2017). Understanding the transgenerational orientation of family businesses: The role of family governance and business family identity. *Journal of Business Economics*, *87*(6), 749–777. doi:10.100711573-016-0835-3

Chapter 6
Corporate Social Responsibility Definitions and Practice in Emerging Economies

Sorbarikor Lebura
https://orcid.org/0000-0002-4318-0000
Rivers State University, Nigeria

Igazeuma Adikema Okoroba
University of Port Harcourt, Nigeria

ABSTRACT

This chapter looks at the concept of corporate social responsibility (CSR), specifically in terms of the diverse definitions and perspectives of it that currently exist within emerging economies. This is explored from its foundation and the interaction between business and society across different emerging economies. This discourse is linked to the interplay between corporate governance and corporate social responsibility across emerging economies. This is hinged on the influences of both the academia and industry, as the definitions of the former does contribute to the practical application of the concept by practitioners and vice versa. The chapter is divided into three sections, which are definitions, perspectives, and case studies, with each of these focusing on the issues as they affect the theme of the chapter.

DOI: 10.4018/978-1-7998-6669-5.ch006

Copyright © 2021, IGI Global. Copying or distributing in print or electronic forms without written permission of IGI Global is prohibited.

INTRODUCTION

The ideological underpinnings of social responsibility and its relationship to emerging societies can be explored through a historical perspective. According to Spector (2008), the roots of the CSR movement trace back to the early years of the old war when companies were encouraged to show why private economic development produced better results than socialist alternatives. The movement was led by academics and executives who advocated on the Harvard Business Review. In defence of free-market capitalism, they advocated for expanded business social responsibility. The pace of advancement in CSR depends on factors such as the continent where business is domiciled, the philosophy of decision makers, government disposition towards business, national cultures and other factors. Due to the influence of globalization, countries review their stakeholder relations policies in the context of local realities. As a result of this, different interpretations of CSR have emerged, differentiating the Western style of CSR from those of developing countries. Frynas (2005) opines that CSR has fallen short mainly due to a synthesis of fundamentally flawed approaches, procedures and inadequate CSR packages often adopted by Multinational Corporations in developing countries. Such flawed approaches contrast with sound business ethics upheld and enforced conscientiously in the home countries of such corporations. Others argue that CSR is but the newest manifestation of business ethics (Blowfield and Frynas, 2005). According to this school of thought, CSR emerged as corporation's response to the increasing campaigns of environmental activists and local communities during the 1980s and 1990s. This new wave of CSR aimed to reduce the agitations from these quarters. These underline the differences that could exist both in the definition and practice of the concept across the globe, but this chapter focuses on the perspectives of the emerging economies.

This chapter aims to achieve the following objectives;

- to provide clarity on the foundations of CSR practice in the emerging economies.
- to contribute will contribute to better understanding what drives CSR in emerging economies by exploring the different perspectives using case studies within emerging economies.
- to stimulate scholars' interest in further research on the subject.

DEFINITIONS OF CORPORATE SOCIAL RESPONSIBILITY (CSR)

The concept known referred to as CSR has attracted a growing and overwhelming interest over the past two decades from both academics and practitioners as can be seen in the various labels given to the concept such as 'Social Responsibility', 'Corporate Sustainability', 'Corporate Citizenship' (Nwaeke & Lebura, 2016), amongst other labels. These different labels and titles given to the concept are further confirmation of the popularity which the concept has garnered over the years, even as Pedersen (2006, p.137) regarded it as "one of the buzzwords of the millennium". The concept of CSR is widely used not only in academia but in the business world. It is therefore applied in many corporate business models, even though there is no clear definition as to what the term represents. This popularity of the concept which has led to increased awareness by the public has not really been seen as leading to its clarity (Amaeshi & Adi, 2007), as it is deemed to mean something different for different people, leading to a diversity of meanings (Votaw, 1972).

According to Drebes (2016), a reason for this definitional lack could be that the concept is located at the boundary between social science and practice, and the rather interest-oriented way in which the term has been used in the past has led to this conceptual blurring. Okoye (2009) argues that CSR is an Essentially Contested Concept (ECC) which means that it might not necessarily need to have one universally accepted definition may not serve the best interests of the concept, so long as the various points of view are referring to the same concept. This seems to mean that not having a generally accepted definition is not always a bad thing to happen to a concept, especially in the light of a concept like CSR that has various perspectives that cut across the divides of the western and emerging economies; multinational corporations and SMEs; academia and practitioners. Wan-Jan (2006) argues that the "absence of a clear working definition would only mean that studies on CSR could be based on weak or false understanding of the topic" (p.177). This indicates that in the past the concept's usage has been determined by the user and purpose for which they were using it, which is emphasized by the definitions presented below as posited by different scholars.

As far back as 1927, Dean Donham had argued that businessmen must begin to give consideration to their responsibilities to others, which Bowen (1953) supported by defining CSR as the obligations of businessmen to pursue policies, make decisions and follow lines of action that are in tandem with the objectives and values of society. This definition by Howard Bowen led to Carroll (1999) arguing that he should be called the "Father of Corporate Social Responsibility" (p.270), because he seemed to have prophesied the future importance of the concept which has today become one of the most talked about business concepts across all parts of the globe. Frederick

(1960) regards social responsibilities of businesses as running an economic system that meets the expectations of the public, which means that the utilization of societal resources by companies must be to have broad social impact on society. Davis (1960) regarded it as "businessmen's decisions and actions taken for reasons at least partially beyond the firm's direct economic or technical interest" (p.70). Another definition was that "the idea of social responsibilities supposes that the corporation has not only economic and legal obligations but also certain responsibilities to society which extend beyond these obligations" (McGuire, 1963, p.144). Davis and Blomstrom (1966) defined it as the firm's obligation to give consideration to the impacts of whatever decisions they make on the entire social system. They went further to add that whenever a firm looks beyond their narrow economic and technical interests (p.12) then they have actually been socially responsible. There was the introduction of the relationships angle by Walton (1967) with the definition of the concept as the recognition of the intimate relationships that exist between companies and society, even as both parties pursue their diverse goals and objectives. It could be seen here that taking this relationship into cognizance would mean that each party would be careful not to do anything that could negatively impact on such relationships.

Steiner (1971) defined CSR as "a philosophy that looks at the social interest and the enlightened self-interest of business over the long run as compared with the old, narrow, unrestrained short-run self-interest (p.164). According to Backman (1975, p.2), "Social responsibility usually refers to the objectives or motives that should be given weight by business in addition to those dealing with economic performance (e.g., profits)". Fitch (1976) regarded it as being about a thoughtful attempt by a firm to ensure that there is a solution which it has caused, either partially or fully. Jones (1980) defined as being about a belief that businesses have a responsibility to constituent groups within the environment in which they operate aside from their shareholders and this is not limited to what is captured by the law and contracts. Epstein (1987) defined it as "achieving outcomes from organizational decisions concerning specific issues or problems which (by some normative standard) have beneficial rather than adverse effects on pertinent corporate stakeholders (p.104). Cadbury (2002) added that broadly speaking, CSR emphasizes the sustained existence of firms as tied to a social contract that ensures that companies do not chase their short-term profitability even when it negates the future interests of the society in which they operate. The emphasis here is that while businesses pursue profit maximisation which is their primary objective ab initio, they must not jeopardise the long-term interests of the larger society. The World Business Council for Sustainable Development (WBCSD) (2002) defines CSR as "the commitment of business to contribute to sustainable economic development, working with employees, their families, the local community and society at large to improve their quality of life" (p.2).

Kok, van der Wiele, McKenna and Brown (2001) regarded the concept as "the obligation of the firm to use its resources in ways to benefit society, through committed participation as a member of society, taking into account the society at large, and improving welfare of society at large independent of direct gains of the company" (p.288). This definition emphasizes that businesses that undertake CSR are supposed to do so without considerations of what gains they can derive from it, which was confirmed by Porter and Kramer (2006) when they insisted that companies must integrate CSR plans and programmes into their strategies in order to maximise them. Kotler and Lee (2005) regarded it as being about improving the welfare of societal members, while Eweje (2006) agreed with the improvement of societal welfare but adding that the firm also gets improved. Ojo (2009) insisted that the lack of a universally accepted definition does not take away from the focus which was now about improving the lives of stakeholders of companies. There seemed to be a movement over the years from the vague reference to CSR as being about looking outside of the business to actually identifying that there are specific stakeholders

It is noteworthy to state at this point that it is almost impossible to have a CSR discussion without mentioning or alluding to stakeholders in some way. In this vein, Smith (2003) defined CSR as the obligation of a business to the society in which it operates, as represented by its stakeholders, that is those persons or groups that are affected by the firm's policies and practices. Hopkins (2003, p 10) agreed that the concept is mainly about stakeholders even as he defined it as 'treating the stakeholders of the firm ethically or in a responsible manner'. The European Commission's Green Paper on CSR (2001) defined CSR as the voluntary integration of social and environmental concerns by firms in their business operations, especially as they interact with their various stakeholders. Carroll (1979) added that 'for a definition of social responsibility to fully address the entire range of obligations business has to society, it must embody the economic, legal, ethical and discretionary categories of business performance' (p.499). This view has come to be accepted as being the most comprehensive of all the views on CSR as it addresses issues concerning the different stakeholders of the firm, which are the shareholders and employees (economic responsibilities); the government (legal responsibilities); customers and clients (ethical responsibilities); and host communities (ethical and discretionary responsibilities. Interestingly, these seem to be arranged in an order that tends to indicate how attention should be given to the different stakeholders to whom the firm owes the various obligations highlighted above.

Considering that this book is about corporate governance, it is also important to present a definition of the concept that touch on the idea of corporate governance. According to Schuchard (2010), 'CSR is the integration of environmental, social, and good governance practices into everything that business does, and the recognition of material aspects of nonfinancial issues that are integral to overall strategy and operations'. There is claimed to be a very strong connection between Corporate Governance and Corporate Social Responsibility (CSR), which makes them reinforce each other in the running of business operations of any firm (Ararat, 2004). It can be seen that the practice of CSR would to a great extent depend on the Corporate Governance structure of the company, so that if a company has on its board individuals who think business only about profit making or has policies and processes that do not ensure ethical operations then it is most likely going to have issues with the practice of CSR.

From the definitions above, it would seem like every scholar that has contributed to the CSR discourse has deemed it necessary for businesses to engage in its practice but that is not the case, as some authors have argued that it is an unnecessary burden on the firm. One of such critics of the whole idea of CSR is Friedman (1970) who claimed that 'the only one responsibility of business towards society is the maximisation of profits to the shareholder within the legal framework and ethical custom of the country' (p.32). This angle of looking at CSR is one that does not entirely oppose the practice of the concept by businesses, but underlines that economic maximization must be done within the confines of regulation while ethical considerations are also made within the specific context of operation. In support of Friedman's position, there is also the view by Knox, Maklan and French (2005) that engaging in CSR in any guise is actually a tax that leads to the reduction of the general wealth. According to Henderson (2004), CSR is a 'radically new model of corporate behaviour' which aims to disrupt the functionality of the market by compelling firms to give needless considerations to societal issues that seeks to change the way the market operates by forcing corporations to give unnecessary attention to public welfare. These positions by these scholars and others reinforce the importance of different definitions and perspectives when it comes to the concept of CSR, as this only further enriches the discourse of both academics and practitioners.

Perspectives of CSR in Emerging Economies

The plethora of definitions available on the concept as seen above have been attributed to the diversities of those involved with both its research and practice, even as these definitions are influenced by the various perspectives that they hold of the concept (Lebura, 2009). It is very interesting to find that majority of the definitions presented above have their origin in more advanced economies of Europe and the Americas, most of which have been exported wholesale to the rest of the world. This has mainly been the way CSR has been explored over the last four decades, even as it has been widely criticized as largely driven by the concerns and priorities of western countries, thereby making it insensitive to the context of developing countries. This lopsided approach to the CSR discourse seems to have triggered the need for the emergence of a South-centred CSR agenda. This is further supported by the growing evidence that non-Western firms from emerging economies such as Nigeria, South Africa and Malaysia are as aware of CSR issues and are striving to become good corporate citizens. The extant literature on CSR in other developing economies in the South contend with the distinction between CSR practices enabled by private morality and those propped by international institutions.

CSR as Philanthropy

Since the 1990s, corporate and scholarly attention has shifted to viewing the concept of CSR from the angle of 'corporate citizenship'. Carroll (1991) strongly argued in favour of the idea of companies that are socially responsible becoming good corporate citizens, by ensuring that they endeavour to make profit by operating within the ambits of the law, being ethical in operations and being a good corporate citizen. This perspective has been mainly practitioner driven, with the emphasis being on the firm being a good neighbour or citizen that contributes to the wellbeing of the community in all areas. This perspective to the practice of CSR which has been around since the 1950s has been the predominant approach of companies operating in emerging economies. Most of the companies operating in the developing world practice CSR as the broad responsiveness to societal needs and expectations, especially in the form of charitable giving. In Europe, the notion of philanthropy is often dismissed and not regarded as part of core CSR activities, but firms in many emerging economies are expected to actively assist their local communities.

CSR can serve as a vehicle for improving Human Development Index (HDI) in emerging economies, though this does not seem to be the case so far. Amaeshi, Adi, Ogbechie and Amao (2006) have argued that this limited impact by CSR could be attributed to the perspective of 'giving back' to the society. Muthuri (2007) actually noted that this was the very first approach to community development projects by companies operating in Africa. This meant that companies made donations to their host communities which could be cash donations or the building of infrastructures such as schools, hospitals, health centres, potable water projects, amongst others. This usually involves the identification of a project by the company's department responsible for the execution of such projects and programmes, the approval of funds and the implementation of whatever projects have been earmarked. The communities to benefit from such projects are not usually involved in decisions relating to the project to be sited in their communities, neither are they involved in how such projects are executed in their communities which has led to projects not aligned to the people's immediate needs being donated to them. Lebura (2013) noted that in a particular instance, the company undertook to build a borehole in the community to ease the burden on the women of that community when it comes to fetching water, without any consultation with the women. After spending money to build the borehole, it was discovered that the borehole was not being put to use by the women of the community and follow-up investigation revealed that the women preferred to go to the stream as a way of taking a break from household chores and catching up with the latest information in town.

CSR as philanthropy in emerging societies is linked to the influences of culture and religion, as these societies have a certain sense of family and kinship (Amaeshi, *et al.* 2006; Adi, 2006). The influence of Islam has been evident at government level in countries like Bangladesh. Several Islamic financial institutions, such as Islamic banks, were set up and in 1984, the Bangladeshi government established the semi-official Zakat Fund Committee to collect Zakat (Momin & Parker, 2013). According to Sharia Law, Zakat was an imposed payment of surplus wealth to be managed by financial institutions and spent on pro-poor projects such as schools, health centres, etc. This imposed a philanthropic responsibility on individuals and corporations in Bangladesh based on an Islamic principle of poor people's rights to rich peoples' savings. This practice is responsible for the adoption of CSR as philanthropy in Islamic-dominated countries.

Philanthropy is voluntary on the part of businesses; however, there is always the societal expectation that businesses provide it (Carroll, 1991). The difference between philanthropy and ethical responsibility is that the former is not expected in an ethical or moral sense. Beyond mitigating community unrest and disruptions for companies dependent on natural resources, the relevance of corporate philanthropy to organisations in emerging economies has not been established in literature. The position therefore remains that companies do not gain much from corporate philanthropy, so while it is good to do good and be a good citizen, this must be done in collaboration with the beneficiaries of such philanthropy.

CSR as a Vehicle for Filling Institutional Voids

One of the key challenges of CSR in emerging economies has been the overload of pressure on companies operating in these countries to do things that ordinarily should be the responsibility of governments in these countries. This lackluster attitude of government to its primary responsibilities and obligations across emerging economies has shifted the focus, as society now seems to blame the corporations operating in their environment, especially multinationals. Eweje (2007) emphasized this point by indicating that host communities within the oil rich Niger Delta region now assume that everything that they need to improve their welfare and standard of living should be provided by the oil companies operating there.

This has affected the approach taken by companies operating in these economies when it comes to the practice of CSR over the years as there has been a focus on basic amenities that would normally be taken for granted in the western economies. For the West, CSR practices are now about the impact of the business on the long-term aspirations of society, such as environmental sustainability and climate change. Emerging economies cannot afford to be trapped in this limited perspective due to the absence of good governance systems that provide basic amenities. Multinational companies operating in these emerging economies, specifically across Africa generally fill socio-economic voids created by poor governance and weak institutions. These voids cut across most aspects of the people's lives and wellbeing, such as education, health, social and basic infrastructure, amongst many others (Eweje, 2007; Idemudia, 2009; Ojo, 2009). These companies have built and equipped schools at all levels; primary, secondary and tertiary educational institutions. They have also sponsored capacity building and scholarships for teachers working in these schools, some local and others foreign. In terms of health, they have built health centres and clinics, as well as equipped government hospitals and provided necessary drugs. They also make contributions to microcredit schemes, potable water schemes, electrification projects, building of community halls, markets and road infrastructure development. Interestingly, these initiatives are voluntarily undertaken by these companies, albeit increasingly expected by stakeholders. Companies may partner with NGOs to undertake projects, employ experts in local culture and community development, and adopt standards or guidelines proffered by international associations.

In Nigeria, an oil-dependent and highly unequal country, SPDC's host communities have looked to the company to provide infrastructure such as water, electricity and roads that the country's government had failed to provide, creating a situation in which local communities depended on Shell for basic amenities. Remarkably, as much as the company has contributed to the economy both in terms of royalties paid and the CSR projects undertaken over her seven decades of operations in Nigeria since it first struck oil in commercial quantities, it is still not deemed to have done much by the host communities in the Niger Delta region. This could be attributed to government not living up to expectation in terms of the basic amenities that it should provide for the people. Owing to such government absence in regard to development actions, it is now a commonly held notion in the communities that host oil and gas operations in the Niger Delta that '*Shell is the government we know*'.

CSR in India negotiates contradictory notions of moral and economic imperatives. The CSR concept is governed by section 135 of the Companies Act of 2013. India's economy is the fastest growing in the world, but stark inequalities exist in the indicators of development. The national government, to address development disparities mandated all enterprises above a certain size, both public and private, to commit 2% of profits to CSR programmes and projects. However, emerging evidence shows that this practice is unlikely to be more successful in filling institutional voids of the country. One of the stated rationales for the CSR law is to drive innovation, but firms claim that government rules and regulations increasingly dictated how they spent CSR budgets and mostly channeled them towards activities the government ought to address. The practice of the CSR law which was sold to the companies with the aim of attaining sustainability goals and stakeholder activism in nation building seems to have been hijacked by political interference forcing business enterprises to take on quasi-government roles. This may be a wrong approach to the contribution of business when it has to do with national development. So, as much as businesses are expected to play an integral role in the development of emerging economies, they are not supposed to take over the duties and responsibilities of governments in the guise of CSR.

CSR as Public Relations

It is widely reported that developing countries endowed with natural resources are caught in the paradox of plenty. Their populations endure decaying infrastructure, annual increase in unemployment rates, devastation and hardship for communities that host such vast mineral resources. The persistence of these conditions gave rise to human right violation protests and demands for the restoration of lost livelihoods. The pressure upon corporations operating in such environments, motivated by the agitations of communities led to the adoption of approaches which serve to protect or repair the image and reputation of the business. In the developing world, especially in oil rich countries like Nigeria, Angola and Brazil, there have been attempts by multinational corporations to launder their battered image and reputation by engaging in CSR activities in the environments where they have caused such damage.

Reputation and legitimacy arguments maintain that firms may strengthen their legitimacy and enhance their reputation by engaging in CSR activities (Carroll & Shabana, 2010). An example of a CSR activity directed at developing reputation and legitimacy is cause marketing. Cause marketing is a strategy where emphasis is given to the company's products and services while linked to appeals for charitable giving. Companies use cause marketing to demonstrate they can, mutually pursue profitability goals and meet the needs of the different stakeholders as well. It is important to note here that when public relations form the main focus of a company's engagement in CSR activities or projects, there is a high dependence on the media. In these days of social media, it becomes commonplace to find companies associated with one good cause or the other which they tend to get involved with to enhance their reputation with the public. It is also common to find that CSR practices of parent companies of Multinational corporations in the West are not being replicated in subsidiaries located in developing countries. When such firms risk being sanctioned by regulators in the home country, internal legitimacy also serves as a primary motivation for CSR practice.

Organizations often focus on financial targets in their operating environments and financial reporting becomes critical for business survival. In South Africa, the culture of financial reporting and disclosures extends to the social sector. Companies like AngloGold Ashanti with a geographically diverse shareholder base which includes some of the world's largest financial institutions, traditionally provide financial reporting to shareholders. However, the practice of non-financial performance reporting has now extended to their other stakeholders. A study by Ackers (2015), showed that CSR in South Africa is significantly motivated by regulatory compliance. The requirement for CSR reporting is being institutionalised by the King Code of Governance [King III] where all JSE-listed companies not only disclose their CSR performance, but also to ensure that such disclosures have been independently assured.

Reputational motives CSR performance may be helpful in the short term but it results in a check the box approach which is unsustainable over time. When CSR is not integrated in a company philosophy it is seen as an addition to the marketing function used to boost brand image or perform damage control when there is a crisis. This type of CSR often leads to 'green washing', which in the long run leads to a sense of distrust between the company and its stakeholders.

CSR as a Transactional Relationship

The primary way local people in emerging economies directly benefit from exploration or any mining activity is the relationship between the value of the community development or CSR projects and the wealth taken from the community in the form of natural resources. This perspective compares CSR project values with the multiple negative impacts that mining produces for local communities and often results in give and take arrangements commonly known as community relations. In today's world, almost every company uses some form of marketing to reach their audience. The transactional marketing orientation is a strategy adopted where there is high concern for operations and short-term solutions are sought. The transactional orientation is an old approach used in the deployment of CSR which arose to consider the gap between the organization's publics view of its performance and the organization's actual performance. This practice involved firms identifying, evaluating and responding to those social and political issues which may impact significantly upon its operations. The approach is also known as issues management.

Societal license to operate is another approach to transactional CSR. Eweje (2006) discussed the concept of a societal license to operate which the multinational oil companies in the Niger Delta region of Nigeria always seek to secure to avoid disruptions to their operations. This license is deemed to be more valued than the legal license granted by the government and it is granted by the host communities in the environments where these companies operate. As a result, CSR projects and activities in this instance are used as some form of currency to ensure continued exploration of natural resources. This introduces the angle of an exchange that takes place between the parties involved, even as each party tries to secure as much benefits as it can from the other party. It is also important to add that a societal license to operate (SLO) is dependent on a community's perceptions of the acceptability of a company and its local operations. SLO's focus on perceptions of the relationship than on perceptions of the impacts puts the weighting of impacts in the hands of the stakeholder, thereby tilting the balance of power in favour of the stakeholder.

Boutilier (2017) argues that the assumption in the concept is that if stakeholders see the impacts as bad, the relationship will be viewed negatively as well. Looking directly at the perceptions of the quality of the relationship avoids the necessity of companies having to make assumptions on what is important to the stakeholders. While social license might present prospects for greater recognition by the stakeholder, it can also be abused when IOCs operating in the region consciously implement CSR for merely the sole aim of securing the societal license to operate. This ambivalent practice can undermine CSR because it substitutes adherence to environmental standards with maintaining a favourable community relationship. An example is where SPDC in Nigeria commits to release funds for CSR activities on the condition that host communities guarantee there will be no disruption of her operations within a given period. This may seem strategic in a sense but then it tends to make the relationship all about what can be gotten from it, with little or no consideration for the greater good of society. Nwaeke & Lebura (2016) agreed that when this happens these relationships are now viewed as games played by the different parties involved in the relationship, as they make decisions on the basis of their expected outcome from the game .

The use of binding agreements such as Memoranda of Understanding (MoUs) and Global Memoranda of Understanding (GMoUs) is another way firms deploy CSR in a transactional manner. Despite allegedly benevolent intentions of CSR executed through instruments such as MoUs and GMoUs, there is a strong imbalance and a structural misalignment between the firm's goals and its contribution to society due to power relations. Foucault, Dreyfus and Rabinow (1982) described power as the expression of a complex strategic situation in a society without which social interaction and communication could not exist. When power relations play out during the use of enforceable agreements, multinational corporations (which do not 'have' power) act in certain ways they exert power over the actions of others, for example host communities. This uneven relationship between them reinforces the corporation's ability to achieve operational goals in the short-term while communities believe they have been 'settled'.

CSR as a Business Strategy

CSR as a business strategy is informed by the agency theory which presents the firm as being run by an agent that has to always protect the interests of their principal and this influences every decision and action that they take. Drucker (1984) argued that businesses must intentionally convert every social responsibility activity or project into a business opportunity. This may not seem very ethical, especially considering Carroll's (1991) ethical responsibility which represents norms, standards or expectations that reflect a concern for what consumers, employees, shareholders, and the community regard as fair or morally right. However, it can become a strong motivation or driver for companies to undertake CSR. Porter and Kramer (2006) argued that companies must start to be proactive by including their CSR plans as part of their business strategies in order to maximise the benefits that come with such.

A strategy approach is different from measures developed under the presumption that CSR is a beneficial add-on. This broad view of CSR often eludes many firms in emerging economies that are narrowly focused on their core activities, with CSR treated as an afterthought that is given attention when there is either a crisis to manage or image to launder. CSR as a business strategy is easily linked with impact because corporations look at their social investments and link them to their business objectives. In deploying a business strategy approach to CSR, a firm identifies CSR projects best aligned with their corporate objectives and undertakes that. Also, the different stakeholders are given a sense of ownership in the decisions surrounding the CSR projects that the firm decides to undertake, which they jointly execute and thereby create shared values. It is important to add here that the specifics of what will constitute a company's CSR will depend on the particular case and the context of the CSR project, as well as sector peculiarities.

CSR as a business strategy is a critical shift for emerging societies which answers to concerns raised by scholars and practitioners that the demands of stakeholders presents potential threats to organization's viability. When CSR is approached as a business strategy, corporate economic interests are served by mitigating the threats through a threshold level of social or environmental performance. For instance, CSR provides equal employment opportunity policies and practices, which can also enhance long-term shareholder value by reducing costs and risks. In the same vein, if a company undertakes to provide educational scholarships to students from their host communities who are interested in studying courses that form the core of their business, then they could as well benefit from employing such persons after they have finished their courses. This becomes a win-win situation for both parties, capacity building and employment for the communities while the company gets the right employees that fit into their business core.

The value creation ability of CSR and attempt to weave the triple bottom-line into business are challenges companies in the emerging economies must consider as part of their business strategy. A factor that potentially influences the uptake of CSR as a business strategy in emerging societies is reporting. Corporate Reporting in emerging economies such as South Africa, Brazil, India and parts of Eastern Europe has the potential to be exceeding standards in some more advanced economies. In Baskin's (2006) analyses, there was not a vast difference in the approach to reported corporate responsibility between leading companies in advanced economies and their emerging economies peers. Beyond reporting, the implementation and outcome of CSR however must be about reciprocal relationships that deliver social value throughout the ecosystem.

CASE STUDIES

This section presents 3 cases of companies that are practicing the different perspectives of CSR across Africa as a way of properly situating this chapter in the context of the emerging economies' business environments.

AngloGold Ashanti: South Africa Case Study

AngloGold Ashanti is the third largest gold producer globally and the largest on the African continent with operations in 11 countries. The company incorporated a structured CSR policy into their mainstream corporate policies in 2007. The company implements a centralized approach to Corporate social investment which guides social investment interventions in each country. The policy outlines the company's approach to identifying projects in which it can be involved, allowing it to make the transition from grant maker and financial enabler to hands-on initiator of projects. In South Africa specifically, its focus areas are geared towards meeting this country's most pressing needs. The company considers education as the key to capacity building that benefits communities long into the future. As such, education forms the company's biggest investment focus area, accounting for almost half of CSR spend.

One of the most significant and multifaceted challenges facing AngloGold Ashanti is that of artisanal and small-scale mining (ASM). The key challenge facing AngloGold Ashanti in managing the issues associated with artisanal and small-scale mining is to develop a strategy which permits co-existence and promotes the development of orderly, viable small-scale mining sectors in collaboration with host communities and governments. Chief among the complex issues of ASM is the Conflict which is common between operators and the safety and environmental risks of the practice.

To address this problem, in 2006 AngloGold Ashanti initiated external baseline studies of ASM in the DRC and Ghana. The company acknowledged that small-scale mining has a legitimate place in the economy and mining sector and engaged the government agencies and communities in allocating land to miners in this sector. This measure was to ensure that such mining activities were done on only land set aside for that purpose. It was believed that this way small-scale miners can access support through appropriate regulatory and administrative procedures. Contracts and collaborative agreements were established with the communities and mining organisations present in all the areas. The 'Good Friends and Neighbours' policy allowed for collaboration with legalised commercial mining activity. At the heart of the programme, artisanal miners were allocated grounds and given legal mining title over the property. In return for this, the miners registered in terms of the local mining regulatory framework and were expected to comply with some basic health and safety and environmental requirements. However, in 2019, the company reports that ASM continues unabated and has escalated in numbers. The complexity of challenges in some areas of the company's operation has necessitated a review of mitigation measures in supporting the concept of ASM formalisation. Advocacy is now ongoing for additional resourcing and extensive dialogue with residents are reliant on ASM-related income to find a lasting solution.

Vizag Steel: India Case Study

India's state-owned enterprises, known as Central Public Sector Enterprises (CPSEs) account for a fifth of India's GDP. They were created with the idea of advancing economic development for the social good. Rashtriya Ispat Nigam Limited, a CPSE is the corporate entity of Visakhapatnam Steel Plant. The company was the first shore-based integrated steel plant in India. The mandatory CSR policy in India aims to get private businesses and CPSE's to spend at least 2 percent on CSR. Before this policy came into place, Rashtriya Ispat Nigam Limited - Visakhapatnam Steel Plant (RINL-VSP) popularly known as 'Vizag Steel', invested significantly in CSR. The company's CSR vehicle, RINL-CSR Foundation was formed in 2007 to hold CSR funds and to transform the rural community.

Every year, annual budget for CSR department was allocated towards donations & Philanthropy, Service to humanity, voluntary service, public awareness programs and contemporary issues like poverty, pollution, energy, waste recycling, water & sanitation, transparency & anti-corruption. Under CSR activities the major initiatives are taken up based on environmental care, health care, peripheral development, education and community development etc. Under environmental care, some of Vizag Steel's CSR activities are the Jaladhara and the Green Visakha programme. Jaladhara project provided safe drinking water to 19 tribal villages of Agency area of

Vizag District. This project provides filtered, perennial drinking water by gravitation method from a rain fed source which is at heights, without using electrical power/energy. About 5500 people in 19 villages benefited. The Green Visakha programme aimed to reduce pollution through the planting of 5,00,000 trees in a period of 5 years commencing from year 2011.

THE NDPI 'THEORY OF CHANGE' MODEL OF CHEVRON NIGERIA

The Niger Delta region of Nigeria produces nearly 75% of Nigeria's foreign exchange earnings. The lack of economic opportunities that persists in the region despite its oil wealth threatens the peace and stability among other issues such as environmental degradation and pollution in the region. Chevron Nigeria Limited is one of the major oil corporations operating under a Joint Venture arrangement with the Nigerian government. In 2010, the company invested $50 million to establish two independent, sister foundations: The Niger Delta Partnership Initiative Foundation (NDPI) based in the United states and the Foundation for Partnership Initiatives in the Niger Delta (PIND), based in Nigeria. The mission of PIND and NDPI was to relieve the region of poverty and promote her development. The organizations were founded on a theory of change model which addresses conflict and poverty as an interrelated phenomenon. Programming was designed so that market conditions and peace building mutually tackle causes of conflict and poverty in a local context.

NDPI and PIND's success to date in the region can be credited to their development of a unique operating model and governance structure – a strong partnership-based approach where organizations developed strong local and international alliances and leveraged these to build extensive social networks in the region. NDPI and PIND then diffuse new best practices, ideas, and technologies (i.e. innovations) throughout these networks by demonstrating their projects. Gradually, stakeholders are encouraged to "crowd in," resulting in new resources being injected into the region. As the regional market actors observe and respond to this scenario, behaviours become self-sustaining, thus resulting in systemic change.

In an assessment of the model, IGD notes that enhanced the attractiveness of the Niger Delta by reducing risk, which paves the way for other development investment in the region. The success factors of the approach are outlined as follows:

- The active role of linking groups and individuals which encourages collaboration and cooperation among different actors, enabling them to identify and access more opportunities.

- Development and providing support for critical cross-sector relationships, partnerships, and alliances.
- The ability to identify change agents – the innovators and early adopters of a population.
- The facilitation rather than support for dependency on donor funding. This is achieved by developing and implementing solutions in three core and interrelated focus areas: economic development, peace building, and creating an enabling Environment.
- The rapid development of a prototype with stakeholders which is tested until the product proves to be competitive or the need to pivot a new approach is discovered.

SOLUTIONS AND RECOMMENDATIONS

The following are some of the recommendations of the authors to help resolve some of the issues surrounding CSR in the emerging economies.

Stakeholder Engagement: Non-governmental organizations (NGOs), activists, communities, governments, media and other institutional forces demand what they consider to be responsible corporate practices. As a result, some corporations need to provide corporate responses to social demands by establishing dialogue with a wide spectrum of stakeholders. Stakeholder dialogue helps to address the question of responsiveness to the generally unclear signals received from the environment. Such dialogue not only enhances a company's sensitivity to their environment but also provides better understanding of the dilemmas facing the organization.

Berman et al. (1999, cited in Okpara & Idowu, 2013) states that being proactive on environmental issues can lower the costs of complying with present and future environmental regulations and may enhance firm efficiencies and drive down operating costs. Environmentally responsible commitments may also reduce the negative impact of social concern. For instance, lawsuits filed in 1999 against 27 well-known retailers on behalf of Saipan garment workers demonstrate the business risk associated with inadequate stakeholder engagement. CSR initiatives can also contribute to strengthening a firm's competitive advantage through enhancing its relationships with its customers, especially when undertaken in a socially responsible manner.

These demands should be seen as opportunities rather than limitations for corporations. Firms should strategically manage their resources to meet these demands and exploit the opportunities associated with them for the benefit of the firm. Competitive advantage has been cited as one of the top two justifications for CSR as reported by Fortune (2003 cited in Carroll & Shabana, 2010) in a survey of business executives. Firms can build their competitive advantage through CSR programs and initiatives by carefully crafting a unique strategy that aligns their corporate strategies with CSR programs. This unique strategy can serve as a basis for setting a firm apart from its competitors and, accordingly, secure its competitive advantage. Such firms do not view CSR as philanthropic activities that distract from the core business.

Sustainable Development: Sustainable development came into widespread use in 1987, when the United Nations World Commission on Environment and Development (United Nations) published a report known as the "Brundtland Report". This report stated that sustainable development seeks to meet the needs of the present without compromising the ability of the future generations to meet their own needs (World Commission on Environment and Development, 1987). Although SD was developed at macro level rather than corporate level, it demands the requisite corporate contribution to be impactful.

The challenge before corporations is the development of processes and implementation strategies that meet corporate sustainable development standards. Business needs to rethink the way it strives to create value and outcomes that are consistent with the ideals of sustainability along social, environmental and economic dimensions. It is suggested that organizations choose their own specific ambition and approach regarding corporate sustainability. This should meet the organization's aims and intentions, and be aligned with the organizational strategy, as an appropriate response to the circumstances in which the organization operates.

Aligning Sustainable Development Goals with Citizen Priorities: Achieving sustainable, systemic change is a process and one that is not accomplished quickly, nor by a single institution or sector. It requires acknowledgement of the complexity involved in fundamentally changing human behavior and the fabric of society. It also requires significant time, as well as sustained commitment and investment to establish and maintain trust and credibility among a large group of stakeholders.

The approach to interventions and measurement alike must be multi-disciplinary, taking into account not just the economic aspects of market development, but more importantly, the sociological, anthropological, and psychological factors as well.

Global Business Citizenship: In the past, the rules and norms of business behavior in most industries were primarily guided by national cultures, social institutions, and legal parameters. Companies typically had a home country and an organizational identity shaped by the home culture. In a global economy, a company will struggle to decide between a multidomestic strategy, which tailors its strategy to local conditions, and a globally integrated strategy, which strives to achieve a unified strategy across all units.

The contentions resulting from this challenged informed the emergence of a new citizenship concept. Wood & Logsdon (2002), proposed the term Global business citizenship (GBC) to incorporate the core moral and social content of CSR and place corporate-community relations and philanthropy among the larger set of rights, duties, and stakeholder relationships. Business citizenship defines a business organization's relationship to nation-states, to other organizations, and to human beings. It is thus an ethical enterprise. GBC addresses the question of which ethics - whose ethics - should prevail by acknowledging varying degrees of ethical certainty about what is the right thing to do. The concept of citizenship if considered in the design of CSR activities holds valuable insights to expand and refine the fundamental elements of CSR into a philosophy to deal with 21st-century challenges in emerging economies.

FUTURE RESEARCH DIRECTIONS

To further drive this discussion on CSR in emerging economies, especially with consideration of the role that Corporate Governance plays in both its definition and practice, it will be important to undertake empirical studies. Such studies would explore the meanings attached to CSR by practitioners and academics in these economies, as well as how the Corporate Governance policies and processes of different companies influence what perspective of CSR that they undertake.

CONCLUSION

This chapter set out to explore the concept of Corporate Social Responsibility (CSR), with a focus on the plethora of definitions and perspectives of it that are available within emerging economies. This was undertaken with a look at the historical aspects of the definitions of the concept globally from the 1920s till the early 2000s. This was followed by a discussion of the five key perspectives that have informed the practice of the concept in the emerging economies, which showed that the different companies that operate in these economies have been forced into undertaking CSR activities and projects. This is either as a result of regulation as in the case of India or government non-performance of their basic duties to provide the very basic amenities. The chapter concludes that while none of the perspectives discussed is written off as bad and not applicable, the business strategy perspective seems to be the most beneficial for all stakeholders and one to attract more shareholder support. This is hinged on the fact that it addresses the various interests of stakeholders that are influenced by the operations of the company in one way or the other.

REFERENCES

Ackers, B. (2015). Ethical considerations of corporate social responsibility: A South African perspective. *South African Journal of Business Management*, *46*(1), 11–21. doi:10.4102ajbm.v46i1.79

Adi, A. B. C. (2006). The moral economy and the possibility of accumulation in Africa: How the IFIs can help. *West Africa Review*, *7*(2), 71–82.

Amaeshi, K., Adi, A. B. C., Ogbechie, C., & Amao, O. O. (2006). *Corporate social responsibility in Nigeria: western mimicry or indigenous influences?* No. 39-2006 ICCSR Research Paper Series.

AngloGold Ashanti. (2019). *Sustainability report*. http://www.aga-reports.com/19/sr

Ararat, M. (2004). Social responsibility in a state-dependent business system. In A. Habisch, J. Jonker, M. Wegner, & R. Schmidpeter (Eds.), *Corporate Social Responsibility across Europe* (pp. 247–260). Springer.

Backman, J. (1975). *Social responsibility and accountability*. New York University Press.

Baskin, J. (2006). Corporate responsibility in emerging markets. *Journal of Corporate Citizenship*, *2006*(24), 29–47. doi:10.9774/GLEAF.4700.2006.wi.00006

Blowfield, M., & Frynas, J. G. (2005). Editorial Setting new agendas: Critical perspectives on Corporate Social Responsibility in the developing world. *International Affairs*, *81*(3), 499–513. doi:10.1111/j.1468-2346.2005.00465.x

Boutilier, R. (2017). *Stakeholder politics: Social capital, sustainable development, and the corporation*. Routledge. doi:10.4324/9781351279727

Bowen, H. R. (1953). *Social Responsibilities of the businessman*. Harper & Row.

Cadbury, A. (2002). *Corporate Governance and chairmanship: A personal view*. Oxford University Press. doi:10.1093/acprof:oso/9780199252008.001.0001

Caroll, A. B. (1991). The pyramid of corporate social responsibility: Toward the moral management of organizational stakeholders. *Business Horizons*, *34*(July-August), 30–48. doi:10.1016/0007-6813(91)90005-G

Carroll, A. B. (1979). A three-dimensional model of corporate performance. *Academy of Management Review*, *4*(4), 497–505. doi:10.5465/amr.1979.4498296

Carroll, A. B. (1999). Corporate Social Responsibility: Evolution of a definitional construct. *Journal of Business and Society*, *38*(3), 268–295. doi:10.1177/000765039903800303

Carroll, A. B., & Shabana, K. M. (2010). The business case for corporate social responsibility: A review of concepts, research and practice. *International Journal of Management Reviews*, *12*(1), 85–105. doi:10.1111/j.1468-2370.2009.00275.x

Davis, K. (1960). Can business afford to ignore Social Responsibilities? *California Management Review*, *2*(3), 70–76. doi:10.2307/41166246

Davis, K., & Blomstrom, R. L. (1966). *Business and its environment*. McGraw- Hill.

Donham, W. B. (1927). The social significance of business. *Harvard Business Review*, *4*(4), 406–419.

Drebes, M. J. (2016). Including the 'Other': Power and postcolonialism as underrepresented perspectives in the discourse on Corporate Social Responsibility. *Critical Sociology*, *42*(1), 105–121. doi:10.1177/0896920513509824

Drucker, P. F. (1984). The new meaning of corporate social responsibility. *California Management Review*, *26*(2), 53–63. doi:10.2307/41165066

Emel, J., Makene, M. H., & Wangari, E. (2012). Problems with reporting and evaluating mining industry community development projects: A case study from Tanzania. *Sustainability*, *4*(2), 257–277. doi:10.3390u4020257

Epstein, E. M. (1987). The corporate social policy process: Beyond business ethics, corporate social responsibility, and corporate social responsiveness. *California Management Review*, *29*(3), 99–114. doi:10.2307/41165254

European Commission (2001). *Green Paper-Promoting a European framework for corporate social responsibility, COM (2001) 366 final*. Brussels: Official publications of the EC.

Eweje, G. (2006). The role of MNEs in Community Development Initiatives in developing countries: Corporate Social Responsibility at work in Nigeria and South Africa. *Business & Society*, *45*(2), 93–129. doi:10.1177/0007650305285394

Eweje, G. (2007). Multinational oil companies' CSR initiatives in Nigeria: The scepticism of stakeholders in host communities. *Managerial Law*, *49*(5/6), 218–235. doi:10.1108/03090550710841340

Fitch, H. G. (1976). Achieving Corporate Social Responsibility. *Academy of Management Review*, *1*(1), 38–46. doi:10.5465/amr.1976.4408754

Foucault, M., Dreyfus, H. L., & Rabinow, P. (1982). Michel Foucault: Beyond structuralism and hermeneutics. *The Subject and Power*, 208-226.

Frederick, W. C. (1960). The growing concern over business responsibility. *California Management Review*, *2*(4), 54–61. doi:10.2307/41165405

Friedman, M. (1970, Sept. 13). The Social Responsibility of Business is to Increase its Profits. *New York Times*.

Frynas, J. G. (2005). The false developmental promise of Corporate Social Responsibility: Evidence from multinational oil companies. *International Affairs*, *81*(3), 581–598. doi:10.1111/j.1468-2346.2005.00470.x

Henderson, D. (2004). *The role of business in the modern world: Progress, pressures and prospects for the market economy*. Institute of Economic Affairs.

Hopkins, M. (2003). *The Planetary bargain*. Earthscan.

Idemudia, U. (2007). *Corporate Partnership and Community Development in the Nigerian oil industry: Strengths and Limitations, UNRISD Markets, Business and Regulation Programme Paper 2*. Geneva: United nations Research Institute for Social Development (UNRISD).

Idemudia, U. (2011). Corporate social responsibility and developing countries: Moving the critical CSR research agenda in Africa forward. *Progress in Development Studies*, *11*(1), 1–18. doi:10.1177/146499341001100101

John, O. O., & Samuel, O. I. (2013). *CSR Sustainability, Ethics & Governance, Challenges, Opportunities and Strategies for 21st Century Leaders*. Springer.

Jones, T. M. (1980). Corporate social responsibility revisited, redefined. *California Management Review*, *22*(3), 59–67. doi:10.2307/41164877

Knox, S., Maklan, S., & French, P. (2005). Corporate Social Responsibility: Exploring stakeholder relationships and programme reporting across leading FTSE companies. *Journal of Business Ethics*, *61*(1), 7–28. doi:10.100710551-005-0303-4

Kok, P. G., van der Wiele, T., McKenna, R., & Brown, A. (2001). A Corporate Social Responsibility audit within a quality management framework. *Journal of Business Ethics*, *31*(4), 285–297. doi:10.1023/A:1010767001610

Kottler, P., & Lee, N. (2005). *Corporate Social Responsibility: Doing the most good for your company and your cause*. John Wiley & Sons.

Kumar, R.A. (2016). A critical study on Corporate Social Responsibility activities of public sector undertakings in India and its financial implications. *IOSR Journal of Business and Management, 18*(10), 31-37.

Lebura, S. (2009). *Corporate Social Responsibility (CSR) and the Nigerian oil industry* [Unpublished MSc dissertation]. De Montfort University, Leicester, UK.

Lebura, S. (2013). *Stakeholder relationships in the Nigerian oil industry* [Unpublished doctoral dissertation]. De Montfort University, Leicester, UK.

McGuire, J. W. (1963). *Business and society*. McGraw-Hill.

Momin, M. A., & Parker, L. D. (2013). Motivations for corporate social responsibility reporting by MNC subsidiaries in an emerging country: The case of Bangladesh. *The British Accounting Review*, *45*(3), 215–228. doi:10.1016/j.bar.2013.06.007

Muthuri, J. N. (2007). Corporate Citizenship and Sustainable Community Development: Fostering Multi-Sector Collaboration in Magadi Division in Kenya. *Journal of Corporate Citizenship*, *28*(28), 73–84. doi:10.9774/GLEAF.4700.2007.wi.00008

Nwaeke, L. I., & Lebura, S. (2016). Stakeholder relationships as games played by stakeholders. *International Journal of Innovative Research and Development*, *5*(4), 1–11.

Ojo, O. (2009). Nigeria: CSR as a vehicle for economic development. In S.O. Idowu & W.L. Filho (Eds.), Global pracitces (pp.393-433). Springer.

Okoye, A. (2009). Theorising Corporate Social Responsibility as an Essentially Contested Concept: Is a definition necessary? *Journal of Business Ethics*, *89*(4), 613–627. doi:10.100710551-008-0021-9

Porter, M. E., & Kramer, M. R. (2006). Strategy and society: The link between competitive advantage and corporate social responsibility. *Harvard Business Review*, *84*(12), 2–17. PMID:17183795

Schuchard, R. (2010). *Understanding the benefits of CSR*. https://www.bsr.org/en/our-insights/blog-view/understanding-the-benefits-of-csr

Smith, N. C. (2003). Corporate Social Responsibility: Whether or how? *California Management Review*, *45*(4), 52–76. doi:10.2307/41166188

Spector, B. (2008). Business Responsibilities in a Divided World: The Cold War Roots of the Corporate Social Responsibility Movement. *Enterprise and Society*, *9*(2), 314.

Steiner, G. A. (1971). *Business and society*. Random House.

Walton, C. C. (1967). *Corporate social responsibilities*. Wadsworth.

Wan-Jan, W. S. (2006). Defining Corporate Social Responsibility. *Journal of Public Affairs. Journal of Public Affairs*, *6*(3-4), 176–184. doi:10.1002/pa.227

Wood, D. J., & Logsdon, J. M. (2002, July). A Global Business Citizenship Process Model. In *Proceedings of the International Association for Business and Society* (Vol. 13, pp. 181-186). 10.5840/iabsproc20021325

World Business Council for Sustainable Development (WBCSD). (2002). *Corporate Social Responsibility: The WBCSD's journey*. http://www.wbcsd.ch/

Chapter 7
Gender Diversity:
An Issue of Concern

Qaiser Rafique Yasser
https://orcid.org/0000-0001-5585-9814
Preston University, Islamabad, Pakistan

Abdullah Al-Mamun
University of Wollongong, Australia

ABSTRACT

Gender diversity is a new and challenging issue of research in business. Women on boards are a heavily discussed topic in developed countries, though this issue has recently appeared to gain the attention of researchers in developing economies as well. However, research on gender diversity in Malaysia is limited. This study aims to examine whether female directors on boards can affect firm performance based on selected public listed companies in Malaysia. In examining the effect of gender diversity on firm performance, Pearson correlation coefficient and regression analysis tests are employed using economic value added (EVA) as a measurement tool. This study found no relationship between gender diversity and firm performance. Given this, future studies should try to consider other aspects of corporate governance.

INTRODUCTION

Growing participation of women in the corporate arena both in developed and developing economies in the last few decades appears to have gained increased attention from scholars and academicians as well as corporate leaders. Though, women's place varies based on social, moral and authoritative status in turn based

DOI: 10.4018/978-1-7998-6669-5.ch007

Copyright © 2021, IGI Global. Copying or distributing in print or electronic forms without written permission of IGI Global is prohibited.

on culture, norms and social values as well as religious sensitivity, gender diversity is considered as a value driver in business strategy and hence has emerged as a challenging issue to researchers as well as regulatory bodies. In general, it's not long ago since the proportion of female members was not at all notable in top positions in firms due to the myth that women are not as capable as men in making decisions, hence unlikely to be effective in the corporate world. However, the effects of female board members with greater performance reflect that an increased number of women in the board room bring firms' higher productivity as well as higher profitability.

A number of studies have been conducted on gender diversity in the board room and these have argued that diversified board perform better compared to non-diversified, from which this study has been inspired to conduct further research in order to produce empirical evidence on developing economies[1]. A survey by Credit Suisse (2012) found that approximately 29% of firms had women board members in 2011 compared to 12% by the end of 2005 in emerging Asia. However, this figure is notable in Europe and North America where 85% of firms had women in their board rooms by 2011, whereas it only was 48% and 73% respectively in 2005. Results also showed a steady increase in share price as well as in return on equity (ROE) of firms with women in the board room from 2005 until 2011. In fact, in order to increase women's participation in board rooms governments around the world have recently started intervening (Credit Suisse, 2012). The report stated that in the past five years, seven countries have passed legislation mandating female board representation and eight have set out non-mandatory targets, while the Norwegian government made it mandatory for large firms to have at least a 40% female presence in the board room (Juana *et al.,* 2010). On the other hand, the Finnish code of corporate governance (2008) requires all public listed firms to have at least one female director on the board starting from 1st January 2010, or otherwise to, explain the reason in their annual report.

Hence, the aim of this study is to examine the effect of gender diversity on firm performance in Malaysia. Moreover, this study aims to suggest whether gender diversity is significant in both of the said economies based on the empirical evidence as most of the empirical evidences on gender diversity have been grounded in developed economies. The next section contains a literature review on gender diversity around the world followed by with sample selection, methodology result analysis and finally the conclusion of the study.

LITERATURE REVIEW

One interesting study area for many researchers over the last few decades has been gender diversity (Elgart, 1983; Wall Street Journal, 1986). Research on female members on boards has gained significant attention in recent years. Though studies have claimed that the number of women is increasing on boards (Heidrick & Struggles, 1986; Vance, 1983), there are still optimistic and pessimistic views as to what this trend represents. The optimistic expression presumes that the increasing number of female Chief Executive Officers (CEOs) or board members is a signal of transition in women's role as top executives (Spencer, 1984), while the pessimistic opinion claims that though the actual number of women on board has been increasing, proportionately it is still not notable (Wall Street Journal, 1986). Those of the latter view claim that women are not an anomaly in the corporate board room as they were just a decade ago, when only 13% of the 1350 major American companies had a female director, while it jumped up to 41% in one year in 1987. However, the recent picture is more surprising, showing that 85% of firms in the US have female board members.

It is speculated that though few rose high enough in their organisations to qualify for service as board members, female members are still concentrated in the lower half of the corporate pyramid (Kesner, 1988). There is an argument that female members are put on the board merely for the sake of firm image, without concern for women's potential contributions. Therefore, women are unlikely to be asked to serve on board positions as powerful as male members and to influence committees. It is predicted that women members on the board will not be given same responsibilities and duties as their counterparts. Kesner (1988) argued that female directors differ from males in terms of occupation, nature, tenure and that would account for their disproportionately lower membership on key committees.

Harrigan (1981) claimed that women's careers are much more diverse unlike men and less business oriented. Subsequently, this statement was supported by Loscocco *et al.,* (1991) and Fischer *et al.,* (1993). Loscocco *et al.,* (1991) concluded that firms owned by men outperform firms owned by women in terms of profitability. Loscocco argued that this is due to the lack of experience of women board members in business and their lower concentration in profitable sectors. Fischer *et al.,* (1993) claimed that male-owned firms are able to generate more sales compared to female-owned firms. From the above discussion it is obvious that occupation and gender are linked. The above mentioned authors also claimed that in terms of productivity, male-owned firms are more productive compared to female-owned firms.

Prasso (1996) argued that there is a significant difference in the way male and female owners run and view their firms: male owners are socially more accepted compared to female owners. Usually men are more competitive, in terms of work efficiency, expanding their business network and firm performance, while Butner & Moore (1997) claimed that women owners tend to focus on the long-term objectives rather than financial performance. As a result, firms controlled by men outperform firms controlled by women. Fasci & Valdez (1998) studied differences between female-owned businesses and male-owned businesses. The study found significant differences in terms of business experience, number of employees, sales volume, revenue and ratio of profit. There were a number of issues at work behind these differences. According to Fasci & Valdez (1998), less experience and lesser business tenure are resultant of all the differences mentioned above. Apart from these, due to having less experience, women lack the networks that are important in business.

Even though women on boards are older than their male counterparts and have a higher level of education, firms controlled by women show significantly lower performance than male-controlled firms due to the lesser business experience of women (Alowaihan, 2004). Subsequently, Shaw *et al.,* (2009) argued that female owners invest approximately one-third of the capital invested by male owners. It significantly undercapitalises the firms. As a result, firms' performance is lower compared to male-owned firms. The land mark-study on gender diversity was published by Joana *et al.,* (2010) based on Denmark and the Netherlands. Though the study claims that gender diverse corporate teams will help bring the global economy back on track during economic recession due to their risk-averse attitudes, the study reported no relationship between women's representation in top corporate positions and firm performance. The study concluded that though the Netherlands imposed a law requiring 40% women on the board in 2006, it might not yet have started to impact performance. The authors claim that it might require longer and future study might include a longer time frame with more variables.

Subsequently, Salim (2011) examined relationships between gender diversity and firm performance based on firms listed on the Indonesia Stock Exchange. The study concluded that there is a negative relationship between women's presence in the board room and return on asset (ROA) as well as market-based performance measure Tobin's Q. The study concluded that female board members being negatively associated with firm performance does not necessarily mean that women on the board destroy shareholders' value. The author suggests encouraging equal opportunity for all groups of employees, including women depending on their expertise, competence and contribution to the organisation.

Based on listed firms in Germany, Jesmin *et al.,* (2012) examine the relationship between gender diversity and firm performance on a time series basis which includes data for five consecutive years. The authors conclude found a U-shaped result on the time series data. The study reported that gender diversity at first negatively affects firm performance and in subsequent years when the proportion of women increased in the board room, it is associated with higher firm performance. Authors suggest that a more gender diverse board composition will only enhance performance if diversity is sufficiently large; they recommended it to be a critical level of 30% women on the board, while very low levels of gender diversity might be associated with reduced firm performance. This could be due to getting approval of decisions taken by female board members or they might not contribute their opinions in board meetings.

However, there are studies which advocate on behalf of female-owned firms. Kalleberg & Leicht (1991) argued that firms owned by women are not less successful than firms controlled by men. The same study found that small firms owned by men show the same performance as those owned by women. A study conducted by Watson (2002) found that there is no significant difference in terms of financial performance between firms owned by men and those owned by women; in fact female-owned firms outperform male-owned firms. Apart from these, Nielsen & Huse (2010) argued that women and men have impact on different tasks at different extent; as a result no overall performance differences can be detected between firms with higher and lower performance of women members in the board.

It is believed that female board members in business are relatively less benefited. Cuba *et al.,* (1983) asserted that firms controlled by women are less successful compared to male-owned firms. Looking back to the survey conducted by Wall Street Journal in 1986 (with reference to Eagly & Carli, (2007)), it is clear that there is an increased trend of women's participation in managerial positions in business. It found that in the US more than 40% of managerial positions are occupied by women compared to 13% in 1986, while Holton, (2000) argued that in the US there is an increased number of women taking roles on corporate boards compared to 20 years ago. The study also claimed that in the Fortune 500, 6% women hold the highest paid executive positions while 2% CEO positions are held by women. Locally, Afza (2011) concluded that there are differences between corporations managed by men and women. The study was conducted based on 182 family-owned firms listed on Bursa Malaysia and concluded that male owners are more likely to enhance firm performance than female owners. On the other hand, a study conducted in Pakistan, by Mirza *et al.,* (2012) examined gender diversity and firm performance in terms of ROA and earnings per share (EPS). It concluded that firms having women in top positions are negatively associated with reduced firm performance. The authors concluded that the reasons for reduced performance included that women are emotional, aggressive, risk averse, less confident and not well educated and there were some invisible-barriers, which are built by society to keep women in lower positions.

The above literature reviews lead us to mixed findings on gender diversity and firm performance. In fact, evidence shows that women sitting on boards in developed economies affect firm performance to a different extent compared to developing nations. For instance, most of the studies conducted in developing economies reported either no effect or a negative effect of female board members on firm performance (Afza, 2011; Salim 2011; Mirza *et al.,* 2012), whereas studies conducted in developed economies reported both a negative and a positive effect of female directors on firm performance (Jesmin *et al.,* 2012; Joana *et al.,* 2010). However there are similarities in both economies, most of the studies empirically evidenced that women are risk-averse (Afza, 2011; Salim, 2011; Mirza *et al.,* 2012, Credit Suisse, 2012; Jesmin *et al.,* 2012; Joana *et al.*, 2010) as well as even a decade ago female board members hardly had any effect on firm performance. Hence, this study decided to investigate the effect of female board members on firm performance in terms of EVA based on public listed firms in Malaysia. The next section contains the sample selection and data.

SAMPLE AND DATA

This study selected 25 listed companies based on Malaysia, listed in Table 1. The years 2008-2010 were selected which gave 75 observations for three consecutive years. The years 2008-2010 were selected as these are latest years before releasing the Code of Corporate governance (Revised 2012) of Malaysia. Hence, this study seeks to explore the performance before the launch of revised code. The study employs both financial and non-financial data with a sample of 25 listed companies and gathered data from the Bursa Malaysia website. In this study, performance variable EVA was largely computed based on the companies' annual reports. Governance and gender diversity data were also obtained from the audited financial reports. The reason behind using annual reports for data collection is that the reports are audited, have been published and are publicly available. In addition, data can be accessed through the stock exchange website. Furthermore, annual reports of PLCs are presented uniformly and data complies with Bursa Malaysia regulations and the Companies Act 1965.

This study begins with the identification of the population of the study, which includes the sample firms listed on the main market and second board of Bursa Malaysia. There were 843 companies listed in the main market on Bursa Malaysia as of 31st December 2011. From 843 companies, 32 companies are based in Sarawak which is the biggest state in Malaysia. However, due to incomplete financial and corporate governance data, the number of companies was reduced to 25 from 32. The final list of the sample contains 25 PLCs for this study, and in total 75 observations for three consecutive years. PLCs were selected because of their publicly published annual reports which are available on Bursa Malaysia website.

Table 1. Sector wise distribution of sample

Industry	Number of Firm(s)
Cement	1
Building & Construction	9
Food & Consumable Goods	5
Glass & Ceramics	1
Manufacturing	4
Mining & Refining	3
Retailing	1
Shipping & Steel	4
Wire & Cable	2
Others	2
Total	**32**

Note(s): Number of observation (N) is 75. Sig. represents the significant value (2-tailed). (*) (**) indicates that correlation is significant at the 0.05 level (2-tailed) and 0.01 level (2-tailed), respectively.

RESEARCH DESIGN

The study was designed to conduct descriptive statistics, Pearson correlation coefficient and linear regression analysis. The following section contains the variables measurement and hypotheses development.

Board Gender Diversity

Board gender diversity is measured in three different dimensions in this study: (1) if there is at least one female member on the board, it is valued at one, otherwise zero; (2) if the CEO is female, it is valued at one, otherwise zero; and (3) the proportion of female directors on the board.

H_0: There is no relationship between board gender diversity and firm performance;
H_1: There is a relationship between board gender diversity and firm performance.

Board Size

Board size in this study refers to the number of executive, non-executive and independent directors serving on the board. The distinction between the roles of inside and outside directors is significant, as both have their specific merits and demerits. Easy access of inside directors to inside information is as significant as the expertise and knowledge of the outside directors in evaluating managers' decisions (Vincent & Peter, 2011).

Board size is a central component of the corporate governance mechanism that affects firm performance. Recommendations on corporate governance require boards to be comprised exclusively of non-executive directors (Cadbury Committee Report, 1992; Hampel Committee Report, 1998; OECD, 2004). The same recommendations were also found in the revised code on corporate governance in Malaysia (2007) as well as the Malaysian Code on Corporate Governance (2012). This is due to the investors' consideration that boards comprised of non-executive directors are an important determinant of firm performance.

Though the study employed both agency and stewardship theory; it found that agency theory is applicable to board size. Jensen & Meckling (1976) found that separation of ownership and management is one of the features of corporations, which is established in agency theory, as the management seem to attain control in the firm by pursuing various activities that tend to benefit the managers but not the owners. As a result, the board's primary role is to safe guard shareholders' interests (Fama & Jensen, 1983). Therefore, agency theory states that boards comprised of a majority of non-executive directors or outsiders tend to stick with the primary role.

Furthermore, empirical evidence of agency theory suggests that non-executive directors with their knowledge, experience and expertise can offer advice, solidity in business, and a green signal when the firm is doing well (Chamsy & Patrick, 2006). Apart from this, non-executive directors play a significant role in supporting shareholders, while controlling the board for tendering offers, hostile takeovers, poison pills, as well as reducing possible fraud in financial statements (Byrd & Hickman, 1992; Beasley, 1996). Byrd & Hickman (1992) found a positive relationship between board size and firm performance, as outsiders are better monitors which can help in reducing fraud while insiders have inside information on the firm which is helpful in firm decision making.

On the other hand, stewardship theory is based on the concept that management are intrinsically trustworthy, are not keen on misappropriation of the organisation's resources (Donaldson & Davis, 1991), while Donaldson & Preston (1995) found that good stewards (managers) in corporations work assiduously aiming to achieve a higher level of profitability and return on the shareholders' investment. Moreover, solicitors of stewardship theory claim that higher firm performance is linked to a majority of executive directors as they have better knowledge of the business compared to non-executive directors. Hence, executive directors work to maximize the return on shareholders' investment (Donaldson & Devis, 1994). Therefore, there is a minimum agency cost, due to the trustworthiness of executive directors and that they are unlikely to deteriorate shareholders' return (Donaldson & Devis, 1994) and stewardship theory proposes the board to be comprised of a majority of executive directors in order to make effective decisions.

Accordingly, executive directors also tend to have a positive effect on firm performance, as they possess inside knowledge and information on the company operation. Insider directors add value to the firm by engaging themselves such activities as are likely to reduce the risk shareholders face. As a result, it reduces the firms cost of capital and increases market value and confidence because of their reputation. All these are possible as the executive directors' work as arbiters in disagreements among internal managers, reducing firms' risk by monitoring various selection processes as for managers and CEOs. And from this, it is suggested that if the board is comprised of a majority of executive directors, the firm is likely to have higher profitability (Donaldson & Devis, 1994). However, board insiders and outsiders comprise the whole board and the Malaysian code on corporate governance states that the board should examine its size determining the impact of the number upon its effectiveness. From this statement it is obvious that corporate governance suggests firms have a board with a balance of executive and non-executive directors. To be effective, boards should be of moderate size, neither too big nor too small. From the empirical study, it has been found that the board should have eight or ten members (Jensen, 1993; Lipton & Lorsch, 1992; Abdullah, 2004; MSWG-NUBS, 2007).

The previously held literature review was mixed on board size and firm performance. According to the theories discussed above and corporate governance, board size might either be positively linked or not linked with firm performance. Both sides are empirically argued in this study. The relationship between board size and firm performance has been reported by a number of studies previously, and according to the arguments stated in this study, there are mixed findings on both executive and non-executive directors and firm performance. Hence, the study measured board size as the number of executive and non-executive directors on the board and suggests the following hypotheses:

H_0: there is no relationship between board size and firm performance;
H_2: there is a relationship between board size and firm performance.

MEASURING FIRM PERFORMANCE

Ratios are widely used around the world as well as in Malaysia. However, ratios are not able to measure and capture the economic profit as well as value created on shareholders' investment (Abdullah, 2004). In fact, Issham (2011) claims that Malaysia is suffering from having a suitable performance measurement tool which can help investors assess the value created on their investment. Given this, the study has been inspired to employ a value-based performance measurement tool for this study, hence selected EVA for this study.

This study measured the economic profit of Sarawak-based public listed companies. EVA is "a measurement of the true economic profit generated by a firm" (Sharma & Kumar, 2010; Stewart, 1994 p. 73) and is calculated by comparing a firm's net operating profit after tax (NOPAT) to the total cost of all its forms of capital including debt. If NOPAT exceeds the cost of capital, it gives a positive EVA and vice Versa. The word capital includes all the assets invested in the firm taking into consideration the deduction of the current liabilities which are not entitled to any interest from those assets and the equity.

This study employs two methods. Firstly, proposed study will calculate the EVA of selected public listed companies in Malaysia. Adjustments will be made on financial data (Stewart, 1991). Though 164 adjustments are suggested, only 15-25 are adjusted due to lack of information and data availability. The number of adjustments is as few as five in real life business (Mouritsen, 1998; Stern, Stewart & Chew, 1997; Young, 1997). In fact, depending on the industry in which the firm is operating, firms might not be required to make any adjustment in calculating EVA (Hoque *et al.,* 2004). However, this study intends to make as many adjustments as possible based on data availability at the time.

This study used the model proposed by Stewart (1991) to calculate EVA[2]. The proposed model is as follows:

$$\text{EVA} = \text{NOPAT} - (\text{WACC x Invested Capital}) \quad (1)$$

WACC stands for weighted average cost of capital. Capital charges are calculated by multiplying the cost of debt and the cost of equity with companies' invested capital. This generates unadjusted form; EVA is equivalent to what is generated by subtracting the cost of capital from net income and that is called economic profit which is residual income from an accountant's perspective (Young, 1997). The only difference between EVA and residual income is the accounting adjustments based on company's generally accepted accounting principles based on financial statements.

EVA FORMULA AND CALCULATION

Stewart (1991) stated that EVA is the deduction of cost of capital from NOPAT. In this calculation, firms are required to make as many adjustments as possible based on the accounting figures from financial statements. The EVA model proposed by Stewart (1991) requires following number of steps in order to figure out EVA:

Gathering Required Data

EVA is calculated based on the financial data of firms where income statements, balance sheets, cash flow statement and other financial notes are available. All the annual reports were collected from the Bursa Malaysia website. A total of 32 selected PLCs were taken as a sample based on Sarawak.

Adjustment and NOPAT

NOPAT is a measure of the company's operating profit. However, before arriving at NOPAT, it requires making as many adjustments as possible on accounting figures based on data availability (Young, 1997). Therefore, this study made adjustments on depreciation, interest expense, and goodwill. NOPAT is also called earnings before interest and tax (EBIT). Operating income is calculated by subtracting all operating expenses (cost of sales, selling, general and administrative expenses) from sales. Finally, deducting tax from EBIT, generates NOPAT (Yahaya & Mahmood, 2011).

Invested Capital

Invested capital is the sum of money invested in a firm. There is more than one approach proposed in calculating invested capital (Young & O'Byrne, 2001). However, this study used the formula proposed by Young & O'Byrne (2001) as follows in order to calculate invested capital.

$$\text{Invested capital} = \text{total debt (short-term debt + long-term debt)} + \text{total equity} \tag{2}$$

Cost of Debt

EVA requires calculation of cost of debt in order to consider the tax benefit of debt[3]. The study stated that the portion of interest is exposed in an income statement and subtracted from taxable income before tax liability is calculated, whereas cost of debt is calculated on an after tax basis and cost of equity is calculated on a before tax basis.

A recent study argued that the determination of cost of capital should be based on marginal borrowing rate. However, in real life, it is difficult to identify the marginal rate as firms generate debts from more than one source for different purposes with different interest rates. This is because the firm might have good relations with the lenders or banks, who are willing to issue loans on lower interest charges. Therefore, in order to make the calculation more realistic this study has decided to find the average interest rate for each company based on their different terms of loan.

Cost of debt (K_d) = average interest rate * (1 – Tax) (3)

Cost of Equity Capital

Stewart (1991) asserted that investment in firms has opportunity cost that shareholders forgo by making investment and the opportunity cost is represented by cost of capital. Measuring cost of capital is relatively difficult as there are arguments against and for cost of capital. However, Roztocki & Needy (2008) proposed a formula in calculation of cost of capital, the formula as below:

Cost of capital (K_e) = Risk free rate + Risk premium.. (4)

Risk free rate is defined as return and risk models, in finance start off with an asset. Risk free rate is nothing but the investors expect the return on that asset investment. However, there is always risk on investment; either it is low or comparatively more. Expected returns on risky investment are measured as relatively risk free rate based on the expected risk premium that is added to the risk free rate. The variance in actual returns and the expected returns are used for the view of risk in finance.

However, only government possesses the control on the currency printing, hence that is the only security bonds those have chance of being risk free. Liebenberg (2004) suggested the average return on government security for risk free rate. Therefore, this study employed interest rates of treasury bills issued by the bank Negara Malaysia in order to determine the risk free rate.

Risk premium reflects the risk which results from investing in the equity of a firm. Roztocki & Needy (2010) stated the level of risk a company can bear depends on the ability to repay their current liability. The term current liability was used because, long-term debt may not be the concern as firms can finance for long-term liability through various sources. However, for short-term debts cash flow is the source to repay. Therefore, the level of risk premium a firm can bear depends on their net cash held at the end of the year to repay their debt. Roztocki & Needy (2010) suggested several risk premium ranges depending on investment risk which are tabulated in Table 2.

The fluctuation of cash flow is estimated by looking at the result of the cash and cash equivalents held at year end. According to Roztecki & Needy (2010), investment bears extremely low risk and suggested risk premium is 6 per cent or less

Table 2. Risk premium range

Risk Premium Range	Investment Risk
6% and less	Extremely low risk, established profitable company with extremely stable cash flows
6% - 12%	Low risk, established profitable company with relatively low fluctuation in cash flows
12%-18%	Moderate risk, established profitable company with moderate fluctuation in cash flows
18% and above	High business risk
Source: Rozkocki & Needy (2010)	

for that specific company, if the cash flow of the company is extremely stable. The company which has low fluctuations in cash flow is categorised as a risk premium level in between 6% and 12%. Accordingly, the company that possesses moderate fluctuation in cash flow has been labelled between 12% and 18% of risk premium. Finally, the riskier investment with vulnerable cash flow has been categorised as the high business risk premium with 18% and above.

Cost of Capital

Sharma & Kumar (2010) argued that if the firms are unable to identify the true cost of capital, they actually destroy value, as they generate less than the total cost of capital. In real life, firms usually do not realise the true cost of capital. Firms, employing traditional performance measures, are healthy in terms of profitability, as they fail to measure costs of capital. However in reality, those firms are unlikely to create value for shareholders' investment. The most common two types of capital employed by firms are borrowed loan and equity. The cost of borrowed loans is the interest charged on those loans provided by the lenders, whereas equity capital is provided by shareholders (Yahaya & Mahmood, 2011).

Therefore, this study used the following formula to calculate WACC:

$$WACC = [K_d \text{ x Debt/ (Debt + Equity)}] + [K_e \text{ x Equity/ (Debt + Equity)}] \ldots\ldots\ldots \quad (5)$$

EVA

EVA results are interpreted according to Stewart (1991)

EVA> 0

This term depicts that return on invested capital is higher than the cost of capital. In other words a firm has created true profit leading to increase in shareholder value.

EVA < 0

On the other hand, the above term presents that return on invested capital is lower than the cost of capital. In other words, firms who generated less EVA than the cost of capital created negative true profit for and hence destroyed shareholders' wealth.

REGRESSION MODEL

This study developed the following regression model to examine the association between gender diversity, board size and firm performance:

$$EVA = \beta_0 + \beta_1 FCEO + \beta_2 FPRO + \beta_3 GDIV + \beta_4 BSIZ + \in \quad (2)$$

Where:

EVA = economic value added;
FCEO = if the CEO is female, it is valued at one, otherwise 0;
FPRO = number of female board members/total board of directors on the board;
GDIV = if at least one female director is on the board it is valued at one, otherwise 0;
BSIX = number of members on the board.

Descriptive Statistics

Table 3 depicts descriptive statistics results for the variables employed in this study. The mean EVA is 3.5% of total invested capital. Results show that the mean proportion of female CEOs is 7% which indicates that on average 7% listed firms possess female CEO in Malaysia. Accordingly the mean proportion of women on boards is 9% which states that there is a presence of 9% female directors on the boards of public listed firms in Malaysia. On the other hand, 56% public listed firms have female directors on their boards which are quite notable. Average board size in Malaysia is 8.77, which represents a moderate board size and hence is consistent with empirical suggestions.

Pearson Correlation Coefficient

Table 3. Descriptive statistics

	Minimum	Maximum	Mean	Std. Deviation	
Female CEO	0.00	1.00	0.07	0.25	
Female proportion	0.00	0.33	0.09	0.10	
Gender diversity	0.00	1.00	0.56	0.50	
Board size	4.00	14.00	8.77	2.44	
EVA	-0.89	0.35	.035	0.15	
Note: Number of observation (N) is 75.					

Pearson correlation coefficient was applied in this study to indicate the relationship between independent variables (board gender diversity and board size) and dependent variable (EVA). There is a perfect positive linear relationship, when the r value is at the level of +0.01. On the other hand, there is a negative relationship between variables, if the r value is at the level of -0.05. However, in this study there is also a positive relationship between variables, when the r value is at the level of +0.05.

In statistics, one-tailed test is specified as that in which the critical area of a distribution is one-sided, or in other words it is either higher than or lesser than a certain value, but does not specify both sides. If the tested sample results in a one-sided critical area, the alternative hypothesis is accepted instead of the null hypothesis. On the other hand, two-tailed test refers to a critical area of a distribution which is two-sided and tests whether a sample is either higher than or lesser than a certain range of values (Wayne *et al.,* 1997; Robert, 1998). The hypotheses in this study are also developed in two-sided critical areas of distribution in which it is tested whether the sample is either greater or lesser than the certain range of values. Hence, this study employed two-tailed significance analysis to test the hypotheses developed.

Table 4 shows Pearson correlation coefficient for all the variables employed in this study, where it examined the association between governance variables (independent variables) and performance variable (dependent variable). Table 4 presents the overall correlations for three consecutive years; where the correlations were low, there are number of statistically significant relationships found in this examination.

The result shows that the female CEO was not significantly correlated with performance variable EVA over the years, but there was a significant relationship between female CEO and board size, proportion of female board members as well

Table 4. Pearson correlations coefficient

Correlation (Sig.)					
	FCEO	GDIV	FPRO	BSIZ	EVA
FCEO	1.00				
GDIV	0.24* (0.04)				
FPRO	0.41** (0.000)	0.751** (0.000)	1.00		
BSIZ	-0.416** (0.000)	0.083 (0.477)	-0.246* (0.033)	1.00	
EVA	-0.027 (0.820)	-0.052 (0.656)	-0.100 (0.394)	0.239* (0.039)	1.00

as gender diversity, $r = -0.416$, p (two-tailed) < 0.01, $r = 0.411$, p (two-tailed) < 0.01, and $r = 0.237$, p (two-tailed) < 0.05 respectively. From the results it appears that there is a significant negative association between female CEO and board size and the rest are having positive relationship with female CEO.

On the other hand, gender diversity is significantly correlated with proportion of female board members. The significant correlation shows that $r = 0.751$, p (two-tailed) <0.01 level. But the result does not show any association with performance variable. Third independent variable, proportion of female board member is also not association firm performance EVA, while it is negatively associated with board size at the level of $r = -0.246$, p (two-tailed) < 0.05. The only independent variable positively associated with firm performance is board size. The result shows significant positive relationship between board size and EVA, $r = 0.239$, p (two-tailed) <0.05.

LINEAR REGRESSION ANALYSIS

Table 5 shows the summary of Linear Regression which has been conducted based on the study results between gender diversity, board size (independent variables) and EVA (Dependent Variable). An examination of t-value indicates governance mechanisms' contribution to the prediction of firm performance (Coakes & Steed, 2003). In other words, t-values predict the level of contribution will be held on performance (EVA) by governance mechanisms (gender diversity and board size). The contribution level is shown in Table 5. On the other hand, beta (*b*) value in unstandardized and standardized coefficients is a measure of how strongly each predictor variable (governance mechanism) influences the criterion variable (firm performance) (Brace *et al.*, 2006; Field, 2009). For instance, in Table 5 *b* of board is 1.8 per cent states that a change of one standard deviation in the board size will result in a change of 1.8 per cent standard deviation in the firm performance.

Hence, a higher *b* value indicates a greater impact of the independent variable on the dependent variable.

Table 5. Coefficients

	Unstandardized Coefficients			t	Sig.
	B	Std. Error	Beta		
(Constant)	-0.112	0.077		-1.453	0.151
Female CEO	0.072	0.080	0.121	0.899	0.372
Female Proportion	0.013	0.306	0.009	0.043	0.966
Gender Diversity	-0.033	0.057	-0.113	-0.587	0.559
Board Size	0.018	0.008	0.301	2.164	0.034
R Square	0.074				
Adjusted R Square	0.021				
F- Value	1.390				
Sig. F	0.246				

Note: Dependent Variable is EVA

RESULTS

It logically follows that if a variable significantly predicts an outcome, then it should have a *b*- value significantly different from *zero* (Field, 2009). The author further states that it is significant when the result gains confidence in the hypothesis that the value of *b* is significantly different from 0 and that the predictor variable contributes significantly to the test ability to estimate values of the outcome.

From the result analysis, the model of the study was found to be statistically significant at the level of 5% ($p < 0.05$). According to Table 4, Regression results found on dependent and independent variables (EVA and gender diversity, board size) were not significantly correlated except for board size. From Table 4, it can be seen that not all variables are strongly related to each other. At a given time, board size and firm performance were shown to be significantly correlated, while other variables (female CEO, gender diversity and female proportion) were seen to have no relationship with EVA, based on the results neither were all the alternative hypotheses accepted nor all the null hypotheses rejected.

For instance, if there is an increase in the number of directors on the board, this might reflect positively on EVA in 1.8 per cent. In other words, by the introduction of an additional member on the board, EVA will increase by 1.8 per cent at the year end. However, none of the other variables are correlated with firm performance. The significance level is 3.4 per cent between board size and EVA. This represents that there is a significant relationship between board size and firm performance. Therefore, the study rejected null hypothesis and accepted the alternative hypothesis (H2).

DISCUSSION

The results found in this study reported no significant relation between gender diversity and firm performance in Malaysia. Accordingly, there has been very limited research conducted on this issue in Malaysia or in other developing economies, which results in very limited evidence to support the findings. This study reported that gender diversity, female CEO as well as proportion of female board members do not have any influence on value-based firm performance EVA. This finding is consistent with earlier studies conducted by Loscocco *et al.,* (1991), Fischer *et al.,* (1993), Prasso (1996), Butner & Moore (1997), Fasci & Valdez (1998), Alowaihan, (2004), and Shaw *et al.*, (2009).

Harrigan (1981) concluded that women are unable to influence firm performance due to their diverse career path, while Loscocco *et al.,* (1991) and Fischer *et al.,* (1993) added that lack of experience in business and lesser concentration on the profitable sectors are also the reason for women being less successful in business compared to men. Alowaihan (2004) also blamed lack of business experience among women for holding them back in making decisions that could influence firm performance. However, Shaw *et al.,* (2009) summarised that female owners invest less compared to their male counter-parts, and such investment undercapitalises firms, which holds back firm growth as well as firm performance.

In contrast, Nielsen & Huse (2010) concluded that there is no difference between-male and female-owned firm performance, which contradicts findings in this study. Authors claimed that this is due to women and men having impact on different tasks at different extents among multiple tasks; as a result no overall performance differences can be detected between firms higher for women members on the board. Accordingly, Salim (2011) reported a negative relationship between women's presence in the board room and return on asset (ROA) as well as market-based performance measure Tobin's Q. A similar result has been found in Pakistan by Mirza *et al.*, (2012). The authors blamed this on the fact that women are more emotional, aggressive, risk averse, less confident and not well educated and some invisible barriers, which are built by society to keep women in lower positions.

On the other hand, Joana *et al.,* (2010) reported no relationship between board gender diversity and firm performance, which is consistent with this study. Similarly Afza (2011) concluded that male owners are more likely to enhance firm performance than female owners in Malaysia. Hence, this study accepts the null hypothesis which states that there is no relationship between gender diversity and firm performance. However, the study found a significant relationship between board size and firm performance.

Results from descriptive statistics and Pearson Correlation Coefficient analysis reported a significant positive relationship between board size and firm performance in Malaysia by public listed companies. Quite a number of studies have indicated that board size has a positive influence on firm performance. Yermack (1996) reported that board size leads to effective performance. Dalton *et al.,* (1999) acknowledged that board size and firm size are correlated and board size is related to firm performance (Kiel & Nickolson, 2003). Agency theory suggests larger firms require bigger boards in order to control and monitor the actions taken by management. There have been some suggestions on the number of member that should be on the board. According to Jensen (1993), an optimal limit should be around eight directors, while previously Lipton & Lorsch (1992) recommended the maximum number of board members should be ten, due to the perception that interference by a higher greater number of board members with group dynamics may hinder performance. This leads to minimized agency costs and increased performance. The results showed that the majority of the firms had experienced positive EVA hence leading to enhanced shareholders' value (Abdullah *et al.,* 2012).

However, there is a claim that a larger board is more effective in solving problems with the expertise of its members, which was supported by Haleblian & Finklestein (1993); they reported that a larger board is more beneficial as it can provide more information and knowledge in critical situations in order to solve problems. The finding is consistent with results in this study on board size and firm performance. Mir & Souad (2008) also found a positive and significant relationship between board size and value-based performance measure EVA, where the researchers claimed that board members' expertise has a big impact on firm performance which is reflected through positive EVA.

There are also some studies to the contrary which found no relationship between board size and firm performance. Aggarwal *et al.,* (2007) found no evidence to support board size having an effect on firm performance. Accordingly, a larger board may lead to more conflicts of interest in arriving at a decision and research claims that there is an ideal board size, exceeding which leads to decreased firm value (Jensen, 1993). These findings are consistent with the results found in this study, as the mean board size is 8.77.

Abdullah's (2004) study which favours large board size also found that board size is positively associated with firm performance, where Sulong & Nor (2009) concluded that larger boards are effective in oversight duties relative to small boards and are capable of monitoring the actions of top management. Therefore, it can be concluded that higher profitability for firms in Malaysia is due to better management which is the result of better monitoring of boards; hence this study accepts the alternative hypothesis rejecting the null hypothesis.

CONCLUSION

Female board directors influencing firm performance have gained a huge amount of attention recently. However, most of the empirical evidence reported that women are more risk-averse, extra careful in making investment decisions and lack business experience affecting their capability of decision making, which is less likely to have an effect on firm performance as has been found in this study. From the results found in this study based on gender diversity and EVA, the study concludes that there is no relationship between female board members and firm performance in Malaysia, which is consistent with past research. The study identifies some reasons notably the lower proportion of female board members, risk-averseness, making lesser investment as well as the views towards women in society. Hence, it is hard to decide whether gender diversity is an issue to be concerned with or not, as there are a number of issues work behind the finding. However, the study suggests further research is necessary with a larger sample size for longer period of time, which might give a different picture as the number of female board members is increasing day by day.

REFERENCES

Abdullah, A. M., Entebang, H., Shazali, A., & Qaiser, R. Y. (2012). *Financial performance of public listed companies in Sarawak*. Paper presented at the postgraduate conference on social science and humanities, Kuching.

Abdullah, S. N. (2004). Board composition, CEO duality and performance among Malaysian listed companies. *Corporate Governance*, *4*(4), 47–61. doi:10.1108/14720700410558871

Afza, N. A. (2011). The Effect of owner's gender and age to firm performance: A review on Malaysian public listed family businesses. *Journal of Global Business and Economics*, *2*(1), 104–116.

Aggarwal, R., Erel, I., Stulz, R. M., & Williamson, R. G. (2007). *Do U.S. firms have the best corporate governance? A cross country examination of the relation between corporate governance and shareholder wealth*. Fisher College of Business working paper no. 2006-03-06.

Alowaihan, A. K. (2004). Gender and business performance of Kuwaiti small firms: A comparative approach. *International Journal of Commerce and Management, 14*(3/4), 69–82. doi:10.1108/10569210480000185

Beasley, M. S. (1996). An empirical analysis of the relation between the board of director composition and financial statement fraud. *The Accounting Review, 71*, 443–465.

Brace, N., Kemp, R., & Snelgar, R. (2006). *SPSS for Psychologists*. Palgrave Macmillan.

Butner, E. H., & Moore, D. P. (1997). Women's organizational exodus to entrepreneurship: Self-reported motivations and correlates with success. *Journal of Small Business Management, 35*(1), 34–46.

Byrd, J. W., & Hickman, K. A. (1992). Do outside directors monitor managers? Evidence from tender offer bids. *Journal of Financial Economics, 32*(2), 195–222. doi:10.1016/0304-405X(92)90018-S

Cadbury, A. (1992), Report on the Committee on the Financial Aspects of Corporate Governance. Gee.

Chamsy, O., & Patrick, H. (2006). *Critical theories of globalization*. Palgrave Machmillan.

Coakes, J. S., & Steed, G. L. (2003). SPSS Analysis without Anguish. John Wiley & Sons Australia Ltd.

Cuba, R., Decenzo, D., & Anish, A. (1983). Management practices of successful female business owners. *American Journal of Small Business, 2*(8), 40–46. doi:10.1177/104225878300800208

Dalton, D. R., Daily, C. M., Johnson, J. L., & Ellstrand, A. E. (1999). Number of directors and financial performance: A meta analysis. *Academy of Management Journal, 42*, 674–686.

Donaldson, L., & Davis, J. (1991). Stewardship theory or agency theory: CEO governance and shareholder returns. *Australian Journal of Management, 16*(1), 49–64. doi:10.1177/031289629101600103

Donaldson, L., & Davis, J. (1994). Board and company performance: Research challenges the conventional wisdom. *Corporate Governance, 2*(3), 151–160. doi:10.1111/j.1467-8683.1994.tb00071.x

Donaldson, T., & Preston, L. (1995). The stakeholder theory of the corporation: Concepts, evidence, and implications. *Academy of Management Review, 20*(1), 65–91. doi:10.5465/amr.1995.9503271992

Eagly, A. H., & Carli, L. L. (2007). Women and the labyrinth of leadership. *Harvard Business Review*, 1–2. PMID:17886484

Elgart, L. D. (1983). Women on Fortune 500 Boards. *California Management Review, 24*(4), 121–127. doi:10.2307/41165036

Fama, E. F., & Jenson, M. (1983). Separation of ownership and control. *The Journal of Law & Economics, 26*(2), 301–325. doi:10.1086/467037

Fasci, M. A., & Valdez, J. (1998). A performance contrast of male and female owned small accounting practices. *Journal of Small Business Management, 36*(3), 1–7.

Ferguson, A. M., Heritage, T., Jonathon, P., Pack, S. E., Philips, S., Ragon, J., & Snaith, P. J. (1997). EVA: A new theoretically based molecular descriptor for use in QSAR/QSPR analysis. *Journal of Computer-Aided Molecular Design, 11*(2), 143–152. doi:10.1023/A:1008026308790 PMID:9089432

Fiend, A. (2009). *Discovering statistics using SPSS*. Sage.

Fischer, E. M., Reuber, A. R., & Dyke, L. S. (1993). A theoretical review and extension of research on sex, gender, and entrepreneurship. *Journal of Business Venturing, 8*(3), 151–168. doi:10.1016/0883-9026(93)90017-Y

Haleblian, J., & Finkelstein, S. (1993). Top management team size, CEO dominance and firm performance: The moderating roles of environmental turbulence and discretion. *Academy of Management Journal, 36*(4), 844–863.

Harrigan, K. R. (1981). Numbers and positions of women elected to corporate boards. *Academy of Management Journal, 24*, 619–625.

Heidrick & Struggles, Inc. (1986). *The Changing board*. Heidrick & Struggles Inc.

Herzberg, M. M. (1998). Implementing EBO/EVA analysis in stock selection. *Journal of Investing, 7*(1), 45–53. doi:10.3905/joi.1998.408447

Issham, I. (2011). Company performance in Malaysia after the 1997 economic crisis: Using Economic Value Added (EVA) as a predictor. *African Journal of Business Management, 5*(7), 3012–3018.

Issham, I., Samad, A. M. F., Siew, Y. H., Kamil, A. A., & Ayub, M. A. (2008). Economic value added (EVA) as a performance measurement for GLCs vs Non-GLCs: Evidence from Bursa Malaysia. *Prague Economic Papers*, *3*(2), 168–179. doi:10.18267/j.pep.328

Jasmin, J., Kerstin, P., & Karin, V. (2010). *Gender diversity in the boardroom and firm performance: What exactly constitutes a critical mass?* Retrieved from https://papers.ssrn.com/sol3/papers.cfm?abstract_id=2009234

Jensen, M. C. (1993). The Modern Industrial Revolution, Exit, and the Failure of Internal Control Systems. *The Journal of Finance*, *48*, 831–880.

Jensen, M. C., & Meckling, W. H. (1976). Theory of Firm: Managerial behaviour, agency costs and ownership structure. *Journal of Financial Economics*, *3*(4), 305–350. doi:10.1016/0304-405X(76)90026-X

Joana M., Janneke P., & Chantal R., (2010). *Gender diversity and firm performance: Evidence from Dutch and Danish boardrooms*. Tjalling C. Koopmans Research Institute, Discussion paper series no. 10-03.

Kalleberg, A., & Leicht, K. (1991). Gender and organizational performance: Determinants of small business survival and success. *Academy of Management Journal*, *34*(1), 136–161.

Kesner, I. F. (1988). Directors' characteristics and committee membership: An investigation of type, occupation, tenure, and gender. *Academy of Management Journal*, *31*(1), 66–84.

Kiel, G. C., & Nicholson, G. J. (2003). Board composition and corporate performance: How the Australian experience informs contrasting theories of corporate governance. *Corporate Governance*, *11*(3), 189–205. doi:10.1111/1467-8683.00318

Knight, J. A. (1998). *Value based management: Developing a systematic approach to creating shareholder value*. McGraw-Hill.

Lipton, M., & Lorsch, J. W. (1992). A modest proposal for improved corporate governance. *Business Lawyer*, *48*(53), 89–77.

Loscocco, K. A., Robinson, J., Hall, R. H., & Allen, J. K. (1991). Gender and small business success: An inquiry into women's relative disadvantage. *Social Forces*, *70*(1), 65–85. doi:10.2307/2580062

Madden, B. J. (1999). *CFROI valuation: A total system approach to valuing the firm*. Butterworth-Heinemann.

Minority Shareholder Watchdog Group and Nottingham University Business School Corporate Governance Survey Report. (2007). Minority Shareholder Group.

Mir, A. E., & Souad, S. (2008). Corporate governance and the relationship between EVA and created shareholder value. *Corporate Governance*, *8*(1), 46–58. doi:10.1108/14720700810853392

Mirza, H. H., Shahid, M., Sumaira, A., & Farzana, R. (2012). Gender diversity and firm performance: Evidence from Pakistan. *Journal of Social and development. The Sciences*, *3*(5), 161–166.

Nielsen, S., & Huse, M. (2010). The contribution of women on boards of directors: Going beyond the surface. *Corporate Governance*, *18*(2), 136–148. doi:10.1111/j.1467-8683.2010.00784.x

Prasso, S. (1996). Poll: Women in office, not offices. *The Commercial Appeal*, 7B.

Ramana, V. D. (2004). *Market value added and economic value added: Some empirical evidences*. Retrieved from https://papers.ssrn.com/sol3/papers.cfm?abstract_id=871404

Robert, G. N. (1998). Two-sided confidence intervals for the single proportion: Comparison of seven methods. *Statistics in Medicine*, *17*, 857–872.

Salim, D. (2011). Board diversity and firm performance: The Indonesian evidence. *Corporate Ownership and Control*, *8*, 1–39.

Shaw, E., Marlow, S., Lam, W., & Carter, S. (2009). Gender and entrepreneurial capital: Implications for firm performance. *International Journal of Gender and Entrepreneurship*, *1*(1), 25–41. doi:10.1108/17566260910942327

Silverman, I. H. (2010). Valuing technology stocks with EVA: A bridge too far? *Journal of Business Case Studies*, *6*(2), 9–20. doi:10.19030/jbcs.v6i2.863

Spencer, G. (1984). Female executives foresee gains. *Best of Business*, *6*(2), 49.

Stewart, G. B. (1991). *The Quest for Value: A Guide for Senior Managers*. Harper Business.

Suisse, C. (2012). *Gender diversity and corporate performance*. Retrieved from https://infocus.creditsuisse.com/data/_product_documents/_shop/360145/csri_gender_diversity_and_corporate_performance.pdf

Sulong, Z., & Nor, M. F. (2009). *The effective of corporate governance mechanisms in Malaysian listed firms: A panel data Analysis*. Paper presented at the meeting of 11th MFA 2009, Bayiew Breach Resort, Penang.

Vance, S. C. (1983). *Corporate leadership: Boards, directors, and strategy*. McGraw-Hill Book Co.

Vincent, O., & Peter, O. (2011). Effects of selected corporate governance characteristics on firm performance: Empirical evidence from Kenya. *International Journal of Economics and Finance Issues*, *1*(3), 99–122.

Wall Street Journal. (1986, Mar. 24). The board game: More women are becoming directors but it's still a token situation. *Wall Street Journal*, p. 29D.

Watson, J. (2002). Comparing the performance of Male and female controlled businesses: Relating outputs to inputs. *Entrepreneurship Theory and Practice*, *26*(3), 91–100. doi:10.1177/104225870202600306

Wayne, C. D., Joseph, L. P., Joseph, R. S., Richard, D. T., Reich, T., Michael, V., & Marcus, E. R. (1997). Subgedual prefrontal cortex abnormalities in mood disorders. *Letters to Nature*, *386*(6627), 824–827. doi:10.1038/386824a0

Worthington, A. C., & West, T. (2001). Economic value-added: A review of the theoretical and empirical literature. *Asian Review of Accounting*, *9*(1), 67–86. doi:10.1108/eb060736

Yermack, D. (1996). Higher market valuation of companies with a small board of directors. *Journal of Financial Economics*, *40*(2), 185–211. doi:10.1016/0304-405X(95)00844-5

Young, D. (1997). Economic value added: A primer for European managers. *European Management Journal*, *15*(4), 335–343. doi:10.1016/S0263-2373(97)00014-5

ENDNOTES

1. For instance, Elgart (1983), Wall Street Journal (1986), Heidrick & Struggles (1986), Vance (1983), Salim (2011), Jesmin (2010), and Credit Suisse (2012).
2. Previously this model has been supported by Young (1997), Issham *et al.* (2008) and Silverman (2010).
3. Refer to the study of Hall & Geyser (2004).

Chapter 8
Governance Practices and CEO Hubris:
An Italian Banking Case

Paola Ferretti
University of Pisa, Italy

Cristina Gonnella
University of Pisa, Italy

ABSTRACT

This chapter analyzes the connection between CEO hubris and corporate governance contingencies, including a case study of an Italian bank for which the state of financial distress shall be linkable also to bad governance. The main objective is to verify whether, in presence of hubristic CEO, the internal control mechanisms, set to ensure the board vigilance and limit the overconfidence of the leader, are implemented, and if so, whether such mechanisms, even when formally respected, may be not so appropriate to guarantee a good governance. Particularly, the existence of a CEO hubris could neutralize their positive expected balancing effects on the power dynamics between CEO and board, such as to give prevalence to substance over form. Therefore, it may occur that some governance mechanisms (e.g., independence, non-duality), even if formally implemented, are unable to stem the managerial entrenchment of the CEO, who succeeds in enhancing immoderately his substantial power in the decision-making process.

DOI: 10.4018/978-1-7998-6669-5.ch008

Copyright © 2021, IGI Global. Copying or distributing in print or electronic forms without written permission of IGI Global is prohibited.

INTRODUCTION

The many calls for banks' sound internal governance as one of the fundamental drivers for achieving institutions stability underline the relevance of corporate governance issues, which recently receive increased attention from scholars as well as international authorities (e.g., EBA, 2017). In the wake of such scenario of growing interest, and considering the various perspectives of analysis of corporate governance of banks, the authors decided to focus their attention on the CEO psychological pattern attributable to hubris, trying to understand whether such pattern could enable the CEO to strengthen immoderately his power, thereby weakening the effectiveness of board vigilance mechanisms, set to contribute to the protection of the decision process from a CEO hubris, and, ultimately, to a sound and prudent management.

The concept of hubris, defined originally by studies in mythology as the disproportionate, blind and arrogant presumption of man in the face of the unsurpassable limits decreed by the gods (Cantarella, 2002; Cerinotti, 2018; Cipolla, 2011; Graves, 2014), has been progressively extended to other disciplines, such as the economic and financial one (Hayward & Hambrick, 1997; Malmendier & Tate, 2008; Roll, 1986). Within the latter line of research and focusing particularly on the connection with the role of the CEO, the existing literature (Brennan & Conroy, 2013; Petit & Bollaert, 2012) identifies the presuppositions of hubris, on one side, with overconfidence together with narcissism, and on the other side, with CEO substantial power. It becomes therefore crucial to understand the essence of hubris from a strictly managerial perspective, and whether it could negatively affect the managerial procedures, among which the governance practices cover a role of primary importance.

In order to give a contribution to this debate, this study analyzes the complex question of hubris, in terms of definition and conceptualization (e.g., it is almost frequent the overlapping with overconfidence and narcissism), as well as in connection with some corporate governance contingencies (e.g., independence of directors, non-duality, ownership). Then, the authors examine such issues considering a case study of an Italian bank for which the financial distress may be linkable also to its inadequate governance. The focus on the banking sector is explained in the light of the above-mentioned interest for internal governance matters, currently increasing also in response to the global financial crisis. Additionally, the limited number of studies on CEO hubris within the banking sector (Brennan & Conroy, 2013; Lawrence et al., 2011; Wray, 2016) calls for further investigation, in respect of which this study intends give a contribution. Particularly, the case study undertakes to verify the existence of hubristic traits in the CEO of an Italian bank, in order to answer the research question: "Is there evidence of CEO hubris?". Secondly, it attempts to examine the presence of board vigilance mechanisms, that literature suggests as suitable to contrast the distortions derivable from a possible pathological behavior of the CEO. Indeed, the hubristic pattern could allow the CEO to exercise strong decisional power within the bank if no obstacles are set in the restrictions placed on his discretion. The board of directors is charged with the responsibility of the development and implementation of appropriate control mechanisms. This is the essence of board vigilance, in presence of effective mechanisms the board should be able to monitor and discipline the management in general and the CEO in particular; otherwise, the top executive could tend to self-serve, especially in the case of hubris (Park et al., 2018). It is therefore important to take into account both the behavior of a leader potentially inebriated with power, and the ability of the board to comprehend, react to and moderate hubristic tendencies. These aspects are examined in this study in order to provide response to the second research question: "What is the weakness of the governance mechanisms which does not halt the imbalance of the power dynamics between the CEO and the board, especially in the case of hubris?".

In line with Petit and Bollaert (2012), the authors expect hubris to manifest in the CEO's relations with the self, with the others and with the world. To investigate such aspects the authors collected information from internal and external sources (e.g., statements from the CEO, press releases, daily newspaper, and reports of the authorities). Additionally, they gathered information on awards and media praises during his tenure. The analysis of the case study appears to confirm the existence of traits of hubris in the CEO, so that it is possible to answer affirmatively to the first research question.

As for the second research question, the examination seems to show that the formal compliance with some governance practices, alone, may not be enough to ensure the effectiveness of the board oversight. The compliance with formal rules has been examined within the case study with particular reference to independence, non-duality, tenure and mechanisms for nominating directors, and block ownership, by gathering data from the financial statements, curricula vitae of directors, and press releases.

This chapter contributes to the existing literature along two dimensions. In consideration of the limited number of studies on CEO hubris and its connection with governance practices within banks, authors try to provide a contribution in this respect. Secondly, while most studies are focused on the relationship between hubris and default or performance (Brennan & Conroy, 2013; Park et al., 2018), this study considers the CEO hubris from a corporate governance perspective, particularly focused on the relations with the board.

The implications for policy makers are also important. In the current scenario good governance practices represent one of the crucial levers for the stability of banks: hence, authorities should work on corporate governance matters adopting different approaches, and thus, also avoiding that substance takes precedence over form, particularly concerning the effectiveness of the internal control mechanisms, set to contribute to the sound and prudent management of banks.

This chapter is structured as follows. Section 2 focuses on the main features of the concept of hubris considering the managerial approach. Section 3 presents a review of the literature on the contingencies of corporate governance and their connection with hubris. Section 4 shows the case study: research questions and results. Finally, Section 5 concludes.

THE QUESTION OF HUBRIS: DISTINCTIVE FEATURES

The term hubris owes its semantic and heuristic poignancy to studies in mythology, in which it expressed the disproportionate, blind and arrogant presumption of man in the face of the unsurpassable limits decreed by the gods (Cantarella, 2002; Cerinotti, 2018; Cipolla, 2011; Graves, 2014). This connotation inspired the first studies in the field of psychology (e.g., Owen & Davidson, 2009), from which the economic and financial literature borrowed the concept (e.g., Brennan & Conroy, 2013; Petit & Bollaert, 2012). Within this line of research, Petit and Bollaert (2012) looked specifically at the role of the CEO. They suggested a definition of hubris that draws on the concept of Owen and Davidson (2009), elucidating its cognitive and behavioral levels and further developing it through the identification of relations with the self, with others and with the world. They also analyzed the ethical consequences of hubristic conduct and then they provided a theoretical framework of CEO hubris, which helps, among other things, to untangle several conceptual overlapping between the psychological constructs of narcissism, overconfidence and hubris, which are often treated interchangeably as a result of a lack of clear definitions (e.g., Buyl et al., 2019; Hayward & Hambrick, 1997; Park et al., 2018; Roll, 1986).

The existing literature (Brennan & Conroy, 2013; Owen & Davidson, 2009; Petit & Bollaert, 2012) recognizes as presuppositions of the hubristic attitude, on one hand, the overconfidence together with narcissism (Chatterjee & Hambrick, 2007; Finkelstein et al., 2009; Kroll et al., 2000) and, on the other hand, substantial power. One of the most common elements between hubristic and narcissistic constructs is the overconfidence (Brennan & Conroy, 2013; Chatterjee & Hambrick, 2007; de Vries, 2004; Hayward & Hambrick, 1997; Kets de Vries, 1994; Kroll et al., 2000; Maccoby, 2000; Owen & Davidson, 2009). However, narcissistic construct is meanly characterized by a dependence on the recognition of others, as the narcissist requires a constant exchange with the context of reference, because of the extreme and ineluctable need to find confirmation for his false and grandiose sense of self (Kets de Vries, 1994; Petit & Bollaert, 2012), thus contributing to his narcissistic supply (Buyl et al., 2019; Chatterjee & Hambrick, 2007; Tang et al., 2018).

As a further prerequisite, hubristic pattern needs recognition and social attention (e.g., awards and media praises; Hayward & Hambrick, 1997), but unlike the narcissist, the hubristic individual perceives a very limited need to engage with others, whatever their company, social or institutional role might be (Godfrey, 2005). As such, he trusts in his own capabilities (Li & Tang, 2010), overestimates his resource endowments (Malmendier & Tate, 2005), and believes that the fate is entirely in his own hands (Tang et al., 2018). For this reason, hubristic CEO tends to believe in his superiority and self-sufficiency and is less other-oriented. These considerations underline the specific presence of overconfidence in the hubristic pattern.

Studies show that the presence of a moderate CEO overconfidence could be linked also to positive behavioral patterns (Kets de Vries, 1994; Maccoby, 2000; Vilanova, 2017). In the case of researches on narcissism, findings reported a strong entrepreneurial sense in addition to the ability to seize opportunities within the CEO economic context of reference (Maccoby, 2000; Lawrence et al., 2011; Tang et al., 2018). Such a CEO is hence able to create an aura of charisma, consensus and admiration, both inside and outside the company (Brennan & Conroy, 2013; Maccoby, 2000; Tang et al., 2018; Vilanova, 2017).

When, however, the overconfidence is taken to extremes and is accompanied by substantial power – and this is the realm of hubris – it appears that potential benefits tend to be cancelled out (Kroll, 2000; Lawrence et al., 2011; Park et al., 2018; Tang et al., 2018). In accordance with a greater or lesser degree of overconfidence, a CEO has the tendency to engage in more or less risky operations (Black & Gallemore, 2013; Buyl et al., 2019; Ho et al., 2016; Lawrence et al., 2011; Niu, 2010; Obitade, 2013; Suntheim & Sironi, 2012; Tang et al., 2011). These findings emerged from empirical evidence on banks which show that a high level of CEO overconfidence tends to be associated with policies that favor an expansion of lending by reducing credit quality standards (Black & Gallemore, 2013; Buyl et al., 2019; Ho et al., 2016; Lawrence et al., 2011), with greater investment in non-core innovative activities (Buyl et al., 2019; Obitade, 2013) and with an increased leverage (Ho et al., 2016; Suntheim & Sironi, 2012). Some studies have further shown that banks whose decision-making processes in years prior to the 2008 crisis were dominated by CEOs with exaggerated self-confidence experienced more serious defaults (Ho et al., 2016; Obitade, 2013). CEO overconfidence can then be included as a factor able to worsen a situation of instability, such as that of the recent international financial crisis (Buyl et al., 2019; Ho et al., 2016).

As mentioned, literature identifies the existence of substantial power as another presupposition of hubristic pattern (Brennan & Conroy, 2013; Owen & Davidson, 2009; Petit & Bollaert, 2012). It therefore becomes important to understand which elements contribute to a CEO's rise to high levels of substantial power (Finkelstein, 1992), in circumstances in which the board of directors does not impose conditions on or offers resistance to his actions (Boyd et al., 2011; Ghaemi et al., 2016; Park et al., 2018; Sadler-Smith, 2016; Sadler-Smith et al., 2017). Thus, a CEO can gradually achieve dominance in the decision-making process vis-à-vis a board (Shleifer & Wishny, 1989), which seems to be not fully able to understand the damaging effects of overconfidence on the company (; Blaug, 2016; Petit & Bollaert, 2012; Schwizer et al., 2014). For this reason and to better understand the impacts of overconfidence on a company, it is necessary to take into account the inefficiencies of the board to comprehend, react to and moderate hubristic tendencies (Buyl et al., 2019; Park et al., 2018; Schwizer et al., 2014; Suntheim & Sironi, 2012).

CONTINGENCIES OF CORPORATE GOVERNANCE AND CONNECTION WITH HUBRIS: A LITERATURE REVIEW

Agency theory is one of the main theoretical paradigms on corporate governance (Fama & Jensen, 1983; Jensen & Meckling, 1976; Walsh & Seward, 1990). According to it, a CEO can behave opportunistically and act against the interests of shareholders. For this reason, literature on corporate governance has taken upon itself the task of defining the mechanisms capable of attenuating the impact of CEO power on company performance; the aim is to bring the respective interests of the CEO and the company in line (Buyl et al., 2019; Park et al., 2018; Walsh & Seward, 1990). Because a CEO's level of freedom to affect company behavior will be higher when he is not effectively monitored (Hambrick et al., 2015; van Essen et al., 2013; Zhu & Chen, 2015), the literature calls for a series of internal control mechanisms, with the board of directors charged with the responsibility of their implementing and developing (Walsh & Seward, 1990).

The topic of CEO hubris can be, therefore, included within the framework of agency theory, given the negative effects that through his behavior a such CEO can have on company performance (Petit & Bollaert, 2012). In particular, according to the findings of Obitade (2013) and Ho et al. (2016), the psychological predisposition toward hubris can be considered as one of the determining factors of the behavior of a CEO in a conflict of interests.

Empirical studies on hubris have therefore come to consider internal control mechanisms identified by agency theory literature as moderating variables on the behavior of hubristic CEOs (Buyl et al., 2019; Park et al., 2018; Schwizer et al., 2014; Suntheim & Sironi, 2012). Such variables should act as safeguards of the board's vigilance and include parameters as the non-duality, the independence of directors and the ownership (Buyl et al., 2019; Park et al., 2018; Schwizer et al., 2014; Suntheim & Sironi, 2012).

Non-duality refers to the separation of the roles of CEO and board chairman (Finkelstein & D'Aveni, 1994; Petrovic, 2008). Combining these two leadership roles in a single person can lead to a decrease in the effectiveness and objectivity of the chair, on the one hand, and to managerial entrenchment of the CEO, on the other (Finkelstein & D'Aveni, 1994; Grove et al., 2011; Hayward & Hambrick, 1997; Park et al., 2018). As Finkelstein and D'Aveni (1994) have argued, CEO duality can exacerbate problems of managerial entrenchment because chair-CEOs are able to dominate the agendas and contents of board meetings, control the most valuable information emerging from board meetings, and strengthen their power by selecting and facilitating consideration of directors who are loyal to them (Hayward & Hambrick, 1997; Park et al., 2018). In the case of CEO hubris, empirical analyses show that non-duality can prevent a CEO from excessive investment in high-risk projects (Hayward & Hambrick, 1997), with positive results on corporate financial performance (Park et al., 2018).

The effectiveness of board vigilance on management activities is also ensured by independent directors. Outside directors (Buyl et al., 2019; Finkelstein & D'Aveni, 1994; Grove et al., 2011; Hayward & Hambrick, 1997; Park et al., 2018) are individuals not otherwise affiliated with the firm on whose board they sit (Finkelstein & D'Aveni, 1994): when they meet certain requirements (e.g., not being personally related to management – Combs et al., 2007), they are able to guarantee operations in the exclusive interest of the company, and not in that of individual stakeholders (Cheng et al., 2015; Ho et al., 2016). As Petrovic affirms (2008, p. 1375), their distance from the day-to-day affairs "makes them instrumental in providing an external view to help develop the company's strategy and bringing in fresh perspectives." Outside directors, then, can contribute to increasing the board's independence, in that they – among other things – have a greater interest in protecting their own reputations as board members (Finkelstein & D'Aveni, 1994; Park et al., 2018). In addition, to the end of guaranteeing the effectiveness of the monitoring functions which they perform, independent directors are more likely to oppose the CEO in case of anomalies in the conduct of sound and prudent company management (Finkelstein & D'Aveni, 1994; Park et al., 2018). By contrast, in such circumstances "inside" directors could be more inclined to support the CEO's initiatives (Graham et al., 2017; Hayward & Hambrick, 1997; Hermalin & Weisbach, 2003; Walsh & Seward, 1990). With specific regard to CEO hubris, empirical analyses show that a greater percentage of independent board directors weakens the correlation between the cognitive character of the hubristic CEO and results in terms of company performance (Park et al., 2018; Schwizer et al., 2014).

Finally, concerning the point of ownership, on the one hand, CEO ownership may reduce contrasts between shareholders and CEO interests (Jensen & Meckling, 1976; Walsh & Seward, 1990), thereby preventing potential conflicts of interest;

on the other, especially in the case of CEO overconfidence, such a circumstance could have damaging effects (Fama & Jensen, 1983; Walsh & Seward, 1990). Park et al. (2018) have looked at the relation between hubristic CEO's ownership and company performance, finding that significant ownership held by the CEO can generate behavior associated with managerial entrenchment, thereby reinforcing the negative correlation between hubris and performance. Conversely, in presence of block-holders owning at least 5% of share capital, the interest on creating company value may weaken the positive correlation between overconfidence and riskiness of policies by opposing the CEO's discretionary power through a concentrated ownership (among others, Buyl et al., 2019).

If it is important to analyze the presence of corporate governance mechanisms, it is also important to test their real capacity to ensure a good and sound governance. This is relevant because their only formal presence could not ensure such goal, not being able substantially to avoid a power imbalance between CEO and board.

Some studies that have attempted to test the effectiveness of internal control mechanisms provided for matching CEO interests with company interests have produced ambiguous findings (Huse, 2005; Morck, 2008). The reason for such mixed results lies, among other things, in the focus of the studies on the compliance of governance mechanisms with formal rules (such as the independence of directors and non-duality), while neglecting analysis of the behavioral processes and dynamics that characterize the CEO and board relations. As Hermalin and Weisbach (2003) argue, a board dominated by a CEO will not carry out efficient vigilance in spite of formal conditions: indeed, formal governance attributes such as directors' independence have been shown to be ineffective if not associated with motivation and intense activity (e.g., Chen & Zhou, 2007). For example, even while respecting the requirement of independence of a part of the board, an entrenched CEO could manage to create a board with individuals who do not oppose his opinions, as in the case of independent directors with previous experience on passive boards or who are unable to make the proper degree of commitment to the position entrusted to them (Zajac & Westphal, 1996). Such directors may turn out to be less diligent and more subservient to managerial power or may simply show full trust in a powerful CEO (Cormier et al., 2016). Thus, if internal control mechanisms that appear strong actually turn out to be ineffective, this circumstance may reinforce and facilitate CEO hubris (Cormier et al., 2016).

It therefore also becomes important to consider informal rules, that is, the spirit with which the formal rules are implemented in company (Daily et al., 2003; Hermalin & Weisbach, 2003; Huse, 2005; Schwizer et al., 2014; Tosi, 2008; Van Ees et al., 2009). Analysis of interpersonal relationships between key actors within the bank – in group dynamics and behavioral processes – could reveal situations in which the discipline of internal control mechanisms turns out to be insufficiently forceful in guaranteeing effective monitoring. A consideration of such elements would be even more important in the case of CEO hubris. The crucial moment for blocking managerial entrenchment could be located in the initial stages of a CEO's tenure in which he is still seeking legitimation and acceptance on the part of the board (Shen, 2003; Park et al., 2018). In this stage, it is necessary to find mechanisms of governance able to counter the persuasive effect of a charismatic CEO on board members and the development of excessively close ties that often emerge between top managers and board members (Hermalin & Weisbach, 2003; Walsh & Seward, 1990). It is these close interpersonal connections that can guarantee to the CEO the power to influence the composition of the board without the need to violate formal requirements.

The present study forms part of this branch of research by analyzing an Italian bank for which poor governance contributed to its instability. The objective is to understand if it is possible to discover traces of CEO hubris and the presence of corporate governance mechanisms suggested by the literature; if so, the authors try to ascertain if the substance tends to prevail over the form due to the CEO hubris.

CEO HUBRIS AND BOARD VIGILANCE: A CASE STUDY OF AN ITALIAN BANK

In the wake of existing literature (e.g., Brennan & Conroy, 2013; Lawrence et al., 2011; Wray, 2016) the present study undertakes, first of all, to ascertain the existence of hubristic pattern in the CEO of a distressed Italian bank. Studies on the existence of traits of hubris in CEOs have considered both the factors which fuel the psychological pattern, (e.g., awards and media praises) (Hayward & Hambrick 1997; Lawrence et al., 2011; Park et al., 2018) and the psychological disposition of the individual (Brennan & Conroy, 2013; Cormier et al., 2016; Wray, 2016). To this end, the authors investigate the various aspects of framework of Petit and Bollaert (2012) together with criteria for hubris syndrome (Owen & Davidson, 2009). They also examine the factors (awards and media praises) that could develop CEO hubris during CEO tenure (Hayward & Hambrick, 1997; Lawrence et al., 2011; Park et al., 2018). The aim here is to validate the first research question: "Is there evidence of CEO hubris?".

Then, the study attempts to understand the main shortcomings of board vigilance of the bank, to the end of validating the second research question: "What is the weakness of the governance mechanisms which does not halt the imbalance of the power dynamics between the CEO and the board, especially in the case of CEO hubris?". In particular, this part of the study concerns research of independent directors and CEO-chair non-duality; furthermore, the study focuses on the tenure of some directors, the criteria for the nomination of directors, and the ownership.

The Italian bank (whose anonymity we will guarantee, referring to it as "Banca Alfa") was chosen because of its state of severe difficulty and the undoubtable role played by inadequate governance in bringing it into these circumstances. As highlighted by Barbagallo (2017): "The critical situation which emerged [at Banca Alfa] is ultimately attributable to the shortcomings of [its] corporate governance and, in this light, to the self-referentiality of the management. These weaknesses aggravated a situation made precarious by an economic recession whose seriousness and breadth had never been experienced in the postwar period. Loans granted with levity or in contexts of conflicts of interest contributed to the decline of the quality of credit following the effects of the crisis, bringing [the Bank] close to ruin."

To track elements of hubris in the CEO of Banca Alfa, the authors collected information from documents mentioning both Banca Alfa and its CEO. In particular, relevant data have been gathered from the statements given by the CEO, press releases of the Bank and sources beyond the control of the CEO and the Bank, such as daily newspapers, and documents pertaining to inspection reports of the supervisory authorities[1]. Accordingly with the literature on hubris triggers (Brennan & Conroy, 2013; Hayward & Hambrick, 1997; Kroll et al., 2000; Lawrence et al., 2011; Owen, 2011; Park et al., 2018) the authors also collected information on CEO awards as well as media praises referring to him during his tenure. For the structure of several internal control mechanisms the authors manually collected information on the composition of the board during the CEO's tenure. Data required to conduct this part of the study were taken from the Banca Alfa charter, financial statements, curricula vitae of board members and press releases.

The CEO of Banca Alfa headed the institution from 29 January 2008 to 25 April 2014. Before 2008, he held various positions as he rose through the bank hierarchy, from department head manager to deputy general manager; from 1997 he was general manager, a position he held a second time from April 2014 to July 2015, after which his working relations with Banca Alfa were definitively severed.

From the analysis carried out, the CEO of the Banca Alfa seems to satisfy three criteria among those defined by Owen and Davidson (2009) and taken up by Petit and Bollaert (2012) with regard to relations with the self: i) a messianic manner of talking about current activities and a tendency to exaltation; ii) a tendency to speak in the third person or use the royal "we"; and iii) exaggerated self-belief, bordering on a sense of omnipotence, in what he personally can achieve. These results emerge from a series of newspaper reports and press releases from the period 2008-2014, which provide examples of successes of Banca Alfa that the CEO attributed to himself. The idea is that the CEO perception of the Bank's scenario was often distorted, as several tendencies typical of those affected by hubris become evident. To name a few, an overestimation of one's own abilities and a propensity to take credit for successes while blaming others for failures (e.g., Black & Gallemore, 2013; Ho et al., 2016); an overestimation of one's own power and of the probability that one's decisions will be successful (Obitade, 2013); and the belief that a single person can have all the necessary information to be able to take decisions to guarantee positive performance, while downplaying the possibility of negative events (Vilanova, 2017). These forms of overconfidence seem to persuade the CEO of Banca Alfa to persevere in pursuing strategies which made him successful and to repeat past actions without effectively determining their suitability for the future (e.g., Lawrence et al., 2011). In this context, for example, Banca Alfa showed a marked nonchalance in lending policies, especially for the benefit of its home region: in the period 2007-2011 – which saw an initial phase of economic crisis followed by a temporary recovery – the Bank reported high rates of increase in its investments, even greater than the average of the banking system. The result was a decline in the quality of credit (Barbagallo, 2017), with a subsequent dizzying increase in non-performing loans over the next five years (2012-2017). In addition to factors of economic difficulty faced by the borrowing companies, this poor standing has been attributed to conduct which tended to provide indiscriminate financial support to businesses in the market of reference of Banca Alfa (Barbagallo, 2017). If this strategy may have also been adopted by other banks, especially local ones, it is beyond doubt that it was favored by those tendencies present in the overconfident CEO of Banca Alfa. In essence, an imprudent investment policy, one based excessively on speculation, was pursued, as it is also revealed by inspections of the supervisory authorities.

In addition to affecting lending policies, the hubristic behavior seems to have impacted various strategic choices, such as those regarding dimensional growth. The literature on this point suggests that a hubristic CEO is more likely to pay a higher price for target companies (Hayward & Hambrick, 1997; Roll, 1986) and make more acquisitions than a non-overconfident CEO (Malmendier & Tate, 2005). Such decisions are made in a context in which a hubristic CEO tends to see his world primarily as an arena in which to exercise power and seek glory. The project of a grandiose "banking empire" (Kroll et al., 2000) expressed by Banca Alfa CEO moved in this direction, especially when he defined the acquisitions and mergers in the national context as his "Italian campaign". This project of aggressive expansion on the national level was considered by many as excessively risky and unjustifiable, so much so that in 2009 the supervisory authorities discovered anomalies and refused authorization for new acquisitions until the operations for consolidating those already underway had been completed (Barbagallo, 2017).

Concluding the analysis of the relation with the self, it also appears that the Banca Alfa CEO was convinced that he was uniquely qualified to run the company (Petit and Bollaert 2012). In essence, his behavior seems to be aimed at consolidating managerial entrenchment, to which can be linked passive delegative legitimation on the part of the board (Barbagallo, 2017). The CEO held a position of absolute and individual dominance on the board that played a passive role with respect to the decision-making process, which was completely in the hands of the CEO frequently called "dominus" of the Banca Alfa. Moreover, the board had no power to check the appropriateness of decisions in front of a CEO who acted as an "absolute monarch".

Other important aspects linked to relations with the self are the CEO tardy resignation and his failure to accept removal from position of power. He was reluctant to step down, for example, in the wake of the inspections of the supervisory authorities, who on several occasions (specifically, once in 2009 and twice in 2013) brought to light that management of the Bank was excessively concentrated in the figure of the CEO with the resulting weakness of the system of governance and control. In spite of the undue centralization of power in the hands of the CEO – reinforced by his close relationship to the Bank's chairman and the near absence of counterbalance on the part of the board – and in spite of the explicit request made by the authorities to bring thorough change to the composition of the bank's governing bodies, the CEO persisted in refusing to resign. Having received a request by the authorities to carry out "a change in its corporate governance as a matter of urgency," the Bank responded with measures that were not effective in making a break with the past or producing a radical reform of the governance. In the face of the inadequacy of these steps, in 2014 the authorities again urged the Bank to make the necessary changes. At this point the Bank took more far-reaching measures, without, however, completely excluding the CEO: in April 2014, on the occasion of the re-election of the governing bodies, he was in fact confirmed, although in the position of general manager. Yet neither a new CEO nor an executive committee was nominated. These decisions clearly indicate the tendency of the overconfident CEO to maintain his power and his failure to accept removal from position. Furthermore, even when he stepped down from all Banca Alfa top positions, the Court of Cassation cited the presumed tendency of the CEO to continue to influence the bank following his resignation.

The consolidation of power, so far linked to the relationship with the self, can also be analyzed with reference to the relationship with others and with the world. In the first case it is expressed through situations of management by fear vis a vis employees and in the second case through the contempt towards authority. Examples of management by fear are given by the statements-made by "victims" (e.g., Bank's employees) of the CEO abuse of power that show the CEO tendency to manage through fear (e.g., threat of job loss) and intimidation. On the other hand, the CEO presented manifestations of contempt towards the authorities, as in the case he claimed that the decision (required by authorities) to step down was a way to send a signal to supervisors that change formally was occurring, in the hope that they exerted less pressure. This suggests the extent to which he came to see himself and his work as being somehow above and beyond the jurisdiction of the authorities.

Lastly, the CEO hubris was further ascertained by finding those factors which can fuel this psychological pattern during his tenure. The case study shows that during his tenure the CEO was recognized as having made awards and praises by the media. Specifically, in 2005 he was granted an honorary degree, while in 2008 he received honorary citizenship from the township in which Banca Alfa was headquartered. On the second occasion in particular, the CEO was eulogized for having promoted and developed local entrepreneurship. Banca Alfa's CEO also received significant positive media attention in relation to the successes of the Banca Alfa; indeed, some examples of positive media coverage include newspapers praising the CEO and identifying his key role in the Bank.

The second step of the research was carried out by examining some characteristics of the Banca Alfa board aimed at understanding the main shortcomings of board vigilance in presence of CEO hubris: independent directors, CEO-Chairman non-duality, tenure of some directors, criteria for nominating directors, and ownership.

Generally speaking, a central role in guaranteeing adequate governance is played by independent directors, to whom is entrusted the task of monitoring management with autonomous judgement, thus contributing to ensuring the interests of the company, as required by regulations. In the case of Banca Alfa, however, this control was not so adequate, as stated, for example, in a report by the supervisory authorities following an inspection of the Bank: shortcomings regarding governance included "inconsistency in the role of the independent directors". This observation emerged despite the statutory provision of Banca Alfa of criteria underlying the independence of directors. This seems to suggest that members of the board expected to fulfill formal requirements of independence were often persons "loyal to the CEO." This seems to underscore the weakness of regulations with regard to independent directors. Indeed, norms in many countries, including Italy, do not provide an unambiguous definition, thus leaving broad autonomy to businesses to draft and interpret their charters. As in the case of Banca Alfa, such a situation may constitute a presupposition for a divergence of form and substance: in the presence of a hubristic CEO, formal practices of governance can be respected, while in reality these are not sufficient for ensuring efficient board oversight. As a result, the quality of governance can be compromised, to the point of contributing to corporate default.

Similarly, with regard to norms regulating non-duality between CEO and chairman, Banca Alfa never formally allowed for the same person to hold both of these positions. Nonetheless, the analysis reveals that a solid, symbiotic relationship existed between the chairman and the CEO: this connection dates to 1997, when the latter held the position of general manager. The chairman may therefore have witnessed the course of the development of the CEO's self-perception and could even have unconsciously been led to fuel the confidence of CEO by sharing in his operative and strategic decisions without critically evaluating their consequences. This attitude may have gradually produced the circumstances which allowed the CEO to consolidate his self-referentiality once he reached the apex of the hubristic psychological pattern. Some examples indeed suggest that a condition of non-duality – even if respected on a formal level – was inconsistent in practice, giving rise to distorsions and power manipulations.

Another crucial element regards the analysis of the composition of the board at Banca Alfa, including the tenure of some directors. This part of the investigation is necessary to understand whether during the CEO's tenure the board was characterized by the presence of a solid core of directors faithful to him, who therefore contributed to strengthening his substantial power. In the years during which the CEO held his position (namely from 2008 to 2013) nine directors were re-nominated (out of a total of 13 for 2008, 2009 and 2010; of 15 for 2011 and 2012; and of 12 for 2013). Each of these remained in that role for the entire period under consideration, thus representing a majority that did not change with time. Such a high number of directors holding their positions over a continuous and extensive period created a strong sense of continuity and conservatism on the board. It can therefore be assumed that these nine directors (whom we can label as "faithful to the CEO") gradually conformed to the decisions of the CEO during the years in which his grandiose sense of self grew stronger and stronger. It is likewise probable that in prior years, when the individual in question was not yet CEO but general manager (from 1997 to 2008), these persons – some of whom were already board directors – had been taken in (perhaps again unconsciously, as is the case with self-deception) by his charisma and talents, thus allowing him to promote "a vision that is appealing and motivating to followers" (Shipman & Mumford, 2011: 662). It could be therefore possible to affirm – in particular – that these directors became subservient to the CEO's intoxication of power: faced with an individual who was excessively overconfidence, they developed an attitude of "awareness of, and orientation to, the leader's psychological needs" (Blaug, 2016). Representing a solid nucleus, their presence on the board could have therefore allowed its composition to become the expression of the CEO's needs, playing the roles that Park et al. (2018) define as compliant directors: these are persons loyal to the CEO who do not hinder his intentions, thus allowing him to gradually increase his substantial power and thereby to further neutralize the effectiveness of board oversight.

The possibility of guaranteeing the permanence of a compact core of compliant directors is also the result – in authors view – of the distorted application of the mechanisms for nominating the directors. During the CEO's tenure, it indeed happened that following the resignation of several directors before the end of their mandates, their replacements were nominated by cooptation. In essence, the board directly identified a new colleague to take the place of the one who had resigned; subsequently, the endorsement and nomination of the new director was approved by the assembly of shareholders at the first possible meeting (which typically coincided with the approval of the annual report).

This continued holding of directorships on the part of persons "faithful to the CEO" further reinforced his position of leadership, especially given the absence of block ownership in the shareholder composition of Banca Alfa. The concentration of CEO power seems to be thus facilitated by the fragmentation of share capital together with the confidence expressed by shareholders, especially about the CEO and his talent. Indeed, the shareholding structure does not seem to have constituted an obstacle to the carrying out of the will of the company's highest echelons but rather to have reinforced it by expressing its confidence and nominating the proposed candidates without presenting alternatives.

CONCLUSION

This chapter focuses on the connection between CEO hubris and governance practices in banks, including a case study of an Italian bank. The main objective of this study is to verify whether, in presence of hubristic traits in the CEO, the internal control mechanisms, set to ensure the board vigilance and limit the overconfidence of the leader, are implemented, and if so, whether such mechanisms, even when formally respected, may be not so appropriate to guarantee a good governance. Particularly, the existence of a CEO hubris could neutralize their positive balancing effects on the power dynamics between CEO and board, such as to give prevalence to substance over form. Therefore it may occur, as results from the case study, that governance mechanisms concerning board oversight (e.g., independence, non-duality), even if formally implemented, are unable to stem the managerial entrenchment of the CEO, who through his psychological traits succeeds in enhancing immoderately his power in the decision-making process in absence of "real" restrictions placed on his discretion. This is detrimental to the balance between the various corporate bodies as well as to the soundness of banks. In fact, on the one side, there could be negative impacts, among others, on the composition of the board; for example, even while respecting the requirement of independence, an entrenched CEO could indeed manage to nominate directors who – for various reasons – succumb to his influence (compliant directors). On the other side, such a CEO could tend to engage in more risky activities: in this respect, the analysis shows particularly the easing of credit standards.

In sum, neglecting the analysis of behavioral processes and dynamics characterizing the board of directors could have a distorting effect for a clear understanding of the good governance practices. In this sense, the case study foregrounds the need to guarantee, especially in the presence of a CEO hubris, the importance of an effective board oversight, if good governance is to be ensured.

However, this study suffers some limitations that need to be overcome, first of all by extending the governance contingencies to be analyzed. Additionally, a comparison between banks, having different features (as regards the size, ownership, gender diversity in the board, to name a few), could be subject of future research, in order to test whether the results could be confirmed or not in presence of some diversities.

REFERENCES

Barbagallo, C. (2017). *Veneto Banca e Banca Popolare di Vicenza*. Academic Press.

Black, D. E., & Gallemore, J. (2013). Bank executive overconfidence and delayed expected loss recognition. Working Paper. https://papers.ssrn.com/sol3/papers.cfm?abstract_id=2144293

Blaug, R. (2016). Pathologies of power and cognition. In G. Robinson & P. Garrard (Eds.), *The Intoxication of Power* (pp. 75–88). Palgrave Macmillan.

Bollaert, H., & Petit, V. (2010). Beyond the dark side of executive psychology: Current research and new directions. *European Management Journal*, *28*(5), 362–376. doi:10.1016/j.emj.2010.01.001

Boyd, B. K., Haynes, K. T., & Zona, F. (2011). Dimensions of CEO–board relations. *Journal of Management Studies*, *48*(8), 1892–1923. doi:10.1111/j.1467-6486.2010.00943.x

Brennan, N. M., & Conroy, J. P. (2013). Executive hubris: The case of a bank CEO. *Accounting, Auditing & Accountability Journal*, *26*(2), 172–195. doi:10.1108/09513571311303701

Buyl, T., Boone, C., & Wade, J. B. (2019). CEO narcissism, risk-taking, and resilience: An empirical analysis in US commercial banks. *Journal of Management*, *45*(4), 1372–1400. doi:10.1177/0149206317699521

Cantarella, E. (2002). *Itaca: eroi, donne, potere tra vendetta e diritto*. Feltrinelli Editore.

Cerinotti, A. (2018). *Miti greci e di Roma antica*. Giunti.

Chatterjee, A., & Hambrick, D. C. (2007). It's all about me: Narcissistic chief executive officers and their effects on company strategy and performance. *Administrative Science Quarterly*, *52*(3), 351–386. doi:10.2189/asqu.52.3.351

Chen, K. Y., & Zhou, J. (2007). Audit committee, board characteristics, and auditor switch decisions by Andersen's clients. *Contemporary Accounting Research*, *24*(4), 1085–1117. doi:10.1506/car.24.4.2

Cheng, I. H., Hong, H., & Scheinkman, J. A. (2015). Yesterday's heroes: Compensation and risk at financial firms. *The Journal of Finance*, *70*(2), 839–879. doi:10.1111/jofi.12225

Cipolla, P. (2011). La hybris di Serse nei Persiani di Eschilo tra destino e responsabilità. In A. Rotondo (Ed.), *Humanitas e cristianesimo. Studi in onore di Roberto Osculati* (pp. 29–39). Viella.

Combs, J. G., Ketchen, D. J. Jr, Perryman, A. A., & Donahue, M. S. (2007). The moderating effect of CEO power on the board composition–firm performance relationship. *Journal of Management Studies*, *44*(8), 1299–1323. doi:10.1111/j.1467-6486.2007.00708.x

Cormier, D., Lapointe-Antunes, P., & Magnan, M. (2016). CEO power and CEO hubris: A prelude to financial misreporting? *Management Decision*, *54*(2), 522–554. doi:10.1108/MD-04-2015-0122

Daily, C. M., Dalton, D. R., & Cannella, A. A. Jr. (2003). Corporate governance: Decades of dialogue and data. *Academy of Management Review*, *28*(3), 371–382. doi:10.5465/amr.2003.10196703

de Vries, M. K. (2004). Organizations on the Couch: A clinical perspective on organizational dynamics. *European Management Journal*, *22*(2), 183–200.

EBA. (2017). Final Report Guidelines on internal governance under Directive 2013/36/EU, September 26.

Fama, E. F., & Jensen, M. C. (1983). Separation of ownership and control. *The Journal of Law & Economics*, *26*(2), 301–325. doi:10.1086/467037

Finkelstein, S. (1992). Power in top management teams: Dimensions, measurement, and validation. *Academy of Management Journal*, *35*(3), 505–538. PubMed

Finkelstein, S., Cannella, S. F. B., Hambrick, D. C., & Cannella, A. A. (2009). *Strategic leadership: Theory and research on executives, top management teams, and boards*. Oxford University Press.

Finkelstein, S., & D'aveni, R. A. (1994). CEO duality as a double-edged sword: How boards of directors balance entrenchment avoidance and unity of command. *Academy of Management Journal*, *37*(5), 1079–1108.

Ghaemi, S. N., Liapis, C., & Owen, D. (2016). The psychopathology of power. In *The Intoxication of Power* (pp. 17–37). Palgrave Macmillan.

Godfrey, P. C. (2005). The relationship between corporate philanthropy and shareholder wealth: A risk management perspective. *Academy of Management Review*, *30*(4), 777–798. doi:10.5465/amr.2005.18378878

Graham, J. R., Kim, H., & Leary, M. T. (2017). CEO Power and Board Dynamics. Working Paper. doi:10.2139srn.2938120

Graves, R. (2014). *I miti greci*. Longanesi & C.

Grove, H., Patelli, L., Victoravich, L. M., & Xu, P. (2011). Corporate governance and performance in the wake of the financial crisis: Evidence from US commercial banks. *Corporate Governance*, *19*(5), 418–436. doi:10.1111/j.1467-8683.2011.00882.x

Hambrick, D. C., Misangyi, V. F., & Park, C. A. (2015). The quad model for identifying a corporate director's potential for effective monitoring: Toward a new theory of board sufficiency. *Academy of Management Review*, *40*(3), 323–344. doi:10.5465/amr.2014.0066

Hayward, M. L., & Hambrick, D. C. (1997). Explaining the premiums paid for large acquisitions: Evidence of CEO hubris. *Administrative Science Quarterly*, *42*(1), 103–127. doi:10.2307/2393810

Hermalin, B. E., & Weisbach, M. S. (2003). Boards of directors as an endogenously determined institution: A survey of the economic literature. *Economic Policy Review*, *9*, 7–26.

Ho, P. H., Huang, C. W., Lin, C. Y., & Yen, J. F. (2016). CEO overconfidence and financial crisis: Evidence from bank lending and leverage. *Journal of Financial Economics*, *120*(1), 194–209. doi:10.1016/j.jfineco.2015.04.007

Huse, M. (2005). Accountability and creating accountability: A framework for exploring behavioural perspectives of corporate governance. *British Journal of Management*, *16*(s1), S65–S79. doi:10.1111/j.1467-8551.2005.00448.x

Jensen, M. C., & Meckling, W. H. (1976). Theory of the firm: Managerial behavior, agency costs and ownership structure. *Journal of Financial Economics*, *3*(4), 305–360. doi:10.1016/0304-405X(76)90026-X

Kets de Vries, M. F. (1994). The leadership mystique. *The Academy of Management Perspectives*, *8*(3), 73–89. doi:10.5465/ame.1994.9503101181

Kroll, M. J., Toombs, L. A., & Wright, P. (2000). Napoleon's tragic march home from Moscow: Lessons in hubris. *The Academy of Management Perspectives*, *14*(1), 117–128. doi:10.5465/ame.2000.2909844

Lawrence, D. Y., Pazzaglia, F., & Sonpar, K. (2011). The introduction of a non-traditional and aggressive approach to banking: The risks of hubris. *Journal of Business Ethics*, *102*(3), 401–420. doi:10.1007/s10551-011-0821-1

Li, J., & Tang, Y. I. (2010). CEO hubris and firm risk taking in China: The moderating role of managerial discretion. *Academy of Management Journal*, *53*(1), 45–68. doi:10.5465/amj.2010.48036912

Maccoby, M. (2000). Narcissistic leaders. *Harvard Business Review*, *78*(1), 69–77.

Malmendier, U., & Tate, G. (2005). Does overconfidence affect corporate investment? CEO overconfidence measures revisited. *European Financial Management*, *11*(5), 649–659. doi:10.1111/j.1354-7798.2005.00302.x

Malmendier, U., & Tate, G. (2008). Who makes acquisitions? CEO overconfidence and the market's reaction. *Journal of Financial Economics*, *89*(1), 20–43. doi:10.1016/j.jfineco.2007.07.002

Morck, R. (2008). Behavioral finance in corporate governance: Economics and ethics of the devil's advocate. *The Journal of Management and Governance*, *12*(2), 179–200. doi:10.1007/s10997-008-9059-4

Niu, J. (2010). The effect of CEO overconfidence on bank risk taking. *Economic Bulletin*, *30*(4), 3288–3299.

Obitade, O. P. (2013). CEO Overconfidence and Bank Failure. Working Paper. doi:10.2139srn.2352053

Owen, D., & Davidson, J. (2009). Hubris syndrome: An acquired personality disorder? A study of US Presidents and UK Prime Ministers over the last 100 years. *Brain*, *132*(5), 1396–1406. doi:10.1093/brain/awp008 PubMed

Owen, L. D. (2011). Psychiatry and politicians–afterword: Commentary on… psychiatry and politicians. *The Psychiatrist*, *35*(4), 145–148. doi:10.1192/pb.bp.110.031708

Park, J. H., Kim, C., Chang, Y. K., Lee, D. H., & Sung, Y. D. (2018). CEO hubris and firm performance: Exploring the moderating roles of CEO power and board vigilance. *Journal of Business Ethics*, *147*(4), 919–933. doi:10.1007/s10551-015-2997-2

Petit, V., & Bollaert, H. (2012). Flying too close to the sun? Hubris among CEOs and how to prevent it. *Journal of Business Ethics*, *108*(3), 265–283. doi:10.1007/s10551-011-1097-1

Petrovic, J. (2008). Unlocking the role of a board director: A review of the literature. *Management Decision*, *46*(9), 1373–1392. doi:10.1108/00251740810911993

Roll, R. (1986). The hubris hypothesis of corporate takeovers. *The Journal of Business*, *59*(2), 197–216. doi:10.1086/296325

Sadler-Smith, E. (2016). Hubris in business and management research: A 30-year review of studies. In G. Robinson & P. Garrard (Eds.), *The Intoxication of Power* (pp. 39–74). Palgrave Macmillan.

Sadler-Smith, E., Akstinaite, V., Robinson, G., & Wray, T. (2017). Hubristic leadership: A review. *Leadership*, *13*(5), 525–548. doi:10.1177/1742715016680666

Schwizer, P., Carretta, A., & Soana, M. G. (2014). Can high quality independent Directors reduce CEO overconfidence [Paper presentation]. European Financial Management Association, 25–28 June 2014, *Annual Meeting*, Rome, Italy.

Shen, W. (2003). The dynamics of the CEO-board relationship: An evolutionary perspective. *Academy of Management Review*, *28*(3), 466–476. doi:10.5465/amr.2003.10196776

Shipman, A. S., & Mumford, M. D. (2011). When confidence is detrimental: Influence of overconfidence on leadership effectiveness. *The Leadership Quarterly*, *22*(4), 649–665. doi:10.1016/j.leaqua.2011.05.006

Shleifer, A., & Vishny, R. W. (1989). Management entrenchment: The case of manager-specific investments. *Journal of Financial Economics*, *25*(1), 123–139. doi:10.1016/0304-405X(89)90099-8

Suntheim, F., & Sironi, A. (2012). CEO Overconfidence in Banking. Working Paper. https://ssrn.com/abstract=2250344

Tang, J., Crossan, M., & Rowe, W. G. (2011). Dominant CEO, deviant strategy, and extreme performance: The moderating role of a powerful board. *Journal of Management Studies*, *48*(7), 1479–1503. doi:10.1111/j.1467-6486.2010.00985.x

Tang, Y., Mack, D. Z., & Chen, G. (2018). The differential effects of CEO narcissism and hubris on corporate social responsibility. *Strategic Management Journal*, *39*(5), 1370–1387. doi:10.1002/smj.2761

Tosi, H. L. Jr. (2008). Quo Vadis? Suggestions for future corporate governance research. *The Journal of Management and Governance*, *12*(2), 153–169. doi:10.1007/s10997-008-9054-9

Van Ees, H., Gabrielsson, J., & Huse, M. (2009). Toward a behavioral theory of boards and corporate governance. *Corporate Governance*, *17*(3), 307–319. doi:10.1111/j.1467-8683.2009.00741.x

van Essen, M., Van Oosterhout, J., & Heugens, P. P. (2013). Competition and cooperation in corporate governance: The effects of labor institutions on blockholder effectiveness in 23 European countries. *Organization Science*, *24*(2), 530–551. doi:10.1287/orsc.1120.0742

Vilanova, L. (2017). Does CEO Overconfidence Always Hurt Organizational Performance? A Social and Deception-Based Theory [Paper presentation]. *XXVIe Conference Internationale de Management Strategique*, Lyon.

Walsh, J. P., & Seward, J. K. (1990). On the efficiency of internal and external corporate control mechanisms. *Academy of Management Review*, *15*(3), 421–458. doi:10.5465/amr.1990.4308826

Wray, T. (2016). The role of leader hubris in the decline of RBS and Lehman Brothers. In G. Robinson & P. Garrard (Eds.), *The Intoxication of Power* (pp. 229–251). Palgrave Macmillan.

Zajac, E. J., & Westphal, J. D. (1996). Director Reputation, CEO–Board Power, and the Dynamics of Board Interlocks. *Administrative Science Quarterly*, *41*(3), 507–529. doi:10.2307/2393940

Zhu, D. H., & Chen, G. (2015). CEO narcissism and the impact of prior board experience on corporate strategy. *Administrative Science Quarterly*, *60*(1), 31–65. doi:10.1177/0001839214554989

ENDNOTE

1 Sources recalling explicitly and exclusively Banca Alfa and/or its CEO have not been intentionally reported in the paper in order to guarantee anonymity; they may be made available upon request. Besides, the authors present a summary of the main investigations carried out; even in such case, the details may be made available.

Chapter 9
Corporate Citizenship:
Moving Beyond Philanthropy

Reena Agrawal
Jaipuria Institute of Management, Lucknow, India

ABSTRACT

The last few decades have witnessed serious sustainability challenges such as economic uncertainty, depletion ozone layer, increase in pollution, urban decay, overpopulation, degradation, and shortage of natural resources, etc. The increasing pace of change and rising competition has posed unknown challenges and unparalleled pressure on the corporates not only to prosper, but also to sustain in future. With customers, investors, and other stakeholders becoming increasing aware and critical about sustainable practices, the companies are forced to think past short term monetary gains. As there exists an interdependence, integration, and co-creation among the three basic tenets of sustainability-people, planet, and profits. There is a global call on companies to pursue socially responsible conduct and adopt innovative practices which create value for people, planet, as well as economy.

INTRODUCTION

Last few decades have witnessed serious sustainability challenges such as economic uncertainty, depletion ozone layer, increase in pollution, urban decay, overpopulation, degradation and shortage of natural resources etc. Ever increasing pace of change and rising competition has posed unknown challenges and unparalleled pressure on the corporates not only to prosper, but also to sustain in future. With customers, investors and other stakeholders becoming increasing aware and critical about sustainable practices, the companies are forced to think past short term monetary

DOI: 10.4018/978-1-7998-6669-5.ch009

Copyright © 2021, IGI Global. Copying or distributing in print or electronic forms without written permission of IGI Global is prohibited.

gains. As there exists an interdependence, integration and co- creation among the three basic tenets of sustainability-people, planet and profits. There is a global call on companies to pursue socially responsible conduct and adopt innovative practices which create value for people, planet as well as economy.

Companies cannot exist short of support from society, hence they are indebted to repay to the society. It is their social obligation to engage in socially and legally responsible behavior while they pursue profits. The companies should be anticipatory and preventative in their approach, rather being reactive and curative. The companies should have progressive and sustainable outlook and adopt strategies that are inclusive in nature. As companies have ownership on productive resources without their support, society will never attain sustainable development. Thus it is essential that companies should become responsible corporate citizens.

Changing Role of Corporate

Though governance still reposes with governments over the period of time role of state governance has deteriorated at regional level, national level, and international levels. Today corporate engagement in society is unavoidable due to numerous reasons. In the modern world, no single government can have resources to do all. The increased pace of globalization, technological advancements, quick flow of information, have negated the significance of political boundaries. Increasing issues and challenges at regional, national and international level require localized as well as global solutions and the deployment of resources needed may be beyond the capacity of any single government.

Political power has its own limitations and as power of the state tapered, the influence of business seems to be widening. Companies engage in delivery of health, education, employment of employees and their children. Corporations have all pervasive impact right from air quality to the availability of life-saving drugs. They are integral to the existence of governments and can create political stability at regional and national level.

Business enterprises are growing at a fast pace, many companies from emerging nations have become global entities. Thus, the impact of companies on societies, on the lives of peoples, and on the environment has suddenly enlarged. This major shift in the power game means that just as societies and citizens look up to state for leadership and solutions, now they will appeals for help from corporates. Thus, there is a need for a more holistic conceptualization of corporate engagement that integrates at various levels.

Corporate Citizenship: Theoretical Background

Companies always influence the society both in good as well as bad ways. Increase in scope and extent of their rippling effect necessitates increased focus on their responsibility towards the society and environment. During 1990s companies realized that "social embeddedness" was essential as well as desirable. This led to the evolution of the term Corporate Citizenship.

The term Corporate Citizenship was used to "connect business activity to broader social accountability and service for mutual benefit," highlighting the philosophy that a corporation is an entity with equivalent to a human being. Corporate Citizenship thus encompasses actions and methods embraced by businesses to meet their societal responsibilities while pursuing their dreams for profits.

Corporate citizenship can be simply defined as being about 'business taking greater account of its social, environmental and financial footprints. (Simon 2001).

Corporate Citizenship wants corporations to become more knowledgeable and enlightened part of society and appreciate both private and public entities. As they are generated by society and they derive their validity from societies in which they function. They need to express their role, scope and purpose in a manner that they fulfill social and environmental responsibilities as well. (McIntosh et al, 2003)

Often Corporate Social Responsibility and Corporate Citizenship are considered as synonyms and used in inter-changeably, while the reality is that the latter is symbolic of a holistic approach adopted by businesses, where the improved consciousness of their role, responsibility and influence in society, is incorporated in all the commercial decisions and is further supplemented by the stakeholder engagement.

Matten et al., (2003) presented three perspectives of "corporate citizenship": (a) "narrow view" that paralleled Corporate Citizenship with the Philanthropy or Charity; (b) "the equal view" that paralleled Corporate Citizenship with Corporate Social Responsibility; and (c) "the comprehensive view," which stated Corporate Citizenship was "re-conceptualization of the relationship between the business and the society".

Citizenship means sense of identification and obligation towards common good, which outspreads one's own interest (Peterson and Seligman, 2004). Citizenship contains display of loyalty, social commitment, and solidarity. Just as individual the Corporate Citizenship also need to focus certain obligations and accountabilities in their course of profit generation. Corporate Citizenship stresses three forms of responses: identification, compliance and internalization. Corporate Citizenship means self-regulation imbibed into business model. Like any individual citizen a good corporate citizen is also obliged to display of the character strength of citizenship.

One school of thought is companies are not citizens rather they are merely entities enjoying legal status, constituted to carry out business activities providing they satisfy some social obligations. Society take away the right to operate, if companies show a misconduct. While the other school of thought says a company will be regarded as good corporate citizen only when it is socially responsible and it abides all laws. Corporate Citizenship is not a check on business activities but rather inspires “reciprocity of relationships” with the society. Citizenship strengths helps the corporates decision-making, to resolve social issues, to develop relationships, and to nurture trust among people. Corporate Citizenship is comprehending and handling company’s widespread influence on society and environment for the benefit of the system as a whole.

A good Corporate Citizen is one which capitalizes on its competencies and value system to exploit

opportunities by integrating social and environmental concerns in its core vision and strategies. Corporate Citizenship thus talks of integration of ethical, social, environmental, philanthropic and economic values in the core decision making processes. The basic traits that can strengthen ethos of Corporate Citizenship, include loyalty, social responsibility, teamwork, moral behavior and progressive leadership. Corporate Citizen may also imbibe human qualities such as compassion, dignity, equality, autonomy and fairness. Focus should be positioned more on aspects that augment ethical thinking.

RELEVANT THEORIES

Wide range of theories have been proposed covering a vivid panorama from neo classical view to more contemporary schools of thoughts, which clearly bring out the expectations form corporates.

Shareholder Approach

A classical view is that primary obligation of any business is to enhance the profits and worth for its owner (Friedman, 1962; Quazi and O’Brien, 2000). Friedman said that the sole responsibility of any company is to use resources, engage in business activities, within the legal framework, and participate in competition to generate profits.

Stakeholder Approach

This approach explained that the companies are not solely answerable to its owners. They should also think about the other stakeholders who will be affected by their decisions. The other stakeholders includes employees, customers, suppliers of raw materials, the community, the government, the environment, and other associated groups (Freeman, 1984; Evan and Freeman, 1988).

Social Contract Theory

Shocker and Sethi (1973) said any social organization, business being no exception, get to function in society through social acceptance and contract, either expressed or implied, where its existence and growth depend on delivery of socially desirable things and equitable dispersal of social, economic, or political benefits to groups from whom it gets its power. According to Thomas Hobbes (1649), the motivation should be to create a social system where each treat the other with respect and abide some basic rules for the benefit of both the entities.

System Thinking

This theory states that only when we understand the relationship between elements, can we comprehend the behavior of the whole. Because business and society are interrelated and interdependent hence the need is to adopt systems thinking, well-thought-out decision are taken based on organizational objectives and needs of the larger goal (Senge,1990). Stacey (2011) said systems thinking basically strives to understand the whole, which is made of numerous parts with the help of strategic thinking.

Social Impact Hypothesis Theory

This theory points out that the companies need to be conscious of the implicit needs of its various stakeholder. Failing to meet the less explicit demands of stakeholders may result in to severe market blows (e.g. product recalls or litigation), and it may also destroy reputation of the company. This in turn may negatively impact the financial performance and the value of the company (Cornell & Shapiro, 1987; Salzmann et al., 2005).

Good Management Theory

According to Waddock and Grave (1997) if company's financial returns improves, enough resources shall be available with the company to enable it to conduct activities for society, employee, community and environment. Such activities develop the competitive advantage and also enhance the company's image, reputation, segmentation, and long term gain. This theory also proposes that the company`s performance shall inevitably improve when the company meets the needs of its various stakeholders.

Instrumental Stakeholder Theory

This theory is based on combination of economic theory, the stakeholder theory, ethics and behavioral science. The theory states that moral ideologies such as trust and cooperation can result in momentous competitive gain for the companies who adopt good conduct and are thoughtful in all their decision and actions (Donaldson & Preston, 1995; Freeman, 1984).

Legitimacy Theory

According to this theory existence enjoyed by any company is possible because of the allowance and legitimacy provided to it by the system whose part it is. Thus if there arises inequality – potential or existing, between the two systems that might create a threat for right to existence and hence it is crucial that companies respect the existing system (Dowling and Pfeffer, 1975). Thus if company`s intends to play a long innings there should be harmony between the company`s ethos with that of the society.

Responsibilities of Corporate Citizen

As business and integral part of society, environment and economy it influence all the three. The diagram below gives a bird eye view of the responsibilities of the companies as responsible Corporate Citizen:

The companies can create social impacts, by partnering with the government and the local communities in order to ensure equal opportunity, education, food, job and health and other amenities facilities for all.

Environmental impact can be created by addressing concerns by adopting sharing of resources, working on the principle of reduce, reuse, recycle, creating sustainable infrastructure, using sustainable technologies, reducing carbon footprints and taking measures to preserve the biodiversity, making use of renewable sources of energy, etc.

Figure 1.

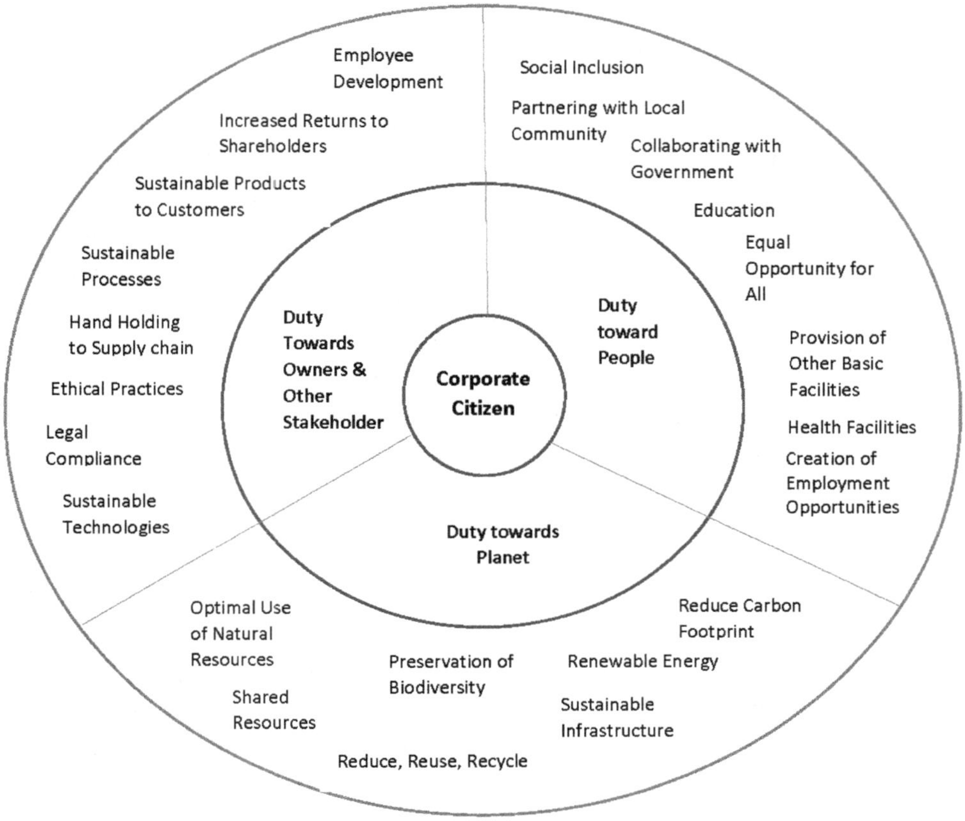

Similarly economic impact can be created by taking care labour norms, human rights issues, adopting moral codes, creating sustainable processes, legal compliance, supporting supply chains players, beings fairs with customers and employees, training and engaging employee for public good.

PRINCIPLES OF CORPORATE CITIZENSHIP

There are ten basic principles that have been developed for building efficient corporate citizenship are:

1. The companies need to extend corporate responsibilities beyond their core business. They need to integrate `citizenship` concept throughout the company. The need is to cultivate a culture where everyone regardless of his/her role and

status, should have duties beyond their stated jobs. Their codes and charters of good practice and behaviour should include: participation, compliance, good governance, ethical behaviour, environment and social obligation, law abidance, and commitment towards public welfare.

2. Business should be able to engage and interact with local communities. They need to visualize bigger social picture and work towards "creating of prosperous communities". First, they need to identify and articulate exactly for whom it wants to work, to be able to do well. The second challenge, is to appreciate and comprehend the diversity of the communities and after that design strategies and plan activities to take advantage of on that diversity in order to augment values and returns for business as well the community.
3. Use of local knowledge to be able to contribute beyond their core business expertise. They should be able to contribute, in decisions related to local communities, their basic amenities, funding for local charities, school etc.
4. The companies should try to find ways to reduce the divide between private and public in order to understand the bigger picture and engage as part of a broader picture and with consciousness about the larger social and environmental effects of their actions.
5. The companies need to go beyond compliance, and try to make sure that markets, government, customers and other stakeholders are aware about that. The companies should send strong signal to the world, customer and clients.
6. The companies should empower the people involved in the business. They should support and encourage personal development beyond the required tasks. This shall increase self-esteem and self-worth amongst all its staff irrespective of their role and position in the workstation.
7. The companies should try to bring cultural change in business through education in the workplace and rather through official directive from "top management". It should be in the "agenda item" at each stage or level of any business. It should encourage reflection and thinking about itself, like to think about health, safety, marketing, procurement, coordination, social good etc
8. The companies need not only to operate morally but it also needs to think ethically in order to prevent range of corporate scandals and collapses. Thinking ethics is mainly pertinent for developing good corporate citizenship, for the reason that lest extensive thought is given by business as to how to show, that it is a morally aware and conscious business. Again, this require change in culture, merely the compliance of set of rules developed by others unthoughtful adherence would not serve the purpose.
9. The companies should try to create ownership for staff in any new expansions. Everyone engaged in the business must have ownership of growths, policies, education, practices that will reassure improved organizational citizenship.

10. The companies need to ensure that each one in business contributes to the creation of new value. Everyone such as employees, customers, management, communities, irrespective of the part and position in the workplace must create new value for that business and should be recognized and rewarded for the same.

BENEFITS OF CORPORATE CITIZENSHIP

Corporate Citizenship and Sustainability

Corporate sustainability means integration of financial goals, environmental safety, and social obligation in business management and operations. The spells out the need to blend the triple bottom line of people, planet, and profits to attain sustainability. In today's highly competitive environment, the question that often is being asked is can engaging in sustainability bring benefit to the organization. Business leaders have started perceiving corporate sustainability as an opportunity instead of a necessity- steadily revisioning and creating value. Many empirical studies uncovered the constructive relationship between Corporate Citizenship and financial benefit. Businesses and organizations should operate in a socially responsible manner. Value for organizations is possible when organizations integrate sustainability practices into their core business strategy. If companies invest in local and global communities, interact with stakeholders, and respond to their needs, it shall result in long-term viability.

Increased Financial Returns

Profit and sustainability can go hand in hand. Researches have proved that companies that adopt sustainable practices record higher return on capital invested, return on equity and earnings per share in contrast to those who do not. Companies with higher social and environmental performance tend to record higher financial gains, in comparison to those who score lower scores achieve lower ones. Disclosure of nonfinancial information enhances the firm's ability to access finance in capital markets, reduces volatility in returns and its cost of capital. Integration of social and environmental obligation in the corporate strategies and practices reduces the risk for the company. The adoption of ecofriendly business strategies and essential disclosures have positive impact on the value of the company. Long term investors are very conscious and considerate about social and environmental conduct of the company while making their investment decisions. Studies have shown that Corporate Citizenship strategies can help companies in obtaining better resources, better employees. It can open unforeseen opportunities, improve their acceptance in local community, enhance their value, reputation, image in the eyes of the stakeholders and also enhance its competitiveness.

Employees

There are various benefits arising out of Corporate Citizenship. Some of them are employee engagement within the company and the improvement of motivation. Leaders and boards of directors who integrate social and community concerns in company's core philosophy and strategies participate in community development and consider it to be as vital as other company functions. It helps in attracting prospective candidates, improves employee morale and retention, builds relationships with communities and government, helps to create healthier communities, increases employee productivity, and improve public image.

Resilience for Future

The sustainability landscape is constantly changing. Day to day new issues emerge and it is expected from the company to resolve the same. No one can predict future contingencies that it will be expected to encounter over the next decade. The rapidly changing environment is prime reason why all companies need to review, refresh and update their strategies: new opportunities emerge expectations increase. Amid all these external stresses and understandings, businesses should not lose track of the need to create value for all.

Corporate Citizenship encourages companies to develop sustainability strategies: by identifying core strength and weakness, look for new opportunities and potential risk, engage all stakeholders through meaningful dialogue and feedback. Thoughtful decision making and sustainability initiatives bring increased returns. By harnessing the unique capabilities the company can create value for society and itself and are resilient during turbulence. Companies who do not create value, might face risks during tough times. The evidences show that the companies which as socially and environmentally responsible are more resilient.

CONCLUSION

The lack of responsible behaviour can shorten the survival of the human race. An improvement in the life of humanity and preserving nature, while creating profitability outcomes results can go hand in hand. Businesses and organizations should operate in a socially responsible manner. Socially responsible behaviors must be anticipatory and preventative, rather than reactive and restorative.

REFERENCES

Abshire, M. (2003). State of Corporate Citizenship: Survey. *Corporate Philanthropy Report, 18*(8), 1–3.

Aguilera, R. V., Williams, C. A., Conley, J. M., & Rupp, D. E. (2006). Corporate governance and social responsibility: A comparative analysis of the UK and the US. *Corporate Governance, 14*(3), 147–158. doi:10.1111/j.1467-8683.2006.00495.x

Ameer, R., & Othman, R. (2012). Sustainability Practices and Corporate Financial Performance: A Study Based on the Top Global Corporations. *Journal of Business Ethics, 2012*(108), 61–79. doi:10.100710551-011-1063-y

Andriof, J., & Marsden, C. (n.d.). *Corporate Citizenship: What Is It and How to Assess It?* WP Corporate Citizenship Unit, Warwick Business School. http://users.wbs.warwick.ac.uk/group/ccu/research/dimensions

Archie, B. (1991). Understanding Stakeholder Thinking. *Business Ethics: A European Review,* 46–51.

Asif, M., Searcy, C., Zutshi, A., & Ahmad, N. (2011). An integrated management systems approach to corporate sustainability. *European Business Review, 23*(4), 353–367. doi:10.1108/09555341111145744

Bansal, P. (2005). Evolving sustainably: A longitudinal study of corporate sustainable development. *Strategic Management Journal, 26*(3), 197–218. doi:10.1002mj.441

Barr, S. (2016). *Environment and Society: Sustainability, Policy and the Citizen.* Routledge. doi:10.4324/9781315579986

Baumgartner, R. J. (2014). Managing corporate sustainability and CSR: A conceptual framework combining values, strategies and instruments contributing to sustainable development. *Corporate Social Responsibility and Environmental Management, 21*(5), 258–271. doi:10.1002/csr.1336

Berthon, B., Abood, D. J., & Lacy, P. (2010). *Can business do well by doing good? Outlook.* Retreived from http://www.accenture.com/SiteCollectionDocuments/PDF/Accenture_Outlook_Can_Business_Do_Well_by_Doing_Good_Sustainability.pdf

Birch, D. (2008). Ten principles of corporate citizenship. *Social Responsibility Journal, 4*(1-2), 129–135. doi:10.1108/17471110810856893

Blank, H. D., & Carty, C. M. (2005). The Eco- Efficiency Anomaly. *Journal of Investing*.

Bodhanwala, S., & Bodhanwala, R. (2018). Does corporate sustainability impact firm profitability? Evidence from India. *Management Decision*, *56*(1), 1734–1747. Advance online publication. doi:10.1108/MD-04-2017-0381

Brannmark, M., & Benn, S. (2012). A proposed model for evaluating the sustainability of continuous change programmes. *Journal of Change Management*, *12*(2), 231–245. doi:10.1080/14697017.2012.672449

Busch, T., & Friede, G. (2018). The Robustness of the Corporate Social and Financial Performance Relation: A Second-Order Meta-Analysis. *Corporate Social Responsibility and Environmental Management*, *25*(4), 583–608. Advance online publication. doi:10.1002/csr.1480

Buttel, F. H. (2003). Environmental sociology and the explanation of environmental reform. *Organization & Environment*, *16*(3), 306–344. doi:10.1177/1086026603256279

Callan, S. J., & Thomas, J. M. (2009). Corporate Financial Performance and Corporate Social Performance: An Update and Reinvestigation. *Corporate Social Responsibility and Environmental Management*, *16*(2), 61–78. doi:10.1002/csr.182

Campblell, D., Craven, B., & Shrives, P. (2002). Voluntary social reporting in three FTSE sectors: A comment on perception and legitimacy. *Accounting, Auditing & Accountability Journal*, *16*(4), 558–581. doi:10.1108/09513570310492308

Carroll, A. B. (2015). Corporate social responsibility: The centerpiece of competing and complementary frameworks. *Organizational Dynamics*, *44*(2), 87–96. doi:10.1016/j.orgdyn.2015.02.002

Carter, N. (2001). *The Politics of the Environment: Ideas, Activism and Policy*. Cambridge University Press. doi:10.1017/CBO9781139163859

Cellier, A., & Chollet, P. (2011). *The Impact of Corporate Social Responsibility Rating Announcement on Stock Price: An Event Study on European Markets*. Universitè Paris-Est.

Cheng, B., Ioannou, I., & Serafeim, G. (2014). Corporate social responsibility and access to finance. *Strategic Management Journal*, *35*(1), 1–23. doi:10.1002mj.2131

Cho, S. Y., Lee, C., & Pfeiffer, R. J. Jr. (2013). Corporate social responsibility performance and information asymmetry. *Journal of Accounting and Public Policy*, *32*(1), 71–83. doi:10.1016/j.jaccpubpol.2012.10.005

Cornell, B., Alan, C., & Shapiro, A. C. (1987). Corporate stakeholders and corporate finance. *Financial Management, 16*(1), 5–14. doi:10.2307/3665543

Cramer, J. (2003). Corporate Social Responsibility: Lessons Learned. *Environmental Quality Management, 13*(2), 59–66. doi:10.1002/tqem.10110

Dawson, S. (2004). Balancing Self-Interest and Altruism: Corporate governance alone is not enough. *Corporate Governance, 12*(2), 130–133. doi:10.1111/j.1467-8683.2004.00351.x

Diaz, C. G. (2011). Corporate culpability as a limit to the overcriminalization of corporate criminal liability: The interplay between self-regulation, corporate compliance and corporate citizenship. *New Criminal Law Review, 14*(1), 78–96. doi:10.1525/nclr.2011.14.1.78

Diltz, J. D. (1995). The Private Cost of Socially Responsible Investing. *Applied Financial Economics, 5*(2), 69–77. doi:10.1080/758529174

Donaldson, T., & Preston, L. E. (1995). The stakeholder theory of the corporation: Concepts, evidence, and implications. *Academy of Management Review, 20*(1), 65–91. doi:10.5465/amr.1995.9503271992

El Ghoul, S., Guedhami, O., Kwok, C. C., & Mishra, D. R. (2011). Does corporate social responsibility affect the cost of capital? *Journal of Banking & Finance, 35*(9), 2388–2406. doi:10.1016/j.jbankfin.2011.02.007

Epstein, M. J., & Buhovac, A. R. (2014a). *Making sustainability work: Best practices in managing and measuring corporate social, environmental, and economic impacts* (2nd ed.). Berrett-Koehler.

Evan, W. E., & Freeman, R. E. (1988). A Stakeholder Theory of the Modern Corporation: Kantian capitalism. In T. L. Beauchamp & N. E. Bowie (Eds.), *Ethical Theory and Business* (3rd ed.). Prentice Hall Press.

Freeman, A. M. III, Herriges, J. A., & Kling, C. L. (2014). *The Measurement of Environmental and Resource Values: Theory and Methods*. Routledge. doi:10.4324/9781315780917

Freeman, R. E. (1984). *Strategic Management: A Stakeholder Approach.* Pitman Publishing Inc.

Friedman, M. (1962). *Capitalism & Freedom.* University of Chicago.

Frooman, J. (1999). Stakeholder influence strategies. *Academy of Management Review, 24*(2), 191–205. doi:10.5465/amr.1999.1893928

Gardiner, L., Rubbens, C., & Bonfiglioli, E. (2003). Big Business, Big Responsibilities. *Corporate Governance*, *3*(3), 67–77. doi:10.1108/14720700310483451

Global Reporting Initiative. (2011). *Sustainability Reporting Guidelines*. GRI.

Goodin, R. (1992). *If People Were money*. Free Movement. Harvester Wheatsheaf.

Haffar, M., & Searcy, C. (2017). Classification of Trade-offs Encountered in the Practice of Corporate Sustainability. *Business Ethics (Oxford, England)*, *2017*(140), 495–522.

Hansen, E., Grobe-Dunker, F., & Reichwald, R. (2009). Sustainability innovation cube. A framework to evaluate sustainability-oriented innovations. *Int. J. Innov. Manag.*, *13*(4), 683-713.

Hashmi, M. A., & Al-Habib, M. (2013). Sustainability and carbon management practices in the Kingdom of Saudi Arabia. *Journal of Environmental Planning and Management*, *56*(1), 140–157. doi:10.1080/09640568.2012.654849

Henao, R., Sarache, W., & Gómez, I. (2018). Lean Manufacturing and Sustainable Performance: Trends and future challenges. *Journal of Cleaner Production*, *208*(20), 99–116.

Herzig, C., & Schaltegger, S. (2011). *Corporate sustainability reporting: an overview. Sustainability Accounting and Reporting*. Springer Netherlands. doi:10.1007/978-94-007-1697-1_14

Hillman, A., & Keim, G. (2001). Shareholder value, stakeholder management, and social issues: What's the bottom line? *Strategic Management Journal*, *22*(2), 125–139. doi:10.1002/1097-0266(200101)22:2<125::AID-SMJ150>3.0.CO;2-H

Horisch, J., Freeman, R. E., & Schaltegger, S. (2014). Applying stakeholder theory in sustainability management: Links, similarities, dissimilarities, and a conceptual framework. *Organization & Environment*, *27*(4), 328–346. doi:10.1177/1086026614535786

Ivancevich, Skinner, & Crosby. (1997). Management Quality & Competitiveness (2nd ed.). Chicago: Irwin.

Jizi, M., Nehme, R., & Salama, A. (2016). Do social responsibility disclosures show improvements on stock price? *Journal of Developing Areas*, *50*(2), 77–95. doi:10.1353/jda.2016.0075

Jo, H., & Na, H. (2012). Does CSR reduce firm risk? Evidence from controversial industry sectors. *Journal of Business Ethics, 110*(4), 441–456. doi:10.100710551-012-1492-2

Kassel, K. (2012). The circle of inclusion: Sustainability, CSR and the values that drive them. *Journal of Human Values, 18*(2), 133–146. doi:10.1177/0971685812454482

Kelman, H. C. (1958). Compliance, identification, and internalization: Three processes of attitude change. *The Journal of Conflict Resolution, 2*(1), 51–60. doi:10.1177/002200275800200106

Kiron, D., Kruschwitz, N., Haanaes, K., & Velken, I. S. (2012). Sustainability nears a tipping point. *MIT Sloan Management Review*, (2), 69.

Klein, J. (2015b). Velveeta & Volkswagen: sustainability is a moving target. *Journal of Property Management*, (2), 12. Retrieved from http://www.jpm-digital.org

Kothari, S. P., Li, X., & Short, J. E. (2009). The effect of disclosures by management, analysts, and business press on cost of capital, return volatility, and analyst forecasts: A study using content analysis. *The Accounting Review, 84*(5), 1639–1670. doi:10.2308/accr.2009.84.5.1639

Kumar, S., Teichman, S., & Timpernagel, T. (2012). A green supply chain is a requirement for profitability. *International Journal of Production Research, 50*(5), 1278–1296. doi:10.1080/00207543.2011.571924

Kurucz, E., Colbert, B., & Wheeler, D. (2008). The business case for corporate social responsibility. In A. Crane, A. McWilliams, D. Matten, J. Moon, & D. Siegel (Eds.), *The Oxford handbook of corporate social responsibility*. Oxford University Press. doi:10.1093/oxfordhb/9780199211593.003.0004

Lee, D. D., & Faff, R. W. (2009). Corporate sustainability performance and idiosyncratic risk: A global perspective. *Financial Review, 44*(2), 213–237. doi:10.1111/j.1540-6288.2009.00216.x

Lin, C. P. (2010). Modeling corporate citizenship, organizational trust, and work engagement based on attachment theory. *Journal of Business Ethics, 94*(4), 517–531. doi:10.100710551-009-0279-6

Lindblom, C. K. (1994). *The implications of organizational legitimacy for corporate social performance and disclosure*. Critical Perspective on Accounting Conference, New York, NY.

Lo, S. F. (2010). Performance evaluation for sustainable business: A profitability and marketability framework. *Corporate Social Responsibility and Environmental Management, 17*(6), 311–319. doi:10.1002/csr.214

Lo, S. F., & Sheu, H. J. (2007). Is corporate sustainability a value-increasing strategy for business? *Corporate Governance, 15*(2), 345–358. doi:10.1111/j.1467-8683.2007.00565.x

Lourenço, I. C., Branco, M. C., Curto, J. D., & Eugénio, T. (2012). How Does the Market Value Corporate Sustainability Performance? *Journal of Business Ethics, 2012*(108), 417–428. doi:10.100710551-011-1102-8

Ludema, J. D., Laszlo, C., & Lynch, D. L. (2012). Embedding sustainability: How the field of organization development and change can help companies harness the next big competitive advantage. *Research in Organizational Change and Development, 20*, 265–299. doi:10.1108/S0897-3016(2012)0000020011

MacAdam, R., & Leonard, D. (2003). Corporate Social Responsibility in a Total Quality Management Context: Opportunities for sustainable growth. *Corporate Governance, 3*(4), 36–45. doi:10.1108/14720700310497104

Marti, C. P., Rovira-Val, M. R., & Drescher, L. G. J. (2015). Are Firms that Contribute to Sustainable Development Better Financially? *Corporate Social Responsibility and Environmental Management, 22*(5), 305–319. doi:10.1002/csr.1347

Martínez-Ferrero, J., & Frías-Aceituno, J. V. (2015). Relationship Between Sustainable Development and Financial Performance: International Empirical Research. *Business Strategy and the Environment, 24*(1), 20–39. doi:10.1002/bse.1803

Matten, D., Crane, A., & Chapple, W. (2003). "Behind the Mask", op. cit. Other terms appear in this decade, namely sustainable company or triple-bottom-line approach. *Journal of Business Ethics, 44*(2/3), 95–105.

McIntosh, Leipziger, & Coleman. (2003). Living Corporate Citizenship: Strategic routes to socially responsible business. FT Prentice Hall.

McWilliams, A., & Siegel, D. (2000). Corporate social responsibility and financial performance: Correlation or misspecification? *Strategic Management Journal, 21*(5), 603–609. doi:10.1002/(SICI)1097-0266(200005)21:5<603::AID-SMJ101>3.0.CO;2-3

Micah, L. C., & Umobong, A. A. (2013). Corporate governance and sustainable development in Nigeria: A study of oil companies in the Niger Delta Region. *International Journal of Business and Management, 8*(7), 127–132. doi:10.5539/ijbm.v8n7p127

Mingers, J., & White, L. (2010). A review of recent contribution of systems thinking to operational research and management science. *European Journal of Operational Research, 207*(3), 1147–1161. doi:10.1016/j.ejor.2009.12.019

Moneva, J. M., & Cuellar, B. (2009). The value relevance of financial and non-financial environmental reporting. *Environmental and Resource Economics, 44*(3), 441–456. doi:10.100710640-009-9294-4

Murphy, M. E. (2009). Restoring trust in corporate America: Toward a republican theory of corporate legitimacy. *New York University Journal of Law and Business, 5*(2), 415–484.

Nawrocka, D., & Parker, T. (2009). Finding the connection: Environmental management systems and environmental performance. *Journal of Cleaner Production, 17*(6), 601–607. doi:10.1016/j.jclepro.2008.10.003

O'Rourke, A. (2003). A New Politics of Engagement: Shareholder activism for corporate social responsibility. *Business Strategy and the Environment, 12*(4), 227–239. doi:10.1002/bse.364

Orlitzky, M., Schmidt, F. L., & Rynes, S. L. (2003). Corporate Social and Financial Performance: A Meta-analysis. *Organization Studies, 24*(3), 403–441. doi:10.1177/0170840603024003910

Peterson, C., & Seligman, M. E. P. (2004). *Character strengths and virtues: A handbook and classification.* Oxford University Press.

Petrovich, M. K. (2014). Social factors of sustainable development of the regional rural territories. *Society: Politics, Economics, Law*, (2), 1-5.

Quazi, A. M., & O'Brien, D. (2000). An Empirical Test of a Cross-National Model of Corporate Social Responsibility. *Journal of Business Ethics, 25*(1), 33–52. doi:10.1023/A:1006305111122

Reverte, C. (2009). Determinants of corporate social responsibility disclosure ratings by Spanish listed firms. *Journal of Business Ethics, 88*(2), 351–366. doi:10.100710551-008-9968-9

Richerson, S. (2013). A road map or turning sustainability goals into action. *Journal for Quality and Participation, 24*(1), 12–21.

Rivera, J. M., Munoz, M. J., & Moneva, J. M. (2017). Revisiting the Relationship Between Corporate Stakeholder Commitment and Social and Financial Performance. *Sustainable Development (Bradford)*, *25*(6), 482–496. doi:10.1002d.1664

Salzmann, O., Ionescu-Somers, A., & Steger, U. (2005). The business case for corporate sustainability. *European Management Journal*, *23*(1), 27–36. doi:10.1016/j.emj.2004.12.007

Schaltegger, S., Gibassier, D., & Zvezdov, D. (2013). Is environmental management accounting discipline? A bibliometric literature review. *Meditari Accountancy Research*, *21*(1), 4–31. doi:10.1108/MEDAR-12-2012-0039

Semenova, N., Hassel, L. G., & Nilsson, H. (2010). The Value Relevance of Environmental and Social Performance: Evidence from Swedish SIX 300 Companies. *Liiketaloudellinen Aikakauskirja, 3*.

Senge, P., Smith, B., Kruschwitz, N., Laur, J., & Schely, S. (2010). *The necessary revolution: How individuals and organizations are working together to create a sustainable world*. Doubleday.

Sinkin, C., Wright, C. J., & Burnett, R. D. (2008). Layoff announcements and stockholder wealth. *Journal of Accounting and Public Policy*, *27*(2), 167–176. doi:10.1016/j.jaccpubpol.2008.01.003

Sosik, J. J. (2015). *Leading with character: Stories of valor and virtue and the principles they teach* (2nd ed.). Information Age Publishing.

Sosik, J. J., & Cameron, J. C. (2010). Character and authentic transformational leadership behavior: Expanding the ascetic self towards others. *Consulting Psychology Journal*, *62*(4), 251–269. doi:10.1037/a0022104

Stacey, R. D. (2011). *Strategic management and organizational dynamics: The challenge of complexity*. FT Prentice-Hall.

Voser, P. (2012). *Sustainability Report 2012*. Retrieved from https://reports.shell.com/sustainability-report/2012/servicepages/welcome.html

Waddock, S. A., & Graves, S. B. (1997). The corporate social performance-financial performance link. *Strategic Management Journal*, *18*(4), 303–319. doi:10.1002/(SICI)1097-0266(199704)18:4<303::AID-SMJ869>3.0.CO;2-G

Wang, J., Qin, S., & Cui, Y. (2010). Problems and Prospects of CSR System Development in China. *International Journal of Business and Management*, *5*(12), 128–134. doi:10.5539/ijbm.v5n12p128

Wang, Y. J., Tsai, Y. H., & Lin, C. P. (2013). Modeling the relationship between perceived corporate citizenship and organizational commitment considering organizational trust as a moderator. *Business Ethics (Oxford, England)*, *22*(2), 218–233. doi:10.1111/beer.12019

Wood, D. J. (1991). Corporate social performance revisited. *Academy of Management Review*, *16*(4), 691–718. doi:10.5465/amr.1991.4279616

Yu, M., & Zhao, R. (2015). Sustainability and firm valuation: An international investigation. *International Journal of Accounting and Information Management*, *23*(3), 289–307. doi:10.1108/IJAIM-07-2014-0050

Zadek, S. (2001). The Civil Corporation: The new economy of corporate citizenship. *Earthscan, London, 2001*, 7.

Zahid, M., & Ghazali, Z. (2017). Corporate Sustainability Practices and Firm's Financial Performance: The Driving Force of Integrated Management System. *Global Business and Management Research*, 9.

Chapter 10
Corporate Governance Mechanisms on the Internal Relations Between Managers and Subordinates

Qudsia Aziz
Preston University, Pakistan

ABSTRACT

The concept of governance is as old as human civilization. However, recently the usage of this term has increased multifarious. A broader concept of corporate governance involves a set of relationships amongst the organization's stakeholders. A stakeholder is any person, organization, social group, or society at large that has a stake in the business. Recognizing the importance of corporate governance, most of the countries in the world have developed their own corporate governance mechanism known as corporate governance models. The mechanism of corporate governance depends upon various indigenous factors such as legal framework, regulatory framework, the pattern of shareholding, breadth, and depth of financial markets.

CONCEPT OF CORPORATE GOVERNANCE

The Organization for Economic Cooperation and Development defines corporate governance as (OECD 1999, cited in Clarke, 2010), the system by which business corporations are directed and controlled. The corporate governance structure specifies the distribution of rights and responsibilities among different participants in the corporation, as the board of directors, managers, shareholders, and other

DOI: 10.4018/978-1-7998-6669-5.ch010

Copyright © 2021, IGI Global. Copying or distributing in print or electronic forms without written permission of IGI Global is prohibited.

stakeholders, explaining the rules and procedures for corporate decision-making, and provides the structure and foundation of the establishment of objectives, the means to achieve and ways to monitor their implementation.

According to Freeman (1984), stakeholders are individuals or groups who can affect or be affected by the purposes and business success, however, several scholars have suggested that this definition is too broad because in the final analysis all social players are directly or indirectly affected by the actions of the company. What has given rise to different classifications of stakeholders, has suggested that they are primary and secondary, according to the degree of impact on the organization in terms of achieving its mission and objectives of the company (Clarkson, 1995). Others have suggested that the stakeholders are all parts that are positively or negatively affected by the operations of the company those involve risks and therefore gain or lose by the results of corporate activities (The Clarkson Centre for Business Ethics School Joseph Rotman Management, University of Toronto, 1999, in Principles of Stakeholder Management, 2002).

In literature, the concept of corporate governance has been an approach in various contexts. The UK's Cadbury Committee on corporate governance as "(It is) the system by which companies are directed and controlled." In 2004, the definition from Organization for Economic Cooperation and Development (OECD) gives us an insight into the philosophy of corporate governance. Corporate governance involves a set of relationships between a company's management, its board, its shareholders and other stakeholders. Corporate governance also provides the structure through which the objectives of the company are set, and the means of attaining those objectives and monitoring performance are determined (OECD, 2004).

The World Bank (1992) defined Governance as: "Governance is a method through which power is exercised in the management of a country's political, economic, and social resources for development." The Asian Development Bank, in 1995, is defined as Governance is the manner in which power is exercised in the management of a country's social and economic resources for development. UNDP defined it as Governance is the exercise of economic, political, and administrative authority to manage a country's affairs at all levels. It comprises the mechanisms, processes, and institutions through which citizens and groups articulate their interests, exercise their legal rights, meet their obligations and mediate their differences.

The comprehensive definition of Corporate Governance is presented by Sir Adrian Cadbury, which states as Corporate Governance is defined as holding the balance between economic and social goals and also between individual and communal goals. The governance framework is there to encourage the efficient use of resources and equally to require accountability for the stewardship of the resources. The aim is to align as nearly as possible the interest of individuals, corporations, and society.

The incentive for states is to strengthen their economies and discourage fraud and mismanagement.

A broader concept of corporate governance involves a set of relationships amongst the organization's stakeholders. A stakeholder is any person, organization, social group, or society at large that has a stake in the business. The stakeholders can be internal or external to the business. Stakeholders may affect a business, or that they may be affected by a business. A stake is a primary interest in the business or its activities. It can include ownership and property interests, legal interests and obligations, moral rights, and social implications. A legal obligation includes the duty to pay for wages or to honor contacts. A moral right may include the right of a consumer not to be intentionally harmed by business activities. Corporate governance is not restricted to these relationships but it holds may other dimensions to this subject. Rather, corporate governance provides you increased transparency into the structure, business operations, business ethics, and corporate social responsibility and across the board accountability.

Corporate Governance in Pakistan

The SEC, since it took over the responsibilities and powers of the Corporate Law Authority in 1999, has been acutely alive to the changes taking place in the international business environment, which directly: and indirectly impact local businesses. As part of its multidimensional strategy to enable Pakistan's corporate sector to meet the challenges raised by the changing global business scenario and to build capacity, the SEC has focused, in part, on encouraging businesses to adopt good corporate governance practices. This is expected to provide transparency and accountability in the corporate sector and to safeguard the interests of stakeholders, including the protection of minority shareholders' rights and strict audit compliance. Parties involved in corporate governance include the regulatory body (e.g., the Chief Executive Officer, the board of directors, management, and shareholders). Other stakeholders who take part include suppliers, employees, creditors, customers, and the community at large. In corporations, the shareholder delegates decision rights to the manager to act in the principal's best interests. This separation of ownership from control implies a loss of effective control by shareholders over managerial decisions. Partly as a result of this separation between the two parties, a system of corporate governance controls is implemented to assist in aligning the incentives of managers with those of shareholders. With the significant increase in equity holdings of investors, there has been an opportunity for a reversal of the separation of ownership and control problems because ownership is not so diffuse. Corporate governance in Pakistan has recently started scratching the surface. Due to many distortions in the economy, market forces do not reward good governances or punish unethical practices. The large part of the undocumented economy discourages the promotion of transparency and accountability in the organization. The overall management structure is also not conducive to establishing the norms of good governance. Many companies in the listed Stock Exchange are not fully practicing the code of good governance. Tightly held ownership, lack of professional skills, missing change agents, audit dependability and overall structural weaknesses are bottlenecks in developing corporate governance in organizations.

Characteristics of Good Governance

United Nation Economic and Social Commission explains that Good Governance has eight major distinguishable features. These are accountability, transparency, follow the rule of law, responsiveness, equitable and inclusive, participation, efficient and effective, and consensus-oriented.

1. Good Governance is accountable. Accountability is the key to governance. In corporate governance, shareholders elect directors to run the affairs of an organization. It has been witnessed that lack of accountability of directors has resulted in the failure of various big organizations like ENRON etc.
2. Good Governance believes in transparency. In corporate governance framework, transparency is being enforced through financial disclosure and audit requirements.
3. Following the rule of law is essential for good governance.
4. Good Governance is responsive. A timely and reasonable response is required and expected from an institution to all stakeholders. Such responsiveness is less available from public sector organizations in Pakistan.
5. Good Governance exhibits equity and inclusiveness.
6. Good Governance is participatory.
7. Good Governance is efficient and effective.
8. Governance process consists of various formal and informal economic agents, therefore, good Governance demands the mediation of various interest groups and therefore, it is believed that good governance is consensus-oriented.

OECD principles for Corporate Governance

The Organization for Economic Cooperation and Development (OECD) is one of the earliest organization to work on governance principles in the corporate sector. OECD in its report recognizes that good corporate governance is not an end in itself, rather, It is a means to create an integration in businesses across markets and thus confidence. This market trust is essential for companies that need access to equity capital for long term investment.

OECD presented the first version of governance principles in 1999 and later on, it was updated in 2004. The current review has been carried out under the auspices of the OECD Corporate Governance Committee in 2016. This review was benefited from experts from key international institutions, notably the Basel Committee, the FSB, and the World Bank Group have also participated actively in the review. Although the recent version maintains many of the governance recommendations from earlier versions, however, they also introduce some new issues and bring greater emphasis or additional clarity. One size does not fit all therefore some of the recommendations may not be more appropriate for all sizes of organizations. OECD Principles provide guidance about the following six elements:

- **Ensuring the Basis for an Effective Corporate Governance Framework:** OECD principles consider the role of corporate governance framework very critical factor in promoting transparent and fair markets, and the efficient allocation of resources. These focus on the quality and consistency the different elements of regulations that influence corporate governance practices and the division of responsibilities between authorities, along with the quality of supervision and enforcement.
- **The Rights and Equitable Treatment of Shareholders and Key Ownership Functions:** OECD principles give prime importance to the rights of a shareholder, their right to have information and active participation in strategic decisions. OECD also gives critical consideration to the disclosure of control structures through different voting rights, the participation of shareholders in the various meeting using information technology, the procedures for approval of related party transactions and shareholder participation in decisions on executive remuneration.
- **Institutional Investors, Stock Markets and Other Intermediaries:** This element addresses the need for sound economic incentives throughout the investment chain, with a particular focus on institutional investors acting in a fiduciary capacity. The importance of disclose and minimize conflicts of interest that may compromise the integrity of proxy advisors, analysts, brokers, rating agencies and others that provide analysis and advice that is relevant to investors is also emphasized in these principles. OECD provides new principles with respect to cross border listings and the importance of fair and effective price discovery in stock markets.
- **The Role of Stakeholders in Corporate Governance:** The OECD Principles encourage active cooperation between corporations and stakeholders and underline the importance of recognizing the rights of stakeholders established

by law or through mutual agreements. Timely access to information on a regular basis and shareholders right to obtain redress for violations of their rights are also emphasized.

- **Disclosure and Transparency:** Key areas to ensure transparency and accountability such as disclosure of financial and operating results, company objectives, the major share ownership, remuneration, related party transactions, risk factors, board members have critical importance in these principles.

Corporate Governance Systems

Recognizing the importance of corporate governance, most of the countries in the world have developed their own corporate governance mechanism known as corporate governance models. The mechanism of corporate governance depends upon various indigenous factors such as legal framework, regulatory framework, the pattern of shareholding, breadth and depth of financial markets, etc. Irrespective of dissimilarities of corporate governance in various counties, the majority of de facto and de jure factors affect the corporate sector in a reasonably analogous way. Taking advantage of such similarity, academia and policymaker have outline corporate governance models for various groups of countries. Two broad categories of corporate governance models are the outsider model and the insider model. Outsider model can be referred to as Shareholder oriented model. Such a mechanism generally exists in Anglo-Saxon counties like the USA, UK, etc. On the contrary, the Insider model also referred to as Stakeholder oriented model, can be further categorized into three sub-models known as the German model, Japanese model and Family/State-based model.

Outsider Model

Outsider model is also known as Shareholder model or Anglo-Saxon model is based on the unitary board model approach where all directors contribute to the decision-making process while in a single board. The idea behind this model is that shareholders are the rightful owner of the company and therefore the ultimate objective of the corporation should be the maximization of their (i.e. Shareholders') wealth. In this model, the idea of Principal-Agent a relationship exists, being shareholders as Principal whereas directors perform their services as Agents of the shareholders. One distinguishing characteristic of this model is investors, in highly dispersed ownership pattern, who are not affiliated with the corporation. The day-to-day operations of the corporation are run by professional and the board generally does not interfere in management. This situation depicts the separation of ownership and control.

This model operates under a well-developed legal framework wherein the duties and responsibilities of key players, i.e. shareholder, directors and executives have been properly defined in relatively less complicated environment.

The Anglo American Model

Such corporate model generally can be seen in the United States, United Kingdom, Canada, Australia, New Zealand, etc. The corporate structure of certain Asian counties, being part of the colonial regime, essentially resembles with the Anglo-Saxon model.

Insider Model

The insider model is also known as the Stakeholder model. The fundamental rationale behind this model lies in the belief that the corporation must ensure the benefits

Figure 1.

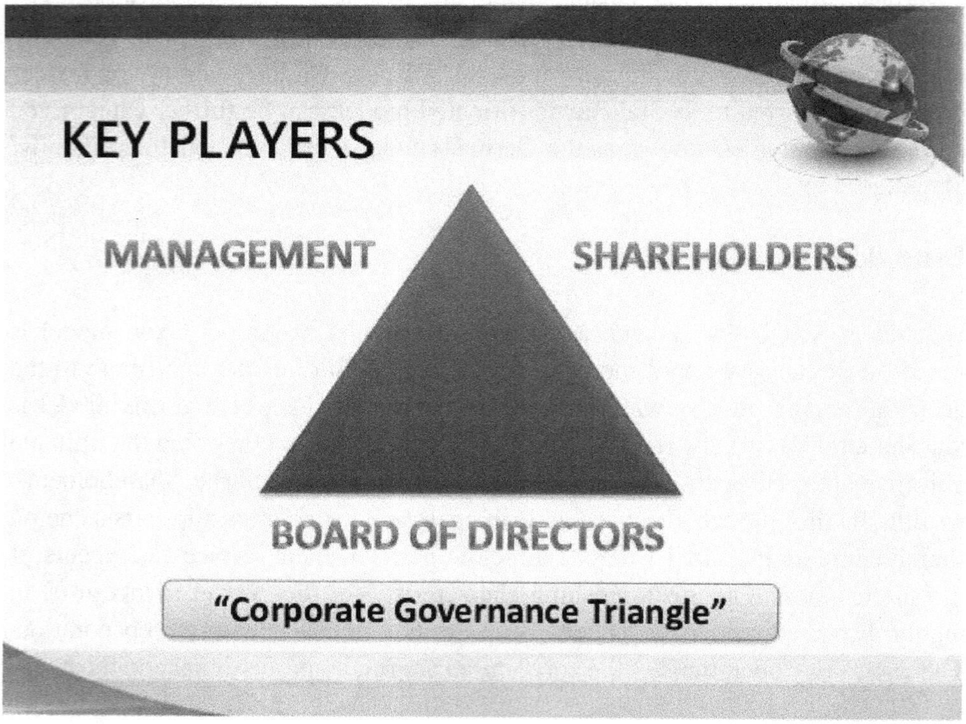

Figure 2.

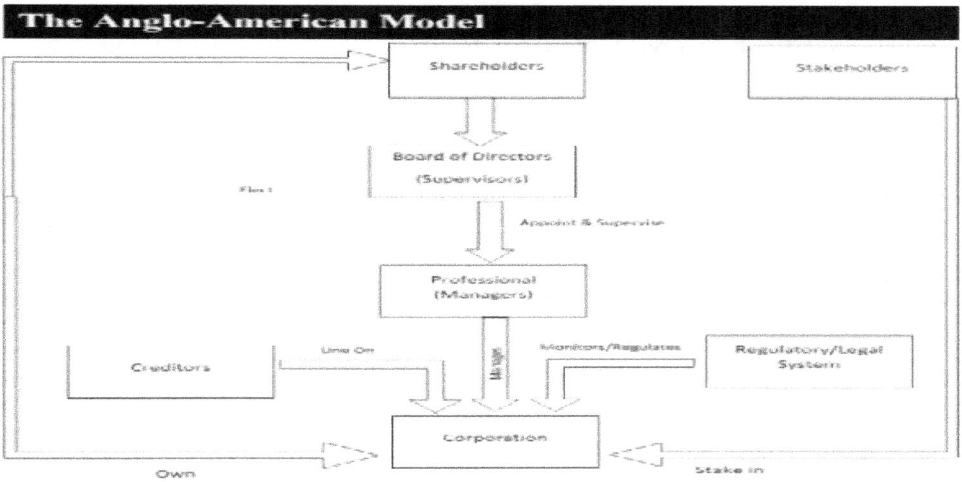

accrue to other stakeholders as well in addition to shareholders. This approach considers that stakeholders (i.e. creditors, employees, unions etc.) participate in the production process and corporations are socially responsible towards them. This model can be further categorized into three types:

- German Model
- Family/State-based Model
- Japanese Model.

The distinguishing characteristic of such model include less-dispersed ownership structure, relatively less strong capital markets, interlocking structure and directorship, less disclosure in financial reporting, high leverage firms.

The term insiders, here, include family interest, institutional interest, banking interest, and holding companies' interest. Contrary to the Anglo-Saxon model, insider plays a dominant role in the governance of the firm in this arrangement, and agency cost is significantly reduced. Controlling shareholders (i.e. family, the state, or institutions, etc.) manage the corporations, thus the agency cost under such a model is almost irrelevant. However, the conflict of interest between controlling interest holders and minority shareholder, i.e. expropriation problem, is very much relevant in this corporate arrangement.

German Model

German model is based on the two-tier board model. In this model, banks hold long-term stakes and their representatives are elected to sit in boards. Large German banks, both private and public sector, play a major role in being key shareholder incorporation and their existence in the board is the reason for relatively fewer agency problems. The German corporate governance exhibits certain significant dissimilarities from, both, the Anglo US and the Japanese model. This model is prevalent in Germany and Austria. Due to its unique characteristics, some corporations in the Netherlands, Scandinavia, France and Belgium is also incorporating some elements of this model. In the German model, two-tier board mechanisms consist of the Supervisory Board and Management Board. Supervisory Board consists of shareholders representatives, union representatives, and the bank obviously. Management Board consists of executives of the organization, i.e. insiders only. Compulsory presence of employees; representative on supervisory board in German firms is one of the most differentiating characteristics of this model in comparison with Anglo-Saxon and the Japanese model. An important characteristic of this two-tier mechanism is that no one is allowed to serve on both boards simultaneously. Another distinguishing fact is that size of the board is fixed according to the law of the land and cannot be changed by shareholders. Voting right restrictions, irrespective of the percentage of shareholding are also part of the legal framework.

These restrictions limit a shareholder to voting a certain percentage of the corporation's total share capital.

Family/State-Based Model

Family-based or State-based model can be mainly observed in East Asian economies and in some emerging economies including Pakistan. The family business is defined as a form of enterprise in which both management and ownership are controlled by a family kinship group, either nuclear or extended and the fruits that remain inside that group, being distributed in some way among its members. Adam Smith, in his book Wealth of Nation implicitly stresses the importance of family business in the following words. Being the managers of other people's money than of their own, it cannot well be expected that [the managers of widely held corporations] should watch over [public investors' wealth] with the same anxious vigilance with which partners in a private copartnery frequently watch over their own. Like the stewards of a rich man, they consider attention to small matters as not for their master's honor and very easily give themselves a dispensation from having it. Negligence and profusion, therefore, must prevail more or less in the management of such a company." Family or State-based models exhibit the following characteristics:

Figure 3.

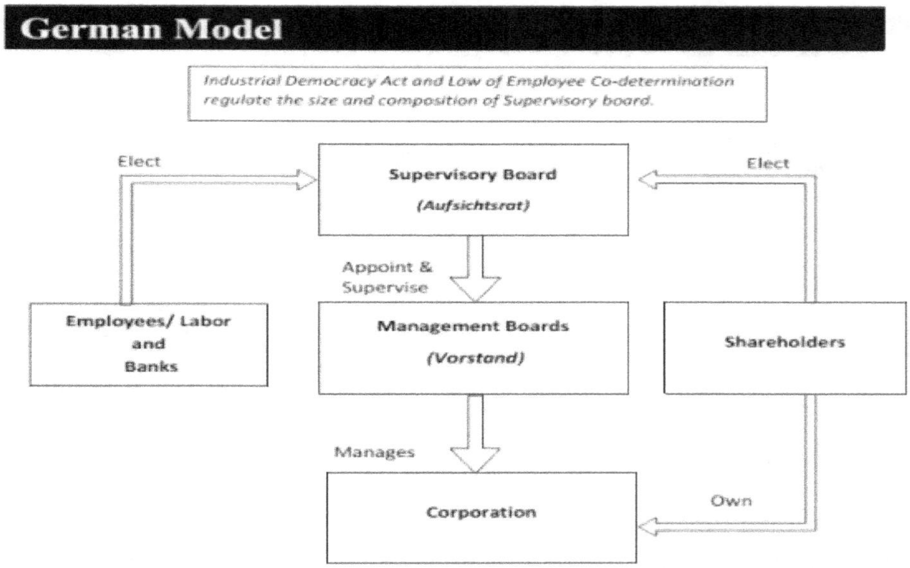

- · Ownership concentrations
- · Prominent shareholding within families
- · Pyramid structure or cross-holdings in various corporations
- · Institutions based on relationship
- · Lack of transparency, less financial reporting disclosure

Conflict of interest within controlling shareholder and minority shareholder Irrespective of certain problems, this model of corporate governance bears certain advantages as well. Some of the advantages include stable ownership, less agency cost, long term commitment of shareholders, etc.

Japanese Model

The Japanese model is characterized by a high level of stock ownership by affiliated banks and companies. The Japanese character of corporate Governance is many-sided centering around the main bank and a financial/ industrial network. The bank provides its corporate clients' with the loan as well as services related to bound issues, equity issues settlement accounts, and related consulting services. The main bank is generally is a major shareholder in the corporation.

Many Japanese corporations also have a strong financial relationship with a network of affiliated companies.

Figure 4.

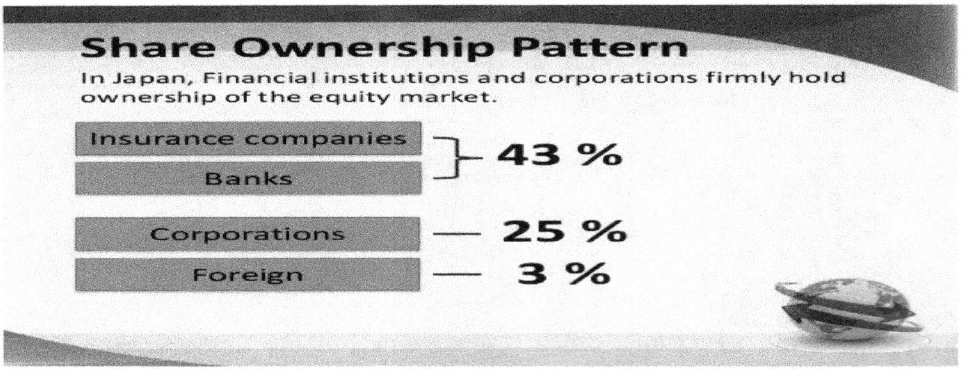

REFERENCES

Clarke, T. (2010). Recurring crises in Anglo-American Corporate Governance. *Contributions to Political Economy*, *29*(1), 9–32. doi:10.1093/cpe/bzq002

Clarkson, M. B. E. (1995). A Stakeholder Framework for Analyzing and Evaluating Corporate Social Performance. *Academy of Management Journal*, *20*(1), 92–118.

Freeman, R. E. (1984). *Strategic Management: A stakeholder Approach*. Pitman.

OECD. (2004). *OECD principles of corporate governance*. OECD.

Chapter 11
Theoretical Disclosure of Board Independence:
Evidence From Pakistan

Aarooj Kiran
International Islamic University, Islamabad, Pakistan

Ayesha Ibrahim
University of Sargodha, Pakistan

ABSTRACT

In the wake of corporate scandals in major companies like Enron, Tyco, and East Asian crisis have emphasized the need of sufficient number of independent directors on the board for proper oversight and functioning of the company. Code of corporate governance recommends the presence of independent directors for better performance of the company. As board independence ensured good corporate governance practices, it is considered that having independent directors on the board is not for better performance but for better governance. In seeking reasonable answer for these arguments, the purpose of this study is to review some of the literature of board independence with respect to corporate governance theories specifically agency theory, stewardship, and resource dependency theory. All these theories have provided mixed evidences in different studies about the impact and importance of board independence and reason behind these mixed evidences might be the institutional context of different organizations in different countries.

DOI: 10.4018/978-1-7998-6669-5.ch011

Copyright © 2021, IGI Global. Copying or distributing in print or electronic forms without written permission of IGI Global is prohibited.

INTRODUCTION / BACKGROUND OF THE STUDY

In recent years, world governance practices have changed significantly. Revisions in corporate governance codes and shareholders engagement practices in the organization all have contributed to the new standards of governance for developed and developing economies. Change in the standards remains robust, because market is continuously reassessing the guidelines to further improve the governance code of conduct (Aifuwa & Embele, 2019). Corporate scandals of major companies like Enron, WorldCom and Tyco, along with that East Asian crisis gave rise to the concern about monitoring and effectiveness of the board. These scandals emphasized that independent board members are vital for the organization and shareholders interest. They should be enough in numbers to oversee management of the company (Mishra, 2018).

Muneer and Allam (2017) explained the concept of board of directors in the firm. According to their study, board of directors includes the CEO, non-CEO, affiliated outside directors and non-affiliated outside directors. CEO is the person who often serves as a chairman of the board, non-CEO is considered as officers of the company. Affiliated directors defined as the directors who are former employees of the company, relatives of the employees of the firm or who have any kind of business relationship with the company, and nonaffiliated outside directors are the individuals having no past or present relationship with the firm.

The board of directors is a collective body that should act in the best interest of their company shareholders. Board is a combination of executive and non-executive directors to pursue the shareholders' interest. The non-executive directors are not the full-time employees of the company as compared to executive directors who are full-time employees and are involved in day to day activities of the company. Role of non-executive directors is to pursue monitoring mechanism of performance and activities of management or executive directors. The non-executive directors on the board prime duty is to provide unbiased judgments, and that is only possible when independent board is vital to exercise their duties. The code of corporate governance and regulators suggests that mere compliance with recommendations is not enough, it is essential that composition of board members should be balanced and independent to perform effectively. In general, the representation and independence of non-executive directors is vital for the board's effectiveness (Fuzia, Halim, & M.K, 2016).

The phrase board characteristics comprises of two concepts in it. Former is the board (usually known as board of directors) is vested with the duty to hire managers and administrating the activities of these managers as well as overall organization. The latter typically means the quality of something or someone. From this concept board characteristics can be explained as internal corporate governance mechanism which expounds on the features of the board (Akeju & Babatunde., 2017). Characteristics of the board are their size, diversity (age, gender, nationality, expertise, educational background, institutional and functional experience), independence, and diligence. Among all these characteristics board independence is considered important for board efficiency and effectiveness (Aifuwa & Embele., 2019).

Monitoring and overseeing of overall performance and functioning of the organization are the basic administrative activities of the board. According to Vafeas (2000), board is responsible for effective monitoring of financial reports and to protect the shareholders interest. As managers have their own interest and incentives to manipulate earnings and this action potentially mislead stockholders. Akeju and Babatunde (2017) opined that board independence as a vital characteristic of board that improves the internal corporate governance mechanism in the firm. Supporting this view D'onza and Lamboglia (2014) emphasized that among all characteristic board independence is unique one to detect any fraud. It is the best suitable monitoring mechanism for organization financial statements.

The major contribution of the board is formulating company's strategy and exercise proper oversight function throughout the company operations (Zinkin, 2010). Independent directors contribute their independent views and actively participate in board discussion. The company appoints independent directors to monitor the performance of executive directors and top managements. As independence person, they must ensure that their presence and performance is free from any kind of influence of insider management. Zinkin (2010) also stated that as non-executive directors represent shareholders on the company's board so, several areas like expertise, industry background should be addressed by independent directors that would contribute to the effective formulation of the company strategy.

Berghe and baelden (2005) studied the construct of board independence and declared from their results that board independence is an important factor in ensuring board effectiveness. Through monitoring and strategizing roles, it can enhance company performance. Foo and Zain (2010) examined the association between disclosure of information and independent board and suggested significant association between these constructs. It means when board is independent more transparency in disclosure is expected which later results in good governance practices. In this context researchers further elaborated that board independence is not just for good performance rather it brings good governance in the firm. They represent shareholders in the firm and understands their responsibility of transparency and thus they strictly monitor all the self-serving activities of management. Therefore, independent directors would not have any chance to do any wrongdoings for their own interest.

The board's ability to monitor management independently has attracted much attention in the research related to corporate governance because of the high-profile corporate collapses in early 2000s, such as the collapse of Enron, WorldCom, and HIH insurance. It is alleged that one cause of these collapses was insufficient monitoring, as the management of these firms had a strong grip on board members leaving the board unable to provide independent advice (Susanto, Pradipta, &, Djashan, 2017). While discussing the board attributes specifically independence, corporate governance theories have received a great deal of attention from investigators. Theoretical paradigms that dominated corporate governance research and importance of board of directors are named as agency theory most common in all (Jensen and Meckling, 1976; Fama and Jensen, 1983; Eisenhardt, 1989a), stewardship theory (Donaldson, 1990; Donaldson and Davis, 1991; 1994) and resource dependence theory (Pfeffer, 1972; 1973; Pfeffer and Salancik, 1978).

Agency theory explained the inherent imperfections in the relationship between capital provider (principals) and fiduciaries (agents) of that capital. It argues that corporate ownership is separated from corporate management. Behaviors, actions and decisions of the managers or inside directors deviate from those required to maximize shareholder value. This divergence creates agency conflict between manager and shareholders. This theory was originated in the 1970s by Michael Jensen, William Meckling, Harold Demsetz and others while propagation in the theory can be seen much earlier during 1932 in the work of Berle and Means. Agency theory remained as a prominent anchor to elaborate the corporate governance practices in the organization (Aguilera, Filatotchev, Gospel, & Jackson, 2008).

The idea of board independence mainly arises from the traditional setting of the agency problem, in the Anglo-American context where there is a distribution of ownership and where managers acts as agents of shareholders, having objective to maximize their shareholders wealth. Independent directors are the person entrusted by shareholders to represent them and help them to reduce agency problem. Agency theorist argued that managers unless restriction to do so, undertake self-serving activities that may be detrimental to economic welfare of the principal (Susanto et al., 2017). The existence of this conflict of interest between principal and agent deviate managers from their objective to maximize shareholders value first.

Several control mechanisms are recommended as part of check and balance to reduce the conflict between the managers and shareholders which can be helpful to achieve the objective of the firm in a cost-effective way. These include external control mechanism such as takeovers and internal control mechanisms as the presence of large shareholders, contracting and independent monitoring board. Among all these mechanisms independent corporate board is the primary and dominant internal corporate mechanism to monitor the management to promote shareholders interest (Rashid, 2014).

In contrast to agency theory, stewardship theory of corporate governance has its roots in psychology and sociology. It was adapted as a theoretical framework for researchers to investigate the decision making, actions, and performance of the executives who are acting as a faithful steward. This theory hypothesized that managers or inside directors are trustworthy individuals and they are good stewards of the resources entrusted to them. As they spend their working lives in the organization the govern, they understand the business better than the outside directors so they can make better decisions to protect shareholders interest (Donaldson, 1990; Donaldson and Davis, 1991; 1994).

Proponents of stewardship theory argues that board attributes and effectiveness that are linked to the better corporate performance is basically relevant to the inside directors rather than outside directors as they naturally work to maximize profits for shareholders. Based on stewardship theorists view, research scholars have investigated that outside directors are not able to make proper decisions for firm even if they are independent to do so. This is because of the reason that outside directors do not have the same access to informal knowledge sources within the firm as inside directors have (Rashid, 2014). Alternatively, opponents of this view suggest that, if there are few inside directors on the board, the board would not be able to fully understand the company and their lack of knowledge can affect decision making process.

Another theory of corporate governance is that of Resource dependence theory, which can explain the concept and importance of the board in an organization under its arguments. This theory has maintained that board attributes have crucial link between the firm and the essential resources that it needs to maximize its performance (Pfeffer, 1973; Pfeffer & Salancik, 1978). This theory has its roots in sociology and management disciplines. There is no universal definition that what actually an important resource is for an organization.

Sociologists concentrated on different type links of resources that an independent board can provide to its organization such as the access that a board provides to a nation's business elite (Useem, 1984), access to capital (Stearns and Mizruchi, 1993) or links to competitors (Mizruchi, 1996). Management scholars tended to take a more generic approach of the theory, Scholars such as palmer and barber (2001) view the board as an important resource for the firm, especially in its link with the external environment. The value of resource is considered as contextual, depending on the urgency of need. Several resources that have been studied because of their perceived value to the firm are information, finance or capital and links to customers and other stakeholders. The ability of the board to access internal information and link its significant resources to that information is seen as one of the key roles for proper decision making and management of organization (Nicholson, Gavin, & Geoffrey, 2007).

As theories of corporate governance have suggested different views for the board and its attributes and considered board effectiveness mandatory for firm functioning and performance. Among all other attributes board independence is considered vital for this study. Thus, the objective of the study is to explore the construct of board attributes specifically board independence under the light of corporate governance theories mainly with respect to agency theory, stewardship theory and resource dependency theory. In order to review the literature of the board independence which has been studied across the world this study is intended to shed light on the theoretical disclosure of the construct. To enhance the understanding of the concept, study will explore the understanding of board independence and its role in the organization and it will further elaborate whether board independence ensured good corporate governance practices or not.

LITERATURE REVIEW: THEORETICAL DISCOURSE

This section will provide insights of board independence impact on different financial variables with respect to corporate governance theories. Firstly, it will provide literature about board independence as a construct and then it will further reveal its impact with respect to agency theory first and then stewardship, resource dependency theory later.

Board Independence as a Construct

The construct of board independence is generally explained as the ability of independent board members to make decisions independently from the firm insider management. As inside managers and other non-independent board members sometimes (referred as affiliated or grey members) responsibilities are tied with the board where they sit. These managers receive substantial monetary benefits for non-director related activities provided to firm on whose board they sit. In this situation outside independent board members are considered more trustworthy even they have limited role with the organization (Yunos, 2011).

Berghe and Baelden (2005) supported the concept of board independence and declared it as important factor for enhancing corporate performance and board effectiveness through the monitoring and strategic roles of the directors. According to the authors, ultimate factor for board independence is by acquiring maximum number of independent directors. Their skills, abilities, willingness and board environment might lead them to pursue independent attitude of each director. Kakabadse, Yang and Sanders (2010) narrated that effectiveness of non-executive directors is determined by their formal independency, competency, incentives provided and information accessibility.

Board independence refers to the participation of outside directors independently. The more the board is independent, more effective it will be in monitoring the management behavior (Afify, 2009). Non-executive directors on the board will not be able to effectively exercise their duties, unless they are independent from management. Independent directors who are free from any kind of influence provides unbiased judgments and make proper and effective decisions. In board discussion independent directors with relevant industry background and wide expertise would be more able to challenge chief executive officers (CEOs) and management team. If these directors only exist and do not perform the expected roles as required by the firm, then their functioning will be ineffective. However, mere compliance with the recommendation is not necessary for these directors they also need to deliver their best in order to functions effectively (Fuzia et al., 2016).

Board independence confirmed good corporate governance practices in the firm. Foo and Zain (2010) investigated that board independence ensured liquidity in the firm. According to their analysis there is a positive association between independent board members and disclosure of information. It means that when board is independent there would be more transparency in the information which later improves the firm's liquidity.

The company appoints independent directors to monitor the performance of firm's top management. Their prime responsibility is to formulate company strategy and exercise proper oversight function throughout the company operations. Independent directors contribute their independent views and actively participate in board discussion. As Independent directors or board members represent shareholders in the company, therefore they pursue the interest of shareholders by maximizing shareholders value (Zinkin, 2010).

Agency Theory: Board Independence

While discussing corporate governance theories board independence has received great deal of attention from investigators. In order to explain the phenomenon of board independence agency theory has got much attention from the researchers. Agency theory explains a conflict of interest between the managers and shareholders of the firm. According to this theory, agency conflict arises between managers and shareholders, because managers actions and behaviors deviate from those required to protect and enhance shareholders interest. In this situation, Independent directors are the person entrusted by shareholders to represent them and will help to reduce agency problems (Akeju & Babatunde, 2017). Different studies have found that agency theory can assist to find out the appropriate impact of board independence.

In line with this, agency theory can help to understand the impact of board independence on firm performance. One study in India showed that effective monitoring mechanism by independent directors in the firm reduced agency problem and enhanced firm performance (Fuzia et al., 2016). Wallison (2006) under this view argued that independent directors on the board are not just for better performance but for better governance. They represent shareholders in the company and monitor the activities of management and executive directors to enhance company performance. Therefore, executive directors would not have any chance for wrongdoings under this monitoring mechanism. This action reduces the agency conflict and improves the firm performance.

Most of the studies conducted in emerging markets found that these markets do not have enough laws and legislation to protect investors interest and governing financial markets. Despite the absence of institutions these markets showed positive effect of board independence on firm performance. A strong relationship was found between board independence and firms' performance in those countries which have no laws and regulation to protect their shareholders and stakeholders' interest. Independent board serve as a shield for shareholders and hinder all the self-serving activities of the manager and mitigate the risk of agency conflict (Mubarak & Hamdan, 2017). This is apparent as Liu et al, (2015) also found positive impact of board independence on firm performance in sixteen thousand firms listed in "Shanghai" stock exchange. They stated that board independence acts as a substitute for laws and regulations and serve the owners right appropriately thus efficiently contribute in the improvement of their performance level.

Garg (2007) identified another perspective of board independence in association with firm performance, stated that board independence did not guarantee firm performance due to poor monitoring roles of independent directors. If independent board members monitoring mechanism is not effective, they cannot reduce agency problem and thus performance of the firm will remain poor. Supporting this view Hermalin and Weisbach (1991) also found that there is no relation between firm performance and the proportion of independent outside directors.

Academics have examined the relationship of board independence and other corporate activities thought to impact shareholder wealth positively (Nicholson, 2007). But a negative relation was found in few studies. Researches which analyzed the relationship between board independence and various activities such as corporate diversification (Baysinger and Hoskisson, 1990), CEO compensation (Fosberg, 1999), the use of long-term incentive plans (Zajac and Westphal, 1994), the adoption of takeover defenses such as poison pills (Coles and Hesterly, 2000) all have produced negative findings, or been unable to identify any correlation at all. Long line researches have provided little consensus that board independence has positive impact on shareholder wealth through different corporate activities

As independent directors represent shareholders in the firm and protect their interest, few researchers contradict from this view argued that independent directors did not enhance shareholders return when their relationship is investigated with earning management in the firm (Johari, Saleh, Jaafar & Hassan, 2008). Earning information is used as a basis to measure firm success or failure in achieving operational goals. This will encourage management to manipulate earning information to make financial statements look good. These actions are basically called earning management. Earning management is the activity of manipulating reported earnings (Goel & Thakor, 2003).

Abdul Rahman and Mohamed Ali (2006) also supported this view from Malaysia and concluded that companies had insignificant relationship between corporate governance mechanisms such as the independence of the board with the earnings management. Susanto and Pradipta, (2016), Nabila and Daljono (2013) and Adıgüzel (2013) also found a negative and significant effect of board independence on earnings management. This showed that board independence is not associated with the earning management even though the proportion of them is one third of the total majority. This means that even though the company had many independent board members it would not increase the shareholders return through controlling earning management. Thus, separation of ownership and control will remain in conflict.

Another study reveals that board independence is effective to resolve agency problems due to its effectiveness in monitoring management (Johnson, Daily, & Ellstrang, 1996). In line with this view, Previous studies have proposed that board independence has positive and significant impact on the timeliness of financial reporting. Afify (2009) suggested positive and significant relationship between independence of the board member and audit report lag. The study implies that monitoring role of the independent board members have positive influence on of timeliness financial reporting. through more effective and efficient audit independent board members can reduce audit report lag and resolve agency conflict.

Abdelsalam and El-Masry (2008) also supported this argument and claimed that independence of directors is positively associated with the timeliness of financial internal reports. The reason behind this positive relationship is that outsider directors usually did not take any advantage from delayed or selective disclosures. Moreover, it was identified that high percentage of independent directors employ expert auditors than less percentage of them. This indicates a positive association between high quality auditors and board independence. Therefore, a more timely financial reporting can be easily achieved (Beasley & Petroni, 2001). In contrast, Wu et al. (2008) believed that existence of independent members in the organization results in longer financial reports lag as they are not the employees working on daily basis in the organization thus, they take more time to monitor and verify firms' events.

Another research stream provided opinion that how board independence can help shareholders to save their interest from managers. For this purpose, board independence is analyzed with the voluntary disclosure of information (Al Maskati & Hamdan, 2017). Board independence has found positive impact when voluntary disclosure of firm exists, it increases transparency of information, and reduces asymmetry of data provided to investors. Ferris et al. (2003) reported that independent directors provide firsthand and rare knowledge and valuable experience which is hard to get from somewhere else. This is true because of their unique experiences that they bring from their mothers' firms and thus they become important advisor for shareholders (Balsmeier et al., 2014).

Among many other reform's agenda, board independence remained a particular interest for the proponents of the agency theory. board willingness and ability to monitor the firm responsibly is a concerned view that has set forth its importance in agency theory (Dalton & Dalton, 2011). the basic argument of agency theory is to protect shareholders interest thus supporting the notion about its importance in theory Brickley and Zimmerman (2010) suggested that Independent board members without any influence can monitor and advised managers to protect shareholders interest.

Hermalin and Weisbach (2003) see the board independence as a market solution that helps mitigate the agency problems that mostly occurs in the organizations. According to Jenfa (2000), independent board members are responsible for a company's internal control systems and operations of the company. They provide high level of advice at the time of risk. Vafeas (2000) also see independent boards as mainly responsible directors for monitoring the quality of information contained in financial reports because managers often have their own interest and incentives with regard to managing earnings and potentially misleading stockholders. Thus, presence of independent directors is vital for an organization.

Stewardship Theory: Board Independence

In contrast to agency theory, another corporate governance theory named as stewardship theory hypothesized that managers are trustworthy individuals in the firm, and they are good stewards of the resources entrusted to them (Donaldson & Davis, 1991). According to the proponents of this theory, inside directors spend their working lives in the organization they govern, they can better understand the need of the business and thus can make better decisions then outside directors (Donaldson & Davis, 1994). As a result, advocates of the theory further stated that superior corporate performance and shareholders interest is not linked to the outside directors rather they suggested that it is linked to the inside directors as they naturally work in the organization to maximize the shareholders interest.

Stewardship theory plays an important role to understand the concept of independent board and their role in the organization. While discussing the impact of board independence on firm performance this theory argues that outside independent board members are not much capable to enhance firm performance. If agency cost is a significant concern for an organization and monitoring is necessary, then proponents proposed that outside or independent directors will lack the proper knowledge, time and resources to monitor management effectively (Fuzia et al.,

2016). This argument is comparable to another study, stated that overemphasis on monitoring is unnecessary for the independent board members to impact corporate performance (Donaldson & Preston, 1995).

In line with this, several other studies explored the concept of board independence in different ways. According to Mubarak and Hamdan (2017) independent board members are less effective for organization financial matters and thus negatively impact the company performance. According to their study board independence negatively affect the firm performance when it is measured using two accounting-based measures: Return on Asset (ROA), and Return on equity (ROE). Based on these inverse results, it was found that internal directors are more effective in enhancing the management and functioning of the organization, as information asymmetry and lack of company specific information leads to the inefficiency of independent directors.

Keeping the view of stewardship theory, another study reveals that organization having large number of independent board members bears excessive management cost related to these members. Their decisions are not effective when they are in majority. While inside directors having no extra management cost at all because they are already employed in the organization. So, this study recommended that non-executive directors on the board should be reduced to reduce excessive management cost (Fahlenbrach et al., 2010).

The code of corporate governance recommended a unique structure of board where outside directors which are mostly referred as non-executive directors (NEDs) are expected to bring independent scrutiny which is free from any kind of influence. This expectation separates the decision management from decision control.But a key argument eradicates this fact is that these directors are selected by the same management and this practice jeopardize the quality of board independence. Because of this practice effectiveness of board towards quality of financial reporting is negatively impacted (shankaraiaha & Amirib, 2017). This point is further supported by another study asserting that the board independence has insignificant relationship with quality of financial reporting. Notwithstanding, very little can be said about the effectiveness of an independent board towards effective financial reporting as the theoretical surmise is far from being displayed practically. Thus, inside board members are more effective than independent board members in the organization (Daoud, Ismail, & lode, 2014).

CEO duality and board independence are inevitably intertwined. Stewardship theorist who prefer CEO duality are in favor of greater inside directors' representation in the board. conversely, proponents of agency theory who oppose CEO duality vehemently prefer that board seats should be occupied by highest percentage of independent members (Yusoff & Alhaji, 2012). Van, Miesing and Kang (2009) found that when board has maximum numbers of insider as a controller, they are more prone to pursue anti hostile takeover moves in order to protect firms from corporate invaders. Donaldson and Davis (1991) found that strong insider representation is associated with significantly higher firm performance, particularly when the board was chaired by the firm's chief executive officer. Similarly, Arthurs, Hoskisson, Busenitz, and Johnson (2008) found that inside directors on board positively effect IPO pricing. Stewardship by its nature infers that insider board members are more motivated then outsiders' independent members thus long-term success of an organization is relevant to the inside management (Davis, Schoorman, & Donaldson, 1997).

Muth and Donaldson (1998) further reinforced this idea with their findings and stated that internal directors are positively related to shareholder wealth and corporate revenue growth. Conversely, agency theorist supported the view that independent board members are the main protector of the shareholders interest, stating that independent directors are the person who can better advocate the shareholders interest because they are independent from management control (Carter, Simkins, & Simpson, 2003). For instance, Mayers, Shivdasani, and Smith, (1997) verified this view in their study and declared that presence of independent outside directors is accompanied with lower operating costs for corporation. This point is further in line with the study of Perry and Shivdasani, (2005) stating that board independence represents significant improvement in operating performance and exert stronger financial performance (Pearce and Zahra, 1991).

Keeping this view Wright, Kroll, and Elenkov (2002) suggested that outside independent board directors are associated with stronger controls over CEO compensation packages. Westphal and Khanna (2003) found that independent directors are more likely to disapprove poison pill clauses than inside directors. They also determined that outside directors are more likely to vote to separate the position of CEO than inside directors. Value-oriented risk taking is an important function of a business and there is indication to suggest that independent board members are seamlessly associated with overall enhancing strategies (Wright, Kroll, Lado, & Van Ness, 2002).

Based on stewardship theory, several studies have opposed the presence of independent board members and disclosed the importance of inside board members presence for rational decision making in the organization. Baysinger and Hoskisson, (1990) found a positive relationship between the ratio of internal managers and the availability of the information in the rationalization of decision making. Managers in the firm are more familiar with the conditions than others and therefore they can make best suitable decisions for organization thus, there is no need to hire external independent members for decision making. Even some studies have questioned the independence of members from outside the firm as internal managers might have an influence on the selection of independent board members that share special interests with them (Coles et al., 2010).

Moreover, multiple appointments of independent outside executives engage them a lot that they could not find time to serve each firm. These busy directors are then unable to serve shareholders interest appropriately. This leads to reluctance of investors to invest in those firm (Fich and Shivdasani, 2006). Some other researchers also provided evidence for this argument and exhibited that independent directors work best for the interest of parent firm in which they belong to and not for the interest of hosting firm. These directors choose to work in firms that increase their own benefits, regardless of the value of the hosting firm. That's why it is suggested that firm should rely more on inside directors (Fahlenbrach et al, 2010).

Resource Dependency Theory: Board Independence

Several other studies explained the construct of board independence in accordance with third major corporate governance theory named as "Resource dependency theory" by Jeffrey Pfeffer and Gerald R. Salancik (1978) that says, resources required by the organizations need to be acquired through a network of contacts and efficiency and effectiveness in bridging these networks will determine the quality of corporate performance. This theory describes that access to essential and scarce resources increase the ability for organizational success (Ulrich & Barney, 1984). Theorists of this theory suggest that corporate boards can help organization in gaining access to these resources otherwise it is beyond their reach (Brown, 2005).

Corporate boards are considered imperative boundary spanners that secure necessary resources, such as capital, knowledge, and venture partnering arrangements (Ruigork, Peck, & Tacheva, 2007). Board characteristics or features like diversity, size, independence and diligence has found to be an important element in this theory to improve financial performance (Waddock & Graves, 1997). According to Abdullah and Valentine, (2009) this theory is centered on the roles of the board that they provide to access the resources for the organization. As a resource provider their characteristics specifically independence and diligence should be considered vital for organization success.

Different Researchers explored the feature of board as independent member and suggested that board independence is positively related to the firm performance and enhance quality of financial reporting. According to them, independent board members are more concerned about stakeholders' interest and they give their best to access all the needed resources for organization and protect all the stakeholders interest without any influence. This activity of members increases the performance of the firm and enhance quality of financial reporting (Ezelibe et al., 2017). In line with this view another study also indicated that an independent board have positive impact on the performance of the business due to their stronger grip on inside and outside environment and organization need as well as help to reduce earnings management (Ilaboya & Lodikero, 2017) and consequently increase the quality of financial reports (Akeju & Babatunde, 2017).

Flowing from extant literature, Klein (2002) does not support this view and hold a stance that independent board members are relevant to different organization they cannot understand the need of the hosting firm thus board independence has a negative relation with financial reporting quality. This study stated that board independence is not statistically and significantly related to quality of financial reporting and overall performance of the firm. Result of this study partially supported Pfeiffer's and Salancik's Resource dependency theory. This finding is consistent with the works of Ahmed et al. (2006), Alkdai and Hanefah (2012), Chalaki et al. (2012) and Goi (2014), however inconsistent with the findings of (Akeju & Babatunde, 2017; Alves, 2014; D'onza & Lamboglia, 2014; Firth, et al., 2007; Holtz & Nieto, 2014; Klai & Omori, 2011; Kantudu & Somalia, 2015; Lara, et al., 2009; Marra et al., 2009; Nesrine & Abdelwahid, 2011).

Sample of studies suggested that resource dependency theorists have not weighed heavily on the issue of board independence, they are likely to agree with agency theorists since a larger number of independent outside board members in the board may increase the access to valuable resources like knowledge, capital, and venture partnering arrangements and they can better protect the interest of shareholders in an organization(Aifuwa & Embele, 2019).

DISCUSSION

In seeking a reasonable answer to the question of whether board independence is important for the organization or adds value to the firm, researchers have extensively depended on number of corporate governance theories, in which most common are agency theory, stewardship theory and resource dependence theory. These theories have undoubtedly assisted to understand the role of independent directors that they may play in contributing firm performance and their impact on different elements in the organization. Different studies have provided different insights of board independence with respect to different theories of corporate governance mentioned above.

The main premise of stewardship theory is that executive inside managers are best stewards of their firm, thus there is no need of outside independent directors monitoring. Pursuant to this theory, it is argued that inside directors spend their working lives in the company they govern, they better understand the businesses than outside or independent directors, they have more knowledge and information which allow them to evaluate the need for the organization, outsiders rely more on insiders to make decisions including access to the information necessary to achieve their monitoring role So, inside directors can make superior decisions than outside independent directors . This theory further suggests that board independence in isolation is not able for good monitoring role it required a skilled and knowledgeable insider management. All the arguments in favor of inside directorship suggests that superior firm performance is linked to the insider management because they work for the organization.

Despite this fact, there is a dearth of studies examining the beneficial impact of inside directors. Evidence prevail in literature that less independent board members can sometimes be more effective at monitoring than inside directors. Similarly, it is further emphasized that inside directors are in great demand externally, and the fact is that outsider directors are infect the insiders of another firm. This notion can be further supported from the insights that inside directors improve board performance but outside directorships if it is independent is vital source of inside director incentives.

In sharp contrast with stewardship theory, agency theory supported the notion that board independence adds value to the firm. It argues that as managers gain control in the firm, they pursue those actions that benefit themselves but not the firm owners. Theorists argued that independent board act as an effective monitor and it ensured that management is acting in the best interest of the company .These members will contribute to the reduction of agency costs, protect the interest of the shareholders and will not be involved in quotidian operational (management) activities.

These non-management directors who are unaffiliated with the corporation and considered as independent directors provides superior performance benefits to the firm due to their strong commitment to their independence role. Board independence in the form of representation of outside independent directors do not have any material interest in the firm thus, effectively perform the controlling role of the board. These directors provide important monitoring functions to resolve the agency conflict between management and shareholders and they are more vigilant than inside directors, as their primarily focus is on the firm's financial performance. According to this theory, an independent board will be able to exercise its role as a controller, which will add value to the firm.

Another theory of corporate governance named as resource dependency theory also played an important role to understand the concept of board independence. Apart from stewardship and agency theory, resource dependence theory is concerned about the external resources and their access from external environment. This theory incorporates the directors' backgrounds, such as their age, tenure, skills, knowledge, expertise, managerial, industrial and functional experience for the access of resources for organization. These theorists argued that outside independent directors have valuable resources, such as objectivity and technical expertise that they can use to enhance firm performance. Supporting this notion this study contended that outside independent board members with their strong expertise influence the board decisions and add value to the firm. Therefore, according to this theory perspective regarding board independence is that outside independent directors may act as a means of facilitating the acquisition of external resources such as advice, legitimacy and council that are considered critical for an organization success.

Literature has revealed that corporate governance theories provided insights regarding board independence, but these theories skipped other aspects to clarify the construct to some extent. Rather providing holistic view these theories displayed narrow view of board independence to some extent according to their perspective. From literature this study can predict that agency theory offer a glimpse effect of one aspect of board independence with performance relationship focusing that shareholders are the prime responsibility of board, similarly resource dependency theory perspective concentrates on single aspect of board role that is basically engaging with the external environment to access critical resources. This view ignores alternative activities of the board such as providing advice, monitoring, strategizing.

CONCLUSION AND FUTURE RECOMMENDATIONS

The major contribution of the board is to formulate company strategy and exercise proper oversight function in the company. Board independence among all characteristics is considered vital for board effectiveness. Code of corporate governance recommended that board should consist of Non-executive independent directors in order to bring proper scrutiny and management in the company. In seeking a reasonable answer, researchers have extensively depended on number of theories of corporate governance with most common named as agency theory, stewardship and resource dependency theory. These theories have provided different insights of board independence according to their perspective. Literature argued that theorists of these theories provided a narrow view of board independence rather providing a holistic view.

After delving into the literature this study also concluded that board independence positive and negative impacts showed that it might base on institutional context. An individual's willingness as an agent, to act as a steward or as a self-serving agent, or a resource provider may be contingent on the institutional context. Furthermore, an individual's capacity to act as an independent director is entirely based on situational factor and may vary across firms, institutional settings and industries as well as across the roles, power and stakes of the key internal external actors that could be shareholders, managers, creditors and employees. Thus, whether the board acts as an effective monitor, or ineffective rubber stamp is totally depends on the institutional context.

Moreover, it is concluded that governance may differ from country to country due to their various cultural values, political, social and historical circumstances. Further recommendation suggests that board independence as a construct can be analyzed with other corporate governance theories such as stakeholder theory, transaction cost theory, and it can be further investigated with other approaches of different disciplines in different developed and developing economies. It is believed that this study contributed to the literature by shedding light on how future studies might be strengthened and reduce the degree of ambiguity.

REFERENCES

Abdelsalam, O., & El-Masry, A. (2008). The impact of board independence and ownership structure on the timeliness of corporate internet reporting of Irish- listed companies. *Managerial Finance*, *34*(12), 907–918. doi:10.1108/03074350810915842

Abdul Rahman, R., & Mohamed Ali, F. H. (2006). Board, audit committee, culture and earnings management: Malaysian evidence. *Managerial Auditing Journal*, *21*(7), 783–804. doi:10.1108/02686900610680549

Abdullah, H., & Valentine, B. (2009). Fundamental and ethics theories of corporate governance. *Middle Eastern Finance and Economics*, 4.

Adıgüzel, H. (2013). Corporate governance, family ownership and earnings management: Emerging market evidence. *Accounting and Finance Research*, *2*(4), 17–33. doi:10.5430/afr.v2n4p17

Afify, H. A. E. (2009). Determinants of audit report lag: Does implementing corporate governance have any impact? Empirical evidence from Egypt. *Journal of Applied Accounting Research*, *10*(1), 56–86. doi:10.1108/09675420910963397

Aguilera, R. V., Filatotchev, I., Gospel, H., & Jackson, G. (2008). An organizational approach to comparative corporate governance: Costs, contingencies, and complementarities. *Organization Science*, *19*(3), 475–492. doi:10.1287/orsc.1070.0322

Ahmed, K., Hossain, M., & Adams, M. (2006). The Effects of Board Composition and Board Size on the Informativeness of Annual Accounting Earnings. *Corporate Governance*, *14*(5), 418–431. doi:10.1111/j.1467-8683.2006.00515.x

Aifuwa, H. O., & Embele, K. (2019). Board Characteristics and Financial Reporting. *Journal of Accounting and Financial Management*, *5*(1), 30–44.

Akeju, J. B., & Babatunde, A. A. (2017). Corporate governance and financial reporting quality in Nigeria. *International Journal of Information Research and Review*, *4*(2), 3749–3753.

Al Maskati, M., & Hamdan, A. (2017). Corporate governance and voluntary disclosure: Evidence from Bahrain. *International Journal of Economics and Accounting*, *8*(1), 1–28. doi:10.1504/IJEA.2017.084876

Alkadai, H, K. H, & Hanefah, M. M. (2012). Audit committee characteristics and earnings management in Malaysian Sharia-compliant companies. *Business and Management Review, 2*(2), 52-61.

Alves, S. M. (2014). The effect of the board independence on the earnings quality: Evidence from Portuguese listed companies. *Australian Accounting. Business and Finance Journal*, *8*(3), 23–44.

Arthurs, J. D., Hoskisson, R. E., Busenitz, L. W., & Johnson, R. A. (2008). Managerial agents watching other agents: Multiple agency conflicts regarding underpricing in IPO firms. *Academy of Management Journal*, *51*(2), 277–294. doi:10.5465/amj.2008.31767256

Balsmeier, B., Buchwald, A., & Stiebale, J. (2014). Outside Directors on the Board and Innovative Firm Performance. *Research Policy*, *43*(1), 1800–1815. doi:10.1016/j.respol.2014.06.003

Baysinger, B., & Hoskisson, R. (1990). The Composition of Boards of Directors and Strategic Control: Effects on Corporate Strategy. *Academy of Management Review*, *15*(1), 72–87. doi:10.5465/amr.1990.4308231

Beasley, M. S., & Petroni, K. R. (2001). Board independence and audit-firm type. *Auditing*, *20*(1), 97–114. doi:10.2308/aud.2001.20.1.97

Berghe, V. D & Baelden, T. (2005). The complex relation between director independence and board effectiveness. *Corporate Governance, 5*, 61-83.

Berle, A. A., & Means, G. C. (1932). *The modern corporation and private property*. Commerce Clearing House.

Brickley, J. A., & Zimmerman, J. L. (2010). Corporate governance myths: Comments on Armstrong, Guay, and Weber. *Journal of Accounting and Economics*, *50*(2-3), 235–245. doi:10.1016/j.jacceco.2010.10.002

Brown, W. (2005). Exploring the Association Between Board and Organizational Performance in Nonprofit Organizations. *Nonprofit Management & Leadership*, *15*(3), 317–339. doi:10.1002/nml.71

Carter, D., Simkins, B., & Simpson, W. (2003). Corporate Governance, Board Diversity, and Firm Value. *Financial Review, 38*(1), 33–53. doi:10.1111/1540-6288.00034

Chalaki, P., Didar, H., & Rianezhad, M. (2012). Corporate Governance Attributes and Financial Reporting Quality: Empirical Evidence from Iran. *International Journal of Business and Social Science, 3*(15), 1–7.

Coles, J., Daniel, N., & Naveen, L. (2010). *Co-opted Boards.* http://papers.ssrn.com/sol3/papers.cfm?abstractid=1699272

Coles, J., & Hesterly, W. (2000). Independence of the Chairman and Board Composition: Firm Choices and Shareholder Value. *Journal of Management, 26*(2), 195–214. doi:10.1177/014920630002600202

Committee and Financial reporting Quality of Oil Marketing Firms: Evidence from Nigeria. *Journal of Finance, Accounting and Management, 6*(2), 34-50.

D'onza, G., & Lamboglia, R. (2014). *The Relation between the Corporate Governance Characteristics and Financial Statement Frauds: An Empirical Analysis of Italian Listed Companies.* Academic Press.

Dalton, D. R., & Dalton, C. M. (2011). Integration of micro and macro studies in governance research: CEO duality, board composition, and firm performance. *Journal of Management, 37*(2), 404–411. doi:10.1177/0149206310373399

Daoud, K. A. A., Ismail, K., Izah, K. N., & Lode, N. A. (2014). The timeliness of financial reporting among Jordanian companies: Do company and board characteristics, and audit opinion matter? *Asian Social Science, 10*(13), 191–201. doi:10.5539/ass.v10n13p191

Donaldson, L. (1990). The ethereal hand: Organizational economics and management theory. *Academy of Management Review, 15*(3), 369–381. doi:10.5465/amr.1990.4308806

Donaldson, L., & Davis, J. H. (1991). Stewardship theory or agency theory: CEO governance and shareholder returns. *Australian Journal of Management, 16*(1), 49–64. doi:10.1177/031289629101600103

Donaldson, L., & Davis, J. H. (1994). Boards and company performance - research challenges the conventional wisdom. *Corporate Governance, 2*(3), 151–160. doi:10.1111/j.1467-8683.1994.tb00071.x

Donaldson, T., & Preston, L. E. (1995). The stakeholder theory of the corporation: Concepts, evidence, and implications. *Academy of Management Review*, *20*(1), 65–91. doi:10.5465/amr.1995.9503271992

Eisenhardt, K. M. (1989a). Agency theory: An assessment and review. *Academy of Management Review*, *14*(1), 57–74. doi:10.5465/amr.1989.4279003

Ezelibe, C. P., Nwosu, O., & Orazulike, S. (2017). Empirical investigation of corporate governance and financial reporting quality of quoted companies in Nigeria. International *Journal of Economics. Business and Management Research*, *1*(5), 117–137.

Fahlenbrach, R., Low, A., & Stulz, R. M. (2010). The dark side of outside directors: Do they quit when they are most needed? (No. w15917). National Bureau of Economic Research. doi:10.3386/w15917

Fama, E. F., & Jensen, M. C. (1983). Separation of ownership and control. *The Journal of Law & Economics*, *26*(2), 301–325. doi:10.1086/467037

Ferris, S. P., Jagannathan, M., & Pritchard, A. C. (2003). Too busy to mind the business? Monitoring by directors with multiple board appointments. *The Journal of Finance*, *58*(3), 1087–1111. doi:10.1111/1540-6261.00559

Fich, E., & Shivdasani, A. (2006). Are Busy Boards Effective Monitors? *Journal of Finance*, 61 (2), 689–724.Fosberg, R. H. (1999). Leadership structure and CEO compensation. *American Business Review*, *17*(1), 50.

Firth, M., Fung, P., & Rui, O. (2007). Ownership, two-tier Board Structure, and the Informativeness of Earnings: Evidence from China. *Journal of Accounting and Public Policy*, *26*(4), 463–496. doi:10.1016/j.jaccpubpol.2007.05.004

Foo, Y. B., & Zain, M. M. (2010). Board independence, board diligence and liquidity in Malaysia: A research note. *Journal of Contemporary Accounting & Economics*, *6*(2), 92–100. doi:10.1016/j.jcae.2010.10.001

Fosberg, R. H. (1999). Leadership structure and CEO compensation. *American Business Review*, *17*(1), 50–56.

Fuzia, S. F. S., Halim, S. A. A., & Julizaerma, M. K. (2016). Board independence and firm performance. *Procedia Economics and Finance*, *37*, 460–465. doi:10.1016/S2212-5671(16)30152-6

Garg, A. K. (2007). Influence of board size and independence on firm performance: A study of Indian companies. *Vikalpa*, *32*(3), 39–60. doi:10.1177/0256090920070304

Goel, A. M., & Thakor, A. V. (2003). Why do firms smooth earnings? *The Journal of Business*, *76*(1), 151–192. doi:10.1086/344117

Gois, C.G. (2014). Financial Reporting Quality and Corporate Governance: The Portuguese Companies Evidence. *Instituto Superior De Contabilidade e Administracao De Coimbra*, 1-25.

Hamdan, A. M. M., & Al Mubarak, M. M. S. (2017). The impact of board independence on accounting-based performance. *Journal of Economic and Administrative Sciences*.

Hermalin, B., & Weisbach, M. (1991). The Effect of Board Composition and Direct Incentives on Firm Performance. *Financial Management*, *21*(4), 101–112. doi:10.2307/3665716

Hermalin, B., & Weisbach, M. (2003). Boards of Directors as an Endogenously Determined Institution: A Survey of the Economic Literature. *Economic Policy Review*, *9*(1), 7–26.

Hill, C., & Snell, S. (1988). External Control, Corporate Strategy, and Firm Performance in Research intensive Industries. *Strategic Management Journal*, *9*(6), 577–590. doi:10.1002mj.4250090605

Holtz, L., & Neto, A. S. (2014). *Effect of board of directors' characteristics on the quality of Accounting information in Brazil.* Paper presented at the VII Anpcont congress, Fortaleza, CE, Brazil. 10.1590/1808-057x201412010

Ilaboya, J. O., & Lodikero, O. (2017). Board independence and financial statement fraud: A moderating effect of female gender diversity. *Accounting and Taxation Review, 1*(1), 196-221.

Jenfa, B. I. (2000). *Elements of Professionalism and Practice of Accountancy*. Ehindero Nigeria Ltd.

Jensen, M. C., & Meckling, W. H. (1976). Theory of the firm: Managerial behavior, agency costs and ownership structure. *Journal of Financial Economics*, *3*(4), 305–360. doi:10.1016/0304-405X(76)90026-X

Johari, N. H., Saleh, N. M., Jaffar, R., & Hassan, M. S. (2009). The influence of board independence, competency and ownership on earnings management in Malaysia. *International Journal of Economics and Management*, *2*(2), 281–306.

Johnson, J. L., Daily, C. M., & Ellstrang, A. E. (1996). Boards of directors: A review and research agenda. *Journal of Management*, *22*(3), 409–438. doi:10.1177/014920639602200303

Kakabadse, N. K., Yang, H., & Sanders, R. (2010). The effectiveness of non-executive directors in Chinese state-owned enterprises. *Management Decision*, *48*(7), 1063–1079. doi:10.1108/00251741011068770

Kantudu, A. L., & Samaila, I. A. (2015). *Board Characteristics*. Independent Audit.

Kemebradikemor Embele, H. O. A. (2019). Board Characteristics and Financial Reporting Quality. *Journal of Accounting and Financial Management ISSN*, *5*(1).

Klai, N., &Omri, A. (2011). *Corporate Governance and Financial Reporting Quality: The Case of Tunisian Firms*. International Business Research.

Klein, A. (2002). Audit Committee, Board of Director Characteristics and Earnings Management. *Journal of Accounting and Economics*, *33*(3), 375–400. doi:10.1016/S0165-4101(02)00059-9

Lara, J. M. G., Osma, B. G., & Penalva, F. (2009). Accounting conservatism and corporate governance. *Review of Accounting Studies*, *14*, 161–201.

Liu, Y., Miletkov, M., Wei, Z., & Yang, T. (2015). Board independence and firm performance in China. *Journal of Corporate Finance*, *30*(1), 223–244. doi:10.1016/j.jcorpfin.2014.12.004

Marra, A., Mazzola, P., & Prencipe, A. (2011). Board monitoring and earnings management pre and post IFRS. *The International Journal of Accounting*, *7*(3), 235–256.

Mayers, D., Shivdasani, A., & Smith, C. Jr. (1997). Board Composition and Corporate Control: Evidence from the Insurance Industry. *The Journal of Business*, *70*(1), 33–62. doi:10.1086/209707

Mishra, S. (2018). *Global governance- board independence standard and practices*. Retrieved from https://corpgov.law.harvard.edu/2018/06/01/global-governance-board-independence-standards-and-practices/

Mizruchi, M. S. (1996). What do interlocks do? An analysis, critique, and assessment of research on interlocking directorates. *Annual Review of Sociology*, *22*, 271–298.

Muth, M., & Donaldson, L. (1998). Stewardship theory and board structure: A contingency approach. *Corporate Governance*, *6*(1), 5–28. doi:10.1111/1467-8683.00076

Nabila, A., & Daljono, D. (2013). Pengaruh proporsi dewan komisaris independen, komite audit, dan reputasi auditor terhadap manajemen laba. *Diponegoro Journal of Accounting*, 99-108.

Nesrine, K., & Abdelwahed, O. (2011). Corporate Governance and Financial Reporting Quality: The Case of Tunisian Firm. *International Business Research*, *4*(1), 158–166.

Nicholson, G. J., & Kiel, G. C. (2007). Can directors impact performance? A case-based test of three theories of corporate governance. *Corporate Governance*, *15*(4), 585–608. doi:10.1111/j.1467-8683.2007.00590.x

Palmer, D., & Barber, B. M. (2001). Challengers, elites, and owning families: A social class theory of corporate acquisitions in the 1960s. *Administrative Science Quarterly*, *46*(1), 87–120. doi:10.2307/2667126

Pearce, J., & Zahra, S. (1991). The Relative Power of CEOs and Boards of Directors: Associations with Corporate Performance. *Strategic Management Journal*, *12*(2), 135–153. doi:10.1002mj.4250120205

Perry, T., & Shivdasani, A. (2005). Do Boards Affect Performance? Evidence from Corporate Restructuring. *The Journal of Business*, *78*(4), 1403–1431. doi:10.1086/430864

Pfeffer, J. (1972). Size and composition of corporate boards of directors: The organization and its environment. *Administrative Science Quarterly*, *17*(2), 218–228.

Pfeffer, J. (1973). Size, composition, and function of hospital boards of directors: A study of organization-environment linkage. *Administrative Science Quarterly*, *18*, 349–364.

Pfeffer, J., & Salancik, G. R. (1978). *The external control of organizations. Resource dependence perspective*. Harper & Row.

Rahman, R. A., & Ali, F. H. M. (2006). Board, audit committee, culture and earnings management: Malaysian evidence. *Managerial Auditing Journal*, *21*(7), 783–804. doi:10.1108/02686900610680549

Rashid, A. (2015). Revisiting agency theory: Evidence of board independence and agency cost from Bangladesh. *Journal of Business Ethics*, *130*(1), 181–198. doi:10.100710551-014-2211-y

Ruigrok, W., Peck, S., & Tacheva, S. (2007). Nationality and gender diversity on Swiss corporate boards. *Corporate Governance*, *15*(4), 546–557. doi:10.1111/j.1467-8683.2007.00587.x

Shankaraiah, K., & Amiri, S. M. S. (2017). Audit committee quality and financial reporting quality: A study of selected Indian companies. *Journal of Accounting and Business Dynamics*, *4*(1), 1–18. doi:10.24815/jdab.v4i1.6653

Stearns, L. B., & Mizruchi, M. S. (1993). Board composition and corporate financing: The impact of financial institution representation on borrowing. *Academy of Management Journal, 36*(3), 603-618.

Susanto, Y. K., & Pradipta, A. (2016). Corporate governance and real earnings management. *International Journal of Business. Economics and Law*, *9*(1), 17–23.

Susanto, Y. K., Pradipta, A., & Djashan, I. A. (2017). Free cash flow and earnings management: board of commissioner, board independence and audit quality. *Corporate Ownership and Control, 14*(4-1), 284-288.

Ulrich, D., & Barney, J. B. (1984). Perspectives in organizations: Resource dependence, efficiency, and population. *Academy of Management Review*, *9*(3), 471–481. doi:10.5465/amr.1984.4279680

Useem, M. (1984). *The inner circle: Large corporations and the rise of business political activity in the U.S. and U.K.* New York: Oxford University Press.

Vafeas, N. (2000). On audit committee appointments. *Auditing: A Journal of Practice & Theory*, 197-207.

Vafeas, N. (2000). Board structure and the informativeness of earnings. *Journal of Accounting and Public Policy*, *19*(2), 139–160. doi:10.1016/S0278-4254(00)00006-5

Van den Berghe, L. A. A., & Baelden, T. (2005). The complex relation between director independence and board effectiveness. *Corporate Governance: The International Journal of Business in Society*.

Van Ness, R. K., Miesing, P., & Kang, J. (2009). Understanding governance and corporate boards: Is theory a problem. *European Journal of Management*, *7*(9), 186–199.

Waddock, S. A., & Graves, S. B. (1997). The corporate social performance–financial performance link. *Strategic Management Journal*, *18*(4), 303–319. doi:10.1002/(SICI)1097-0266(199704)18:4<303::AID-SMJ869>3.0.CO;2-G

Wallison, P. J. (2006). All the Rage: Will Independent Directors Produce Good. *Corporate Governance*.

Westphal, J., & Khanna, P. (2003). Keeping Directors in Line: Social Distancing as a Control Mechanism in the Corporate Elite. *Administrative Science Quarterly*, *48*(3), 361–398. doi:10.2307/3556678

Wright, P., Kroll, M., & Elenkov, D. (2002). Acquisition Returns, Increase in Firm Size, and Chief Executive Officer Compensation: The Moderating Role of Monitoring. *Academy of Management Journal, 45*(3), 599–608.

Wright, P., Kroll, M., Lado, A., & Van Ness, B. (2002). The Structure of Ownership and Corporate Acquisition Strategies. *Strategic Management Journal, 23*(1), 41–53. doi:10.1002mj.208

Wu, C. -H., Wu, C., & Liu, V. W. (2008). The release timing of annual reports and board characteristics. *The International Journal of Business of Finance Research, 2*(1).

Yunos, R. M. (2011). *The effect of ownership concentration, board of directors, audit committee and ethnicity on conservative accounting: Malaysian evidence* (Doctoral thesis). School of Accounting, Finance and Economics Faculty of Business and Law, Australia.

Yusoff, W. F. W., & Alhaji, I. A. (2012). Insight of corporate governance theories. *Journal of Business and Management, 1*(1), 52–63.

Zajac, E., & Westphal, J. (1996). Director Reputation, CEO-Board Power, and the Dynamics of Board Interlocks. *Administrative Science Quarterly, 41*(3), 507–529.

Zald, M. N. (1969, July). The Power and Functions of Boards of Directors: A Theoretical Synthesis. *American Journal of Sociology, 75*(1), 97–111. doi:10.1086/224747

Zinkin, J. (2010). Independent directors must learn to ask CEOs the right questions. *The Star*.

Chapter 12
Leveraging Women on Boards in Asia:
Insights From Thailand

Narupon Duangwises
https://orcid.org/0000-0001-5585-9814
University of Kent, UK

ABSTRACT

Diverse boards have been seen as providing impetus for initiating change. This study focuses on the relationship between female representation on boards of directors and its effect on firm performance, based on evidence from the Thailand. The authors use empirical data on SET 100 Index firms observed in 2015 to 2019. The result indicate that at least one female director in the board is associated with the firm financial performance, while the female CEO/Chairman or higher percentage of females in board having no firm performance association.

INTRODUCTION

Research has shown that men and women behave differently and have different talents and perspectives. With respect to behavioural differences, Croson and Gneezy (2009) based on a literature survey; argue that women differ from men with respect to risk, social and competitive preferences. In particular, they argue that women are more risk-averse, less overconfident and more sensitive to social signals in determining appropriate behaviour. With respect to differences in talents and perspectives, Hillman et al. (2002) find that female directors are more likely to come from non-business backgrounds, are more likely to hold advanced degrees and join multiple boards at

DOI: 10.4018/978-1-7998-6669-5.ch012

This chapter published as an Open Access Chapter distributed under the terms of the Creative Commons Attribution License (http://creativecommons.org/licenses/by/4.0/) which permits unrestricted use, distribution, and production in any medium, provided the author of the original work and original publication source are properly credited.

a faster rate. Singh et al. (2008) report that adding women to the board increases international diversity. They also show that women are significantly more likely to be experienced board members, as they have fulfilled several of these positions, especially in smaller firms.

Brammer et al. (2007) also argue that greater equality of representation provides the firm with benefits that arise from alignment with the demographic characteristics of key stakeholder groups such as customers, employees and investors. However there is not general consensus in the board diversity literature with scholars arguing, appointing female directors in response to regulatory pressure has, at best, a limited effect on firm value (Adams and Ferreira, 2009; Gregory-Smith et al., 2014). We expect that women's prospects and ability to exercise influential corporate leadership may vary based on their social, moral and authoritative status which in turn is determined by culture, societal norms and values as well as religious sensitivity (Grosvold and Brammer, 2011; Adams and Ferreira, 2009; Terjesen and Singh, 2008). Accordingly, acknowledging the socio-economic context within which women exercise their board roles can be informative for identifying the mechanisms through which female directors influence shareholder value. Therefore, we signify the performance implications of gender diversity in the context of developing economies, where less is known about the contextual validity of insights for understanding female corporate leadership contributions in Asia's fast-developing economies.

One positive attribute assigned to female directors is their superior ability, compared to male directors, to recognise and control risk (Erhardt et al, 2003; Carter et al., 2010; Schwartz-Ziv, 2015). Excessive risk taking and poor risk management are commonly cited causes of the recent global financial crisis and it is not surprising that many firms identified by irresponsible risk decisions had boards that consisted mostly of male members. The recent growing participation of women in the corporate arena, both in developed and developing economies, has gained increased attention from scholars, corporate leaders, and policy-makers but evidence of their effectiveness, particularly in Asian economies, is sparse. Therefore, this study seeks to investigate the level of female participation in corporate roles in one of Asia's fastest growing economies, Thailand, and determine whether link between female board participation, reduced enterprise risk and enhanced overall corporate performance exists.

A substantial body of evidence from Western corporate contexts suggests that appointing women on boards of directors has a positive influence on firm outcomes and shareholder value (Erhardt et al., 2003; Nielsen and Huse, 2010; Ahern and Dittmar, 2012). However, the opportunity for women to influence corporate leadership in the context of Asian economy firms has been explored by only limited studies. Thailand presents as an important research environment given it is one of the fastest developing economies in Asia Pacific and a society where the recognition of female leadership contribution is rapidly evolving.

LITERATURE REVIEW

A considerable body of empirical evidence maintains a positive relationship between female involvement in upper management, particularly the board of directors, and enhanced outcomes for firms. The assertion of a firm-level benefit from gender diversity is based on theoretical streams shared by the sociology, management, organisational and corporate governance literatures. Herring (2009) provides a good summary of the literature and concludes proponents of diversity argue it enhances firm performance for three reasons. Firstly, diversity improves workplace outcomes as, compared to homogeneous work teams; diverse work teams have greater resources and insights for problem solving (Cox, 2001; Adams and Ferreira, 2009). Secondly, innovation depends less on homogeneous individuals than on diverse groups working together and capitalising on their individuality (Page, 2007). Thirdly, diversity can influence customers' perceptions and purchasing practices (Sen and Battacharya, 2001).

Additional support for board gender diversity is provided by the corporate governance literature. In particular, Stakeholder theory posits that as the board's function is to represent its stakeholders it is more efficient when it is representative of those stakeholders (Huse and Rindova, 2001; Ahern and Dittmar, 2012). Resource dependency theory also holds that board gender diversity increases networks that link the firm to important external resources (Ruigrok et al., 2006). Other researchers argue benefits of gender diversity in upper management come from the enhanced creativity, knowledge and innovation that divergent views of females bring to the board (Carter et al., 2003; Wiersema and Bantel, 1992; Carter et al., 2010); their more inclusive and collaborative management style (Van Knippenberg et al., 2004) and their superior ability to recognise and control risk (Erhardt et al., 2003). Recent Australian evidence is provided by Hutchinson, Mack and Plastow (2014) who report that greater board gender diversity moderates firm risk which in turn improves firms' financial performance.

By recruiting female directors companies may also derive benefits from greater linkage with their external stakeholders (Singh and Vinnicombe, 2004) with the provision of legitimacy highlighted in the gender diversity literature. For example, female directors have been shown to provide a valuable form of legitimacy in the eyes of potential and current employees with female directors also symbolising career possibilities to prospective recruits (Hillman et al., 2007). The appointment of female directors to governance committees has also been shown to be indicative of a flexible board that includes high ability individuals in governance o enhance firm performance (Smale and Miller, 2015).

In recognition of the abilities and opportunities of women a number of developed countries, such as Norway and Denmark, have mandated regulations that prescribe fixed quota percentages for women on corporate boards (Joana, Jannekeand Chantal, 2010; Isidro and Sobral, 2014). While researchers claim that the increased number of women on boards (Vance, 1983; Heidrick and Struggles, 1986; Grosvold and Brammer, 2011; Ahern and Dittmar, 2012) and the increasing number of female Chief Executive Officers (CEOs) is a signal of the transition of women to top executive roles (Spencer, 1984) others argue that though the actual number of women on board has been increasing, proportionately it is still not notable (Gregory-Smith, Main and OReilly, 2014).

However, emerging economies are lagging behind in mandating legislation or promoting policies that encourage increased female participation in the board room with participation rates remaining low. While the empirical evidence documents mixed findings on women's ability to influence corporate leadership and performance in the context of western economies, the situation in fast growing Asian economies has barely been examined (Alowaihan, 2004; Afza, 2011; Abdullah et al., 2015). Therefore, the main focus of this study is to examine the extent to which women are appointed to corporate boards in Thailand, the corporate governance characteristics of firms that appoint them and to investigate their impact on firm outcomes.

Yet there are other studies that do not find any significant relationship between female board representation and firm performance. Using a panel dataset of 300 firms from Fortune 1000 firms over the period 1990-1999 with Poisson regression, Farrell and Hersch (2005) found that the addition of female directors to the board has no significant impact on the return on assets. Carter et al. (2010) also found that the number of female directors is not significantly related to Tobin's Q or return on assets in S&P indexed companies. Moreover, Rose (2007) shows there is no significant link between firm performance and board gender diversity with a sample of Danish firms for years 1998-2001. Adams and Ferreira (2009) found that although female directors are more diligent monitors of the firm, they appear to have a negative impact on Tobin's Q. Ahearn and Dittmar (2012) found that imposing a 40% female director quota in Norway results in lower Tobin's Q. They argue that the reason might be that the law forces firms to pick younger or less experienced females as their board directors.

The literature on how female board members affect governance decisions is scarce. Adams and Ferreira (2009) document that female directors generally have fewer attendance problems, suggesting that female directors are more active monitors compared their male counterparts.

HYPOTHESES DEVELOPMENT

Within a corporate governance framework, the composition of corporate boards is crucial to aligning the interest of all stakeholders, to providing information for monitoring and counselling, and to ensuring effective decision-making (Becht, Bolton and Röell, 2002; Hermalin and Weisbach, 2003). Gender diversity, together with board size, age dispersion and the share of directors chosen by the employees, all relate to board decision-making processes (Bøhren and Strøm, 2007).

In western economies diversity issues have taken centre stage on account of the following reasons; first, many institutional investors are implementing diversity aspects as part of their investment practices and commitment to diversity in employment is part of socially responsible investment indices (Yasser, 2012). Also board gender diversity is desired by customers, employees and other stakeholders since it demonstrates the sensitivity of management to stakeholder preferences, aspirations and concerns (Ibid, 2012). Lastly, board gender diversity has been the subject of discussions for best practices in corporate governance.

Smith et al. (2006) found that female employee elected directors have a positive impact on firm performance, while female shareholder elected directors have the opposite effect. A significant part of the shareholder elected female directors is found to have family ties to firm owners.

Carter et al. (2003) explain the relationship between board gender diversity and firm performance based on the agency theory and they posit that board gender diversity enhances the board's ability to monitor top management. In addition to this, they argue that increasing the number of female directors may increase board's independence since women tend to ask questions that male directors may not ask.

In addition, Smith et al. (2006), posit that board gender diversity enhances problem solving as a variety of perspectives arise hence more alternatives are evaluated in the process. Furthermore, a more gender diverse board may also improve a firm's competitive advantage provided it improves the image of the firm and if this has a positive effect on customers' behaviour and thus on a firm's performance (Smith et al., 2006). Based on the above arguments, we hypothesis that:

Hypothesis 1: Does gender diversity in a firm impact positively on firm performance?

Since the marketplace itself is diverse, higher proportionate of female directors will make it easy for firms to penetrate these markets. Robinson and Dechant (1997) also noted that a higher percentage of female directors in boards increase creativity and innovation. This view therefore states that the attitudes, beliefs and cognitive functioning of humans are not distributed in a random pattern but appear to be systematically distributed with variables like gender, race and age. It is further noted that diversity especially in terms of gender leads to greater problem solving. This is because many alternatives are carefully evaluated in terms of pros and cons.

Carter et al. (2003) examined the relationship between board gender diversity and firm value for the Fortune 1000 firms. Using Tobin's Q as a measure of firm value, they found statistically significant positive relationships between the percentage of women on the board of directors and firm value as well as presence of women on the board of directors and firm value. In line with these findings, this research argues that it is likely that higher percentage of female directors in the boardroom, as measured, may influence firm performance. Brammer et al. (2007) suggest that higher female proportion in boards is shaped by a close proximity to stakeholders, such as customers, employees, labour unions and investors as the firm's external business environment whose demands are for a greater diversity. Broome and Krawiec (2008) assume this is because firms need to signal that they are committed to equality, although it is argued that this practice may lead to a negative reputational cost for the firms as an impact of an inability to give meaning to the higher diversity (Shin and Gulati, 2011). Lindstädt et al. (2011) show that positive significant performance effects of female supervisory board members are only attained in firms with a high proportion of females in the workforce or in firms in the business to customer (B2C) business. Torchia et al. (2011) document that having three or more women on boards positively influence firm innovation through board strategic tasks. We propose the following hypothesis:

Hypothesis 2: Does female proportion in a firm impact positively on firm performance?

We also find that women directors with senior corporate experience are associated with higher firm performance relative to women directors with non-corporate or junior corporate backgrounds. This is consistent with women directors with senior corporate experience having greater monitoring and advising capability and being better informed given their background and business connections. This may also indicate that women directors with senior corporate experience are able to elicit value adding incremental monitoring efforts from other board members.

Literature (for example, Bliss and Potter, 2002, Wei, 2007), notes that women, in addition to being more risk averse, worry more about the way the company money is spent and normally extract less personal benefits from the company than men. Laakso (2010) complement this information, stating that women make more ethical decisions in the workplace than men on CEO position. Based on the above, our first null hypothesis is proposed:

Hypothesis 3: Does female CEO/Chairman impact positively on firm performance?

METHODOLOGY

The focus of the study is a sample of the largest 100 companies listed on the Stock Exchange Thailand for the years 2014-2019. This allows for a sufficient lag for firms to adjust their board nomination practices and enables a comparison of Thailand corporate governance pre and post the Code. As previously mentioned the revised Code of Corporate Governance had a particular emphasis on increasing female presence on Thai boards[1].

The final sample comprises 500 observations over five consecutive years with each company investigated for increases in female board member appointment. Using annual reports for data collection is preferred as these reports are audited, have been published and are publicly available. Furthermore, annual reports of public listed companies are presented uniformly and disclosures must comply with SET. There were 843 companies listed in the main market on Thailand as of 31st December 2018, from which100 large companies are taken for this study for each of five consecutive years.

The study employs non-financial data relating to the sample of 100 listed companies and data gathered from the SET website. We employ financial measures for performance including ROA (return on asset) and ROE (return on equity). These are derived from the relevant firm financial reports. Data on gender diversity and other board characteristics are also obtained from the audited annual reports. In this study, we also control for board size (total number of board members) and firm size (natural log of total assets held by the firm). We use three measures of female board representation, i.e. the number of female directors, the percentage of female directors and a dichotomous variable that equals 1 when a female is CEO or Chairman and 0 otherwise.

FINDINGS

In order to increase female participation in board rooms, governments and regulators around the world have recently started intervening (Credit Suisse, 2012; Isidro and Sobral, 2014), Thailand among them. However there is scarce empirical research on the issue in Thailand and in other developing economies. To date, our preliminary findings suggest that as few as 9% of our sample of 100 large Thai firms disclose the existence of female directors on the board. The presence of female CEOs, the proportion of female board members and their influence on firm performance will be examined in the next stage of this study.

Earlier studies have also found minimal presence of women on boards including Loscocco et al. (1991), Fischer et al. (1993), Prasso (1996), Butner and Moore (1997),

Fasci and Valdez (1998), Ahern and Dittmar (2012), Alowaihan (2004) and Shaw et al. (2009). In addition we will investigate corporate governance characteristics of those firms that appoint female directors with an important focus on the examination of the influence of female board members on firm performance, measured in terms of ROA and ROE. Building on the work of extant studies, we examine how (H1) female presence on board and (H2) the percentage of female board members and (H3) the presence of a female CEO/Chairman status on firm performance.

Descriptive statistics explain the primary characteristics of quantitative data acquired during the data collection process to summarize the data (Hair et al. 2003). Table 1 presents the statistics of the gender diversity and performance. We see from the table that, the mean values of gender diversity in board is 28%, 34%, 27%, 38% and 28% from 2015 to the 2019 respectively. While the female percentage in board is 5.5% on average and CEO/Chairman status of female is 5% with a standard deviation of 18.5%.

Table 1. Descriptive statistics

Variables	2015	2016	2017	2018	2019	Total	S.D.
Gender Diversity in Board	0.28	0.34	0.27	0.38	0.28	0.31	0.44
Female Proportionate in Board	5.2	5.6	5.1	5.9	5.2	5.5	11.12
CEO/Chairman Gender Status	0.04	0.05	0.04	0.06	0.04	0.05	0.185
Firm Size	5.26	5.35	5.27	5.36	5.42	5.38	1.65
Board Size	8.71	8.90	7.89	8.05	8.12	8.41	3.26
Return on Assets	2.32	3.15	2.89	2.99	2.83	2.94	4.31
Return on Equity	5.69	7.05	6.21	6.66	5.89	6.32	5.58

The ROA reflects the profitability of firms based on accounting numbers taken from the financial reports. The ROA is a ratio of net income and total assets. On average, from 2015 to 2019, the value of ROA was 2.94%. However, the ROE is a ratio of net income and total equity. On average, from 2015 to 2019, the value of ROE was 6.32% with a standard deviation of 5.58.

The results of correlation coefficient analysis (Table 2) indicate that gender diversity is positively associated with the return on assets. Except that, there is no association with the variables in the data set.

Table 3 indicates the regression analysis of the gender diversity issue of the Thai 100 indexed companies. The result indicate that at least one female director in the board is positively associated with the firm financial performance in line with the results of Adams and Ferreira (2009) and Wei (2007). The higher percentage of

Table 2. Correlation coefficient analysis

	Variables	1	2	3	4	5	6	7
1.	Gender Diversity	1						
2.	Female Proportionate	0.10	1					
3.	Female CEO/Chairman	0.59	2.32	1				
4.	Board Size	1.26	0.89	0.69	1			
5.	Firm Size	1.11	0.10	0.22	-.51	1		
6.	ROA	0.02**	0.32	-.46	0.56	0.43	1	
7.	ROE	0.19	0.22	0.59	1.17	0.66	0.33	1

female directors and female as CEO or the chairman of the board is not associated with any performance indicator by taking the performance as ROE and ROA. The corporate landscape of Thailand is different from the European context and the presence of the female CEO/Chairman and the selection criteria of different gender are also different from the European constitution as examined by Smith at al. (2006). However, firm size is also having a positive association with the firm financial performance. There is no apparent effect on the firm financial performance by changing the board numbers.

DISCUSSION AND IMPLICATIONS

The role of females as board members and top corporate executive in a company, CEO, in driving firm performance has become a very topical issue, especially in the

Table 3. Regression analysis

	ROA	ROE
Gender Diversity	0.12**	0.85
Female Proportionate	0.42	1.10
Female CEO/Chairman	0.97	1.08
Board Size	2.39	2.15
Firm Size	2.28**	1.97**
R^2	36%	42%
Adj. R^2	31%	34%
F-Statistics	5.125	6.235
Prob.	0.00	0.00

current times of economic catastrophe in which largely attributed to unsound risk management practices, there is debate if the global economic picture would have looked less grim, had there been more women on boards of directors in the distressed financial institutions. The results of this study suggest that female directors not only contribute more types of expertise than male counterparts do but also offer particular sets of expertise currently missing in the incumbent corporate boards. Therefore, adding women directors, with their unique skill contribution, to corporate boards would increase heterogeneity of board skills. This skill heterogeneity increase would, in turn, enhance the overall advisory effectiveness of the board and improve firm value (Kim and Starks, 2015).

This study uses social identity theory and resource dependence theory to examine factors in relation to female presence in the corporate board rooms in a fast-growing developing Asian economy, Thailand. We examine the social identity aspect of gender diversity in establishing a theoretical foundation for listed firms in Thailand where board diversity has been emphasised by the regulators.

In providing empirical evidence for the drivers of and benefits of gender diversity on corporate boards in an emerging economy, our findings evidence several implications for practice, policy, theory and the future research agenda. These findings in particular will allow policy makers and stakeholder groups to evaluate current board diversity recommendations and provide evidence to firms to strengthen their corporate governance through greater female participation.

LIMITATION AND FUTURE RESEARCH

Even though the sample focuses on Thai large firms whose practices should be expected to comply regulations the transferability of our findings to other jurisdictions may be limited by the idiosyncratic characteristics of Thailand. If preliminary findings of no relation between female presence on board and performance hold we suggest future research to investigate the relationship in other emerging economy firms.

REFERENCES

Abdullah, S. N., Ku Ismail, K., & Nachum, L. (2015). Does having women on boards create value? The impact of societal perceptions and corporate governance in emerging markets. *Strategic Management Journal*, *38*(3), 334–354.

Adams, R. B., & Ferreira, D. (2009). Women in the boardroom and their impact on governance and performance. *Journal of Financial Economics*, *94*(2), 291–309. doi:10.1016/j.jfineco.2008.10.007

Afza, N. A. (2011). The Effect of owner's gender and age to firm performance: A review on Malaysian public listed family businesses. *Journal of Global Business and Economics*, *2*(1), 104–116.

Ahern, K. R., & Dittmar, A. K. (2012). The changing of the boards: The impact on firm valuation of mandated female board representation. *The Quarterly Journal of Economics*, *127*(1), 137–197. doi:10.1093/qje/qjr049

Ahern, K. R., & Dittmar, A. K. (2012). The changing of the boards: The impact on firm valuation of mandated female board presentation. *The Quarterly Journal of Economics*, *127*(1), 137–197. doi:10.1093/qje/qjr049

Alowaihan, A. K. (2004). Gender and business performance of Kuwaiti small firms: A comparative approach. *International Journal of Commerce and Management*, *14*(4), 69–82. doi:10.1108/10569210480000185

Becht, M., Bolton, P., & Röell, A. (2002). *Corporate Governance and Control*. ECGI—Finance Working Paper # 02, 2002. http://ssrn.com/abstract=343461

Bliss, R., & Potter, M. (2002). Mutual Fund managers: Does gender matter? *Journal of Business and Economic Studies*, *8*(1), 1–15.

Bøhren, Ø. & Strøm, R.Ø. (2007). *Aligned, informed and decisive: Characteristics of value-creating boards*. Ljubljana Meetings Paper.

Brammer, S., Millington, A., & Pavelin, S. (2007). Gender and ethnic diversity among UK corporate boards. *Corporate Governance*, *15*(2), 393–403. doi:10.1111/j.1467-8683.2007.00569.x

Broome, L. L., & Krawiec, K. D. (2008). Signalling through board diversity: Is anyone listening', University of Cincinnati Law Review. *Twenty-First Annual Corporate Law Symposium*.

Butner, E. H., & Moore, D. P. (1997). Women's organizational exodus to entrepreneurship: Self-reported motivations and correlates with success. *Journal of Small Business Management*, *35*(1), 34–46.

Carter, D., D'Souza, F., Simkins, B. J., & Simpson, W. (2010). The gender and ethnic diversity of US boards and board committees and firm financial performance. *Corporate Governance*, *18*(5), 396–414. doi:10.1111/j.1467-8683.2010.00809.x

Carter, D., Simkins, B., & Simpson, W. (2003). Corporate governance, board diversity and firm value. *Financial Review*, *38*(1), 33–53. doi:10.1111/1540-6288.00034

Carter, D. F., D'Souza, B., Simkins, J., & Simpson, W. (2010). The gender and ethnic diversity of US boards and board committees and firm financial performance. *Corporate Governance*, *18*(5), 396–414. doi:10.1111/j.1467-8683.2010.00809.x

Cox, T. (2001). *Creating the multicultural organization: A strategy for capturing the power*. Jossey-Bass.

Credit Suisse. (2012). *Gender diversity and corporate performance*. Retrieved from https://infocus.creditsuisse.com/data/_product_documents/_shop/360145/csri_gender_diversity_and_corporate_performance.pdf

Croson, R., & Gneezy, U. (2009). Gender differences in preferences. *Journal of Economic Literature*, *47*(2), 448–474. doi:10.1257/jel.47.2.448

Erhardt, N. L., Werbel, J. D., & Shrader, C. B. (2003). Board of director diversity and firm financial performance. *Corporate Governance*, *11*(2), 102–111. doi:10.1111/1467-8683.00011

Farrell, K. A., & Hersch, P. L. (2005). Additions to Corporate Boards: The Effect of Gender. *Journal of Corporate Finance*, *11*(1-2), 85–106. doi:10.1016/j.jcorpfin.2003.12.001

Fasci, M. A., & Valdez, J. (1998). A performance contrast of male and female owned small accounting practices. *Journal of Small Business Management*, *36*(3), 1–7.

Fischer, E. M., Reuber, A. R., & Dyke, L. S. (1993). A theoretical review and extension of research on sex, gender and entrepreneurship. *Journal of Business Venturing*, *8*(3), 151–168. doi:10.1016/0883-9026(93)90017-Y

Gregory-Smith, I., Main, B. M., & O'Reilly, C. A. III. (2014). Appointments, pay and performance in UK boardrooms by gender. *Economic Journal (London)*, *124*(574), F109–F128. doi:10.1111/ecoj.12102

Grosvold, J., & Brammer, S. (2011). National institutional systems as antecedents of female board representation: An empirical study. *Corporate Governance*, *19*(2), 116–135. doi:10.1111/j.1467-8683.2010.00830.x

Hair, J. F., Babin, B., Money, A. H., & Samouel, P. (2003). *Essentials of business research methods*. John Wiley & Sons.

Heidrick & Struggles, I. (1986). *The changing board*. Chicago: Heidrick and Struggles Inc.

Hermalin, B. E., & Weisbach, M. S. (2003). Boards of directors as an endogenously determined institution: A survey of the economic literature. *Economic Policy Review*, *9*(1), 7–26.

Herring, C. (2009). Does diversity pay? Race, gender and the business case for diversity. *American Sociological Review*, *74*(2), 208–224. doi:10.1177/000312240907400203

Hillman, A., Canella, A. A., & Harris, I. C. (2002). Women and racial minorities in the boardroom: How do directors differ? *Journal of Management*, *28*(6), 747–763. doi:10.1177/014920630202800603

Hillman, A. J., Shropshire, C., & Canella, A. A. (2007). Organizational predictors of women on corporate boards. *Academy of Management Journal*, *50*(4), 941–952. doi:10.5465/amj.2007.26279222

Huse, M., & Rindova, V. P. (2001). Stakeholders' expectations of board roles: The case of subsidiary boards. *The Journal of Management and Governance*, *5*(2), 153–178. doi:10.1023/A:1013017909067

Hutchinson, M., Mack, J., & Plastow, K. (2014). Who selects the 'right' directors? An examination of the association between board selection, gender diversity and outcomes. *Accounting and Finance*. Advance online publication. doi:10.1111/acfi.12082

Isidro, H., & Sobral, M. (2014). The effects of women on corporate boards on firm value, financial performance, ethical and social compliance. *Journal of Business Ethics*, 1–19.

Joana, M., Janneke, P. & Chantal, R. (2010). *Gender diversity and firm performance: Evidence from Dutch and Danish boardrooms*. Tjalling C. Koopmans Research Institute, Discussion paper series no. 10-03.

Kim, D., & Starks, L. T. (2015). *Board heterogeneity of expertise and firm performance*. Working paper.

Laakso, E. (2010). *Stock market participation and household characteristics in Europe*. Master Thesis, Aalto University, School of Economics. http://epub.lib.aalto.fi/en/ethesis/pdf/12385/hse ethesis 12385.pdf

Lindstädt, H., Wolff, M., & Fehre, K. (2011). *Frauen in Führungspositionen: Auswirkungen auf den Unternehmenserfolg*. Bundesministerium für Familie, Senioren, Frauen und Jugend.

Loscocco, K. A., Robinson, J., Hall, R. H., & Allen, J. K. (1991). Gender and small business success: An inquiry into women's relative disadvantage. *Social Forces, 70*(1), 65–85. doi:10.2307/2580062

Nielsen, S., & Huse, M. (2010). The contribution of women on boards of directors: Going beyond the surface. *Corporate Governance, 18*(2), 136–148. doi:10.1111/j.1467-8683.2010.00784.x

Page, S. (2007). *The difference: How the power of diversity creates better groups, firms, schools and societies*. Princeton University Press.

Prasso, S. (1996). Poll: Women in office, not offices. *The Commercial Appeal*, 7B.

Robinson, G., & Dechant, K. (1997). Building a business case for diversity. *The Academy of Management Executive, 11*(3), 21–30. doi:10.5465/ame.1997.9709231661

Rose, C. (2007). Does female board representation influence firm performance? The Danish evidence. *Corporate Governance, 15*(2), 404–413. doi:10.1111/j.1467-8683.2007.00570.x

Ruigrok, W., Peck, S., Tacheva, S., Greve, P., & Hu, Y. (2006). The determinants and effects of board nomination committees. *The Journal of Management and Governance, 10*(2), 119–148. doi:10.100710997-006-0001-3

Schwartz-Ziv, M. (2015). Does the gender of directors matter? *Journal of Financial and Quantitative Analysis.*

Sen, S., & Bhattacharya, B. (2001). Does doing good always lead to doing better? consumer reactions to corporate social responsibility. *JMR, Journal of Marketing Research, 38*(2), 225–243. doi:10.1509/jmkr.38.2.225.18838

Shaw, E., Marlow, S., Lam, W., & Carter, S. (2009). Gender and entrepreneurial capital: Implications for firm performance. *International Journal of Gender and Entrepreneurship, 1*(1), 25–41. doi:10.1108/17566260910942327

Shin, P. S., & Gulati, M. (2011). Showcasing diversity. *North Carolina Law Review, 89*, 1017–1054.

Singh, V., & Vinnicombe, S. (2004). Why so few women directors in top UK boardrooms? Evidence and theoretical explanations. *Corporate Governance, 12*(4), 479–489. doi:10.1111/j.1467-8683.2004.00388.x

Smale, A., & Miller, C. C. (2015, March 6). Germany sets Gender Quota in Boardrooms. *The New York Times*. Retrieved from: https://www.nytimes.com/2015/03/07/world/europe/germanlaw-requires-more-women-on-corporate-boards.html?_r=0

Smith, N., Valdemar, S., & Mette, V. (2006). Do women in top management affect firm performance? A panel study of 2,500 Danish firms. *International Journal of Productivity and Performance Management*, *55*(7), 569–593. doi:10.1108/17410400610702160

Spencer, G. (1984). Female executives foresee gains. *Best of Business*, *6*(2), 49–58.

Terjesen, S., & Singh, V. (2008). Female presence on corporate boards: A multi-country study of environmental context. *Journal of Business Ethics*, *83*(1), 55–63. doi:10.100710551-007-9656-1

Torchia, M., Calabrò, A., & Huse, M. (2011). Women directors on corporate boards: From tokenism to critical mass. *Journal of Business Ethics*, *102*(2), 299–317. doi:10.100710551-011-0815-z

Van Knippenberg, D., De Dreu, C., & Homan, A. (2004). Work diversity and group performance: An Integrated model and research agenda. *The Journal of Applied Psychology*, *89*(6), 1008–1022. doi:10.1037/0021-9010.89.6.1008 PMID:15584838

Vance, S. C. (1983). *Corporate leadership: Boards, directors, and strategy*. McGraw-Hill Book Co.

Wei, X. (2007). Wage Compensation for job-related illness: Evidence from a matched employer and employee survey in the UK. *Journal of Risk and Uncertainty*, *34*(1), 85–99. doi:10.100711166-006-9000-7

Wiersema, M., & Bantel, K. (1992). Top management team demography and corporate strategic change. *Academy of Management Journal*, *35*(1), 91–121.

Yasser, Q. R. (2012). Affects of female directors on firms performance in Pakistan. *Modern Economy*, *3*(07), 817–825. doi:10.4236/me.2012.37104

ENDNOTE

1 The board should establish a policy formalising its approach to boardroom diversity. The board through its Nominating Committee should take steps to ensure that women candidates are sought as part of its recruitment exercise. The board should explicitly disclose in the annual report its gender diversity policies and targets and the measures taken to meet those targets.

Chapter 13
The Impact of Conservatism Accounting on Audit Fees: Evidence From Portugal and Spain

Sandra Alves
School of Accountancy and Administration, University of Aveiro, Portugal

ABSTRACT

For a sample of listed Portuguese and Spanish firms from 2010 to 2018, this study draws on audit pricing, substitution, signaling, and complementary theories to evaluate the impact of conservatism accounting on audit fees. Using fixed effects technique, the author finds a positive relationship between conservatism accounting and audit fees. The results suggest that firms with more conservative accounting (with strong internal corporate governance) could be more likely to demand high-quality audit to strengthen investor confidence in financial information and, thus pay higher audit fees. Therefore, this study supports signaling and complementary theories. The results also suggest that Big 4, growth, firm size, and leverage are positively related with audit fees. To Spain, audit risk and ROA are also positively related with audit fees.

INTRODUCTION

Management is responsible for providing stakeholders with information regarding various entity activities, which can be achieved through financial reporting (Baker & Al-Thuneibat, 2011). Nevertheless, the inherent flexibility in many accounting standards facilitates managers to take advantage of it and misrepresent information. Thus, a key element of the financial reporting process is to guarantee an independent

DOI: 10.4018/978-1-7998-6669-5.ch013

Copyright © 2021, IGI Global. Copying or distributing in print or electronic forms without written permission of IGI Global is prohibited.

verification of the financial statements prepared by the firm's management (Chan, Ezzamel, & Gwilliam, 1993). Auditing aims to ensure the credibility of the financial statements. Audit quality is the joint probability that the external auditor detects an irregularity in financial statements, and then reveals it to the external users (DeAngelo, 1981).

Audit pricing theory suggests that in a competitive audit market, audit fee is a function of audit effort and the auditor's client-specific business risk (Simunic, 1980; Simunic & Stein, 1996). Audit effort is driven by audit risk. According to International Auditing and Assurance Standards Board, audit risk is defined as the risk that the auditor expresses an inappropriate audit opinion when the financial statements are materially misstated. The client's business risk is also expected to influence audit effort. Thus, for a client presenting a higher risk level, the auditor asks for higher fees to cover higher audit effort (costs) (Simunic & Stein, 1996).

Auditors risk losing reputation capital when audit market participants perceive that they have allowed misreporting (Skinner & Srinivasan, 2012; Weber, Willenborg, & Zhang, 2008). Prior research finds evidence that restatements harm auditors' reputation by triggering auditor dismissals (Hennes, Leone, & Miller, 2014). Litigation exposes auditors to direct financial penalties, while lost reputation impairs the ability to retain and attract clients (DeFond, Lim, & Zang, 2016). In the case of wrong opinions or a failure to discover breaches, auditors suffer significant damages to their brand reputation and high litigation costs if sued (Becker, DeFond, Jiambalso, & Subramanyam, 1998; DeAngelo 1981; Francis & Krishnan 1999; Khurana & Raman, 2004). Therefore, a client's business risk is expected to be associated with audit fees.

Audit quality is reflected by financial reporting quality, and accounting conservatism is one of the key factors that determine financial reporting quality (Lim, 2011; Watts, 2003a, b). Therefore, auditors may also consider the level of conservatism in financial reporting to avoid legal liability and promote shareholder interest, which reduces audit risk and, thereby, decreases audit fees.

Accounting conservatism enhances financial statement usefulness by reducing residual losses arising from asymmetric information between managers and other parties to the firm (Ahmed & Duellman, 2007). This is achieved by restricting managers' opportunistic payments to themselves and other parties, minimising agency problems associated with managerial investment decisions, improving the efficiency of debt and other contracting, better facilitating the monitoring of contracts and reducing litigation and political costs (Ball & Shivakumar, 2005; Watts, 2003a). Conservative reporting reduces the potential for overstatements by mitigating aggressive managerial estimates (Basu, 1997; Holthausen & Watts, 2001; Khan & Watts, 2009; Watts, 2003a). Accounting conservatism also reduces managements' tendency to misreport (LaFond & Watts, 2008; Watts, 2003a); thereby reducing the chances that auditors will fail to prevent misreporting, which adversely affect the auditor's ability to attract and retain clients (Hennes et al., 2014; Weber et al., 2008). Thus, the client's conservative reporting is expected to reduce the risks of material misstatements. Consequently, the client's conservative reporting is expected to influence audit fees.

Audit pricing theory suggests that auditors might charge lower fees to less riskier clients. Client's conservative reporting leads to lower risk. Therefore, it is expected that the conservative reporting induces lower audit fees.

External auditors are considered an important role in corporate governance by giving credibility to published financial reports. Thus, as a form of external governance, independent auditing can alleviate agency conflicts among stakeholders and reduce agency costs. Effective internal corporate governance reduces agency costs, and consequently the external auditor's risk (Carcello, Hermanson, Neal, & Riley, 2002). This implies less effort by external auditor and in turn lower fees. Therefore, substitution theory suggests that a significant part of external audit is substituted by effective internal corporate governance that results in high quality financial reporting. This is expected to reduce external auditor's risk of providing inaccurate audit opinion (Beasley, Carcello, Hermanson, & Neal, 2009; Krishnan & Visvanathan, 2009). As a result, due to the positive roles of conservatism in mitigating agency costs and reducing litigation and reputation risks, it is expected that the conservative reporting (effective internal corporate governance) induces lower audit fees. Recent research demonstrates that auditors demand lower fees if a client's accounting is more conservative (e.g. DeFond et al., 2016; Lee, Li, & Sami, 2015).

Conversely, signaling theory argues that managers signal high-level corporate governance to external stakeholders by inviting high-quality auditing. Audit quality leads to higher audit fees. Complementary theory predicts that good internal governance mechanisms are related to high-quality audit (Srinidhi, He, & Firth, 2014). Companies with strong corporate governance pay higher audit fees (Wu, 2012). This theory suggests that conservatism accounting and audit are complementary governance mechanisms. Therefore, according to signaling and complementary theories, it is expected a positive relationship between conservatism accounting and audit fees.

Using a sample of non-financial listed Portuguese and Spanish firms-year from 2010 to 2018, this study draws on audit pricing, substitution, signaling and complementary theories to examine the effect of conservatism accounting on audit fees.

The study makes some contributions to the existing literature. First, although many studies have examined the factors influencing audit fees, the relationship between conservative accounting and audit fees is only now beginning to receive research attention, mainly in the United States (DeFond et al., 2016; Lee et al., 2015). There is no evidence concerning the impact of conservatism accounting on audit fees in Iberian Peninsula countries. This paper attempts to fill that gap in our knowledge. Second, this study contributes to the literature in corporate governance by showing that conservatism accounting affects an important external governance mechanism. This study also contributes to prior literature on audit pricing and financial accounting choices by showing how conservatism accounting can influence auditors' perceptions of client risk and, in turn, affect audit fees. Third, the US auditors when compared to other countries' auditors faced significantly higher litigation risk (Chung, Firth, & Kim, 2003; Francis, 2006). Therefore, since Portugal and Spain have a lower litigation risk environment (Beveridge, Nott, & Stephen, 2018), it is possible that accounting conservatism would have little impact on audit fees. That is, whether or not accounting conservatism affects audit fees in environments with lower litigation risk and lower demand for accounting quality - in code-law countries such as Portugal and Spain- remains an open question. Fourth, this paper represents the first known study examining the association between and conservatism accounting and audit fees in Portugal and Spain. Fifth, the Portuguese and Spanish capital markets present a unique case in the study of auditing, because the ownership in Portuguese and Spanish listed firms is highly concentrated, in contrast with the ownership in the US listed firms, which is widely diffused (Shleifer & Vishny, 1997). Sixth, this study also contributes to the limited Portuguese and Spanish corporate governance literature by examining the impact of conservatism accounting on audit fees. Seventh, the findings of this study can provide useful information for auditors, regulators, standard setters and shareholders, mainly whether accounting conservatism affects audit fees, especially in countries with a lower litigation risk environment, which is likely to eliminate the deep pockets incentive for investors, and in firms with highly concentrated equity ownership. Finally, findings based on Portuguese and Spanish data also help build a more expansive international understanding of the effect of conservatism accounting on audit fees.

LITERATURE REVIEW AND TESTABLE HYPOTHESES

Conservatism Accounting and Audit Fees

A key element of the financial reporting process is to guarantee an independent verification of the financial statements prepared by the firm's management (Chan et al., 1993). External audit adds credibility to the financial statements of management.

Audit fee is the price of audit services provided by external auditors. The amount of cost of external audit or the audit fees can vary greatly (DeAngelo, 1981). Audit pricing theory suggests that in a competitive audit market, audit fee is a function of audit effort and the auditor's client-specific business risk (Simunic, 1980; Simunic & Stein, 1996).

Audit effort is driven by audit risk. The higher the audit risk associated with a particular client firm the more time and effort the audit firm is likely to devote to the audit of the client firm's financial statements and this in turn will more than likely lead to an increased level of audit fees (Gul, Chen, & Tsui, 2003). The client's business risk is normally defined as the probability that an auditor will suffer loss because of a client relationship. This risk can affect the reliability of the financial statements and the auditor's expected losses. Such losses may arise e.g. from litigation, sanctions imposed by regulatory bodies, impaired reputation capital or failure to collect fees (Niemi, 2002). This potential loss motivates the auditor to conduct more costly audit testing, resulting in a more defensible audit, and/or charge an additional premium to cover the higher expected costs associated with potential litigation and reputational declines (Stanley, 2011). In this vein, Bedard & Johnstone (2004) show that auditors respond to greater risk by adjusting audit procedures, increasing planned audit effort, and increasing audit fees. Bell, Landsman, & Shackelford (2001) and Charles, Glover, & Sharp (2010) find that audit firms charge higher fees to clients where the auditor faces increased litigation risk. Therefore, riskier companies have larger audit fees.

Accounting conservatism is one of the key factors that determine financial reporting quality (Lim, 2011; Watts, 2003a, b). Watts (2003a) claims that conservatism accounting is important to constrain management's opportunistic financial reporting behaviour and to offset biases introduced in financial reports. Previous empirical studies show that firms with conservative accounting are less likely to engage in earnings management (Goa, 2013; Khalifa & Othman, 2015). Conservative reporting reduces the potential for overstatements by mitigating aggressive managerial estimates (Basu, 1997; Khan & Watts, 2009; Watts, 2003a). Therefore, conservatism is likely to reduce litigation risk because auditors are primarily sued for allowing overstatements or when clients declare bankruptcy (Barrow, Pratt, & Stice, 2001). Understating profits is less dangerous than making an overstatement. In this vein, DeFond et al. (2012) find that client conservatism lowers auditors' litigation risk. Liu & Elayan (2015) also show that higher conservatism in financial reporting leads to lower litigation risk. Biddle, Ma, & Song (2016) show that conservatism mitigates bankruptcy risk by constraining earnings management.

Accounting conservatism also decreases managements' tendency to misreport (LaFond & Watts, 2008; Watts, 2003a); thus, reducing the chances that auditors will fail to prevent misreporting, which adversely affect the auditor's ability to attract and retain clients (Hennes et al., 2014; Weber et al., 2008). DeFond et al. (2012; 2016) find that conservative audit clients are less likely to issue accounting restatements.

The above discussion suggests that, the level of conservatism accounting may be a factor in the determination of the audit risks associated with a particular client firm. The lower the audit risk associated with a particular client firm the less time and effort the audit firm is likely to devote to the audit of the client firm's financial statements and this in turn will more than likely lead to a decreased level of audit fees.

Thus, according to audit pricing theory auditors might charge lower fees to less riskier clients. Client's conservative reporting leads to lower risk. Therefore, it is expected that the conservative reporting induces lower audit fees.

In the corporate governance literature, substitution theory also suggests a negative relationship between conservative accounting and audit fees. External auditors are considered an important role in corporate governance by giving credibility to published financial reports. Thus, as a form of external governance, independent auditing can alleviate agency conflicts among stakeholders and reduce agency costs. Effective internal corporate governance reduces agency costs, and consequently the external auditor's risk (Carcello et al., 2002). This implies less effort by external auditor and in turn lower fees. Good corporate governance may decrease the demand for extensive audit services, reducing the audit fees. In this vein, Cohen & Hanno (2000) find that auditors reduce substantive testing in the presence of stronger corporate governance. Therefore, substitution theory suggests that a significant part of external audit is substituted by effective internal corporate governance that results in high quality financial reporting. This is expected to reduce external auditor's risk of providing inaccurate audit opinion (Beasley et al., 2009; Krishnan & Visvanathan, 2009).

Firms with good governance practices would use conservative accounting to alleviating agency problem and increasing earnings quality. Conservatism accounting inhibits the opportunistic behavior of the managers, and then improves the accuracy and reliability of financial reporting. So, conservatism accounting may to help mitigate financial reporting risk, including earnings management risk. This leads probability auditors tend to invest less audit resources to ensure the quality of auditing, which could decrease audit fees. That is, if external auditors perceive that they can rely on good governance practices, such as conservative accounting, to help control the quality of financial reporting, they may decrease audit effort and charge lower audit fees. As a result, due to the positive roles of conservatism in mitigating agency costs, improving financial reporting quality, reducing litigation and reputation risks, it is expected that the conservative reporting (lower client risk) induces lower audit fees. Recent research demonstrates that auditors demand lower fees if a client's accounting is more conservative (DeFond et al., 2016; Lee et al., 2015).

Hence, under the audit pricing and substitution theories perspective it is expected that conservatism accounting will be more likely to affect audit fees negatively:

Hypothesis 1a (Audit pricing/Substitution theories): The level of conservatism accounting will be negatively associated with audit fees.

External auditors are expected to reduce information asymmetry. Audit quality is considered as a signal quality of the integrity of financial information (Datar, Feltham, & Hughes, 1991; Mukhlasin, 2018). Signaling theory argues that managers signal high-level corporate governance to external stakeholders by inviting high-quality auditing. That is, according to signaling theory firms are more likely to demand high-quality audit to assure and signal investors about the quality of financial reporting even they have a strong corporate governance structure. Audit quality leads to higher audit fees. Thus, signaling theory suggests that firms with more conservative accounting could be more likely to demand high-quality audit to strengthen investor confidence in financial information and, thus pay higher audit fees.

In the corporate governance literature, complementary theory also suggests a positive relationship between conservative accounting and audit fees. Complementary theory predicts that good internal governance mechanisms are related to high-quality audit (Srinidhi et al., 2014). That is, complementary theory considers that in order to effectively supervise the implementation of internal control, the governance layer of the firms with higher internal control quality will actively require auditors to expand the audit scope, and hire the audit firms with high-quality services. Strong corporate governance firms are more likely to engage high-quality auditors and pay larger audit fees (DeFond & Zhang, 2014; Watts & Zimmerman, 1983; Wahab, Zain, & James, 2011). Therefore, firms with strong internal corporate governance pay higher audit fees (Srinidhi et al., 2014; Wahab et al., 2011; Wu, 2012). Previous empirical research also suggests that more effective governance mechanisms lead to higher conservatism accounting (Ahmed & Duellman, 2007; Ahmed & Henry, 2012; Beekes, Pope, & Young, 2004; Goh & Li, 2011; Lobo & Zhou, 2006; Majeed, Zhang, & Wang, 2017; Nasr & Ntim, 2018; Wistawan, Subroto, & Ghofar, 2015). Thus, complementary theory suggests that firms with good governance practices (more conservative accounting) are more likely to demand an extensive audit service and pay higher audit fees.

Therefore, according to signaling and complementary theories, it is expected a positive relationship between conservatism accounting and audit fees.

Hypothesis 1b (Signaling/Complementary theories): The level of conservatism accounting will be positively associated with audit fees.

SAMPLE AND RESEARCH DESIGN

Sample Selection

Our sample includes all the non-financial listed firms of Euronext Lisbon and the Madrid Stock Exchange for the period 2010-2018. Table 1 details how the selection criteria resulted in a final total unbalanced panel of 934 firm-year observations over the 2010 to 2018 period.

The data used in this paper come from the following sources. The Amadeus, a database managed by Bureau Van Dijk and Informa D&B, S.A., the Portuguese Securities Market Supervisory Authority [Comissão de Mercado de Valores Mobiliários (CMVM)] and the Spanish Securities Market Supervisory Authority [Comisión Nacional del Mercado de Valores (CNVM)], which provide the accounting information from annual accounts.

Table 1. Sample selection criteria during the years 2010-2018

Sample selection	Number of firm years		
	Portugal	Spain	Total
Non-financial firms listed	483	1.000	1.483
(-) Football club companies	(36)	-	(36)
(-) Firms with missing data	(135)	(378)	(513)
Number of firm-year observations in the final sample	312	622	934

Research Design

Measuring Audit Fees

Following most audit fee studies (e.g. Barroso, Ali, & Lesage, 2018; Ghafran & O'Sullivan, 2017; Stanley, 2011), the audit fees are measured by the natural log of audit fees paid by the company for audit services during the year (*Audit_Fee*).

Measuring Conservatism Accounting

Following previous studies, this study uses an accrual-based proxy to measure accounting conservatism. Therefore, in line with Ahmed, Billings, Morton, & Stanford-Harris (2002), Ahmed & Duellman (2007), Ahmed & Henry (2012),

Alkurdi, Al-Nimer, & Dabaghia (2017), Givoly & Hayn (2000) and Kim, Pan, & Zuo (2013) the accrual-based measure of conservatism, CONS_ACC, is the income operations plus depreciation less cash flows from operations deflated by average total assets, multiplied by negative one. Positive values of CONS_ACC indicate greater conservatism. The intuition underlying this measure is that conservative accounting results in persistently negative accruals (Givoly & Hayn, 2000; Watts, 2003a).

Control Variables

Given that the *Conservatism Accounting* is not the only factor affecting audit fees, several control variables are introduced to isolate other factors that may influence the audit fees. Previous research suggests that audit risk, Big 4, free cash flow, growth, ROA, leverage and firm size are associated with audit fees (Chung, Firth, & Kim, 2005; Fleischer & Goettsche, 2012; Francis, 2004; Griffin, Lont, & Sun, 2010; Gul & Tsui, 1998; Habib, Bhuiyan, & Rahman, 2018; Mohammadi, Kardan, & Salehi, 2018; Shailer, Cummings, Vatuloka, & Welch, 2004; Simunic, 1980).

Audit risk (Aud_Risk). Higher audit fees are expected with higher audit risk. Certain assets are perceived as being riskier to audit, resulting in higher audit fees. Previous studies suggest that larger amount of inventory and receivables is a signal for higher audit risk (Gandía & Huguet, 2019; Habib et al. 2018; Stanley, 2011).

Big 4. DeAngelo (1981) suggests that large auditors earn higher audit fees because of their higher degrees of perceived quality. Fleischer & Goettsche (2012), Francis (2004), Gandía & Huguet (2019), Mohammadi et al. (2018), Shailer et al. (2004) and Simunic (1980) find that Big audit firms charge high audit fees.

Free Cash Flow (FCF). Jensen (1986) asserts that FCF creates agency problems because of the increased likelihood of value destroying investments. Literature also suggests that the earnings of firms with high agency costs of free cash flow are of low quality (Bukit & Iskandar, 2009; Chung et al., 2005; Rahman & Mohd-Saleh, 2008). Chung et al. (2005) find that managers of firms with high FCF have the incentives to camouflage their activities by increasing reported earnings through income-increasing discretionary accruals. Consequently, auditors may react by judging firms with high FCF as having higher probability of misstatements and require greater effort. As a result, auditors would impose higher level of audit fees. Griffin et al. (2010) and Gul & Tsui (1998) find that high FCF companies have higher audit fees.

Growth. High-growth firms are by nature more difficult to monitor due to the existence of discretionary investments and measurement problems associated with future assets (Myers, 1977). Managers in high-growth firms are more likely to have opportunistic behaviour (Skinner, 1993; Watts & Zimmerman, 1986). High-growth firms are more likely to engage in earnings management, which will further aggravate the situation of lower observability in growth firms (Chen, Elder, & Hung 2010; Zalata, Tauringana, & Tingbani, 2018). In addition, discretionary accruals increase audit risk because they are inherently more difficult to audit (Gul et al., 2003). Therefore, high growth firms can also be more difficult to audit, which can increase audit fees. Griffin et al. (2010) and Gul & Tsui (1998) find that high growth firms have higher audit fees.

ROA. High profitability firms tend to pay more audit fees to their auditors (Simunic, 1980). Highly profitable firms pay more fees because higher profits may require rigorous auditing testing of the validity for the recognition of revenue and expenses which requires more audit time (Joshi & AL-Bastaki, 2000).

Leverage. Highly levered firms have agency problems between lenders and equity investors. These conflicts increase the risk of default. The risk of default may aggravate the underinvestment problem (Jensen, 1986; Myers, 1977). Therefore, high levered firms can rise the likelihood of financial distress. This likelihood increases audit risk, which can increase audit fees. Joshi & AL-Bastaki (2000) find a positive relationship between debt ratio and audit fees.

Firm Size (Size). Larger firms are normally more complex and difficult to control. Therefore, firm size may affect audit fees because reviewing the firms will require additional effort from the auditing firm (Palmrose, 1986; Simunic, 1980). Chen et al. (2005), Gandía & Huguet (2019) and Mohammadi et al. (2018) find that larger firms pay larger audit fees.

Regression Model

The association between conservatism accounting and audit fees is examined by estimating the following regression:

$$Audit\_Fee_{it} = \lambda_0 + \lambda_1 (CONS\_ACC_{it}) + \lambda_2 (Aud\_Risk_{it}) + \lambda_3 (Big4_{it}) + \lambda_4 (FCF_{it}) + \lambda_5 (Growth_{it}) + \lambda_6 (ROA_{it}) + \lambda_7 (Leverage_{it}) + \lambda_8 (Size_{it}) + \varepsilon_{it} \quad (1)$$

where:

$Audit\_Fee_{it}$ = is the natural log of audit fees paid by the firm *i* for audit services during the period *t*;

$CONS\_ACC_{it}$ = is the income operations plus depreciation less cash flows from operations deflated by average total assets for firm *i* for period *t*;

Aud_Risk_{it} = is the sum of inventories and accounts receivables divided by total assets for firm *i* for period *t*;

$Big4_{it}$ = value of 1 if firm is audited by a Big 4 audit firm and 0 otherwise;

FCF_{it} = is the ratio between the operating cash flows and the total assets of firm i for period t;

$Growth_{it}$ = is the market to book of firm *i* for period *t*;
ROA_{it} = is the net income deflated by total assets of firm *i* for period *t*;
$Leverage_{it}$ = ratio between the book value of all liabilities and the total assets of firm *i* for period *t*;
$Size_{it}$ = logarithm of market value of equity of firm *i* for period *t*.

RESULTS AND DISCUSSION

Descriptive Statistics and Correlations

Table 2 presents the sample descriptive statistics for the variables used in this research. Spearman correlations between the explanatory variables are documented in Table 3.

Table 2. Summary of descriptive statistics

	Mean	Median	Min.	Max.
Panel A – Portugal: Number of observations: 312				
CONS_ACC	-0.018	-0.008	-2.989	0.463
Aud_Risk	0.049	0.003	0.000	0.609
Big4	0.721	1.000	0.000	1.000
FCF	0.032	0.032	-2.997	1.544
Growth	1.377	0.732	-0.452	10.017
ROA	2.523	2.193	-56.188	55.356
Leverage	0.471	0.462	0.001	2.517
Size (th EUR)	1.322,4	144,07	0.300	16.345
Panel B – Spain: Number of observations: 622				
CONS_ACC	-0.007	-0.022	-0.491	8.250
Aud_Risk	0.188	0.160	0.000	0.698
Big4	0.811	1.000	0.000	1.000
FCF	0.080	0.067	-1.086	8.225
Growth	3.112	1.442	-9.467	21.499
ROA	3.439	3.021	-58.025	91.200
Leverage	0.600	0.606	0.003	3.721
Size (th EUR)	4.969,4	513,85	0.306	95.167

Table 3. Pearson correlation coefficients matrix

	CONS_ ACC	Aud_ Risk	FCF	Growth	ROA	Leverage	Size
CONS_ACC	1						
Aud_Risk	-0.037**	1					
FCF	0.120***	-0.051	1				
Growth	0.045	-0.267	0.023	1			
ROA	0.160***	-0.071**	0.164***	0.101***	1		
Leverage	0.133***	0.021	-0.054	0.071**	-0.319***	1	
Size	0.025	-0.091**	-0.043	0.072**	0.257***	-0.043	1

CONS_ACC is the income operations plus depreciation less cash flows from operations deflated by average total assets; *Aud_Risk* is the sum of inventories and accounts receivables divided by total assets; *Big4* dummy variable which takes a value 1 if firm is audited by a Big 4 audit firm and 0 otherwise; *FCF* is the ratio between the operating cash flows and the total assets; *Growth* is the market to book of firm; *ROA* is the net income deflated by total assets; *Leverage* represents the ratio between the book value of all liabilities and the total assets; *Size* represents the firm's size.

CONS_ACC is the income operations plus depreciation less cash flows from operations deflated by average total assets; *Aud_Risk* is the sum of inventories and accounts receivables divided by total assets; *FCF* is the ratio between the operating cash flows and the total assets; *Growth* is the market to book of firm; *ROA* is the net income deflated by total assets; *Leverage* represents the ratio between the book value of all liabilities and the total assets; *Size* represents the firm's size.

Regarding Portugal, Panel A in Table 2 shows that, while conservatism, ranges between about -2.989 and 0.463, the mean and median are about -0.018 and -0.008. The mean (median) audit risk is 4.9% (0.3%), with a minimum of 0.0% and a maximum of 60.9%. *Big 4* auditors are used by 72.1% of the sample firms. *FCF* variable represents on average 0.032 of the total assets of the company (with a median of 0.032). The mean (median) *Growth* is 1.377 (0.732), with a minimum of -0.452 and a maximum of 10.017. Panel A in Table 2 also shows that the mean (median) ROA is 2.523 (2.193), with a minimum of -56.188 and a maximum of 55.356. *Leverage* variable represents on average 0.471 of the total assets of the company (with a median of 0.462). The mean of firm size (Size) is about EUR 1.322 million with a minimum of EUR 300 thousand and a maximum of EUR 16.345 million.

Regarding Spain, Panel B in Table 2 shows that, while conservatism, ranges between about -0.491 and 8.250, the mean and median are about -0.007 and -0.022. The mean (median) audit risk is 18.8% (16%), with a minimum of 0.0%

and a maximum of 69.8%. *Big 4* auditors are used by 81.1% of the sample firms. *FCF* variable represents on average 0.080 of the total assets of the company (with a median of 0.067). The mean (median) *Growth* is 3.112 (1.442), with a minimum of -9.467 and a maximum of 21.499. Panel B in Table 2 also shows that the mean (median) ROA is 3.439 (3.021), with a minimum of -58.025 and a maximum of 91.200. *Leverage* variable represents on average 0.6 of the total assets of the company (with a median of 0.606). The mean of firm size (Size) is about EUR 4.969 million with a minimum of EUR 306 thousand and a maximum of EUR 95.167 million.

The analysis of Table 3 shows that there are some significant correlations between the variables. The binary variable *Big4* is not included in the Table 3, given that the Pearson correlation coefficient is not computed to nominal variables.

CONS_ACC is negatively correlated with *Aud_Risk* suggesting that firms with high conservatism accounting tend to have smaller audit risk. *CONS_ACC* is positively correlated with *FCF*, *ROA* and *Leverage*, suggesting that firms with high conservatism accounting have higher *FCF*, *ROA* and *Leverage*. *Aud_Risk* is negatively correlated with both *ROA* and *Size*, suggesting that firms with high audit risk have lower *ROA* and *Size*.

FCF is positively associated with *ROA*, suggesting that firms with high *FCF* have greater *ROA*. *Growth* is positively correlated with *ROA*, *Leverage* and *Size* suggesting that high-growth firms tend to have higher *ROA*, *Leverage* and *Size*. A negative correlation between *Leverage* and *ROA* indicates that firms with high leverage tend to have smaller *ROA*. *Size* is positively associated with *ROA*, suggesting that larger firms have higher *ROA*. Correlation coefficients are, in general, low (below the 0.9 threshold) (Tabachnick & Fidell, 2001), suggesting the absence of serious statistical problems related with multicollinearity.

Regression Results

The author begins with a pooled Ordinary Least Squares (OLS) model, a random effects model and a fixed effects model and the author runs different tests to check the suitability of each model. On one hand, the author compares the results of the pooled OLS model to those of the random effects model by means of the Breusch-Pagan test for random effects. This test revealed that using the random effects model is preferable to the pooled regression model. On the other hand, the author estimates a fixed effects model, and the F test for significance of fixed effects revealed that using fixed effects is also preferable to the pooled regression. Finally, the author uses the Hausman specification test to compare random and fixed effects models and, based on the test results, the fixed effects model is appropriate.

Table 4 presents the results from fixed effects regression for the equation 1.

Table 4. Fixed effects regression results: Period: 2010-2018

	Portugal		Spain		Total sample	
Dependent variable	**Audit Fee**		**Audit Fee**		**Audit Fee**	
Independent variables	**Coefficient**	**t-values**	**Coefficient**	**t-values**	**Coefficient**	**t-values**
Constant	1.123	5.02***	2.005	3.533***	1.576	5.428***
CONS_ACC	0.371	1.913*	1.611	2.994**	1.246	2.178**
Aud_Risk	0.010	1.594	0.689	2.662**	0.782	1.792*
Big4	0.371	1.913*	0.505	2.145**	1.104	3.347***
FCF	0.001	0.194	0.003	1.069	0.066	0.192
Growth	0.790	2.064**	0.454	2.092**	0.529	3.181***
ROA	0.001	0.153	0.003	1.701*	0.105	0.475
Leverage	0.576	2.552**	1.702	3.372***	0.610	2.250**
Size	0.581	3.601***	0.417	2.103***	1.321	4.782***
Observations	312		622		934	
R-squared	33.28%		44.97%		52.59%	
F-statistic	29.923***		39.259***		41.036***	

*** Significant at the 1-percent level; ** Significant at the 5-percent level; * Significant at the 10-percent level.

Audit Fee represents the natural log of audit fees paid by the firm for audit services during the year; *CONS_ACC* is the income operations plus depreciation less cash flows from operations deflated by average total assets; *Aud_Risk* is the sum of inventories and accounts receivables divided by total assets; *Big4* dummy variable which takes a value 1 if firm is audited by a Big 4 audit firm and 0 otherwise; *FCF* is the ratio between the operating cash flows and the total assets; *Growth* is the market to book of firm; *ROA* is the net income deflated by total assets; *Leverage* represents the ratio between the book value of all liabilities and the total assets; *Size* represents the firm's size.

To both Portugal and Spain, the results in Table 4 show that conservatism accounting is positively related to audit fees. The Hypothesis 1*b* predicts a positive relationship between conservatism accounting and audit fees. The findings support this hypothesis, which suggests that firms with more conservative accounting (with strong internal corporate governance) could be more likely to demand high-quality audit to strengthen investor confidence in financial information and, thus pay higher audit fees. Therefore, the results of this study support signaling/complementary theories.

The control variables, audit risk, is positively and significantly associated with audit fees to Spain and to total sample consistent with other studies (e.g. Habib et al. 2018; Stanley, 2011), what is in line with expectations that higher risk firms pay higher audit fees. As in other studies (Barroso et al., 2018; Francis, 2004; Mohammadi et al., 2018; Shailer et al., 2004), Big 4 has a positive and significant effect on audit fees, suggesting that Big audit firms charge high audit fees. As in Griffin et al. (2010) and Gul & Tsui (1998), growth is positively related to audit fees, which is in line with expectations that high growth firms pay higher audit fees. To Spain, as in Gandía & Huguet (2019), Ghafran & O'Sullivan (2017) and Joshi & AL-Bastaki, 2000, ROA is positively associated with audit fees, suggesting that high profitability firms induce more audit fees. To both Portugal and Spain, the results suggest that larger and higher leveraged firms tend to pay greater audit fees consistent with other studies (Chen et al., 2005; Fleischer & Goettsche, 2012; Ghafran & O'Sullivan, 2017; Joshi & AL-Bastaki, 2000; Mohammadi et al., 2018).

DISCUSSION

This study examines the relationship between conservatism accounting and audit fees using audit pricing, substitution, signaling and complementary theoretical frameworks. These theories differ in their assessment of the effect of conservatism accounting on audit fees. Audit pricing theory provides a framework that posits that auditors might charge lower fees to less riskier clients (more conservative clients). Substitution theory argues that a more effective internal governance mechanism substitutes for higher audit quality. Therefore, this theory also suggests that conservatism accounting induces lower audit fees. On the other hand, signaling theory argues that managers signal high-level corporate governance to external stakeholders by inviting high-quality auditing. Complementary theory suggests that firms with good governance practices (such as more conservative accounting) are more likely to demand an extensive audit service and pay higher audit fees.

The findings of this research show evidence that conservatism accounting affects audit fees. In line with signaling and complementary theories perspective, conservatism accounting is positively related to audit fees. Thus, managers signal high-level corporate governance to external stakeholders by inviting high-quality auditing firms. Firms with more conservative accounting are more likely to demand high-quality audit, and pay more audit fees, to assure and signal investors about the quality of financial reporting. Firms with good governance practices are more likely to demand an extensive audit service and pay higher audit fees. Thus, conservatism accounting and external audits are complementary governance mechanisms to improve the quality and credibility of the financial reporting. This study supports the view that the control mechanisms complement each other, where a firm with effective internal governance mechanisms is more likely to demand high audit quality, which ultimately results in higher audit fees.

However, this result is not in line with recent findings of studies of DeFond et al. (2016) and Lee et al. (2015) conducted in USA context, which find that conservatism accounting induces lower audit fees. One potential explanation for the results of this study may be that the ownership in the US listed firms is widely diffused, while the ownership in Portuguese and Spanish listed firms is highly concentrated. In firms with higher ownership concentration, there is usually not enough separation of duties and independent check-and-balance mechanisms to restrain the abuse of power by the controlling owners. Agency problems that are induced by concentrated ownership structure may increase audit risks and, consequently the audit fees. The expropriation risk of minority shareholders is likely to influence the audit fees (Hope, Langli, & Thomas, 2012; Whisenant, Sankaraguruswamy, & Raghunandan, 2003). Consequently, when firms facing opportunistic behaviour of insiders, auditors charge higher fee to compensate the higher inherent risk and higher control risk present in such firms (Jensen, 1986; Khalil, Magnan, & Cohen, 2008). In addition, minority shareholders might demand an extensive audit service to protect themselves from the expropriation of major shareholders (Hay, Knechel, & Ling, 2008) and to reduce information asymmetry with managers (Barroso et al., 2018). Another potential explanation is that firms with concentrated ownership may purchase high-quality audit services to signal non-expropriation behaviour and increase the transparency of the firms (Fan & Wong, 2005; Hay et al., 2008). Future research could address the influence of ownership concentration on audit fees.

SENSITIVITY ANALYSES

To ensure the robustness of results, the author performs several sensitivity checks. The first sensitivity analysis tests the impact of using alternative definition for the conservatism variable on regression results. The accrual-based measure of conservatism (CONS_ACC) is estimate using the Ball & Shivakumar (2006) model. Consequently, conservatism is measured using the following piecewise linear relation between accruals and cash flows:

$$\text{CONS\_ACC}_{it} = \beta_0 + \beta_1 \text{DCFO}_{it} + \beta_2 \text{CFO}_{it} + \beta_3 \text{DCFO}_{it} \text{ x CFO}_{it} + \xi_{it}$$

where, CONS_ACC = accruals scaled by beginning total assets. Accruals are defined as the operating profit after tax minus cash flows from operations. CFO = cash flows from operation scaled by beginning total assets. DCFO = dummy variable that equals 1 if CFO is negative and 0 otherwise.

The results (not reported here) of the regression, using alternative variable to measure CONS_ACC has implications on *ROA* variable, which is now not significant. Therefore, the central findings of this study are similar with the initial ones. The results are also robust to using either the value of assets or reported sales as alternative proxies of firm size.

The second sensitivity analysis examines the effect of influential observations on results. Where outliers are found (namely in the variables *FCF, Growth and ROA*), a winserization method is used to test the robustness of the results. Extreme values (defined as values that are more than three standard deviations away from the mean) are replaced by values that are exactly three standard deviations away from the mean. The results (not reported here) do not differ from results presented previously. Thus, the influential observations do not seem affect the results.

The next sensitivity analysis examines the potential endogeneity problems. An analysis of the impact of conservatism accounting on audit fees may face the endogeneity challenge. Conservatism accounting can cause the firm to demand less (additional) audit services. High earnings quality (more conservative accounting) can cause the firm to demand less audit services. In contrast, the firm could to demand additional audit services (high-quality auditing) to signal high-level corporate governance to external stakeholders.

Conservatism accounting might cause auditors to supply less (additional) services. The presence of conservatism accounting might cause the auditors to undertake less audit procedures. On the other hand, auditors may charge higher audit fees to conservative firms because conservatism accounting increase earnings quality. A high earnings quality sends a signal to market participants that the firm has a higher audit quality, which increase the auditor reputation.

To address the potential endogeneity problem, the author estimates a simultaneous equation system of audit fees and conservatism accounting using the 2SLS method. In the first stage, the author regresses the measure of conservatism on a set of determinants which are taken from previous literature: board composition; leverage, profitability, growth and firm size (Ahmed et al., 2002; Ahmed & Duellman, 2007; Sun & Liu, 2011). Then, in the second stage, the author uses the predicted value for conservatism as instruments, and re-estimate model (1). The main results persist, all coefficient and average coefficient estimates retain their sign and significance levels.

Overall, the several sensitivity analyses conducted largely corroborate the results presented previously.

CONCLUSION

Conservatism is considered an effective mechanism to address agency problem (Watts, 2003a). Accounting conservatism enhances financial statement usefulness by reducing residual losses arising from asymmetric information between managers and other parties to the firm (Ahmed & Duellman, 2007). This research explores the trade-off between conservatism accounting and external governance mechanisms. In particular, this research draws on audit pricing, substitution, signaling and complementary theories to evaluate the impact of conservatism accounting on audit fees. Audit pricing theory suggests that auditors might charge lower fees to less riskier clients (client's conservative reporting). Substitution theory suggests that to the extent that firms with high conservatism accounting experience less agency problems, hiring audit quality (higher audit fees) is less needed. That is, this hypothesis views conservatism accounting as a substitute for external audit quality. On the other hand, signaling theory suggests that firms with more conservative accounting could be more likely to demand high-quality audit to strengthen investor confidence in financial information and, thus pay higher audit fees. Complementary theory suggests that conservatism accounting and audit are complementary governance mechanisms.

Using fixed effects technique, the author finds a positive relationship between conservatism accounting and audit fees. This results are in line with signaling and complementary theories perspective. Firms with more conservative accounting are more likely to demand high-quality audit, and pay more audit fees, to assure and signal investors about the quality of financial reporting. Firms with good governance practices are more likely to demand an extensive audit service and pay higher audit fees. Thus, conservatism accounting and external audits are complementary governance mechanisms to improve the quality and credibility of the financial reporting.

The results of this study make the following contributions. First, this study contributes to the literature in corporate governance by showing that conservatism accounting affects an important external governance mechanism. Therefore, this paper contributes to understanding how conservatism accounting can influence auditors' perceptions of client risk and, in turn, affects audit fees. Second, this study also contributes to the literature by showing that conservatism accounting affects audit fees in environments with lower litigation risk and lower demand for accounting quality - in code-law countries such as Portugal and Spain. Third, this paper has also implications for cross-national governance and auditing price research. The results of this study show that conservatism accounting impacts audit fees in Portugal and Spain. Fourth, the findings are relevant for countries with an institutional environment similar to that of Portugal and Spain. Finally, the results of this study are likely of interest to a broad range of parties, including shareholders, investors, corporate executives, auditors and regulators.

REFERENCES

Ahmed, A. S., Billings, B. K., Morton, R. M., & Stanford-Harris, M. (2002). The role of accounting conservatism in mitigating bondholder-shareholder conflicts over dividend policy and in reducing debt costs. *The Accounting Review*, *77*(4), 867–890. doi:10.2308/accr.2002.77.4.867

Ahmed, A. S., & Duellman, S. (2007). Accounting conservatism and board of director characteristics: An empirical analysis. *Journal of Accounting and Economics*, *46*(2-3), 411–437. doi:10.1016/j.jacceco.2007.01.005

Ahmed, K., & Henry, D. (2012). Accounting conservatism and voluntary corporate governance mechanisms by Australian firms. *Accounting and Finance*, *52*(3), 631–662. doi:10.1111/j.1467-629X.2011.00410.x

Alkurdi, A., Al-Nimer, M., & Dabaghia, M. (2017). Accounting Conservatism and Ownership Structure Effect: Evidence from Industrial and Financial Jordanian Listed Companies. *International Journal of Economics and Financial Issues*, *7*(2), 608–619.

Baker, R. A., & Al-Thuneibat, A. (2011). Audit tenure and equity risk premium: Evidence from Jordan. *International Journal of Accounting and Information Management*, *19*(1), 5–23. doi:10.1108/18347641111105908

Ball, R., & Shivakumar, L. (2006). The role of accruals in asymmetrically timely gain and loss recognition. *Journal of Accounting Research*, *44*(2), 207–242. doi:10.1111/j.1475-679X.2006.00198.x

Ball, R., & Shivakunar, L. (2005). Earnings quality in UK private firms: Comparative loss recognition timeliness. *Journal of Accounting and Economics*, *39*(1), 83–128. doi:10.1016/j.jacceco.2004.04.001

Barroso, R., Ali, C. B., & Lesage, C. (2018). 'Blockholders' ownership and audit fees: The impact of the corporate governance model. *European Accounting Review*, *27*(1), 149–172. doi:10.1080/09638180.2016.1243483

Barrow, O., Pratt, J., & Stice, J. D. (2001). Misstatement Direction, Litigation Risk, and Planned Audit Investment. *Journal of Accounting Research*, *39*(3), 449–462. doi:10.1111/1475-679X.00022

Basu, S. (1997). The conservatism principle and the asymmetric timeliness of earnings. *Journal of Accounting and Economics*, *24*(1), 3–37. doi:10.1016/S0165-4101(97)00014-1

Beasley, M. S., Carcello, J. V., Hermanson, D. R., & Neal, T. L. (2009). The Audit Committee Oversight Process. *Contemporary Accounting Research, 26*(1), 65–122. doi:10.1506/car.26.1.3

Becker, C. L., DeFond, M. L., Jiambalso, J., & Subramanyam, K. R. (1998). The Effect of Audit Quality on Earnings Management. *Contemporary Accounting Research, 15*(1), 1–24. doi:10.1111/j.1911-3846.1998.tb00547.x

Bedard, J. C., & Johnstone, K. M. (2004). Earnings manipulation risk, corporate governance risk, and auditors' planning and pricing decisions. *The Accounting Review, 79*(2), 277–304. doi:10.2308/accr.2004.79.2.277

Beekes, W., Pope, P., & Young, S. (2004). The link between earnings timeliness, earnings conservatism and board composition: Evidence from the UK. *Corporate Governance, 12*(1), 47–59. doi:10.1111/j.1467-8683.2004.00342.x

Bell, T. B., Landsman, W. R., & Shackelford, D. A. (2001). Auditors' perceived business risk and audit fees: Analysis and evidence. *Journal of Accounting Research, 39*(1), 35–43. doi:10.1111/1475-679X.00002

Beveridge, F., Nott, S., & Stephen, K. (2018). *Making Women Count: Integrating Gender into Law and Policy-Making*. Routledge Revivals.

Biddle, G., Ma, M., & Song, F. (2016). *Accounting conservatism and bankruptcy risk*. Working paper, Faculty of Business and Economics, University of Hong Kong, Hong Kong.

Bukit, R. B., & Iskandar, T. M. (2009). Surplus Free Cash Flow, Earnings Management and Audit Committee. *International Journal of Economics and Management, 3*(1), 204–223.

Carcello, J. V., Hermanson, D. R., Neal, T. L., & Riley, R. A. Jr. (2010). Board Characteristics and Audit Fees. *Contemporary Accounting Research, 19*(3), 365–384. doi:10.1506/CHWK-GMQ0-MLKE-K03V

Chan, P., Ezzamel, M., & Gwilliam, D. (1993). Determinants of audit fees for quoted UK companies. *Journal of Business Finance & Accounting, 20*(6), 765–785. doi:10.1111/j.1468-5957.1993.tb00292.x

Charles, S. L., Glover, S. M., & Sharp, N. Y. (2010). The association between financial reporting risk and audit fees before and after the historic events surrounding SOX. *Auditing, 29*(1), 15–39. doi:10.2308/aud.2010.29.1.15

Chen, K. Y., Elder, R. J., & Hung, S. (2010). The investment opportunity set and earnings management: Evidence from the role of controlling shareholders. *Corporate Governance*, *18*(3), 193–211. doi:10.1111/j.1467-8683.2010.00793.x

Chung, R., Firth, M., & Kim, J. B. (2003). Auditor conservatism and reported earnings. *Accounting and Business Research*, *33*(1), 19–32. doi:10.1080/00014788.2003.9729629

Chung, R., Firth, M., & Kim, J. B. (2005). Earnings management, surplus free cash flow, and external monitoring. *Journal of Business Research*, *58*(6), 766–776. doi:10.1016/j.jbusres.2003.12.002

Cohen, J. R., & Hanno, D. M. (2000). Auditors' consideration of corporate governance and management control philosophy in preplanning and planning judgments. *Auditing*, *19*(2), 133–146. doi:10.2308/aud.2000.19.2.133

Datar, S., Feltham, G., & Hughes, J. (1991). The role of audits and audit quality in valuing new issues. *Journal of Accounting and Economics*, *14*(1), 3–49. doi:10.1016/0167-7187(91)90057-R

DeAngelo, L. (1981). Auditor size and auditor quality. *Journal of Accounting and Economics*, *3*(3), 183–199. doi:10.1016/0165-4101(81)90002-1

DeFond, M. L., Lim, C. Y., & Zang, Y. (2012). *Do Auditors Value Client Conservatism?* Working Paper, University of Southern California, Los Angeles, CA.

DeFond, M. L., Lim, C. Y., & Zang, Y. (2016). Client Conservatism and Auditor-Client Contracting. *The Accounting Review*, *91*(1), 69–98. doi:10.2308/accr-51150

DeFond, M. L., & Zang, J. (2014). A review of archival auditing research. *Journal of Accounting and Economics*, *58*(2-3), 275–326. doi:10.1016/j.jacceco.2014.09.002

Fan, J. P. H., & Wong, T. J. (2005). Do external auditors perform a corporate governance role in emerging markets? Evidence from East Asia. *Journal of Accounting Research*, *43*(1), 35–72. doi:10.1111/j.1475-679x.2004.00162.x

Fleischer, R., & Goettscha, M. (2012). Size effects and audit pricing: Evidence from Germany. *Journal of International Accounting, Auditing & Taxation*, *21*(2), 156–168. doi:10.1016/j.intaccaudtax.2012.07.005

Francis, J. R. (2004). The Effect of Auditor Firm Size on Audit Prices: A study of the Australian Market. *Journal of Accounting and Economics*, *6*, 131–151. doi:10.1016/0165-4101(84)90010-7

Francis, J. R. (2006). Are auditors compromised by Nonaudit services? Assessing the evidence. *Contemporary Accounting Research*, *23*(3), 747–760. doi:10.1506/4VD9-AE3K-XV7L-XT07

Francis, J. R., & Krishnan, J. (1999). Accounting Accruals and Auditor Reporting Conservatism. *Contemporary Accounting Research*, *16*(1), 135–165. doi:10.1111/j.1911-3846.1999.tb00577.x

Gandía, J. L., & Huguet, D. (2019). *Audit fees and cost of debt: differences in the credibility of voluntary and mandatory audits*. Economic Research-Ekonomska Istraživanja. doi:10.1080/1331677X.2019.1678501

Gao, P. (2013). A measurement approach to conservatism and earnings management. *Journal of Accounting and Economics*, *55*(2-3), 251–268. doi:10.1016/j.jacceco.2012.10.001

Ghafran, C., & O'Sullivan, N. (2017). The impact of audit committee expertise on audit quality: Evidence from UK audit fees. *The British Accounting Review*, *49*(6), 578–593. doi:10.1016/j.bar.2017.09.008

Givoly, D., & Hayn, C. (2000). The changing time-series properties of earnings, cash flows and accruals: Has financial reporting become more conservative? *Journal of Accounting and Economics*, *29*(3), 287–320. doi:10.1016/S0165-4101(00)00024-0

Goh, B. W., & Li, D. (2011). Internal Controls and Conditional Conservatism. *The Accounting Review*, *86*(3), 975–1005. doi:10.2308/accr.00000041

Griffin, P. A., Lont, D. H., & Sun, Y. (2010). Agency problems and audit fees: Further tests of the free cash flow hypothesis. *Accounting and Finance*, *50*(2), 321–350. doi:10.1111/j.1467-629X.2009.00327.x

Gul, F. A., Chen, C. J. P., Tsui, J. S. L., & University, H. K. P. (2003). Discretionary Accounting Accruals, Managers' Incentives, and Audit Fees. *Contemporary Accounting Research*, *20*(3), 441–464. doi:10.1506/686E-NF2J-73X6-G540

Gul, F. A., & Tsui, J. (1998). A test of the free cash flow and debt monitoring hypotheses: Evidence from audit pricing. *Journal of Accounting and Economics*, *24*(2), 219–237. doi:10.1016/S0165-4101(98)00006-8

Habib, A., Bhuiyan, B. U., & Rahman, A. (2018). "Problem" directors and audit fees. *International Journal of Auditing*, *23*(1), 125–143. doi:10.1111/ijau.12150

Hay, D., Knechel, W. R., & Ling, H. (2008). Evidence on the impact of internal control and corporate governance on audit fees. *International Journal of Auditing*, *12*(1), 9–24. doi:10.1111/j.1099-1123.2008.00367.x

Hennes, K. M., Leone, A. J., & Miller, B. P. (2014). Determinants and Market Consequences of Auditor Dismissals after Accounting Restatements. *The Accounting Review*, *89*(3), 1051–1082. doi:10.2308/accr-50680

Holthausen, R. W., & Watts, R. L. (2001). The relevance of value-relevance literature for financial accounting standard setting. *Journal of Accounting and Economics*, *31*(1/3), 3–75. doi:10.1016/S0165-4101(01)00029-5

Hope, O. K., Langli, J. C., & Thomas, W. B. (2012). Agency conflicts and auditing in private firms. *Accounting, Organizations and Society*, *37*(7), 500–517. doi:10.1016/j.aos.2012.06.002

Jensen, M. C. (1986). Agency costs of free cash flow, corporate finance, and takeovers. *The American Economic Review*, *76*(2), 323–329. https://www.jstor.org/stable/1818789

Joshi, P. L., & AL-Bastaki, H. (2000). Determinants of Audit Fees: Evidence from the Companies Listed in Bahrain. *International Journal of Auditing*, *4*(2), 129–138. doi:10.1111/1099-1123.00308

Khalifa, M., & Othman, H. B. (2015). The effect of conservatism on cost of capital: MENA evidence. *Applied Economics*, *47*(1), 71–87. doi:10.1080/00036846.2014.962223

Khalil, S., Magnan, M. L., & Cohen, J. R., 2008. Dual-class shares and audit pricing: Evidence from the Canadian markets. *Auditing: A Journal of Practice, 27*(2), 199-216. doi:10.2308/aud.2008.27.2.199

Khan, M., & Watts, R. L. (2009). Estimation and empirical properties of a firm-year measure of accounting conservatism. *Journal of Accounting and Economics*, *48*(2-3), 132–150. doi:10.1016/j.jacceco.2009.08.002

Khuruma, I. K., & Raman, K. K. (2004). Litigation Risk and the Financial Reporting Credibility of Big 4 versus Non-Big 4 Audits: Evidence from Anglo-American Countries. *The Accounting Review*, *79*(2), 473–495. doi:10.2308/accr.2004.79.2.473

Kim, Y., Li, S., Pan, C., & Zuo, L. (2013). The Role of Accounting Conservatism in the Equity Market: Evidence from Seasoned Equity Offerings. *The Accounting Review*, *88*(4), 1327–1356. doi:10.2308/accr-50420

Krishnan, G., & Visvanathan, G. (2009). Do Auditors Price Audit Committee's Expertise? The Case of Accounting versus Nonaccounting Financial Experts. *Journal of Accounting, Auditing & Finance*, *24*(1), 115–144. doi:10.1177/0148558X0902400107

LaFond, R., & Watts, R. L. (2008). The Information Role of Conservatism. *The Accounting Review*, *83*(2), 447–478. doi:10.2308/accr.2008.83.2.447

Lee, S., Li, X., & Sami, H. (2015). Conditional Conservatism and Audit Fees. *Accounting Horizons*, *29*(1), 83–113. doi:10.2308/acch-50928

Lim, R. (2011). Are corporate governance attributes associated with accounting conservatism? *Accounting and Finance*, *51*(4), 1007–1030. doi:10.1111/j.1467-629X.2010.00390.x

Liu, Z., & Elayan, F. A. (2015). Litigation risk, information asymmetry and conditional conservatism. *Review of Quantitative Finance and Accounting*, *44*(4), 581–608. doi:10.100711156-013-0428-y

Lobo, G., & Zhou, J. (2006). Did conservatism in financial reporting increase after the Sarbanes-Oxley Act? Initial evidence. *Accounting Horizons*, *20*(1), 57–73. doi:10.2308/acch.2006.20.1.57

Majeed, M. A., Zhang, X. Z., & Wang, Z. (2017). Product market competition, regulatory changes, ownership structure, and accounting conservatism. *Chinese Management Studies*, *11*(4), 658–688. doi:10.1108/CMS-12-2016-0248

Mohammadi, M. T., Kardan, B., & Salehi, M. (2018). The relationship between cash holdings, investment opportunities and financial constraint with audit fees. *Asian Journal of Accounting Research*, *3*(1), 15–27. doi:10.1108/AJAR-07-2018-0016

Mukhlasin, M. (2018). Auditor Tenure and Auditor Industry Specialization as a Signal to Detect Fraudulent Financial Reporting. *Academy of Accounting and Financial Studies Journal*, *22*(5), 1–10.

Myers, S. (1977). Determinants of corporate borrowing. *Journal of Financial Economics*, *5*(2), 147–175. doi:10.1016/0304-405X(77)90015-0

Nasr, M. A., & Ntim, C. G. (2018). Corporate governance mechanisms and accounting conservatism: Evidence from Egypt. *Corporate Governance: The International Journal of Business in Society*, *18*(3), 386–407. doi:10.1108/CG-05-2017-0108

Niemi, L. (2002). Do firms pay for audit risk? Evidence on risk premiums in audit fees after direct control for audit effort. *International Journal of Auditing*, *6*(1), 37–51. doi:10.1111/j.1099-1123.2002.tb00004.x

Palmrose, Z. (1986). Audit fees and auditor size. *Journal of Accounting Research*, *24*(1), 97–110. doi:10.2307/2490806

Rahman, A. F., & Mohd-Saleh, N. (2008). The Effect of Free Cash Flow Agency Problem on the Value Relevance of Earnings and Book Value. *Journal of Financial Reporting and Accounting*, *6*(1), 75–90. doi:10.1108/19852510880000636

Shailer, G., Cummings, L., Vatuloka, E., & Welch, S. (2004). Discretionary Pricing in a Monopolistic Audit Market. *International Journal of Auditing*, *8*(3), 263–277. doi:10.1111/j.1099-1123.2004.00095.x

Shleifer, A., & Vishny, R. W. (1997). A survey of corporate governance. *The Journal of Finance*, *52*(2), 737–783. doi:10.1111/j.1540-6261.1997.tb04820.x

Simunic, D. A. (1980). The pricing of audit services, theory and evidence. *Journal of Accounting Research*, *18*(1), 161–190. doi:10.2307/2490397

Simunic, D. A., & Stein, M. T. (1996). The Impact of Litigation Risk on Audit Pricing: A Review of the Economics and the Evidence. *Auditing*, *15*, 119–134.

Skinner, D. J. (1993). The investment opportunity set and accounting procedure choice: Preliminary evidence. *Journal of Accounting and Economics*, *16*(4), 407–445. doi:10.1016/0165-4101(93)90034-D

Skinner, D. J., & Srinivasan, S. (2012). Audit Quality and Auditor Reputation: Evidence from Japan. *The Accounting Review*, *87*(5), 1737–1765. doi:10.2308/accr-50198

Srinidhi, B. N., He, S., & Firth, M. (2014). The Effect of Governance on Specialist Auditor Choice and Audit Fees in U.S. Family Firms. *The Accounting Review*, *89*(6), 2297–2329. doi:10.2308/accr-50840

Stanley, J. D. (2011). Is the Audit Fee Disclosure a Leading Indicator of Clients' Business Risk? *Auditing*, *30*(3), 157–179. doi:10.2308/ajpt-10049

Sun, J., & Liu, G. (2011). Client-specific litigation risk and audit quality differentiation. *Managerial Auditing Journal*, *26*(4), 300–316. doi:10.1108/02686901111124639

Tabachnick, B. G., & Fidell, L. S. (2001). *Using Multivariate Statistics*. Allyn and Bacon.

Wahab, E. A. A., Zain, M. M., & James, K. (2011). Political connections, corporate governance and audit fees in Malaysia. *Managerial Auditing Journal*, *26*(5), 393–418. doi:10.1108/02686901111129562

Watts, R. L. (2003a). Conservatism in accounting part I: Explanations and Implications. *Accounting Horizons*, *17*(3), 207–221. doi:10.2308/acch.2003.17.3.207

Watts, R. L. (2003b). Conservatism in accounting part II: Evidence and Research Opportunities. *Accounting Horizons*, *17*(4), 287–301. doi:10.2308/acch.2003.17.4.287

Watts, R. L., & Zimmerman, J. L. (1983). Agency problems, auditing, and the theory of the firm: Some evidence. *The Journal of Law & Economics*, *26*(3), 613–633. doi:10.1086/467051

Watts, R. L., & Zimmerman, J. L. (1986). *Positive Accounting Theory*. Prentice-Hall Englewood Cliffs.

Weber, J., Willenborg, M., & Zhang, J. (2008). Does auditor reputation matter? The case of KPMG Germany and ComROAD AG. *Journal of Accounting Research*, *46*(4), 941–972. doi:10.1111/j.1475-679X.2008.00298.x

Whisenant, S., Sankaraguruswamy, S., & Raghunandan, K. (2003). Evidence on the Joint Determination of Audit and Non-Audit Fees. *Journal of Accounting Research*, *41*(4), 721–744. doi:10.1111/1475-679X.00121

Wistawan, M. A. P., Subroto, B., & Ghofar, A. (2015). The Characteristics Board of Directors, Family Ownership and Accounting Conservatism: Evidence from Family Public Firms in Indonesia. *Research Journal of Finance and Accounting*, *6*(22), 113–121. doi:10.21512/bbr.v9i3.4311

Wu, X. (2012). Corporate governance and audit fees: Evidence from companies listed on the Shanghai Stock Exchange. *China Journal of Accounting Research*, *5*(4), 321–342. doi:10.1016/j.cjar.2012.10.001

Zalata, A. M., Tauringana, V., & Tingbani, I. (2018). Audit committee financial expertise, gender, and earnings management: Does gender of the financial expert matter? *International Review of Financial Analysis*, *55*, 170–183. doi:10.1016/j.irfa.2017.11.002

ADDITIONAL READING

Antle, R., & Nalebuff, B. (1991). Conservatism and Auditor-Client Negotiations. *Journal of Accounting Research*, *29*, 31–54. doi:10.2307/2491002

Choi, A., Sohn, B. C., & Yuen, D. (2018). Do auditors care about real earnings management in their audit fee decisions? *Asia-Pacific Journal of Accounting & Economics*, *25*(1-2), 21–41. doi:10.1080/16081625.2016.1231580

Choi, J. H., Kim, J. B., Liu, X., & Simunic, D. A. (2008). Audit pricing, legal liability regimes, and Big 4 premiums: Theory and cross-country evidence. *Contemporary Accounting Research*, *25*(1), 55–99. doi:10.1506/car.25.1.2

Choi, J. H., Kim, J. B., Liu, X., & Simunic, D. A. (2009). Cross-listing audit fee premiums: Theory and evidence. *The Accounting Review*, *84*(5), 1429–1463. doi:10.2308/accr.2009.84.5.1429

Crockett, M., & Ali, M. J. (2015). Auditor independence and accounting conservatism – Evidence from Australia following the corporate law economic reform program. *International Journal of Accounting & Information Management*, *23*(1), 80–104. doi:10.1108/IJAIM-02-2014-0008

Gul, F. A. (1999). Audit prices, product differentiation and economic equilibrium. *Auditing*, *18*(1), 90–100. doi:10.2308/aud.1999.18.1.90

Karaibrahimoglu, Y. (2013). Is Corporate Governance A Determinant of Auditor Choice? Evidence From Turkey. *Ege Academic Review*, *13*(2), 273–284.

Larcker, D. F., & Richardson, S. A. (2004). Fees Paid to Audit Firms, Accrual Choices, and Corporate Governance. *Journal of Accounting Research*, *42*(3), 625–658. doi:10.1111/j.1475-679X.2004.t01-1-00143.x

Leidner, J. J., & Lenz, H. (2017). Client's business risk, public-interest entities, and audit fees: The case of German credit institutions. *International Journal of Auditing*, *21*(3), 1–15. doi:10.1111/ijau.12099

Li, B., & Ma, C. (2018). Can audit fees inhibit accounting misstatements? Moderating effects of auditor reputation from Chinese experience. *Asia-Pacific Journal of Accounting & Economics*, 1–20. doi:10.1080/16081625.2018.1475243

Miah, M. S., Jiang, H., Rahman, A., & Stent, W. (2020). Audit effort, materiality and audit fees: Evidence from the adoption of IFRS in Australia. *Accounting Research Journal*, *33*(1), 186–216. doi:10.1108/ARJ-06-2018-0103

KEY TERMS AND DEFINITIONS

Audit Fee: A fee paid by the firm for audit services during the period.

Audit Quality: Is the joint probability that the external auditor detects an irregularity in financial statements, and then reveals it to the external users.

Audit Risk: Is the risk that the auditor expresses an inappropriate audit opinion when the financial statements are materially misstated.

External Audit: Is an official examination of the accounts of a company or organization conducted by an independent third party (the auditor), to ensure that they have been properly maintained, are accurate and comply with accounting standards and give a true and fair view of the financial state of the entity.

Conservatism Accounting: In accounting, the convention of conservatism, is a policy of anticipating possible future losses but not futures gains. This policy tends to exhibit the potential worst scenarios in financial statements.

Chapter 14
BoD Structure and Corporate Governance Models

Mahboob Ullah
https://orcid.org/0000-0001-5585-9814
Al-Taqwa University, Afghanistan

ABSTRACT

Corporate governance, the soul of every corporate body, is indispensable for the survival, growth, and development of any kind of organization. It has significant impact and influence in attaining the confidence of stakeholder. Good governance leads to instill the confidence of stakeholder. The significance of corporate governance has increased globally in past decades due to financial crises, technology advancement, liberalizations, emergence of financial markets, and liberalization of trade and capital mobilization. Corporate boards, academicians, legislators, and in all businesses, corporate governance are believed to be a mainstream concern in corporate structure.

BOARD OF DIRECTORS

Corporate governance, the soul of every corporate body, which is indispensible for the survival, growth and development of any kind of organization. It has significant impact and influence in attaining the confidence of stakeholder. Good governance leads to instill the confidence of stakeholder. The significance of corporate governance has increased globally in past decades due to financial crises, technology advancement, liberalizations, emergence of financial markets, and liberalization of trade and capital mobilization. Corporate boards, academicians, legislators and in all businesses, corporate governance is believed as a mainstream concern in corporate structure (Claessens, Djankov & Lang, 2000). The significance of corporate

DOI: 10.4018/978-1-7998-6669-5.ch014

Copyright © 2021, IGI Global. Copying or distributing in print or electronic forms without written permission of IGI Global is prohibited.

governance was realized and first time came into fashion in1970s in USA. While in Pakistan, Corporate governance code came into vogue in March 2002 after the operationalization of Securities and Exchange Commission of Pakistan (SECP), in order to make sure prism and accountability in corporate division for safeguarding the stake every stakeholder, particularly those of minority stockholders.

A board of directors (B of D) is an elected group of individuals that represent shareholders. The board is a governing body that typically meets at regular intervals to set policies for corporate management and oversight. Every public company must have a board of directors. Some private and nonprofit organizations also have a board of directors.

In general, the board makes decisions as a fiduciary on behalf of shareholders. Issues that fall under a board's purview include the hiring and firing of senior executives, dividend policies, options policies, and executive compensation. In addition to those duties, a board of directors is responsible for helping a corporation set broad goals, supporting executive duties, and ensuring the company has adequate, well-managed resources at its disposal.

Board Structure

The structure and powers of a board are determined by an organization's bylaws. Bylaws can set the number of board members, the manner in which the board is elected (e.g., by a shareholder vote at an annual meeting), and how often the board meets. While there is no set number of members for a board, most range from 3 to 31 members. Some analysts believe the ideal size is seven.

The board of directors should be a representation of both management and shareholder interests and include both internal and external members.

An insider director is a member who has the interest of major shareholders, officers, and employees in mind, and whose experience within the company adds value. An insider director is not typically compensated for board activity as they are often already a C-level executive, major shareholder, or another stakeholder, such as a union representative.

Independent or outside directors are not involved in the day-to-day inner workings of the company. These board members are reimbursed and usually receive additional pay for attending meetings. Ideally, an outside director brings an objective, independent view to goal-setting and settling any company disputes. It is considered critical to strike a balance of internal and external directors on a board.

Board structure can differ slightly in international settings. In some countries in Europe and Asia, corporate governance is split into two tiers: an executive board and a supervisory board. The executive board is composed of insiders elected by employees and shareholders and is headed by the CEO or managing officer. The executive board is in charge of daily business operations. The supervisory board is chaired by someone other than the presiding executive officer and addresses similar concerns as a board of directors in the United States.

Election and Removal Methods of Board Members

While members of the board of directors are elected by shareholders, which individuals are nominated is decided by a nomination committee. In 2002, the NYSE and NASDAQ required independent directors to compose a nomination committee. Ideally, directors' terms are staggered to ensure only a few directors are elected in a given year.

Removal of a member by resolution in a general meeting can present challenges. Most bylaws allow a director to review a copy of a removal proposal and then respond to it in an open meeting, increasing the possibility of a rancorous split. Many directors' contracts include a disincentive for firing — a golden parachute clause that requires the corporation to pay the director a bonus if they are let go.

A board member is likely to be removed if they break foundational rules; for example, engaging in a transaction that is a conflict of interest, or striking a deal with a third party to influence a board vote.

Breaking foundational rules can lead to the expulsion of a director. These infractions include but are not limited to the following:

- Using directorial powers for something other than the financial benefit of the corporation.
- Using proprietary information for personal profit,
- Making deals with third parties to sway a vote at a board meeting.
- Engaging in transactions with the corporation that result in a conflict of interest.

In addition, some corporate boards have fitness-to-serve protocols.

Roles of Director

Typical duties of boards of directors include;

- governing the organization by establishing broad policies and setting out strategic objectives;
- selecting, appointing, supporting and reviewing the performance of the chief executive (of which the titles vary from organization to organization; the chief executive may be titled CEO, President or Executive Director

- terminating the chief executive;
- ensuring the availability of adequate financial resources;
- approving annual budgets;
- accounting to the stakeholders for the organization's performance;
- setting the salaries, compensation and benefits of senior management;

The legal responsibilities of boards and board members vary with the nature of the organization, and between jurisdictions. For companies with publicly trading stock, these responsibilities are typically much more rigorous and complex than for those of other types.

Typically, the board chooses one of its members to be the chairman (often now called the "chair" or "chairperson"), who holds whatever title is specified in the by laws or articles of association. However, in membership organizations, the members elect the president of the organization and the president becomes the board chair, unless the by-laws say otherwise.

Governance Systems

Corporate governance systems perform a significant role in financial performance as they present mechanism which affect investment's return for external suppliers of finance to corporation (Edwards & Nibler, 2000). The corporate governance systems could vary to great extent depending on mechanism that corporate owners utilize to persuade managers (Davis & Useem, 2000). The system of corporate governance differ amongst countries in diversity of capitalism systems in which they are entrenched (Giurca Vasilescu, 2008). Thus, various models of corporate governance are applied all over world and these models have separate and distinct traits (Hasan, 2009). Nestor and Thompson (2000) have categorized these models in to two kinds:

External models (Unitary system): US and other English language speaking countries also known as Anglo Saxon Model.

Internal Model (Dual System): European Continental Model also known as German Model

With inside regular system of governance and exclusive combination of corporate control, both the systems have grown-up from various environments of regulatory, political and institutions (Babic, 2003). Weimer and Paper (1999) arrived at same group difference between unitary and dual systems of corporate governance. The principal trait of market oriented system is a dynamic outside market for corporate control, a mechanism for influencing decision making of managers as independent shareholders, consisting of stock, labor and hostile takeover markets. Conversely, dual systems, oligarchic class with various recognitions greatly influence decision making of managers by more direct means of sway. Specifically, limited voting rights of independent stockholders, cross stockholders, and interlocking directors' shows orientation of network. According to Shleifer and Vishny (1997), for consideration of corporate governance problems, classification of two systems is necessary. The system includes:

Unitary Systems: In the UK and the USA, which inclined to rely upon compensation of managers and market for corporate control

Dual Systems: Germany, France and Spain, which inclined to utilize control by many incumbent stockholders to support the managers and owners behavior.

Anglo American Model of Corporate Governance (External Model)

Figure 1. Anglo Saxon model of corporate governance
Source: Cernat (2004, p.153)

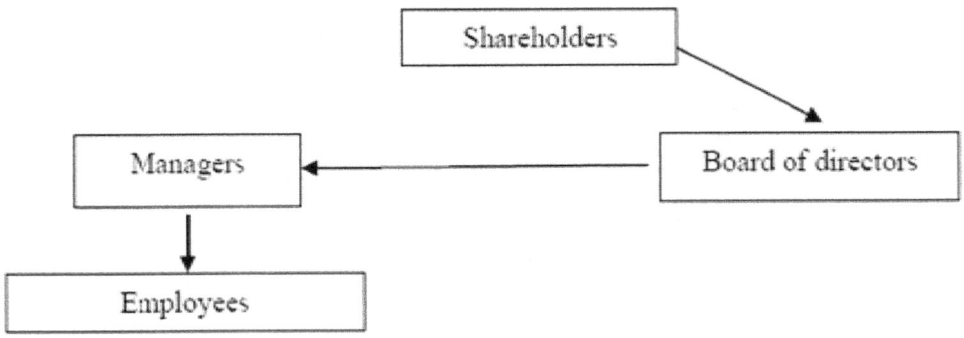

In the Anglo Saxon Model, the corporate notion is based upon fiduciary relation amongst stockholders and manager. The Anglo Saxon model is based on concept that self-stake and decentralized market can perform in a self-controlled, balanced manner and is founded on notion of capitalism market (Cernat, 2004). Therefore, corporations have normally same systems of corporate governance in Anglo American countries: UK, US Australia and Canada. In this model, management activities are monitored and controlled by one independent board of director for improvement. According to Hasan (2009) ownership is concentrated in Anglo Saxon Model, indicated by International Chamber of Commerce, only some people having legitimate power upon the management team and minority investors have meager shelter, who ask for support of independent director, which is made via executive chairman.

The above diagram indicates that Anglo Saxon Model is based on the relation amongst shareholders and managers. Sound legal shield in this model is required by shareholders due to dispersed sound legal protection and the impact of shareholders on management is poor. In this model, the function of corporate governance is to provide safeguarding the stake and right of shareholders (Hasan, 2009).

Continental Model of Corporate Governance (Internal Model)

Donaldson and Preston (1995) described the stakeholder's model that it concentrates on relation standing upon the emphasis of interest maximization of broader group of stakeholders. The internal model of corporate governance (particularly European corporations and Japan) spotlight on stake of crews, managers, clients, suppliers and community, which aid innovations and competitions (Giurca Vasilescu, 2008). Similar notion is applied in France where managers and board of directors detained duties to the company as well as crew, trade union the work council and public (Snyder, 2007). The core principles which are bases for corporate governance continental systems embodied are corporate stakeholder's theory. The continental model of corporate governance concentrate on not only shareholders' stake but also input from the related stakeholders (Cernat, 2004). For corporate governance, several Europeans countries like France, Greece and Germany apply stakeholder's model in several large corporations as element of economic and social structure (Maher and Anderson, 2000).

Iqbal and Mirakhor (2004) argued that the Continental model of corporate governance (insider model) has three foundations on three propositions which are apparently opposite Anglo American Model of Corporate Governance (External Model). These propositions are related to stakeholder's stake, right and responsibilities of managers, summarized as under:

Stake: Enhancing stake of stakeholders not of the shareholders only as Anglo Saxon model

Right: Stakeholders own the right to contribute in company decisions

Responsibilities: Safeguarding the stake of stakeholders is the responsibility of managers

The diagram of continental model exhibits that it has foundation on the relation among stockholders, board of directors, and supervisory board on the basis of important banks role and broad ownership relevant to finance and control (Cernat, 2004). The board of supervisors normally consists several stakeholders comprises investors (stockholders and creditors) customers, crew (group of union), suppliers and appointees of government representation wider part of society (Schilling, 2001; West, 2006). According to Hassan (2009) structure of corporate governance in Germany, primarily concern with some large corporations with greater than two thousand crews, enlisted at stock exchanges and run on two level systems: supervisory and management board system (Hasan, 2009).

Figure 2. Corporate governance of continental model
Source: Cernat (2004, p.153)

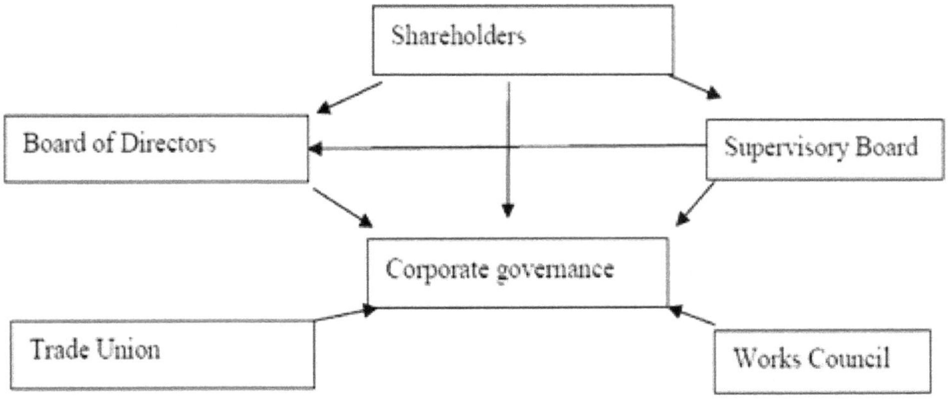

Giurca Vasilescu (2008) described that comparative evaluation of corporate governance models and its pros and cons indicates that corporate governance system of corporations might be maximized due to subsequent factors:

- Corporate governance is influenced by the products and services competiveness
- Corporate performance is identified the capital market's real presentation and management's implicitly with corporate share price level.
- Corporate governance is influenced by the potential force of institutional investors
- Managers labor markets which approve extreme benefits of managers without good performance, by replacing such managers in managing board.

Table 1. Comparison of US and German corporate governance systems

Aspects	U.S	Germany
Executive compensation	High	Moderate
Board of directors	Primarily outsiders	Management/ supervisory
Ownership	Diffuse/ non-corporate	Concentrated: high family/ Corporate/ bank
Capital markets	Very liquid	Relatively illiquid
Takeover/ control market	Major	Minor
Banking system	Fragmented	Universal banking

Source: Kaplan (1997)

Code of Corporate Governance in Pakistan

The Security and Exchange Commission of Pakistan (SECP) has centered its regulatory measures on promoting investors confidence to uphold sound corporate governance to make sure transparency and accountability in the corporate sector and protect the stake of all stakeholders, particularly minority stakeholders. Code of corporate governance for Pakistan was concluded and issued by SECP in March 2002 and at that time Pakistan included amongst those few countries who adopted code of corporate governance. Code of corporate governance was included in the listing regulations of firms in Pakistani stock exchange(s). Pakistan Institute of Corporate Governance in Public Private Partnership was established in 2004 for studying governance practices jointly according to their roles. Pakistan corporate governance project was started by International Finance Corporation in 2006 in order to improve corporate governance practices (Corporate Governance Practices in Pakistan, 2009). In the preceding decade, Pakistani regulators and corporations have made imperative effort for improvement of the level of corporate governance. Corporate governance is a set of sound application to offer a framework with the help which listed corporation at stock exchange(s) of Pakistan can be better directed and controlled.

All the listed corporations in stock exchanges are required to fulfill the codes of corporate governance, revised on March 08, 2013 by SECP Act 1997(XLII of 1997) with sanctioning of central government, in application of power granted by section 43, clause b of companies ordinance 1984 (XLVII of 1984). According to SECP (2018) the key components of code of corporate governance are: Short title, commencement and applicability, Definitions, Composition of the Board, Role of the chairman and chief executive and separation of the two positions, Responsibilities, powers and functions of the Board, Meetings of the Board, Key information to be placed for decision by the Board, Performance evaluation, Related party transactions, Quarterly and Monthly Financial Statements and Annual Report, Board orientation and learning, Formation of Board committees, Chief Financial Officer, Company Secretary and Chief Internal, Auditor - appointment and removal, Role and qualification of Chief Financial Officer and Company Secretary, Requirement to attend Board Meetings, Financial Reporting Framework, Directors' report to the Shareholders, Disclosure of Interests by Directors and Officers, Directors' Remuneration, Responsibility for financial reporting and corporate Compliance, Audit Committee, Internal Audit, External Auditors, Compliance with the rules and Penalty for contravention of the rules.

Key provisions of code of: Composition of the Board, Role of the chairman and chief executive and separation of the two positions and Audit Committee are enumerated in the light of revised SECP, 2019.

Composition of the Board

1. Executive directors, non executive directors, independent directors and of minority stake with required level of knowledge, skills, experience, competency, and approach.
2. Forty percent of total member of a board must be independent directors and in next 2 years it must be increased and it must be kept consequently. The corporation must disclose the executive, non-executive and independent directors in the annual report.
3. Independent directors shall not join in share option or same schemes of corporation which enables him/her to attain any stake in corporation.
4. Directors must replenish any casual position in corporate board before but not later than 90 days.
5. No one can be nominated or elected like director of greater than 5 corporations except their subsidiaries.
6. The listed corporation must initiate essential steps where required, to make sure that a class of minority shareholders are supported by proxy solicitation.
7. Fit and proper criteria must be applied by appointing authorities of government and shareholders for nomination of person(s) in board membership election under the provision companies ordinance 1984.

Role of the Chairman and Chief Executive and Separation of the Two Positions

1. The office and responsibilities shall be separate and distinct of chairman and chief executive officer.
2. The chairman shall:
    a. Ensure the appropriately performance of board as well as the entire matters related to corporation are placed in board meeting's agenda;
    b. Setting up agenda and conducting the board meeting and
    c. Ensuring that board of directors are enable and encourage in totally participation in the discussions and decisions of board. He shall not engage in daily operations of the corporation. He shall be responsible for leading the board, ensuring board effectively carrying out and its constant development.
3. According to the companies ordinance 1984, the CEO is responsible for:
    a. Corporate management and its financial and other matters procedures
    b. Efficient execution of corporate strategies and policies sanctioned by the board
    c. Suitable arrangement of ensuring that corporate funds are other resources are protected properly and utilized efficiently and effectively, according to entire statutory obligations.
4. The chairman shall be elect by the board amongst the suitable non executive directors SECP (2019), *it was made voluntary to elect chairman from independent directors as first its was mandatory)* in order to accomplish right balance of power, enhancing accountability and improving the capacity of board for applying independent evaluation

Audit Committee

1. The board shall set up an audit committee and the member of board shall be finance qualified. Subject to the provision of sub rule
2. Off rule 12, the chairman and majority of audit committee shall be non executive directors
3. Corporate chairman and CEO shall not be the member of the audit committee
4. The CFO, CIA and one representative of outside auditors shall participate in every meeting of audit committee in which accounts and audit matters are discussed, provided that:
    a. The audit committee shall meet the outside directors at least once a year exclusive of
    b. CFO, CIA and other executives being present, to make sure the free communication between audit committee and external auditors:

   c. That audit committee shall meet the CIA and other members of the internal audit function exclusive of CFO and external auditors.
5. Terms of references for audit committee shall be decided by the board in writing, identifying the audit committee mandate. The committee having complete explicit authority to examine accounts and finance issues as mentioned in the terms of references and must be given enough resources and access to entire related information
6. Recommendation regarding the appointment, resignation or removal of corporate external auditor is the responsibility of the audit committee and the board shall proceed in all matters according to the these recommendations, if lacking sound reasons to act. Yet the board must not consider to release itself from the entire responsibility for delegation of functions to audit committee.
7. It may be included in term of reference of the audit committee designed by corporate board:
   a. Correct measures' determination for protection of assets
   b. Reviewing the financial statements, quarterly, semi annually and annually before board sanctioning of
   c. External audit facilitation and discussion of main observations raised by the external auditors or wishing to arise in interim and annual audits
   d. Reviewing letter issued by external auditors and management feed back
   e. Reviewing the internal audit scope and extent and making sure that enough resources are available for internal audit functions and placed appropriately.
   f. Making sure the internal and external auditors coordination
   g. concern of internal investigation main findings and the management feedback
   h. highlighting any main violation
8. Management of relationship with external auditors shall be the responsibility of audit committee
9. Audit committee recommendations regarding the appointment of retired auditors and the reasons for changing the outside directors prior to the lapse of three successive fiscal year shall be contain in director's report.
10. A secretary of the audit committee shall be appointed for circulation of meeting minutes to among all members, directors and CFO within fourteen days of meeting.

REFERENCES

Babic, V. (2003). *Corporate governance problems in transition economies.* Winston-Salem: Wake Forest University (Social Science Research Seminar), http://www.ibrarian.net/navon/paper/corporate_governance_problems_in_transition_econo.pdf?paperid=3696120

Cernat, L. (2004). The emerging European corporate governance model: Anglo-Saxon, Continental, or still the century of diversity? *Journal of European Public Policy*, *11*(1), 147–166. doi:10.1080/1350176042000164343

Claessens, S., & Fan, J. P. H. (2002). Corporate governance in Asia: A survey. *International Review of Finance*, *3*(2), 71–103. doi:10.1111/1468-2443.00034

Davis, G. F., & Useem, M. (2002). Top management, company directors, and corporate control. In A. M. Pettigrew, H. Thomas, & R. Whittington (Eds.), Handbook of strategy and management (pp. 233–259). Academic Press.

Edwards, J., & Nibler, M. (2000). Corporate governance in Germany: The role of banks and insider directors. *Economic Policy*, *15*(31), 237–267. doi:10.1111/1468-0327.00062

Giurca Vasilescu, L. (2008). *Corporate governance in developing and emerging countries: the case of Romania.* Munich Personal RePEc Archive, https://mpra.ub.uni-muenchen.de/11053/

Hasan, Z. (2009). Corporate governance: Western and Islamic perspectives'. *International Review of Business Research Papers*, *5*(1), 277–293.

Iqbal, Z., & Mirakhor, A. (2004). Stakeholders model of governance in Islamic economic system. *Islamic Economic Studies*, *11*(2), 43–63.

Nestor, S., & Thompson, J. (2000). *Corporate governance patterns in OECD economies: is convergence under way?* Academic Press.

OECD. (2001). *Corporate governance in Asia: A comparative perspective*. OECD.

Schilling, F. (2001). Corporate governance in Germany: The move to shareholder value. *Corporate Governance*, *9*(3), 148–151. doi:10.1111/1467-8683.00242

SECP. (2018). www.secp.gov.pk/news/PDF/News_14/PR_Jan13_2014.pdf

Snyder, L. (2007). Filling a position of corporate governance in France: A practical Introduction. *Corporate Governance*, *7*(3), 238–250. doi:10.1108/14720700710756526

Compilation of References

Abdelsalam, O., & El-Masry, A. (2008). The impact of board independence and ownership structure on the timeliness of corporate internet reporting of Irish- listed companies. *Managerial Finance*, *34*(12), 907–918. doi:10.1108/03074350810915842

Abdul Rahman, R., & Mohamed Ali, F. H. (2006). Board, audit committee, culture and earnings management: Malaysian evidence. *Managerial Auditing Journal*, *21*(7), 783–804. doi:10.1108/02686900610680549

Abdullah, A. M., Entebang, H., Shazali, A., & Qaiser, R. Y. (2012). *Financial performance of public listed companies in Sarawak*. Paper presented at the postgraduate conference on social science and humanities, Kuching.

Abdullah, H., & Valentine, B. (2009). Fundamental and ethics theories of corporate governance. *Middle Eastern Finance and Economics*, 4.

Abdullah, S. N. (2004). Board composition, CEO duality and performance among Malaysian listed companies. *Corporate Governance*, *4*(4), 47–61. doi:10.1108/14720700410558871

Abdullah, S. N., Ku Ismail, K., & Nachum, L. (2015). Does having women on boards create value? The impact of societal perceptions and corporate governance in emerging markets. *Strategic Management Journal*, *38*(3), 334–354.

Abshire, M. (2003). State of Corporate Citizenship: Survey. *Corporate Philanthropy Report*, *18*(8), 1–3.

Accenture Strategy. (2019). *Family Businesses in Asia. Accenture Strategy, 2019*. Retreived from https://www.accenture.com/_acnmedia/thought-leadership-assets/pdf/accenture-family-businesses-in-asia-deepening-the-roots-of-trust.pdf

Ackers, B. (2015). Ethical considerations of corporate social responsibility: A South African perspective. *South African Journal of Business Management*, *46*(1), 11–21. doi:10.4102ajbm.v46i1.79

Adams, R. B., & Ferreira, D. (2009). Women in the boardroom and their impact on governance and performance. *Journal of Financial Economics*, *94*(2), 291–309. doi:10.1016/j.jfineco.2008.10.007

Adi, A. B. C. (2006). The moral economy and the possibility of accumulation in Africa: How the IFIs can help. *West Africa Review*, *7*(2), 71–82.

Adıgüzel, H. (2013). Corporate governance, family ownership and earnings management: Emerging market evidence. *Accounting and Finance Research*, *2*(4), 17–33. doi:10.5430/afr.v2n4p17

Afify, H. A. E. (2009). Determinants of audit report lag: Does implementing corporate governance have any impact? Empirical evidence from Egypt. *Journal of Applied Accounting Research*, *10*(1), 56–86. doi:10.1108/09675420910963397

Afza, N. A. (2011). The Effect of owner's gender and age to firm performance: A review on Malaysian public listed family businesses. *Journal of Global Business and Economics*, *2*(1), 104–116.

Aggarwal, R., Erel, I., Stulz, R. M., & Williamson, R. G. (2007). *Do U.S. firms have the best corporate governance? A cross country examination of the relation between corporate governance and shareholder wealth*. Fisher College of Business working paper no. 2006-03-06.

Aggarwal, P. (2013). Impact of Corporate Governance on Corporate Financial Performance. *Journal of Business and Management*, *13*(3), 1–5.

Aggarwal, R., Erel, I., Stulz, R., & Williamson, R. (2009). Differences in governance practices between US and foreign firms: Measurement, causes, and consequences. *Review of Financial Studies*, *22*(8), 3131–3169. doi:10.1093/rfs/hhn107

Aguilera, R. V., Filatotchev, I., Gospel, H., & Jackson, G. (2008). An organizational approach to comparative corporate governance: Costs, contingencies, and complementarities. *Organization Science*, *19*(3), 475–492. doi:10.1287/orsc.1070.0322

Aguilera, R. V., Williams, C. A., Conley, J. M., & Rupp, D. E. (2006). Corporate governance and social responsibility: A comparative analysis of the UK and the US. *Corporate Governance*, *14*(3), 147–158. doi:10.1111/j.1467-8683.2006.00495.x

Ahern, K. R., & Dittmar, A. K. (2012). The changing of the boards: The impact on firm valuation of mandated female board representation. *The Quarterly Journal of Economics*, *127*(1), 137–197. doi:10.1093/qje/qjr049

Ahmed, A. S., Billings, B. K., Morton, R. M., & Stanford-Harris, M. (2002). The role of accounting conservatism in mitigating bondholder-shareholder conflicts over dividend policy and in reducing debt costs. *The Accounting Review*, *77*(4), 867–890. doi:10.2308/accr.2002.77.4.867

Ahmed, A. S., & Duellman, S. (2007). Accounting conservatism and board of director characteristics: An empirical analysis. *Journal of Accounting and Economics*, *46*(2-3), 411–437. doi:10.1016/j.jacceco.2007.01.005

Ahmed, K., & Henry, D. (2012). Accounting conservatism and voluntary corporate governance mechanisms by Australian firms. *Accounting and Finance*, *52*(3), 631–662. doi:10.1111/j.1467-629X.2011.00410.x

Ahmed, K., Hossain, M., & Adams, M. (2006). The Effects of Board Composition and Board Size on the Informativeness of Annual Accounting Earnings. *Corporate Governance*, *14*(5), 418–431. doi:10.1111/j.1467-8683.2006.00515.x

Aifuwa, H. O., & Embele, K. (2019). Board Characteristics and Financial Reporting. *Journal of Accounting and Financial Management*, *5*(1), 30–44.

Akeju, J. B., & Babatunde, A. A. (2017). Corporate governance and financial reporting quality in Nigeria. *International Journal of Information Research and Review*, *4*(2), 3749–3753.

Al Maskati, M., & Hamdan, A. (2017). Corporate governance and voluntary disclosure: Evidence from Bahrain. *International Journal of Economics and Accounting*, *8*(1), 1–28. doi:10.1504/IJEA.2017.084876

Alderson, J. K. (2011). *Understanding the family business*. Business Expert Press. doi:10.4128/9781606491706

Ali, S., Hussain, T., Zhang, G., Nurunnabi, M., & Li, B. (2018). The implementation of sustainable development goals in "BRICS" countries. *Sustainability*, *10*(7), 2513. doi:10.3390u10072513

Alkadai, H, K. H, & Hanefah, M. M. (2012). Audit committee characteristics and earnings management in Malaysian Sharia-compliant companies. *Business and Management Review*, *2*(2), 52-61.

Alkurdi, A., Al-Nimer, M., & Dabaghia, M. (2017). Accounting Conservatism and Ownership Structure Effect: Evidence from Industrial and Financial Jordanian Listed Companies. *International Journal of Economics and Financial Issues*, *7*(2), 608–619.

Almeida, H., Park, S., Subrahmanyam, M., & Wolfenzon, D. (2011). The Structure and Formation of Business Groups: Evidence from Korean Chaebols. *Journal of Financial Economics*, *99*(2), 447–475. doi:10.1016/j.jfineco.2010.08.017

Almeida, H., & Wolfenzon, D. (2006). A Theory of Pyramidal Ownership and Family Business Groups. *The Journal of Finance*, *61*(6), 2637–2680. doi:10.1111/j.1540-6261.2006.01001.x

Alowaihan, A. K. (2004). Gender and business performance of Kuwaiti small firms: A comparative approach. *International Journal of Commerce and Management*, *14*(3/4), 69–82. doi:10.1108/10569210480000185

Alves, S. M. (2014). The effect of the board independence on the earnings quality: Evidence from Portuguese listed companies. *Australian Accounting. Business and Finance Journal*, *8*(3), 23–44.

Amaeshi, K., Adi, A. B. C., Ogbechie, C., & Amao, O. O. (2006). *Corporate social responsibility in Nigeria: western mimicry or indigenous influences?* No. 39-2006 ICCSR Research Paper Series.

Ameer, R., & Othman, R. (2012). Sustainability Practices and Corporate Financial Performance: A Study Based on the Top Global Corporations. *Journal of Business Ethics*, *2012*(108), 61–79. doi:10.100710551-011-1063-y

Andriof, J., & Marsden, C. (n.d.). *Corporate Citizenship: What Is It and How to Assess It?* WP Corporate Citizenship Unit, Warwick Business School. http://users.wbs.warwick.ac.uk/group/ccu/research/dimensions

AngloGold Ashanti. (2019). *Sustainability report.* http://www.aga-reports.com/19/sr

Apple. (2019). *Environmental Responsibility Report 2019.* Apple Inc. Retrieved from https://www.apple.com/environment/pdf/Apple_Environmental_Responsibility_Report_2019.pdf

Ararat, M. (2004). Social responsibility in a state-dependent business system. In A. Habisch, J. Jonker, M. Wegner, & R. Schmidpeter (Eds.), *Corporate Social Responsibility across Europe* (pp. 247–260). Springer.

Archie, B. (1991). Understanding Stakeholder Thinking. *Business Ethics: A European Review,* 46–51.

Arrive, J. T., & Feng, M. (2018). Corporate social responsibility disclosure: Evidence from BRICS nations. *Corporate Social Responsibility and Environmental Management, 25*(5), 920–927. doi:10.1002/csr.1508

Arthurs, J. D., Hoskisson, R. E., Busenitz, L. W., & Johnson, R. A. (2008). Managerial agents watching other agents: Multiple agency conflicts regarding underpricing in IPO firms. *Academy of Management Journal, 51*(2), 277–294. doi:10.5465/amj.2008.31767256

Asif, M., Searcy, C., Zutshi, A., & Ahmad, N. (2011). An integrated management systems approach to corporate sustainability. *European Business Review, 23*(4), 353–367. doi:10.1108/09555341111145744

Astrachan, J. (2010). Strategy in family business: Toward a multidimensional research agenda. *Journal of Family Business Strategy, 1*(1), 6–14. doi:10.1016/j.jfbs.2010.02.001

Babic, V. (2003). *Corporate governance problems in transition economies.* Winston-Salem: Wake Forest University (Social Science Research Seminar), http://www.ibrarian.net/navon/paper/corporate_governance_problems_in_transition_econo.pdf?paperid=3696120

Backman, J. (1975). *Social responsibility and accountability.* New York University Press.

Bain, D. (2015). *The top 500 family businesses in the world.* Retrieved from https://familybusiness.ey-vx.com/pdfs/182-187.pdf

Baker, R. A., & Al-Thuneibat, A. (2011). Audit tenure and equity risk premium: Evidence from Jordan. *International Journal of Accounting and Information Management, 19*(1), 5–23. doi:10.1108/18347641111105908

Baldini, M., Dal Maso, L., Liberatore, G., Mazzi, F., & Terzani, S. (2018). Role of country-and firm-level determinants in environmental, social, and governance disclosure. *Journal of Business Ethics, 150*(1), 79–98. doi:10.100710551-016-3139-1

Ball, R., & Shivakumar, L. (2006). The role of accruals in asymmetrically timely gain and loss recognition. *Journal of Accounting Research, 44*(2), 207–242. doi:10.1111/j.1475-679X.2006.00198.x

Ball, R., & Shivakunar, L. (2005). Earnings quality in UK private firms: Comparative loss recognition timeliness. *Journal of Accounting and Economics, 39*(1), 83–128. doi:10.1016/j.jacceco.2004.04.001

Balsmeier, B., Buchwald, A., & Stiebale, J. (2014). Outside Directors on the Board and Innovative Firm Performance. *Research Policy, 43*(1), 1800–1815. doi:10.1016/j.respol.2014.06.003

Bansal, P. (2005). Evolving sustainably: A longitudinal study of corporate sustainable development. *Strategic Management Journal, 26*(3), 197–218. doi:10.1002mj.441

Barbagallo, C. (2017). *Veneto Banca e Banca Popolare di Vicenza*. Academic Press.

Barbosa, C. D., Francato, A. L., & Barbosa, P. S. (2019). Towards Brazilian Corporations Better Stock Price Valuation and Operational Performance with Corporate Social Responsibility and Environmental Socio Responsibility. In C. Stehr, N. Dziatzko, & F. Struve (Eds.), *Corporate Social Responsibility in Brazil* (pp. 129–146). Springer. doi:10.1007/978-3-319-90605-8_6

Barroso, R., Ali, C. B., & Lesage, C. (2018). 'Blockholders' ownership and audit fees: The impact of the corporate governance model. *European Accounting Review, 27*(1), 149–172. doi: 10.1080/09638180.2016.1243483

Barrow, O., Pratt, J., & Stice, J. D. (2001). Misstatement Direction, Litigation Risk, and Planned Audit Investment. *Journal of Accounting Research, 39*(3), 449–462. doi:10.1111/1475-679X.00022

Barr, S. (2016). *Environment and Society: Sustainability, Policy and the Citizen*. Routledge. doi:10.4324/9781315579986

Baskin, J. (2006). Corporate responsibility in emerging markets. *Journal of Corporate Citizenship, 2006*(24), 29–47. doi:10.9774/GLEAF.4700.2006.wi.00006

Basu, S. (1997). The conservatism principle and the asymmetric timeliness of earnings. *Journal of Accounting and Economics, 24*(1), 3–37. doi:10.1016/S0165-4101(97)00014-1

Baumgartner, R. J. (2014). Managing corporate sustainability and CSR: A conceptual framework combining values, strategies and instruments contributing to sustainable development. *Corporate Social Responsibility and Environmental Management, 21*(5), 258–271. doi:10.1002/csr.1336

Baysinger, B., & Hoskisson, R. (1990). The Composition of Boards of Directors and Strategic Control: Effects on Corporate Strategy. *Academy of Management Review, 15*(1), 72–87. doi:10.5465/amr.1990.4308231

Beasley, M. S. (1996). An empirical analysis of the relation between the board of director composition and financial statement fraud. *The Accounting Review, 71*, 443–465.

Beasley, M. S., Carcello, J. V., Hermanson, D. R., & Neal, T. L. (2009). The Audit Committee Oversight Process. *Contemporary Accounting Research*, *26*(1), 65–122. doi:10.1506/car.26.1.3

Beasley, M. S., & Petroni, K. R. (2001). Board independence and audit-firm type. *Auditing*, *20*(1), 97–114. doi:10.2308/aud.2001.20.1.97

Becht, M., Bolton, P., & Röell, A. (2002). *Corporate Governance and Control*. ECGI—Finance Working Paper # 02, 2002. http://ssrn.com/abstract=343461

Becker, C. L., DeFond, M. L., Jiambalso, J., & Subramanyam, K. R. (1998). The Effect of Audit Quality on Earnings Management. *Contemporary Accounting Research*, *15*(1), 1–24. doi:10.1111/j.1911-3846.1998.tb00547.x

Bedard, J. C., & Johnstone, K. M. (2004). Earnings manipulation risk, corporate governance risk, and auditors' planning and pricing decisions. *The Accounting Review*, *79*(2), 277–304. doi:10.2308/accr.2004.79.2.277

Beekes, W., Pope, P., & Young, S. (2004). The link between earnings timeliness, earnings conservatism and board composition: Evidence from the UK. *Corporate Governance*, *12*(1), 47–59. doi:10.1111/j.1467-8683.2004.00342.x

Bell, T. B., Landsman, W. R., & Shackelford, D. A. (2001). Auditors' perceived business risk and audit fees: Analysis and evidence. *Journal of Accounting Research*, *39*(1), 35–43. doi:10.1111/1475-679X.00002

Berghe, V. D & Baelden, T. (2005). The complex relation between director independence and board effectiveness. *Corporate Governance, 5*, 61-83.

Berghe, L., & Carchon, S. (2002). Family business research: Corporate governance practices in Flemish family businesses. *Corporate Governance*, *10*(3), 225–245. doi:10.1111/1467-8683.00286

Berle, A. A., & Means, G. C. (1932). *The modern corporation and private property*. Commerce Clearing House.

Bernard, C. (2015). *European Family Business Trends*. KPMG Enterprise.

Berthon, B., Abood, D. J., & Lacy, P. (2010). *Can business do well by doing good? Outlook*. Retreived from http://www.accenture.com/SiteCollectionDocuments/PDF/Accenture_Outlook_Can_Business_ Do_Well_by_Doing_Good_Sustainability.pdf

Bettinelli, C. (2011). Board of Directors in Family Firms: An Exploratory Study of Structure and Group Process. *Family Business Review*, *24*(2), 151–169. doi:10.1177/0894486511402196

Beveridge, F., Nott, S., & Stephen, K. (2018). *Making Women Count: Integrating Gender into Law and Policy-Making*. Routledge Revivals.

Bhatia, A., & Makkar, B. (2019). CSR disclosure in developing and developed countries: A comparative study. *Journal of Global Responsibility*, *11*(1), 1–26. doi:10.1108/JGR-04-2019-0043

Bhatia, A., & Tuli, S. (2018). Sustainability reporting: An empirical evaluation of emerging and developed economies. *Journal of Global Responsibility*, *9*(2), 207–234. doi:10.1108/JGR-01-2018-0003

Biddle, G., Ma, M., & Song, F. (2016). *Accounting conservatism and bankruptcy risk*. Working paper, Faculty of Business and Economics, University of Hong Kong, Hong Kong.

Birch, D. (2008). Ten principles of corporate citizenship. *Social Responsibility Journal*, *4*(1-2), 129–135. doi:10.1108/17471110810856893

Black, D. E., & Gallemore, J. (2013). Bank executive overconfidence and delayed expected loss recognition. Working Paper. https://papers.ssrn.com/sol3/papers.cfm?abstract_id=2144293

Blank, H. D., & Carty, C. M. (2005). The Eco- Efficiency Anomaly. *Journal of Investing*.

Blaug, R. (2016). Pathologies of power and cognition. In G. Robinson & P. Garrard (Eds.), *The Intoxication of Power* (pp. 75–88). Palgrave Macmillan.

Bliss, R., & Potter, M. (2002). Mutual Fund managers: Does gender matter? *Journal of Business and Economic Studies*, *8*(1), 1–15.

Blowfield, M., & Frynas, J. G. (2005). Editorial Setting new agendas: Critical perspectives on Corporate Social Responsibility in the developing world. *International Affairs*, *81*(3), 499–513. doi:10.1111/j.1468-2346.2005.00465.x

Bodhanwala, S., & Bodhanwala, R. (2018). Does corporate sustainability impact firm profitability? Evidence from India. *Management Decision*, *56*(1), 1734–1747. Advance online publication. doi:10.1108/MD-04-2017-0381

Bøhren, Ø. & Strøm, R.Ø. (2007). *Aligned, informed and decisive: Characteristics of value-creating boards*. Ljubljana Meetings Paper.

Bollaert, H., & Petit, V. (2010). Beyond the dark side of executive psychology: Current research and new directions. *European Management Journal*, *28*(5), 362–376. doi:10.1016/j.emj.2010.01.001

Botero, I., Cruz, C., De Massis, A., & Nordqvist, M. (2015). Family business research in the European context. *European Journal of International Management*, *9*(2), 139–159. doi:10.1504/EJIM.2015.067858

Boutilier, R. (2017). *Stakeholder politics: Social capital, sustainable development, and the corporation*. Routledge. doi:10.4324/9781351279727

Bowen, H. R. (1953). *Social Responsibilities of the businessman*. Harper & Row.

Bowen, H. R. (1953). *Social Responsibilities of the Businessman*. Harper & Row.

Boyd, B. K., Haynes, K. T., & Zona, F. (2011). Dimensions of CEO–board relations. *Journal of Management Studies*, *48*(8), 1892–1923. doi:10.1111/j.1467-6486.2010.00943.x

Brace, N., Kemp, R., & Snelgar, R. (2006). *SPSS for Psychologists*. Palgrave Macmillan.

Brammer, S., Millington, A., & Pavelin, S. (2007). Gender and ethnic diversity among UK corporate boards. *Corporate Governance*, *15*(2), 393–403. doi:10.1111/j.1467-8683.2007.00569.x

Brannmark, M., & Benn, S. (2012). A proposed model for evaluating the sustainability of continuous change programmes. *Journal of Change Management*, *12*(2), 231–245. doi:10.1080/14697017.2012.672449

Brennan, N. M., & Conroy, J. P. (2013). Executive hubris: The case of a bank CEO. *Accounting, Auditing & Accountability Journal*, *26*(2), 172–195. doi:10.1108/09513571311303701

Brickley, J. A., & Zimmerman, J. L. (2010). Corporate governance myths: Comments on Armstrong, Guay, and Weber. *Journal of Accounting and Economics*, *50*(2-3), 235–245. doi:10.1016/j.jacceco.2010.10.002

Broome, L. L., & Krawiec, K. D. (2008). Signalling through board diversity: Is anyone listening', University of Cincinnati Law Review. *Twenty-First Annual Corporate Law Symposium.*

Brown, W. (2005). Exploring the Association Between Board and Organizational Performance in Nonprofit Organizations. *Nonprofit Management & Leadership*, *15*(3), 317–339. doi:10.1002/nml.71

Bukit, R. B., & Iskandar, T. M. (2009). Surplus Free Cash Flow, Earnings Management and Audit Committee. *International Journal of Economics and Management*, *3*(1), 204–223.

Busch, T., & Friede, G. (2018). The Robustness of the Corporate Social and Financial Performance Relation: A Second-Order Meta-Analysis. *Corporate Social Responsibility and Environmental Management*, *25*(4), 583–608. Advance online publication. doi:10.1002/csr.1480

Butner, E. H., & Moore, D. P. (1997). Women's organizational exodus to entrepreneurship: Self-reported motivations and correlates with success. *Journal of Small Business Management*, *35*(1), 34–46.

Buttel, F. H. (2003). Environmental sociology and the explanation of environmental reform. *Organization & Environment*, *16*(3), 306–344. doi:10.1177/1086026603256279

Buyl, T., Boone, C., & Wade, J. B. (2019). CEO narcissism, risk-taking, and resilience: An empirical analysis in US commercial banks. *Journal of Management*, *45*(4), 1372–1400. doi:10.1177/0149206317699521

Byrd, J. W., & Hickman, K. A. (1992). Do outside directors monitor managers? Evidence from tender offer bids. *Journal of Financial Economics*, *32*(2), 195–222. doi:10.1016/0304-405X(92)90018-S

Cadbury, A. (1992), Report on the Committee on the Financial Aspects of Corporate Governance. Gee.

Cadbury, A. (2002). *Corporate Governance and chairmanship: A personal view.* Oxford University Press. doi:10.1093/acprof:oso/9780199252008.001.0001

Callan, S. J., & Thomas, J. M. (2009). Corporate Financial Performance and Corporate Social Performance: An Update and Reinvestigation. *Corporate Social Responsibility and Environmental Management, 16*(2), 61–78. doi:10.1002/csr.182

Campblell, D., Craven, B., & Shrives, P. (2002). Voluntary social reporting in three FTSE sectors: A comment on perception and legitimacy. *Accounting, Auditing & Accountability Journal, 16*(4), 558–581. doi:10.1108/09513570310492308

Cantarella, E. (2002). *Itaca: eroi, donne, potere tra vendetta e diritto*. Feltrinelli Editore.

Carcello, J. V., Hermanson, D. R., Neal, T. L., & Riley, R. A. Jr. (2010). Board Characteristics and Audit Fees. *Contemporary Accounting Research, 19*(3), 365–384. doi:10.1506/CHWK-GMQ0-MLKE-K03V

Cardamone, P., Carnevale, C., & Giunta, F. (2012). The value relevance of social reporting: Evidence from listed Italian companies. *Journal of Applied Accounting Research, 13*(3), 255–269. doi:10.1108/09675421211281326

Caroll, A. B. (1991). The pyramid of corporate social responsibility: Toward the moral management of organizational stakeholders. *Business Horizons, 34*(July-August), 30–48. doi:10.1016/0007-6813(91)90005-G

Carroll, A. B. (1979). A three-dimensional conceptual model of corporate performance. *Academy of Management Review, 4*(4), 497–505. doi:10.5465/amr.1979.4498296

Carroll, A. B. (1999). Corporate Social Responsibility: Evolution of a definitional construct. *Journal of Business and Society, 38*(3), 268–295. doi:10.1177/000765039903800303

Carroll, A. B. (2015). Corporate social responsibility: The centerpiece of competing and complementary frameworks. *Organizational Dynamics, 44*(2), 87–96. doi:10.1016/j.orgdyn.2015.02.002

Carroll, A. B., & Shabana, K. M. (2010). The business case for corporate social responsibility: A review of concepts, research and practice. *International Journal of Management Reviews, 12*(1), 85–105. doi:10.1111/j.1468-2370.2009.00275.x

Carter, D., D'Souza, F., Simkins, B. J., & Simpson, W. (2010). The gender and ethnic diversity of US boards and board committees and firm financial performance. *Corporate Governance, 18*(5), 396–414. doi:10.1111/j.1467-8683.2010.00809.x

Carter, D., Simkins, B., & Simpson, W. (2003). Corporate Governance, Board Diversity, and Firm Value. *Financial Review, 38*(1), 33–53. doi:10.1111/1540-6288.00034

Carter, N. (2001). *The Politics of the Environment: Ideas, Activism and Policy*. Cambridge University Press. doi:10.1017/CBO9781139163859

Caspar, C., Dias, A., & Elstrodt, H. (2010). Organizational practice: The five attributes of enduring family businesses. *The McKinsey Quarterly, 1*, 1–10.

CED. (1971). *Social Responsibilities of Business Corporations*. Committee for Economic Development.

Cellier, A., & Chollet, P. (2011). *The Impact of Corporate Social Responsibility Rating Announcement on Stock Price: An Event Study on European Markets*. Universitè Paris-Est.

Cerinotti, A. (2018). *Miti greci e di Roma antica*. Giunti.

Cernat, L. (2004). The emerging European corporate governance model: Anglo-Saxon, Continental, or still the century of diversity? *Journal of European Public Policy*, *11*(1), 147–166. doi:10.1080/1350176042000164343

CGA-Canada. (2005). *Measuring Up: A Study on Corporate Sustainability Reporting in Canada*. Certified General Accountants' Association of Canada Burnaby, BC. Retrieved from https://books.scholarsportal.info/viewdoc.html?id=358907

Chalaki, P., Didar, H., & Rianezhad, M. (2012). Corporate Governance Attributes and Financial Reporting Quality: Empirical Evidence from Iran. *International Journal of Business and Social Science*, *3*(15), 1–7.

Chamsy, O., & Patrick, H. (2006). *Critical theories of globalization*. Palgrave Machmillan.

Chan, P., Ezzamel, M., & Gwilliam, D. (1993). Determinants of audit fees for quoted UK companies. *Journal of Business Finance & Accounting*, *20*(6), 765–785. doi:10.1111/j.1468-5957.1993.tb00292.x

Charles, S. L., Glover, S. M., & Sharp, N. Y. (2010). The association between financial reporting risk and audit fees before and after the historic events surrounding SOX. *Auditing*, *29*(1), 15–39. doi:10.2308/aud.2010.29.1.15

Chatterjee, A., & Hambrick, D. C. (2007). It's all about me: Narcissistic chief executive officers and their effects on company strategy and performance. *Administrative Science Quarterly*, *52*(3), 351–386. doi:10.2189/asqu.52.3.351

Chen, J. (2020). Corporate Governance Definition. Investopedia. Retrieved 12 April 2020, from https://www.investopedia.com/terms/c/corporategovernance.asp

Cheng, B., Ioannou, I., & Serafeim, G. (2014). Corporate social responsibility and access to finance. *Strategic Management Journal*, *35*(1), 1–23. doi:10.1002mj.2131

Cheng, I. H., Hong, H., & Scheinkman, J. A. (2015). Yesterday's heroes: Compensation and risk at financial firms. *The Journal of Finance*, *70*(2), 839–879. doi:10.1111/jofi.12225

Chen, K. Y., Elder, R. J., & Hung, S. (2010). The investment opportunity set and earnings management: Evidence from the role of controlling shareholders. *Corporate Governance*, *18*(3), 193–211. doi:10.1111/j.1467-8683.2010.00793.x

Chen, K. Y., & Zhou, J. (2007). Audit committee, board characteristics, and auditor switch decisions by Andersen's clients. *Contemporary Accounting Research, 24*(4), 1085–1117. doi:10.1506/car.24.4.2

Cho, S. Y., Lee, C., & Pfeiffer, R. J. Jr. (2013). Corporate social responsibility performance and information asymmetry. *Journal of Accounting and Public Policy, 32*(1), 71–83. doi:10.1016/j.jaccpubpol.2012.10.005

Chua, J. H., Chrisman, J. J., & Sharma, P. (1999). Defining the family business by behavior. *Entrepreneurship Theory and Practice, 23*(4), 19–39. doi:10.1177/104225879902300402

Chung, R., Firth, M., & Kim, J. B. (2003). Auditor conservatism and reported earnings. *Accounting and Business Research, 33*(1), 19–32. doi:10.1080/00014788.2003.9729629

Chung, R., Firth, M., & Kim, J. B. (2005). Earnings management, surplus free cash flow, and external monitoring. *Journal of Business Research, 58*(6), 766–776. doi:10.1016/j.jbusres.2003.12.002

CII. (2011). *Indian IT/ITeS Industry: Evolving business models for sustained growth*. Confederation of Indian Industry Report.

Cipolla, P. (2011). La hybris di Serse nei Persiani di Eschilo tra destino e responsabilità. In A. Rotondo (Ed.), *Humanitas e cristianesimo. Studi in onore di Roberto Osculati* (pp. 29–39). Viella.

Claessens, S., & Fan, J. P. H. (2002). Corporate governance in Asia: A survey. *International Review of Finance, 3*(2), 71–103. doi:10.1111/1468-2443.00034

Clarke, T. (2010). Recurring crises in Anglo-American Corporate Governance. *Contributions to Political Economy, 29*(1), 9–32. doi:10.1093/cpe/bzq002

Clarkson, M. B. E. (1995). A Stakeholder Framework for Analyzing and Evaluating Corporate Social Performance. *Academy of Management Journal, 20*(1), 92–118.

Coakes, J. S., & Steed, G. L. (2003). SPSS Analysis without Anguish. John Wiley & Sons Australia Ltd.

Cohen, J. R., & Hanno, D. M. (2000). Auditors' consideration of corporate governance and management control philosophy in preplanning and planning judgments. *Auditing, 19*(2), 133–146. doi:10.2308/aud.2000.19.2.133

Coles, J., Daniel, N., & Naveen, L. (2010). *Co-opted Boards*. http://papers.ssrn.com/sol3/papers.cfm?abstractid=1699272

Coles, J., & Hesterly, W. (2000). Independence of the Chairman and Board Composition: Firm Choices and Shareholder Value. *Journal of Management, 26*(2), 195–214. doi:10.1177/014920630002600202

Coluccia, D., Fontana, S., & Solimene, S. (2018). Does institutional context affect CSR disclosure? A study on Eurostoxx 50. *Sustainability, 10*(8), 2823. doi:10.3390u10082823

Combs, J. G., Ketchen, D. J. Jr, Perryman, A. A., & Donahue, M. S. (2007). The moderating effect of CEO power on the board composition–firm performance relationship. *Journal of Management Studies*, *44*(8), 1299–1323. doi:10.1111/j.1467-6486.2007.00708.x

Comi, A., & Eppler, M. J. (2014). Diagnosing capabilities in family firms: An overview of visual research methods and suggestions for future applications. *Journal of Family Business Strategy*, *5*(1), 41–51. doi:10.1016/j.jfbs.2014.01.009

Committee and Financial reporting Quality of Oil Marketing Firms: Evidence from Nigeria. *Journal of Finance, Accounting and Management, 6*(2), 34-50.

Conway, E. (2018). Sustainability, the Triple Bottom Line and Corporate Social Responsibility. In E. Conway & D. Byrne (Eds.), *Contemporary Issues in Accounting* (pp. 15–35). Palgrave Macmillan. doi:10.1007/978-3-319-91113-7_2

Cormier, D., Lapointe-Antunes, P., & Magnan, M. (2016). CEO power and CEO hubris: A prelude to financial misreporting? *Management Decision*, *54*(2), 522–554. doi:10.1108/MD-04-2015-0122

Cornell, B., Alan, C., & Shapiro, A. C. (1987). Corporate stakeholders and corporate finance. *Financial Management*, *16*(1), 5–14. doi:10.2307/3665543

Cox, T. (2001). *Creating the multicultural organization: A strategy for capturing the power*. Jossey-Bass.

Cramer, J. (2003). Corporate Social Responsibility: Lessons Learned. *Environmental Quality Management*, *13*(2), 59–66. doi:10.1002/tqem.10110

Credit Suisse. (2011). *Asian Family Businesses Report*. Zurich, Switzerland: Emerging market research institute. Retrieved from http://www.efiko.org/material/Asian%20Family%20%20Report%20by%20Credit%20Suisse.pdf

Credit Suisse. (2012). *Gender diversity and corporate performance*. Retrieved from https://infocus.creditsuisse.com/data/_product_documents/_shop/360145/csri_gender_diversity_and_corporate_performance.pdf

Croson, R., & Gneezy, U. (2009). Gender differences in preferences. *Journal of Economic Literature*, *47*(2), 448–474. doi:10.1257/jel.47.2.448

Cuba, R., Decenzo, D., & Anish, A. (1983). Management practices of successful female business owners. *American Journal of Small Business*, *2*(8), 40–46. doi:10.1177/104225878300800208

D'onza, G., & Lamboglia, R. (2014). *The Relation between the Corporate Governance Characteristics and Financial Statement Frauds: An Empirical Analysis of Italian Listed Companies*. Academic Press.

Daily, C. M., Dalton, D. R., & Cannella, A. A. Jr. (2003). Corporate governance: Decades of dialogue and data. *Academy of Management Review*, *28*(3), 371–382. doi:10.5465/amr.2003.10196703

Dalton, D. R., Daily, C. M., Johnson, J. L., & Ellstrand, A. E. (1999). Number of directors and financial performance: A meta analysis. *Academy of Management Journal*, *42*, 674–686.

Dalton, D. R., & Dalton, C. M. (2011). Integration of micro and macro studies in governance research: CEO duality, board composition, and firm performance. *Journal of Management*, *37*(2), 404–411. doi:10.1177/0149206310373399

Dana, L., & Smyrnios, K., (2010). *The MGI Australian Family and Private Business Survey: 2010*. Academic Press.

Daoud, K. A. A., Ismail, K., Izah, K. N., & Lode, N. A. (2014). The timeliness of financial reporting among Jordanian companies: Do company and board characteristics, and audit opinion matter? *Asian Social Science*, *10*(13), 191–201. doi:10.5539/ass.v10n13p191

Datar, S., Feltham, G., & Hughes, J. (1991). The role of audits and audit quality in valuing new issues. *Journal of Accounting and Economics*, *14*(1), 3–49. doi:10.1016/0167-7187(91)90057-R

Davies, P. L. (2000). *The Board of Directors: Composition, Structure, Duties and Powers*. Company Law Reform in OECD Countries A Comparative Outlook of Current Trends.

Davis, G. F., & Useem, M. (2002). Top management, company directors, and corporate control. In A. M. Pettigrew, H. Thomas, & R. Whittington (Eds.), Handbook of strategy and management (pp. 233–259). Academic Press.

Davis, K. (1960). Can business afford to ignore social responsibilities? *California Management Review*, *2*(3), 70–76. doi:10.2307/41166246

Davis, K., & Blomstrom, R. L. (1966). *Business and its environment*. McGraw- Hill.

Davis, P. (1983). Realizing the potential of the family business. *Organizational Dynamics*, *12*(1), 47–56. doi:10.1016/0090-2616(83)90026-8

Dawson, S. (2004). Balancing Self-Interest and Altruism: Corporate governance alone is not enough. *Corporate Governance*, *12*(2), 130–133. doi:10.1111/j.1467-8683.2004.00351.x

De Massis, A., Audretsch, D., Uhlaner, L., & Kammerlander, N. (2018). Innovation with limited resources: management lessons from the German Mittelstand. *Journal of Product of Innovation Management, 35*(1), 125-146. Doi:10.1111/jpim.12373

de Vries, M. K. (2004). Organizations on the Couch: A clinical perspective on organizational dynamics. *European Management Journal*, *22*(2), 183–200.

DeAngelo, L. (1981). Auditor size and auditor quality. *Journal of Accounting and Economics*, *3*(3), 183–199. doi:10.1016/0165-4101(81)90002-1

DeFond, M. L., Lim, C. Y., & Zang, Y. (2012). *Do Auditors Value Client Conservatism?* Working Paper, University of Southern California, Los Angeles, CA.

DeFond, M. L., Lim, C. Y., & Zang, Y. (2016). Client Conservatism and Auditor-Client Contracting. *The Accounting Review*, *91*(1), 69–98. doi:10.2308/accr-51150

DeFond, M. L., & Zang, J. (2014). A review of archival auditing research. *Journal of Accounting and Economics*, *58*(2-3), 275–326. doi:10.1016/j.jacceco.2014.09.002

Deloitte Centre for Corporate Governance. (2017). Diversity in the boardroom. Available online at: Retrieved 14 April 2020, from https://www2.deloitte.com/za/en/services/centre-for-corporate-governance.html

Deschênes, S., Rojas, M., Boubacar, H., Prud'homme, B., & Ouedraogo, A. (2015). The impact of board traits on the social performance of Canadian firms. Corporate Governance International Journal of Business in Society., 15(3), 293–305. doi:10.1108/CG-08-2014-0097

Diaz, C. G. (2011). Corporate culpability as a limit to the overcriminalization of corporate criminal liability: The interplay between self-regulation, corporate compliance and corporate citizenship. *New Criminal Law Review*, *14*(1), 78–96. doi:10.1525/nclr.2011.14.1.78

Diltz, J. D. (1995). The Private Cost of Socially Responsible Investing. *Applied Financial Economics*, *5*(2), 69–77. doi:10.1080/758529174

Donaldson, L. (1990). The ethereal hand: Organizational economics and management theory. *Academy of Management Review*, *15*(3), 369–381. doi:10.5465/amr.1990.4308806

Donaldson, L., & Davis, J. (1991). Stewardship theory or agency theory: CEO governance and shareholder returns. *Australian Journal of Management*, *16*(1), 49–64. doi:10.1177/031289629101600103

Donaldson, L., & Davis, J. (1994). Board and company performance: Research challenges the conventional wisdom. *Corporate Governance*, *2*(3), 151–160. doi:10.1111/j.1467-8683.1994.tb00071.x

Donaldson, T., & Preston, L. (1995). The stakeholder theory of the corporation: Concepts, evidence, and implications. *Academy of Management Review*, *20*(1), 65–91. doi:10.5465/amr.1995.9503271992

Donham, W. B. (1927). The social significance of business. *Harvard Business Review*, *4*(4), 406–419.

Donnelley, R. G., (1964). The family business. *Harvard Business Review, 42*(4), 93-105.

Drebes, M. J. (2016). Including the 'Other': Power and postcolonialism as underrepresented perspectives in the discourse on Corporate Social Responsibility. *Critical Sociology*, *42*(1), 105–121. doi:10.1177/0896920513509824

Drucker, P. F. (1984). The new meaning of corporate social responsibility. *California Management Review*, *26*(2), 53–63. doi:10.2307/41165066

Duh, M., Tominc, P., & Rebernik, M. (2009). The Importance of Family Enterprises in Transition Economies: Is It Overestimated? *Eastern European Economics*, *47*(6), 22–42. doi:10.2753/EEE0012-8775470602

Eagly, A. H., & Carli, L. L. (2007). Women and the labyrinth of leadership. *Harvard Business Review*, 1–2. PMID:17886484

EBA. (2017). Final Report Guidelines on internal governance under Directive 2013/36/EU, September 26.

Edwards, J., & Nibler, M. (2000). Corporate governance in Germany: The role of banks and insider directors. *Economic Policy*, *15*(31), 237–267. doi:10.1111/1468-0327.00062

EFB. (2012). *Family Business Statistics. European Family Businesses 2009*. Retrieved from http://www.europeanfamilybusinesses.eu/uploads/Modules/Publications/pp---family-business-statisticsv2.pdf

Eisenhardt, K. M. (1989a). Agency theory: An assessment and review. *Academy of Management Review*, *14*(1), 57–74. doi:10.5465/amr.1989.4279003

El Ghoul, S., Guedhami, O., Kwok, C. C., & Mishra, D. R. (2011). Does corporate social responsibility affect the cost of capital? *Journal of Banking & Finance*, *35*(9), 2388–2406. doi:10.1016/j.jbankfin.2011.02.007

Elgart, L. D. (1983). Women on Fortune 500 Boards. *California Management Review*, *24*(4), 121–127. doi:10.2307/41165036

Emel, J., Makene, M. H., & Wangari, E. (2012). Problems with reporting and evaluating mining industry community development projects: A case study from Tanzania. *Sustainability*, *4*(2), 257–277. doi:10.3390u4020257

Emirates. (2016). *Environment Report 2015-16*. Emirates Group. Retrieved from https://cdn.ek.aero/downloads/ek/pdfs/environment/ENV_REPORT-2015_2016.pdf

Emirates. (2017). *Environment Report 2016-17*. Emirates Group. Retrieved from https://cdn.ek.aero/ae/english/images/environment-report-2016-17_tcm277-4662773.pdf

Epstein, E. M. (1987). The corporate social policy process: Beyond business ethics, corporate social responsibility, and corporate social responsiveness. *California Management Review*, *29*(3), 99–114. doi:10.2307/41165254

Epstein, M. J., & Buhovac, A. R. (2014a). *Making sustainability work: Best practices in managing and measuring corporate social, environmental, and economic impacts* (2nd ed.). Berrett-Koehler.

Erhardt, N. L., Werbel, J. D., & Shrader, C. B. (2003). Board of director diversity and firm financial performance. *Corporate Governance*, *11*(2), 102–111. doi:10.1111/1467-8683.00011

European Commission (2001). *Green Paper-Promoting a European framework for corporate social responsibility, COM (2001) 366 final*. Brussels: Official publications of the EC.

European Commission. (2011). *Communication from the Commission to the European Parliament, the Council, the European Economic and Social Committee and the Committee of the Regions – A renewed EU strategy 2011-14 for Corporate Social Responsibility*. Available from https://eurlex.europa.eu/LexUriServ/LexUriServ.do?uri=COM:2011:0681:FIN:EN:PDF

Evan, W. E., & Freeman, R. E. (1988). A Stakeholder Theory of the Modern Corporation: Kantian capitalism. In T. L. Beauchamp & N. E. Bowie (Eds.), *Ethical Theory and Business* (3rd ed.). Prentice Hall Press.

Eweje, G. (2006). The role of MNEs in Community Development Initiatives in developing countries: Corporate Social Responsibility at work in Nigeria and South Africa. *Business & Society*, *45*(2), 93–129. doi:10.1177/0007650305285394

Eweje, G. (2007). Multinational oil companies' CSR initiatives in Nigeria: The scepticism of stakeholders in host communities. *Managerial Law*, *49*(5/6), 218–235. doi:10.1108/03090550710841340

Ezelibe, C. P., Nwosu, O., & Orazulike, S. (2017). Empirical investigation of corporate governance and financial reporting quality of quoted companies in Nigeria. International *Journal of Economics. Business and Management Research*, *1*(5), 117–137.

Fahlenbrach, R., Low, A., & Stulz, R. M. (2010). The dark side of outside directors: Do they quit when they are most needed? (No. w15917). National Bureau of Economic Research. doi:10.3386/w15917

Fama, E. F., & Jenson, M. (1983). Separation of ownership and control. *The Journal of Law & Economics*, *26*(2), 301–325. doi:10.1086/467037

Family Firm Institute. (2017). *Global Data Points*. Retrieved from the FFI website on o November 27, 2017: https://www.ffi.org/page/globaldatapoints

Fan, J. P. H., & Wong, T. J. (2005). Do external auditors perform a corporate governance role in emerging markets? Evidence from East Asia. *Journal of Accounting Research*, *43*(1), 35–72. doi:10.1111/j.1475-679x.2004.00162.x

Farrell, K. A., & Hersch, P. L. (2005). Additions to Corporate Boards: The Effect of Gender. *Journal of Corporate Finance*, *11*(1-2), 85–106. doi:10.1016/j.jcorpfin.2003.12.001

Fasci, M. A., & Valdez, J. (1998). A performance contrast of male and female owned small accounting practices. *Journal of Small Business Management*, *36*(3), 1–7.

Fenwick, M., McCahery, J. A., & Vermeulen, E. P. (2019). The end of 'corporate' governance: Hello 'platform' governance. *European Business Organization Law Review*, *20*(1), 171–199. doi:10.100740804-019-00137-z

Ferguson, A. M., Heritage, T., Jonathon, P., Pack, S. E., Philips, S., Ragon, J., & Snaith, P. J. (1997). EVA: A new theoretically based molecular descriptor for use in QSAR/QSPR analysis. *Journal of Computer-Aided Molecular Design*, *11*(2), 143–152. doi:10.1023/A:1008026308790 PMID:9089432

Fernandez-Araoz, C., Iqbal, S., & Ritter, J. (2015). Why family firms in East Asia struggle with succession. *Harvard Business Review*. Retrieved from https://hbr.org/2015/03/why-family-firms-in-east-asia-struggle-with-succession

Fernández-Olmos, M., Gargallo-Castel, A., & Giner-Bagües, E. (2016). Internationalization and performance in Spanish family SMES: The W-curve. *BRQ Business Research Quarterly*, *19*(2), 122–136. doi:10.1016/j.brq.2015.07.001

Ferris, S. P., Jagannathan, M., & Pritchard, A. C. (2003). Too busy to mind the business? Monitoring by directors with multiple board appointments. *The Journal of Finance*, *58*(3), 1087–1111. doi:10.1111/1540-6261.00559

Fich, E., & Shivdasani, A. (2006). Are Busy Boards Effective Monitors? *Journal of Finance*, 61 (2), 689–724.Fosberg, R. H. (1999). Leadership structure and CEO compensation. *American Business Review*, *17*(1), 50.

Fiend, A. (2009). *Discovering statistics using SPSS*. Sage.

Finkelstein, S. (1992). Power in top management teams: Dimensions, measurement, and validation. *Academy of Management Journal*, *35*(3), 505–538. PubMed

Finkelstein, S., Cannella, S. F. B., Hambrick, D. C., & Cannella, A. A. (2009). *Strategic leadership: Theory and research on executives, top management teams, and boards*. Oxford University Press.

Finkelstein, S., & D'aveni, R. A. (1994). CEO duality as a double-edged sword: How boards of directors balance entrenchment avoidance and unity of command. *Academy of Management Journal*, *37*(5), 1079–1108.

Finnigan, M. (2014). *Infographic: Spanish family businesses | Campden FB*. Campdenfb.com. Retrieved 8 January 2016, from http://www.campdenfb.com/article/infographic-spanish-family-businesses

Firth, M., Fung, P., & Rui, O. (2007). Ownership, two-tier Board Structure, and the Informativeness of Earnings: Evidence from China. *Journal of Accounting and Public Policy*, *26*(4), 463–496. doi:10.1016/j.jaccpubpol.2007.05.004

Fischer, E. M., Reuber, A. R., & Dyke, L. S. (1993). A theoretical review and extension of research on sex, gender, and entrepreneurship. *Journal of Business Venturing*, *8*(3), 151–168. doi:10.1016/0883-9026(93)90017-Y

Fitch, H. G. (1976). Achieving Corporate Social Responsibility. *Academy of Management Review*, *1*(1), 38–46. doi:10.5465/amr.1976.4408754

Fleischer, R., & Goettscha, M. (2012). Size effects and audit pricing: Evidence from Germany. *Journal of International Accounting, Auditing & Taxation*, *21*(2), 156–168. doi:10.1016/j.intaccaudtax.2012.07.005

Foo, Y. B., & Zain, M. M. (2010). Board independence, board diligence and liquidity in Malaysia: A research note. *Journal of Contemporary Accounting & Economics*, *6*(2), 92–100. doi:10.1016/j.jcae.2010.10.001

Forbes Insights. (2012). Global wealth and family ties. A worldwide study of how fortunes are founded managed and passed on. New York: Author.

Fosberg, R. H. (1999). Leadership structure and CEO compensation. *American Business Review*, *17*(1), 50–56.

Foucault, M., Dreyfus, H. L., & Rabinow, P. (1982). Michel Foucault: Beyond structuralism and hermeneutics. *The Subject and Power*, 208-226.

Francis, J. R. (2004). The Effect of Auditor Firm Size on Audit Prices: A study of the Australian Market. *Journal of Accounting and Economics*, *6*, 131–151. doi:10.1016/0165-4101(84)90010-7

Francis, J. R. (2006). Are auditors compromised by Nonaudit services? Assessing the evidence. *Contemporary Accounting Research*, *23*(3), 747–760. doi:10.1506/4VD9-AE3K-XV7L-XT07

Francis, J. R., & Krishnan, J. (1999). Accounting Accruals and Auditor Reporting Conservatism. *Contemporary Accounting Research*, *16*(1), 135–165. doi:10.1111/j.1911-3846.1999.tb00577.x

Frederick, W. C. (1960). The growing concern over business responsibility. *California Management Review*, *2*(4), 54–61. doi:10.2307/41165405

Freeman, A. M. III, Herriges, J. A., & Kling, C. L. (2014). *The Measurement of Environmental and Resource Values: Theory and Methods*. Routledge. doi:10.4324/9781315780917

Freeman, R. E. (1984). *Strategic Management: A Stakeholder Approach*. Pitman Publishing Inc.

Freeman, R. E. (1984). *Strategic Management: A stakeholder Approach*. Pitman.

Friedman, M. (1970, Sept. 13). The Social Responsibility of Business is to Increase its Profits. *New York Times*.

Friedman, M. (1962). *Capitalism & Freedom*. University of Chicago.

Frooman, J. (1999). Stakeholder influence strategies. *Academy of Management Review*, *24*(2), 191–205. doi:10.5465/amr.1999.1893928

Frynas, J. G. (2005). The false developmental promise of Corporate Social Responsibility: Evidence from multinational oil companies. *International Affairs*, *81*(3), 581–598. doi:10.1111/j.1468-2346.2005.00470.x

Fuzia, S. F. S., Halim, S. A. A., & Julizaerma, M. K. (2016). Board independence and firm performance. *Procedia Economics and Finance*, *37*, 460–465. doi:10.1016/S2212-5671(16)30152-6

Gandía, J. L., & Huguet, D. (2019). *Audit fees and cost of debt: differences in the credibility of voluntary and mandatory audits*. Economic Research-Ekonomska Istraživanja. doi:10.1080/1331677X.2019.1678501

Gao, P. (2013). A measurement approach to conservatism and earnings management. *Journal of Accounting and Economics*, *55*(2-3), 251–268. doi:10.1016/j.jacceco.2012.10.001

Garcia, A. S., Mendes-Da-Silva, W., & Orsato, R. J. (2019). Corporate Sustainability, Capital Markets, and ESG Performance. In W. Mendes-Da-Silva (Ed.), *Individual Behaviors and Technologies for Financial Innovations* (pp. 287–309). Springer. doi:10.1007/978-3-319-91911-9_13

Gardiner, L., Rubbens, C., & Bonfiglioli, E. (2003). Big Business, Big Responsibilities. *Corporate Governance*, *3*(3), 67–77. doi:10.1108/14720700310483451

Garg, A. K. (2007). Influence of board size and independence on firm performance: A study of Indian companies. *Vikalpa*, *32*(3), 39–60. doi:10.1177/0256090920070304

Garriga, E., & Mele, D. (2004). Corporate social responsibility theories: Mapping and territory. *Journal of Business Ethics*, *53*(1/2), 51–74. doi:10.1023/B:BUSI.0000039399.90587.34

Gersick, K. E., & Feliu, N. (2014). Governing the family enterprise: Practices, performance, and research. The Sage Handbook of Family Business, 196-225.

Ghaemi, S. N., Liapis, C., & Owen, D. (2016). The psychopathology of power. In *The Intoxication of Power* (pp. 17–37). Palgrave Macmillan.

Ghafran, C., & O'Sullivan, N. (2017). The impact of audit committee expertise on audit quality: Evidence from UK audit fees. *The British Accounting Review*, *49*(6), 578–593. doi:10.1016/j.bar.2017.09.008

Gill, A. (2008). Corporate Governance as Social Responsibility: A Research Agenda. *Berkeley Journal of International Law*, *26*(2), 452–478.

Giurca Vasilescu, L. (2008). *Corporate governance in developing and emerging countries: the case of Romania*. Munich Personal RePEc Archive, https://mpra.ub.uni-muenchen.de/11053/

Givoly, D., & Hayn, C. (2000). The changing time-series properties of earnings, cash flows and accruals: Has financial reporting become more conservative? *Journal of Accounting and Economics*, *29*(3), 287–320. doi:10.1016/S0165-4101(00)00024-0

Global Reporting Initiative. (2011). *Sustainability Reporting Guidelines*. GRI.

Godfrey, P. C. (2005). The relationship between corporate philanthropy and shareholder wealth: A risk management perspective. *Academy of Management Review*, *30*(4), 777–798. doi:10.5465/amr.2005.18378878

Goel, A. M., & Thakor, A. V. (2003). Why do firms smooth earnings? *The Journal of Business*, *76*(1), 151–192. doi:10.1086/344117

Goh, B. W., & Li, D. (2011). Internal Controls and Conditional Conservatism. *The Accounting Review*, *86*(3), 975–1005. doi:10.2308/accr.00000041

Gois, C.G. (2014). Financial Reporting Quality and Corporate Governance: The Portuguese Companies Evidence. *Instituto Superior De Contabilidade e Administracao De Coimbra*, 1-25.

Gómez, N. A., & García, S. M. (2020). Governance and Type of Industry as Determinants of Corporate Social Responsibility Disclosures in Latin America. *Latin American Business Review*, *21*(1), 1–35. doi:10.1080/10978526.2019.1697185

Goodin, R. (1992). *If People Were money*. Free Movement. Harvester Wheatsheaf.

Google. (2019). Google. *Environment Reporter, 2019*. https://services.google.com/fh/files/misc/google_2019-environmental-report.pdf

Goyal, R., Kakabadse, N., & Kakabadse, A. (2019). Improving Corporate Governance with Functional Diversity on FTSE 350 Boards: Directors' Perspective. *Journal of Capital Markets Studies.*, *3*(2), 113–136. doi:10.1108/JCMS-09-2019-0044

Graham, J. R., Kim, H., & Leary, M. T. (2017). CEO Power and Board Dynamics. Working Paper. doi:10.2139srn.2938120

Graves, R. (2014). *I miti greci*. Longanesi & C.

Gregory-Smith, I., Main, B. M., & O'Reilly, C. A. III. (2014). Appointments, pay and performance in UK boardrooms by gender. *Economic Journal (London)*, *124*(574), F109–F128. doi:10.1111/ecoj.12102

Griffin, P. A., Lont, D. H., & Sun, Y. (2010). Agency problems and audit fees: Further tests of the free cash flow hypothesis. *Accounting and Finance*, *50*(2), 321–350. doi:10.1111/j.1467-629X.2009.00327.x

Grosvold, J., & Brammer, S. (2011). National institutional systems as antecedents of female board representation: An empirical study. *Corporate Governance*, *19*(2), 116–135. doi:10.1111/j.1467-8683.2010.00830.x

Grove, H., Patelli, L., Victoravich, L. M., & Xu, P. (2011). Corporate governance and performance in the wake of the financial crisis: Evidence from US commercial banks. *Corporate Governance*, *19*(5), 418–436. doi:10.1111/j.1467-8683.2011.00882.x

Gul, F. A., Chen, C. J. P., Tsui, J. S. L., & University, H. K. P. (2003). Discretionary Accounting Accruals, Managers' Incentives, and Audit Fees. *Contemporary Accounting Research*, *20*(3), 441–464. doi:10.1506/686E-NF2J-73X6-G540

Gul, F. A., & Tsui, J. (1998). A test of the free cash flow and debt monitoring hypotheses: Evidence from audit pricing. *Journal of Accounting and Economics*, *24*(2), 219–237. doi:10.1016/S0165-4101(98)00006-8

Gulzar, M. A., & Wang, Z. J. (2010). Corporate Governance and Non-Listed Family Owned Businesses: Evidence from Pakistan. *International Journal of Innovation, Management and Technology*, *1*(2), 124–129.

Habib, A., Bhuiyan, B. U., & Rahman, A. (2018). "Problem" directors and audit fees. *International Journal of Auditing*, *23*(1), 125–143. doi:10.1111/ijau.12150

Haffar, M., & Searcy, C. (2017). Classification of Trade-offs Encountered in the Practice of Corporate Sustainability. *Business Ethics (Oxford, England)*, *2017*(140), 495–522.

Hair, J. F., Babin, B., Money, A. H., & Samouel, P. (2003). *Essentials of business research methods*. John Wiley & Sons.

Haleblian, J., & Finkelstein, S. (1993). Top management team size, CEO dominance and firm performance: The moderating roles of environmental turbulence and discretion. *Academy of Management Journal*, *36*(4), 844–863.

Hall, R. E., & Jones, C. I. (1999). Why do some countries produce so much more output per worker than others? *The Quarterly Journal of Economics*, *114*(1), 83–116. doi:10.1162/003355399555954

Hambrick, D. C., Misangyi, V. F., & Park, C. A. (2015). The quad model for identifying a corporate director's potential for effective monitoring: Toward a new theory of board sufficiency. *Academy of Management Review*, *40*(3), 323–344. doi:10.5465/amr.2014.0066

Hamdan, A. M. M., & Al Mubarak, M. M. S. (2017). The impact of board independence on accounting-based performance. *Journal of Economic and Administrative Sciences*.

Hansen, E., Grobe-Dunker, F., & Reichwald, R. (2009). Sustainability innovation cube. A framework to evaluate sustainability-oriented innovations. *Int. J. Innov. Manag.*, *13*(4), 683-713.

Harrigan, K. R. (1981). Numbers and positions of women elected to corporate boards. *Academy of Management Journal*, *24*, 619–625.

Hasan, Z. (2009). Corporate governance: Western and Islamic perspectives'. *International Review of Business Research Papers*, *5*(1), 277–293.

Hashmi, M. A., & Al-Habib, M. (2013). Sustainability and carbon management practices in the Kingdom of Saudi Arabia. *Journal of Environmental Planning and Management*, *56*(1), 140–157. doi:10.1080/09640568.2012.654849

Haunschild, L., & Wolter, H. (2010). *The economic importance of family and women's enterprises*. Institute for SME Research.

Hay, D., Knechel, W. R., & Ling, H. (2008). Evidence on the impact of internal control and corporate governance on audit fees. *International Journal of Auditing*, *12*(1), 9–24. doi:10.1111/j.1099-1123.2008.00367.x

Hayward, M. L., & Hambrick, D. C. (1997). Explaining the premiums paid for large acquisitions: Evidence of CEO hubris. *Administrative Science Quarterly*, *42*(1), 103–127. doi:10.2307/2393810

Heidrick & Struggles, I. (1986). *The changing board*. Chicago: Heidrick and Struggles Inc.

Heidrick & Struggles, Inc. (1986). *The Changing board*. Heidrick & Struggles Inc.

Henao, R., Sarache, W., & Gómez, I. (2018). Lean Manufacturing and Sustainable Performance: Trends and future challenges. *Journal of Cleaner Production, 208*(20), 99–116.

Henderson, D. (2004). *The role of business in the modern world: Progress, pressures and prospects for the market economy*. Institute of Economic Affairs.

Hennes, K. M., Leone, A. J., & Miller, B. P. (2014). Determinants and Market Consequences of Auditor Dismissals after Accounting Restatements. *The Accounting Review, 89*(3), 1051–1082. doi:10.2308/accr-50680

Hermalin, B. E., & Weisbach, M. S. (2003). Boards of directors as an endogenously determined institution: A survey of the economic literature. *Economic Policy Review, 9*, 7–26.

Hermalin, B., & Weisbach, M. (1991). The Effect of Board Composition and Direct Incentives on Firm Performance. *Financial Management, 21*(4), 101–112. doi:10.2307/3665716

Hermalin, B., & Weisbach, M. (2003). Boards of Directors as an Endogenously Determined Institution: A Survey of the Economic Literature. *Economic Policy Review, 9*(1), 7–26.

Herring, C. (2009). Does diversity pay? Race, gender and the business case for diversity. *American Sociological Review, 74*(2), 208–224. doi:10.1177/000312240907400203

Herzberg, M. M. (1998). Implementing EBO/EVA analysis in stock selection. *Journal of Investing, 7*(1), 45–53. doi:10.3905/joi.1998.408447

Herzig, C., & Schaltegger, S. (2011). *Corporate sustainability reporting: an overview. Sustainability Accounting and Reporting*. Springer Netherlands. doi:10.1007/978-94-007-1697-1_14

Hill, C., & Snell, S. (1988). External Control, Corporate Strategy, and Firm Performance in Research intensive Industries. *Strategic Management Journal, 9*(6), 577–590. doi:10.1002mj.4250090605

Hillman, A. J., Shropshire, C., & Canella, A. A. (2007). Organizational predictors of women on corporate boards. *Academy of Management Journal, 50*(4), 941–952. doi:10.5465/amj.2007.26279222

Hillman, A., Canella, A. A., & Harris, I. C. (2002). Women and racial minorities in the boardroom: How do directors differ? *Journal of Management, 28*(6), 747–763. doi:10.1177/014920630202800603

Hillman, A., & Keim, G. (2001). Shareholder value, stakeholder management, and social issues: What's the bottom line? *Strategic Management Journal, 22*(2), 125–139. doi:10.1002/1097-0266(200101)22:2<125::AID-SMJ150>3.0.CO;2-H

Holthausen, R. W., & Watts, R. L. (2001). The relevance of value-relevance literature for financial accounting standard setting. *Journal of Accounting and Economics, 31*(1/3), 3–75. doi:10.1016/S0165-4101(01)00029-5

Holtz, L., & Neto, A. S. (2014). *Effect of board of directors' characteristics on the quality of Accounting information in Brazil.* Paper presented at the VII Anpcont congress, Fortaleza, CE, Brazil. 10.1590/1808-057x201412010

Ho, P. H., Huang, C. W., Lin, C. Y., & Yen, J. F. (2016). CEO overconfidence and financial crisis: Evidence from bank lending and leverage. *Journal of Financial Economics, 120*(1), 194–209. doi:10.1016/j.jfineco.2015.04.007

Hope, O. K., Langli, J. C., & Thomas, W. B. (2012). Agency conflicts and auditing in private firms. *Accounting, Organizations and Society, 37*(7), 500–517. doi:10.1016/j.aos.2012.06.002

Hopkins, M. (2003). *The Planetary bargain.* Earthscan.

Horisch, J., Freeman, R. E., & Schaltegger, S. (2014). Applying stakeholder theory in sustainability management: Links, similarities, dissimilarities, and a conceptual framework. *Organization & Environment, 27*(4), 328–346. doi:10.1177/1086026614535786

Huse, M. (2005). Accountability and creating accountability: A framework for exploring behavioural perspectives of corporate governance. *British Journal of Management, 16*(s1), S65–S79. doi:10.1111/j.1467-8551.2005.00448.x

Huse, M., & Rindova, V. P. (2001). Stakeholders' expectations of board roles: The case of subsidiary boards. *The Journal of Management and Governance, 5*(2), 153–178. doi:10.1023/A:1013017909067

Hutchinson, M., Mack, J., & Plastow, K. (2014). Who selects the 'right' directors? An examination of the association between board selection, gender diversity and outcomes. *Accounting and Finance.* Advance online publication. doi:10.1111/acfi.12082

ICAEW (2004). *Sustainability: The Role of Accountants.* The Institute of Chartered Accountants in England & Wales.

Idemudia, U. (2007). *Corporate Partnership and Community Development in the Nigerian oil industry: Strengths and Limitations, UNRISD Markets, Business and Regulation Programme Paper 2.* Geneva: United nations Research Institute for Social Development (UNRISD).

Idemudia, U. (2011). Corporate social responsibility and developing countries: Moving the critical CSR research agenda in Africa forward. *Progress in Development Studies, 11*(1), 1–18. doi:10.1177/146499341001100101

Ilaboya, J. O., & Lodikero, O. (2017). Board independence and financial statement fraud: A moderating effect of female gender diversity. *Accounting and Taxation Review, 1*(1), 196-221.

Institute for Family Business. (2011). *The UK Family Business Sector.* Oxford Economics.

Institute of Directors in Southern Africa (IoDSA). (2009). King Report on Corporate Governance in South Africa. Retrieved 16 April 2020, from https://www.iodsa.co.za/page/kingIII

Institute of Directors in Southern Africa (IoDSA). (2016). King IV Report on Corporate Governance for South Africa 2016. Retrieved 20 April 2020, from https://www.adams.africa/wp-content/uploads/2016/11/King-IV-Report.pdf

International Labour Organization. (2007). *International Instruments and Corporate Social Responsibility: A Booklet to Accompany Training – The Labour Dimension of CSR: from Principles to Practice.* Available from http://www.ilo.org/wcmsp5/groups/public/@ed_emp/@emp_ent/@multi/documents/instr uctionalmaterial/wcms_101247.pdf

Iqbal, Z., & Mirakhor, A. (2004). Stakeholders model of governance in Islamic economic system. *Islamic Economic Studies*, *11*(2), 43–63.

Isidro, H., & Sobral, M. (2014). The effects of women on corporate boards on firm value, financial performance, ethical and social compliance. *Journal of Business Ethics*, 1–19.

Issham, I. (2011). Company performance in Malaysia after the 1997 economic crisis: Using Economic Value Added (EVA) as a predictor. *African Journal of Business Management*, *5*(7), 3012–3018.

Issham, I., Samad, A. M. F., Siew, Y. H., Kamil, A. A., & Ayub, M. A. (2008). Economic value added (EVA) as a performance measurement for GLCs vs Non-GLCs: Evidence from Bursa Malaysia. *Prague Economic Papers*, *3*(2), 168–179. doi:10.18267/j.pep.328

Ivancevich, Skinner, & Crosby. (1997). Management Quality & Competitiveness (2nd ed.). Chicago: Irwin.

Jasmin, J., Kerstin, P., & Karin, V. (2010). *Gender diversity in the boardroom and firm performance: What exactly constitutes a critical mass?* Retrieved from https://papers.ssrn.com/sol3/papers.cfm?abstract_id=2009234

Jenfa, B. I. (2000). *Elements of Professionalism and Practice of Accountancy*. Ehindero Nigeria Ltd.

Jensen, M. C. (1986). Agency costs of free cash flow, corporate finance, and takeovers. *The American Economic Review*, *76*(2), 323–329. https://www.jstor.org/stable/1818789

Jensen, M. C. (1993). The Modern Industrial Revolution, Exit, and the Failure of Internal Control Systems. *The Journal of Finance*, *48*, 831–880.

Jensen, M. C., & Meckling, W. H. (1976). Theory of Firm: Managerial behaviour, agency costs and ownership structure. *Journal of Financial Economics*, *3*(4), 305–350. doi:10.1016/0304-405X(76)90026-X

Jensen, M. C., & Meckling, W. H. (1976). Theory of the firm: Managerial behavior, agency costs and ownership structure. *Journal of Financial Economics*, *3*(4), 305–360. doi:10.1016/0304-405X(76)90026-X

Jizi, M., Nehme, R., & Salama, A. (2016). Do social responsibility disclosures show improvements on stock price? *Journal of Developing Areas*, *50*(2), 77–95. doi:10.1353/jda.2016.0075

Joana M., Janneke P., & Chantal R., (2010). *Gender diversity and firm performance: Evidence from Dutch and Danish boardrooms*. Tjalling C. Koopmans Research Institute, Discussion paper series no. 10-03.

Joana, M., Janneke, P. & Chantal, R. (2010). *Gender diversity and firm performance: Evidence from Dutch and Danish boardrooms*. Tjalling C. Koopmans Research Institute, Discussion paper series no. 10-03.

Jo, H., & Na, H. (2012). Does CSR reduce firm risk? Evidence from controversial industry sectors. *Journal of Business Ethics*, *110*(4), 441–456. doi:10.100710551-012-1492-2

Johannesburg Stock Exchange Listing Requirements. Service Issue 14. April 2011. Second edition. Johannesburg, South Africa.

Johari, N. H., Saleh, N. M., Jaffar, R., & Hassan, M. S. (2009). The influence of board independence, competency and ownership on earnings management in Malaysia. *International Journal of Economics and Management*, *2*(2), 281–306.

John, O. O., & Samuel, O. I. (2013). *CSR Sustainability, Ethics & Governance, Challenges, Opportunities and Strategies for 21st Century Leaders*. Springer.

Johnson, H. L. (1971). Business in Contemporary Society: Framework and Issues. Belmont, CA: Wadsworth.

Johnson, J. L., Daily, C. M., & Ellstrang, A. E. (1996). Boards of directors: A review and research agenda. *Journal of Management*, *22*(3), 409–438. doi:10.1177/014920639602200303

Jones, T.M., (1980, Spring). Corporate social responsibility revisited, redefined. *California Management Review*, 59-67.

Jones, T. M. (1980). Corporate social responsibility revisited, redefined. *California Management Review*, *22*(3), 59–67. doi:10.2307/41164877

Joshi, P. L., & AL-Bastaki, H. (2000). Determinants of Audit Fees: Evidence from the Companies Listed in Bahrain. *International Journal of Auditing*, *4*(2), 129–138. doi:10.1111/1099-1123.00308

Kakabadse, N. K., Yang, H., & Sanders, R. (2010). The effectiveness of non-executive directors in Chinese state-owned enterprises. *Management Decision*, *48*(7), 1063–1079. doi:10.1108/00251741011068770

Kalleberg, A., & Leicht, K. (1991). Gender and organizational performance: Determinants of small business survival and success. *Academy of Management Journal*, *34*(1), 136–161.

Kantudu, A. L., & Samaila, I. A. (2015). *Board Characteristics*. Independent Audit.

Kassel, K. (2012). The circle of inclusion: Sustainability, CSR and the values that drive them. *Journal of Human Values*, *18*(2), 133–146. doi:10.1177/0971685812454482

Kaufmann, D., Kraay, A., & Mastruzzi, M. (2011). The worldwide governance indicators: Methodology and analytical issues. *Hague Journal on the Rule of Law*, *3*(2), 220–246. doi:10.1017/S1876404511200046

Kelly, M. (2019). The Role of the Board of Directors in Corporate Governance. CPA Ireland. Retrieved 14 April 2020, from https://www.cpaireland.ie/CPAIreland/media/EducationTraining/Study%20Support%20Resources/P1%20Corp%20Laws%20and%20Governance/Relevant%20Articles/p1-corp-governance-the-role-of-the-board-of-directors.pdf

Kelman, H. C. (1958). Compliance, identification, and internalization: Three processes of attitude change. *The Journal of Conflict Resolution*, *2*(1), 51–60. doi:10.1177/002200275800200106

Kemebradikemor Embele, H. O. A. (2019). Board Characteristics and Financial Reporting Quality. *Journal of Accounting and Financial Management ISSN*, *5*(1).

Kesner, I. F. (1988). Directors' characteristics and committee membership: An investigation of type, occupation, tenure, and gender. *Academy of Management Journal*, *31*(1), 66–84.

Kets de Vries, M. F. (1994). The leadership mystique. *The Academy of Management Perspectives*, *8*(3), 73–89. doi:10.5465/ame.1994.9503101181

Khalifa, M., & Othman, H. B. (2015). The effect of conservatism on cost of capital: MENA evidence. *Applied Economics*, *47*(1), 71–87. doi:10.1080/00036846.2014.962223

Khalil, S., Magnan, M. L., & Cohen, J. R., 2008. Dual-class shares and audit pricing: Evidence from the Canadian markets. *Auditing: A Journal of Practice, 27*(2), 199-216. doi:10.2308/aud.2008.27.2.199

Khan, H. (2011). A Literature Review of Corporate Governance. In International Conference on E-business, Management and Economics. IPEDR. IACSIT Press.

Khan, M., & Watts, R. L. (2009). Estimation and empirical properties of a firm-year measure of accounting conservatism. *Journal of Accounting and Economics*, *48*(2-3), 132–150. doi:10.1016/j.jacceco.2009.08.002

Khuruma, I. K., & Raman, K. K. (2004). Litigation Risk and the Financial Reporting Credibility of Big 4 versus Non-Big 4 Audits: Evidence from Anglo-American Countries. *The Accounting Review*, *79*(2), 473–495. doi:10.2308/accr.2004.79.2.473

Kiel, G. C., & Nicholson, G. J. (2003). Board composition and corporate performance: How the Australian experience informs contrasting theories of corporate governance. *Corporate Governance*, *11*(3), 189–205. doi:10.1111/1467-8683.00318

Kim, D., & Starks, L. T. (2015). *Board heterogeneity of expertise and firm performance*. Working paper.

Kim, Y., Li, S., Pan, C., & Zuo, L. (2013). The Role of Accounting Conservatism in the Equity Market: Evidence from Seasoned Equity Offerings. *The Accounting Review*, *88*(4), 1327–1356. doi:10.2308/accr-50420

Kiron, D., Kruschwitz, N., Haanaes, K., & Velken, I. S. (2012). Sustainability nears a tipping point. *MIT Sloan Management Review*, (2), 69.

Klai, N., &Omri, A. (2011). *Corporate Governance and Financial Reporting Quality: The Case of Tunisian Firms.* International Business Research.

Klein, J. (2015b). Velveeta & Volkswagen: sustainability is a moving target. *Journal of Property Management*, (2), 12. Retrieved from http://www.jpm-digital.org

Klein, A. (2002). Audit Committee, Board of Director Characteristics and Earnings Management. *Journal of Accounting and Economics*, *33*(3), 375–400. doi:10.1016/S0165-4101(02)00059-9

Knight, J. A. (1998). *Value based management: Developing a systematic approach to creating shareholder value*. McGraw-Hill.

Knox, S., Maklan, S., & French, P. (2005). Corporate Social Responsibility: Exploring stakeholder relationships and programme reporting across leading FTSE companies. *Journal of Business Ethics*, *61*(1), 7–28. doi:10.100710551-005-0303-4

Kok, P. G., van der Wiele, T., McKenna, R., & Brown, A. (2001). A Corporate Social Responsibility audit within a quality management framework. *Journal of Business Ethics*, *31*(4), 285–297. doi:10.1023/A:1010767001610

Kothari, S. P., Li, X., & Short, J. E. (2009). The effect of disclosures by management, analysts, and business press on cost of capital, return volatility, and analyst forecasts: A study using content analysis. *The Accounting Review*, *84*(5), 1639–1670. doi:10.2308/accr.2009.84.5.1639

Kotler, P., & Lee, N. (2005). Corporate Social Responsibility: Doing the most good for your business. John Wiley & Sons, Inc.

Kottler, P., & Lee, N. (2005). *Corporate Social Responsibility: Doing the most good for your company and your cause*. John Wiley & Sons.

KPMG. (2013). *CII's Family Business Network (India chapter).* Retrieved from http://www.kpmgfamilybusiness.com/family-owned-businesses-backbone-indias-economy

Krishnan, G., & Visvanathan, G. (2009). Do Auditors Price Audit Committee's Expertise? The Case of Accounting versus Nonaccounting Financial Experts. *Journal of Accounting, Auditing & Finance*, *24*(1), 115–144. doi:10.1177/0148558X0902400107

Kroll, M. J., Toombs, L. A., & Wright, P. (2000). Napoleon's tragic march home from Moscow: Lessons in hubris. *The Academy of Management Perspectives*, *14*(1), 117–128. doi:10.5465/ame.2000.2909844

Kulkani, R., & Maniam, B. (2014). Corporate Governance: Indian Perspective. International Journal of Trade. *Economics and Finance.*, *5*(4), 364–368.

Kumar, R.A. (2016). A critical study on Corporate Social Responsibility activities of public sector undertakings in India and its financial implications. *IOSR Journal of Business and Management, 18*(10), 31-37.

Kumar, A., & Das, N. (2018). Sustainability Reporting Practices in Emerging Economies: A Cross-Country Study of BRICS Nations. *Problemy Ekorozwoju, 13*(2), 17–25.

Kumar, S., Teichman, S., & Timpernagel, T. (2012). A green supply chain is a requirement for profitability. *International Journal of Production Research, 50*(5), 1278–1296. doi:10.1080/00207543.2011.571924

Kurtz, M. J., & Schrank, A. (2007). Growth and governance: Models, measures, and mechanisms. *The Journal of Politics, 69*(2), 538–554. doi:10.1111/j.1468-2508.2007.00549.x

Kurucz, E., Colbert, B., & Wheeler, D. (2008). The business case for corporate social responsibility. In A. Crane, A. McWilliams, D. Matten, J. Moon, & D. Siegel (Eds.), *The Oxford handbook of corporate social responsibility*. Oxford University Press. doi:10.1093/oxfordhb/9780199211593.003.0004

L'Huillier, B. M. (2014). What does "corporate governance" actually mean? Corporate Governance International Journal of Business in Society., 14(3), 300–319. doi:10.1108/CG-10-2012-0073

Laakso, E. (2010). *Stock market participation and household characteristics in Europe*. Master Thesis, Aalto University, School of Economics. http://epub.lib.aalto.fi/en/ethesis/pdf/12385/hse ethesis 12385.pdf

LaFond, R., & Watts, R. L. (2008). The Information Role of Conservatism. *The Accounting Review, 83*(2), 447–478. doi:10.2308/accr.2008.83.2.447

Lara, J. M. G., Osma, B. G., & Penalva, F. (2009). Accounting conservatism and corporate governance. *Review of Accounting Studies, 14*, 161–201.

Lawrence, D. Y., Pazzaglia, F., & Sonpar, K. (2011). The introduction of a non-traditional and aggressive approach to banking: The risks of hubris. *Journal of Business Ethics, 102*(3), 401–420. doi:10.1007/s10551-011-0821-1

Le Quang, C., Kwang Soo, K., & Yu, Y. (2014). Effects of Corporate Governance on the Performance of Private Economic Groups in Vietnam. Muyeog Yeon'gu, 10(6), 39–56. doi:10.16980/jitc.10.6.201412.39

Lebura, S. (2009). *Corporate Social Responsibility (CSR) and the Nigerian oil industry* [Unpublished MSc dissertation]. De Montfort University, Leicester, UK.

Lebura, S. (2013). *Stakeholder relationships in the Nigerian oil industry* [Unpublished doctoral dissertation]. De Montfort University, Leicester, UK.

Lee, D. D., & Faff, R. W. (2009). Corporate sustainability performance and idiosyncratic risk: A global perspective. *Financial Review, 44*(2), 213–237. doi:10.1111/j.1540-6288.2009.00216.x

Lee, S., Li, X., & Sami, H. (2015). Conditional Conservatism and Audit Fees. *Accounting Horizons*, *29*(1), 83–113. doi:10.2308/acch-50928

Li, J., & Tang, Y. I. (2010). CEO hubris and firm risk taking in China: The moderating role of managerial discretion. *Academy of Management Journal*, *53*(1), 45–68. doi:10.5465/amj.2010.48036912

Lim, R. (2011). Are corporate governance attributes associated with accounting conservatism? *Accounting and Finance*, *51*(4), 1007–1030. doi:10.1111/j.1467-629X.2010.00390.x

Lin, C. P. (2010). Modeling corporate citizenship, organizational trust, and work engagement based on attachment theory. *Journal of Business Ethics*, *94*(4), 517–531. doi:10.100710551-009-0279-6

Lindblom, C. K. (1994). *The implications of organizational legitimacy for corporate social performance and disclosure*. Critical Perspective on Accounting Conference, New York, NY.

Lindstädt, H., Wolff, M., & Fehre, K. (2011). *Frauen in Führungspositionen: Auswirkungen auf den Unternehmenserfolg*. Bundesministerium für Familie, Senioren, Frauen und Jugend.

Lipton, M., & Lorsch, J. W. (1992). A modest proposal for improved corporate governance. *Business Lawyer*, *48*(53), 89–77.

Li, S., Fetscherin, M., Alon, I., Lattemann, C., & Yeh, K. (2010). Corporate social responsibility in emerging markets. *Management International Review*, *50*(5), 635–654. doi:10.100711575-010-0049-9

Li, S., & Filer, L. (2007). The effects of the governance environment on the choice of investment mode and the strategic implications. *Journal of World Business*, *42*(1), 80–98. doi:10.1016/j.jwb.2006.11.006

Liu, Y., Miletkov, M., Wei, Z., & Yang, T. (2015). Board independence and firm performance in China. *Journal of Corporate Finance*, *30*(1), 223–244. doi:10.1016/j.jcorpfin.2014.12.004

Liu, Z., & Elayan, F. A. (2015). Litigation risk, information asymmetry and conditional conservatism. *Review of Quantitative Finance and Accounting*, *44*(4), 581–608. doi:10.100711156-013-0428-y

Lobo, G., & Zhou, J. (2006). Did conservatism in financial reporting increase after the Sarbanes-Oxley Act? Initial evidence. *Accounting Horizons*, *20*(1), 57–73. doi:10.2308/acch.2006.20.1.57

Lo, S. F. (2010). Performance evaluation for sustainable business: A profitability and marketability framework. *Corporate Social Responsibility and Environmental Management*, *17*(6), 311–319. doi:10.1002/csr.214

Lo, S. F., & Sheu, H. J. (2007). Is corporate sustainability a value-increasing strategy for business? *Corporate Governance*, *15*(2), 345–358. doi:10.1111/j.1467-8683.2007.00565.x

Loscocco, K. A., Robinson, J., Hall, R. H., & Allen, J. K. (1991). Gender and small business success: An inquiry into women's relative disadvantage. *Social Forces*, *70*(1), 65–85. doi:10.2307/2580062

Lourenço, I. C., Branco, M. C., Curto, J. D., & Eugénio, T. (2012). How does the market value corporate sustainability performance? *Journal of Business Ethics*, *108*(4), 417–428. doi:10.100710551-011-1102-8

Ludema, J. D., Laszlo, C., & Lynch, D. L. (2012). Embedding sustainability: How the field of organization development and change can help companies harness the next big competitive advantage. *Research in Organizational Change and Development*, *20*, 265–299. doi:10.1108/S0897-3016(2012)0000020011

Luo, Y., Sun, J., & Wang, S. L. (2011). Comparative strategic management: An emergent field in international management. *Journal of International Management*, *17*(3), 190–200. doi:10.1016/j.intman.2011.05.002

MacAdam, R., & Leonard, D. (2003). Corporate Social Responsibility in a Total Quality Management Context: Opportunities for sustainable growth. *Corporate Governance*, *3*(4), 36–45. doi:10.1108/14720700310497104

Maccoby, M. (2000). Narcissistic leaders. *Harvard Business Review*, *78*(1), 69–77.

Madden, B. J. (1999). *CFROI valuation: A total system approach to valuing the firm*. Butterworth-Heinemann.

Majeed, M. A., Zhang, X. Z., & Wang, Z. (2017). Product market competition, regulatory changes, ownership structure, and accounting conservatism. *Chinese Management Studies*, *11*(4), 658–688. doi:10.1108/CMS-12-2016-0248

Malmendier, U., & Tate, G. (2005). Does overconfidence affect corporate investment? CEO overconfidence measures revisited. *European Financial Management*, *11*(5), 649–659. doi:10.1111/j.1354-7798.2005.00302.x

Malmendier, U., & Tate, G. (2008). Who makes acquisitions? CEO overconfidence and the market's reaction. *Journal of Financial Economics*, *89*(1), 20–43. doi:10.1016/j.jfineco.2007.07.002

Mans-Kemp, N., & Viviers, S. (2015). Investigating Board Diversity in South Africa. *Journal of Economic and Financial Sciences.*, *8*(2), 392–414. doi:10.4102/jef.v8i2.100

Marra, A., Mazzola, P., & Prencipe, A. (2011). Board monitoring and earnings management pre and post IFRS. *The International Journal of Accounting*, *7*(3), 235–256.

Marti, C. P., Rovira-Val, M. R., & Drescher, L. G. J. (2015). Are Firms that Contribute to Sustainable Development Better Financially? *Corporate Social Responsibility and Environmental Management*, *22*(5), 305–319. doi:10.1002/csr.1347

Martín, C. J. G., & Herrero, B. (2018). Boards of directors: Composition and effects on the performance of the firm. Economic Research-Ekonomska Istraživanja., 31(1), 1015–1041. doi: 10.1080/1331677X.2018.1436454

Martínez-Ferrero, J., & Frías-Aceituno, J. V. (2015). Relationship Between Sustainable Development and Financial Performance: International Empirical Research. *Business Strategy and the Environment*, *24*(1), 20–39. doi:10.1002/bse.1803

Matten, D., Crane, A., & Chapple, W. (2003). "Behind the Mask", op. cit. Other terms appear in this decade, namely sustainable company or triple-bottom-line approach. *Journal of Business Ethics*, *44*(2/3), 95–105.

Mayers, D., Shivdasani, A., & Smith, C. Jr. (1997). Board Composition and Corporate Control: Evidence from the Insurance Industry. *The Journal of Business*, *70*(1), 33–62. doi:10.1086/209707

McGuire, J. W. (1963). *Business and society*. McGraw-Hill.

McIntosh, Leipziger, & Coleman. (2003). Living Corporate Citizenship: Strategic routes to socially responsible business. FT Prentice Hall.

McWilliams, A., & Siegel, D. (2000). Corporate social responsibility and financial performance: Correlation or misspecification? *Strategic Management Journal*, *21*(5), 603–609. doi:10.1002/(SICI)1097-0266(200005)21:5<603::AID-SMJ101>3.0.CO;2-3

Micah, L. C., & Umobong, A. A. (2013). Corporate governance and sustainable development in Nigeria: A study of oil companies in the Niger Delta Region. *International Journal of Business and Management*, *8*(7), 127–132. doi:10.5539/ijbm.v8n7p127

Michelberger, K. (2016). Corporate Governance Effects on Firm Performance: A Literature Review. Regional Formation and Development Studies., 3(20), 84–95. doi:10.15181/rfds.v20i3.1346

Mingers, J., & White, L. (2010). A review of recent contribution of systems thinking to operational research and management science. *European Journal of Operational Research*, *207*(3), 1147–1161. doi:10.1016/j.ejor.2009.12.019

Minority Shareholder Watchdog Group and Nottingham University Business School Corporate Governance Survey Report. (2007). Minority Shareholder Group.

Mir, A. E., & Souad, S. (2008). Corporate governance and the relationship between EVA and created shareholder value. *Corporate Governance*, *8*(1), 46–58. doi:10.1108/14720700810853392

Miralles-Quirós, M. D. M., Miralles-Quirós, J. L., & Arraiano, I. G. (2017). Are firms that contribute to sustainable development valued by investors? *Corporate Social Responsibility and Environmental Management*, *24*(1), 71–84. doi:10.1002/csr.1392

Miralles-Quirós, M., Miralles-Quirós, J., & Valente Gonçalves, L. (2018). The value relevance of environmental, social, and governance performance: The Brazilian case. *Sustainability*, *10*(3), 574. doi:10.3390u10030574

Miras-Rodríguez, M. D. M., Martínez-Martínez, D., & Escobar-Pérez, B. (2019). Which corporate governance mechanisms drive CSR disclosure practices in emerging countries? *Sustainability*, *11*(1), 61–81. doi:10.3390u11010061

Mirza, H. H., Shahid, M., Sumaira, A., & Farzana, R. (2012). Gender diversity and firm performance: Evidence from Pakistan. *Journal of Social and development. The Sciences*, *3*(5), 161–166.

Mishra, S. (2018). *Global governance- board independence standard and practices*. Retrieved from https://corpgov.law.harvard.edu/2018/06/01/global-governance-board-independence-standards-and-practices/

Mizruchi, M. S. (1996). What do interlocks do? An analysis, critique, and assessment of research on interlocking directorates. *Annual Review of Sociology*, *22*, 271–298.

Mohammadi, M. T., Kardan, B., & Salehi, M. (2018). The relationship between cash holdings, investment opportunities and financial constraint with audit fees. *Asian Journal of Accounting Research*, *3*(1), 15–27. doi:10.1108/AJAR-07-2018-0016

Molano-León, R. (2011). The roles of the board of directors: The unresolved riddle. *Vniversitas.*, *122*, 541–602.

Momin, M. A., & Parker, L. D. (2013). Motivations for corporate social responsibility reporting by MNC subsidiaries in an emerging country: The case of Bangladesh. *The British Accounting Review*, *45*(3), 215–228. doi:10.1016/j.bar.2013.06.007

Moneva, J. M., & Cuellar, B. (2009). The value relevance of financial and non-financial environmental reporting. *Environmental and Resource Economics*, *44*(3), 441–456. doi:10.100710640-009-9294-4

Morck, R. (2008). Behavioral finance in corporate governance: Economics and ethics of the devil's advocate. *The Journal of Management and Governance*, *12*(2), 179–200. doi:10.1007/s10997-008-9059-4

Mori, N. (2014). Directors' diversity and board performance: Evidence from East African microfinance institutions. *Journal of African Business*, *15*(2), 100–113. doi:10.1080/15228916.2014.920654

Muchemwa, M. R., Padia, N., & Callaghan, C. W. (2016). Board Composition, Board Size and Financial Performance of Johannesburg Stock Exchange Companies. *Suid-Afrikaanse Tydskrif vir Ekonomiese en Bestuurswetenskappe*, *19*(4), 497–513. doi:10.4102/sajems.v19i4.1342

Mudashiru, A., Bakare, I. A. O., Babatunde, Y., & Ishmael, O. (2014). Good Corporate Governance and Organisational Performance: An Empirical Analysis. *International Journal of Humanities and Social Science*, *4*(7), 170–178.

Mukhlasin, M. (2018). Auditor Tenure and Auditor Industry Specialization as a Signal to Detect Fraudulent Financial Reporting. *Academy of Accounting and Financial Studies Journal*, *22*(5), 1–10.

Murphy, M. E. (2009). Restoring trust in corporate America: Toward a republican theory of corporate legitimacy. *New York University Journal of Law and Business*, *5*(2), 415–484.

Muth, M., & Donaldson, L. (1998). Stewardship theory and board structure: A contingency approach. *Corporate Governance*, *6*(1), 5–28. doi:10.1111/1467-8683.00076

Muthuri, J. N. (2007). Corporate Citizenship and Sustainable Community Development: Fostering Multi-Sector Collaboration in Magadi Division in Kenya. *Journal of Corporate Citizenship*, *28*(28), 73–84. doi:10.9774/GLEAF.4700.2007.wi.00008

MyAccountingCourse. (2020). What is a Board Member? Retrieved 02 April 2020, from https://www.myaccountingcourse.com/accounting-dictionary/board-member

Myers, S. (1977). Determinants of corporate borrowing. *Journal of Financial Economics*, *5*(2), 147–175. doi:10.1016/0304-405X(77)90015-0

Nabila, A., & Daljono, D. (2013). Pengaruh proporsi dewan komisaris independen, komite audit, dan reputasi auditor terhadap manajemen laba. *Diponegoro Journal of Accounting*, 99-108.

Nasr, M. A., & Ntim, C. G. (2018). Corporate governance mechanisms and accounting conservatism: Evidence from Egypt. *Corporate Governance: The International Journal of Business in Society*, *18*(3), 386–407. doi:10.1108/CG-05-2017-0108

Nawrocka, D., & Parker, T. (2009). Finding the connection: Environmental management systems and environmental performance. *Journal of Cleaner Production*, *17*(6), 601–607. doi:10.1016/j.jclepro.2008.10.003

Nesrine, K., & Abdelwahed, O. (2011). Corporate Governance and Financial Reporting Quality: The Case of Tunisian Firm. *International Business Research*, *4*(1), 158–166.

Nestor, S., & Thompson, J. (2000). *Corporate governance patterns in OECD economies: is convergence under way?* Academic Press.

Nicholson, G. J., & Kiel, G. C. (2007). Can directors impact performance? A case-based test of three theories of corporate governance. *Corporate Governance*, *15*(4), 585–608. doi:10.1111/j.1467-8683.2007.00590.x

Nielsen, S., & Huse, M. (2010). The contribution of women on boards of directors: Going beyond the surface. *Corporate Governance*, *18*(2), 136–148. doi:10.1111/j.1467-8683.2010.00784.x

Niemi, L. (2002). Do firms pay for audit risk? Evidence on risk premiums in audit fees after direct control for audit effort. *International Journal of Auditing*, *6*(1), 37–51. doi:10.1111/j.1099-1123.2002.tb00004.x

Niu, J. (2010). The effect of CEO overconfidence on bank risk taking. *Economic Bulletin*, *30*(4), 3288–3299.

Nwaeke, L. I., & Lebura, S. (2016). Stakeholder relationships as games played by stakeholders. *International Journal of Innovative Research and Development*, *5*(4), 1–11.

O'Rourke, A. (2003). A New Politics of Engagement: Shareholder activism for corporate social responsibility. *Business Strategy and the Environment*, *12*(4), 227–239. doi:10.1002/bse.364

Obitade, O. P. (2013). CEO Overconfidence and Bank Failure. Working Paper. doi:10.2139srn.2352053

OCED. (2005). *Organization for Economic Cooperation and Development, OECD (2005) Glossary of Statistical Terms*. Retrieved from https://stats.oecd.org/glossary/detail.asp?ID=6778

OECD. (2001). *Corporate governance in Asia: A comparative perspective*. OECD.

OECD. (2004). *OECD principles of corporate governance*. OECD.

Ojo, O. (2009). Nigeria: CSR as a vehicle for economic development. In S.O. Idowu & W.L. Filho (Eds.), Global pracitces (pp.393-433). Springer.

Okoye, A. (2009). Theorising Corporate Social Responsibility as an Essentially Contested Concept: Is a definition necessary? *Journal of Business Ethics*, *89*(4), 613–627. doi:10.100710551-008-0021-9

O'Neill, J. (2001). *Building Better Global Economic BRICs*. Goldman Sachs Global Economics Paper, 66.

Organisation for Economic Cooperation and Development (OECD). (1999). *Principles of Corporate Governance*. OECD.

Orlitzky, M., Schmidt, F. L., & Rynes, S. L. (2003). Corporate Social and Financial Performance: A Meta-analysis. *Organization Studies*, *24*(3), 403–441. doi:10.1177/0170840603024003910

Owen, D., & Davidson, J. (2009). Hubris syndrome: An acquired personality disorder? A study of US Presidents and UK Prime Ministers over the last 100 years. *Brain*, *132*(5), 1396–1406. doi:10.1093/brain/awp008 PubMed

Owen, L. D. (2011). Psychiatry and politicians–afterword: Commentary on… psychiatry and politicians. *The Psychiatrist*, *35*(4), 145–148. doi:10.1192/pb.bp.110.031708

Page, S. (2007). *The difference: How the power of diversity creates better groups, firms, schools and societies*. Princeton University Press.

Palmer, D., & Barber, B. M. (2001). Challengers, elites, and owning families: A social class theory of corporate acquisitions in the 1960s. *Administrative Science Quarterly*, *46*(1), 87–120. doi:10.2307/2667126

Palmrose, Z. (1986). Audit fees and auditor size. *Journal of Accounting Research*, *24*(1), 97–110. doi:10.2307/2490806

Park, J. H., Kim, C., Chang, Y. K., Lee, D. H., & Sung, Y. D. (2018). CEO hubris and firm performance: Exploring the moderating roles of CEO power and board vigilance. *Journal of Business Ethics*, *147*(4), 919–933. doi:10.1007/s10551-015-2997-2

Pearce, J., & Zahra, S. (1991). The Relative Power of CEOs and Boards of Directors: Associations with Corporate Performance. *Strategic Management Journal*, *12*(2), 135–153. doi:10.1002mj.4250120205

Perry, T., & Shivdasani, A. (2005). Do Boards Affect Performance? Evidence from Corporate Restructuring. *The Journal of Business*, *78*(4), 1403–1431. doi:10.1086/430864

Peterson, C., & Seligman, M. E. P. (2004). *Character strengths and virtues: A handbook and classification.* Oxford University Press.

Peterson, M., & Bishop, M. (2015). Sustainability in the BRICS and beyond: an examination of the Sustainability Society Index. In B. L. Kedia & K. Aceto (Eds.), *Emerging Markets and the Future of the BRIC Nations* (pp. 41–64). Edward Elgar Publishing. doi:10.4337/9781783479764.00010

Petit, V., & Bollaert, H. (2012). Flying too close to the sun? Hubris among CEOs and how to prevent it. *Journal of Business Ethics, 108*(3), 265–283. doi:10.1007/s10551-011-1097-1

Petrovich, M. K. (2014). Social factors of sustainable development of the regional rural territories. *Society: Politics, Economics, Law*, (2), 1-5.

Petrovic, J. (2008). Unlocking the role of a board director: A review of the literature. *Management Decision, 46*(9), 1373–1392. doi:10.1108/00251740810911993

Pfeffer, J. (1972). Size and composition of corporate boards of directors: The organization and its environment. *Administrative Science Quarterly, 17*(2), 218–228.

Pfeffer, J. (1973). Size, composition, and function of hospital boards of directors: A study of organization-environment linkage. *Administrative Science Quarterly, 18*, 349–364.

Pfeffer, J., & Salancik, G. R. (1978). *The external control of organizations. Resource dependence perspective.* Harper & Row.

Porter, M. E., & Kramer, M. R. (2006). Strategy and society: The link between competitive advantage and corporate social responsibility. *Harvard Business Review, 84*(12), 2–17. PMID:17183795

Poza, E. J., & Daugherty, M. S. (2013). *Family business* (4th ed.). Cengage Learning.

Prasso, S. (1996). Poll: Women in office, not offices. *The Commercial Appeal*, 7B.

PwC Family Business Survey. (2012). *The family firm: Central to the success pf the Middle East.* Retrieved from https://www.pwc.com/m1/en/publications/documents/family-firm-english.pdf

PwC. (2009). *Family Business Survey 2007-2008, Price Water House Coopers, 2009.* Retrieved from https://www.pwc.com/extweb/home.nsf/docid/1FB68AE4ADAFB42E85257395004EEC89

PwC. (2019a). *Thailand Family Business Survey 2019.* Price Waterhouse Cooper (PwC) Thailand. Retrieved from https://www.pwc.com/th/en/services/epb/thailand-Family-Business-survey-2019.html

PwC. (2019b). *India Family Business Survey.* Price Waterhouse Cooper (PwC). Retrieved from https://www.pwc.in/assets/pdfs/research-insights/fbs/2019/pwc-india-family-business-survey-2019.pdf

PwC. (2019c). *PwC Middle East Family Business Survey.* Price Waterhouse Cooper (PwC). Retrieved from https://www.pwc.com/m1/en/publications/documents/family-business-survey-2019.pdf

Qin, Y., Harrison, J., & Chen, L. (2019). A framework for the practice of corporate environmental responsibility in China. *Journal of Cleaner Production*, *235*, 426–452. doi:10.1016/j.jclepro.2019.06.245

Quazi, A. M., & O'Brien, D. (2000). An Empirical Test of a Cross-National Model of Corporate Social Responsibility. *Journal of Business Ethics*, *25*(1), 33–52. doi:10.1023/A:1006305111122

Rahman, A. F., & Mohd-Saleh, N. (2008). The Effect of Free Cash Flow Agency Problem on the Value Relevance of Earnings and Book Value. *Journal of Financial Reporting and Accounting*, *6*(1), 75–90. doi:10.1108/19852510880000636

Rajesh, R. (2020). Exploring the sustainability performances of firms using environmental, social, and governance scores. *Journal of Cleaner Production*, *247*, 119600. doi:10.1016/j.jclepro.2019.119600

Ralston, D. A., Egri, C. P., Karam, C. M., Naoumova, I., Srinivasan, N., Casado, T., Li, Y., & Alas, R. (2015). The triple-bottom-line of corporate responsibility: Assessing the attitudes of present and future business professionals across the BRICs. *Asia Pacific Journal of Management*, *32*(1), 145–179. doi:10.100710490-014-9376-x

Ramana, V. D. (2004). *Market value added and economic value added: Some empirical evidences.* Retrieved from https://papers.ssrn.com/sol3/papers.cfm?abstract_id=871404

Rashid, A. (2015). Revisiting agency theory: Evidence of board independence and agency cost from Bangladesh. *Journal of Business Ethics*, *130*(1), 181–198. doi:10.100710551-014-2211-y

Rastogi S. & Agrawal, R., (2010). Intention of offspring to join the family enterprise: a study of Indian businesses. *Annals of Innovation & Entrepreneurship 2010, 1*, 5603. Doi:10.3402/aie.v1i1.5603

Raut, S. (2018). *Corporate Governance: Concepts and Issues*. Research Scholar with Institute of Directors.

Refinitiv. (2020). *Environmental, Social and Governance (ESG) Scores from Refinitiv*. Retrieved from https://www.refinitiv.com/content/dam/marketing/en_us/documents/methodology/esg-scores-methodology.pdf

Republic of South Africa. (2003). *The Broad-Based Black Economic Empowerment Act No 53 of 2003*. Government Printers.

Republic of South Africa. (2008). *The Companies Act No 71 of 2008*. Government Printers.

Reverte, C. (2009). Determinants of corporate social responsibility disclosure ratings by Spanish listed firms. *Journal of Business Ethics*, *88*(2), 351–366. doi:10.100710551-008-9968-9

Rexhepi, B. (2015). *Small family business: guarantor of economic and social development (PhD)*. University of Pristina.

Richerson, S. (2013). A road map or turning sustainability goals into action. *Journal for Quality and Participation*, *24*(1), 12–21.

Rivera, J. M., Munoz, M. J., & Moneva, J. M. (2017). Revisiting the Relationship Between Corporate Stakeholder Commitment and Social and Financial Performance. *Sustainable Development (Bradford)*, *25*(6), 482–496. doi:10.1002d.1664

Robert, G. N. (1998). Two-sided confidence intervals for the single proportion: Comparison of seven methods. *Statistics in Medicine*, *17*, 857–872.

Robinson, G., & Dechant, K. (1997). Building a business case for diversity. *The Academy of Management Executive*, *11*(3), 21–30. doi:10.5465/ame.1997.9709231661

Roll, R. (1986). The hubris hypothesis of corporate takeovers. *The Journal of Business*, *59*(2), 197–216. doi:10.1086/296325

Rose, C. (2007). Does female board representation influence firm performance? The Danish evidence. *Corporate Governance*, *15*(2), 404–413. doi:10.1111/j.1467-8683.2007.00570.x

Ruigrok, W., Peck, S., & Tacheva, S. (2007). Nationality and gender diversity on Swiss corporate boards. *Corporate Governance*, *15*(4), 546–557. doi:10.1111/j.1467-8683.2007.00587.x

Ruigrok, W., Peck, S., Tacheva, S., Greve, P., & Hu, Y. (2006). The determinants and effects of board nomination committees. *The Journal of Management and Governance*, *10*(2), 119–148. doi:10.100710997-006-0001-3

Sadler-Smith, E. (2016). Hubris in business and management research: A 30-year review of studies. In G. Robinson & P. Garrard (Eds.), *The Intoxication of Power* (pp. 39–74). Palgrave Macmillan.

Sadler-Smith, E., Akstinaite, V., Robinson, G., & Wray, T. (2017). Hubristic leadership: A review. *Leadership*, *13*(5), 525–548. doi:10.1177/1742715016680666

Salim, D. (2011). Board diversity and firm performance: The Indonesian evidence. *Corporate Ownership and Control*, *8*, 1–39.

Salzmann, O., Ionescu-Somers, A., & Steger, U. (2005). The business case for corporate sustainability. *European Management Journal*, *23*(1), 27–36. doi:10.1016/j.emj.2004.12.007

Schaltegger, S., Gibassier, D., & Zvezdov, D. (2013). Is environmental management accounting discipline? A bibliometric literature review. *Meditari Accountancy Research*, *21*(1), 4–31. doi:10.1108/MEDAR-12-2012-0039

Schilling, F. (2001). Corporate governance in Germany: The move to shareholder value. *Corporate Governance*, *9*(3), 148–151. doi:10.1111/1467-8683.00242

Scholtz, H., & Kieviet, S. (2018). The Influence of Board Diversity on Company Performance of South African Companies. *Journal of African Business*, *19*(1), 105–123. doi:10.1080/15228916.2017.1356065

Schuchard, R. (2010). *Understanding the benefits of CSR.* https://www.bsr.org/en/our-insights/blog-view/understanding-the-benefits-of-csr

Schwartz, M. S., & Carroll, A. B. (2003). Corporate social responsibility: A three-domain approach. *Business Ethics Quarterly, 13*(October), 503–530. doi:10.5840/beq200313435

Schwartz-Ziv, M. (2015). Does the gender of directors matter? *Journal of Financial and Quantitative Analysis.*

Schwizer, P., Carretta, A., & Soana, M. G. (2014). Can high quality independent Directors reduce CEO overconfidence [Paper presentation]. European Financial Management Association, 25–28 June 2014, *Annual Meeting*, Rome, Italy.

Secchi, D. (2007). Utilitarian, managerial and relational theories of corporate social responsibility. *International Journal of Management Reviews, 9*(4), 347–373. doi:10.1111/j.1468-2370.2007.00215.x

SECP. (2018). www.secp.gov.pk/news/PDF/News_14/PR_Jan13_2014.pdf

Semenova, N., Hassel, L. G., & Nilsson, H. (2010). The Value Relevance of Environmental and Social Performance: Evidence from Swedish SIX 300 Companies. *Liiketaloudellinen Aikakauskirja, 3.*

Senge, P., Smith, B., Kruschwitz, N., Laur, J., & Schely, S. (2010). *The necessary revolution: How individuals and organizations are working together to create a sustainable world.* Doubleday.

Sen, S., & Bhattacharya, B. (2001). Does doing good always lead to doing better? consumer reactions to corporate social responsibility. *JMR, Journal of Marketing Research, 38*(2), 225–243. doi:10.1509/jmkr.38.2.225.18838

Shailer, G., Cummings, L., Vatuloka, E., & Welch, S. (2004). Discretionary Pricing in a Monopolistic Audit Market. *International Journal of Auditing, 8*(3), 263–277. doi:10.1111/j.1099-1123.2004.00095.x

Shankaraiah, K., & Amiri, S. M. S. (2017). Audit committee quality and financial reporting quality: A study of selected Indian companies. *Journal of Accounting and Business Dynamics, 4*(1), 1–18. doi:10.24815/jdab.v4i1.6653

Shaw, E., Marlow, S., Lam, W., & Carter, S. (2009). Gender and entrepreneurial capital: Implications for firm performance. *International Journal of Gender and Entrepreneurship, 1*(1), 25–41. doi:10.1108/17566260910942327

Shen, W. (2003). The dynamics of the CEO-board relationship: An evolutionary perspective. *Academy of Management Review, 28*(3), 466–476. doi:10.5465/amr.2003.10196776

Shin, P. S., & Gulati, M. (2011). Showcasing diversity. *North Carolina Law Review, 89*, 1017–1054.

Shipman, A. S., & Mumford, M. D. (2011). When confidence is detrimental: Influence of overconfidence on leadership effectiveness. *The Leadership Quarterly*, *22*(4), 649–665. doi:10.1016/j.leaqua.2011.05.006

Shleifer, A., & Vishny, R. (1997). A Survey of Corporate Governance. *The Journal of Finance*, *52*(2), 737–783. doi:10.1111/j.1540-6261.1997.tb04820.x

Shleifer, A., & Vishny, R. W. (1989). Management entrenchment: The case of manager-specific investments. *Journal of Financial Economics*, *25*(1), 123–139. doi:10.1016/0304-405X(89)90099-8

Signitzer, B., & Prexl, A. (2007). Corporate sustainability communications: Aspects of theory and professionalization. *Journal of Public Relations Research*, *20*(1), 1–19. doi:10.1080/10627260701726996

Silverman, I. H. (2010). Valuing technology stocks with EVA: A bridge too far? *Journal of Business Case Studies*, *6*(2), 9–20. doi:10.19030/jbcs.v6i2.863

Simunic, D. A. (1980). The pricing of audit services, theory and evidence. *Journal of Accounting Research*, *18*(1), 161–190. doi:10.2307/2490397

Simunic, D. A., & Stein, M. T. (1996). The Impact of Litigation Risk on Audit Pricing: A Review of the Economics and the Evidence. *Auditing*, *15*, 119–134.

Singh, V., & Vinnicombe, S. (2004). Why so few women directors in top UK boardrooms? Evidence and theoretical explanations. *Corporate Governance*, *12*(4), 479–489. doi:10.1111/j.1467-8683.2004.00388.x

Sinkin, C., Wright, C. J., & Burnett, R. D. (2008). Layoff announcements and stockholder wealth. *Journal of Accounting and Public Policy*, *27*(2), 167–176. doi:10.1016/j.jaccpubpol.2008.01.003

Skinner, D. J. (1993). The investment opportunity set and accounting procedure choice: Preliminary evidence. *Journal of Accounting and Economics*, *16*(4), 407–445. doi:10.1016/0165-4101(93)90034-D

Skinner, D. J., & Srinivasan, S. (2012). Audit Quality and Auditor Reputation: Evidence from Japan. *The Accounting Review*, *87*(5), 1737–1765. doi:10.2308/accr-50198

Smale, A., & Miller, C. C. (2015, March 6). Germany sets Gender Quota in Boardrooms. *The New York Times*. Retrieved from: https://www.nytimes.com/2015/03/07/world/europe/germanlaw-requires-more-women-on-corporate-boards.html?_r=0

Smith, N. C. (2003). Corporate Social Responsibility: Whether or how? *California Management Review*, *45*(4), 52–76. doi:10.2307/41166188

Smith, N., Valdemar, S., & Mette, V. (2006). Do women in top management affect firm performance? A panel study of 2,500 Danish firms. *International Journal of Productivity and Performance Management*, *55*(7), 569–593. doi:10.1108/17410400610702160

Snyder, L. (2007). Filling a position of corporate governance in France: A practical Introduction. *Corporate Governance*, *7*(3), 238–250. doi:10.1108/14720700710756526

Sosik, J. J. (2015). *Leading with character: Stories of valor and virtue and the principles they teach* (2nd ed.). Information Age Publishing.

Sosik, J. J., & Cameron, J. C. (2010). Character and authentic transformational leadership behavior: Expanding the ascetic self towards others. *Consulting Psychology Journal*, *62*(4), 251–269. doi:10.1037/a0022104

Spector, B. (2008). Business Responsibilities in a Divided World: The Cold War Roots of the Corporate Social Responsibility Movement. *Enterprise and Society*, *9*(2), 314.

Spencer, G. (1984). Female executives foresee gains. *Best of Business*, *6*(2), 49.

Srinidhi, B. N., He, S., & Firth, M. (2014). The Effect of Governance on Specialist Auditor Choice and Audit Fees in U.S. Family Firms. *The Accounting Review*, *89*(6), 2297–2329. doi:10.2308/accr-50840

Stacey, R. D. (2011). *Strategic management and organizational dynamics: The challenge of complexity*. FT Prentice-Hall.

Stanley, J. D. (2011). Is the Audit Fee Disclosure a Leading Indicator of Clients' Business Risk? *Auditing*, *30*(3), 157–179. doi:10.2308/ajpt-10049

Stearns, L. B., & Mizruchi, M. S. (1993). Board composition and corporate financing: The impact of financial institution representation on borrowing. *Academy of Management Journal*, *36*(3), 603-618.

Steel, T. (2017). *Towards a Sustainable Future. Integrated Report and Annual accounts 201-6-17, Tata Steel*. Retrieved from https://www.tatasteel.com/media/4852/csr-2016-17.pdf

Steels, T. (2004). *Corporate Sustainability Report (2003-04) Tata Steels*. Retrieved from https://www.tatasteel.com/files/csr-2003-04/management_sys/ms_07.htm

Stewart, G. B. (1991). *The Quest for Value: A Guide for Senior Managers*. Harper Business.

Stiftung für Familienunternehmen. (2014). *Informationsmaterial Familienunternehmen.* https://www.familienunternehmen.de/media/public/pdf/daten-zahlen-fakten/sfudaten-zahlen-fakten_de.pdf

Suess-Reyes, J. (2017). Understanding the transgenerational orientation of family businesses: The role of family governance and business family identity. *Journal of Business Economics*, *87*(6), 749–777. doi:10.100711573-016-0835-3

Suisse, C. (2012). *Gender diversity and corporate performance*. Retrieved from https://infocus.creditsuisse.com/data/_product_documents/_shop/360145/csri_gender_diversity_and_corporate_performance.pdf

Sulong, Z., & Nor, M. F. (2009). *The effective of corporate governance mechanisms in Malaysian listed firms: A panel data Analysis*. Paper presented at the meeting of 11th MFA 2009, Bayiew Breach Resort, Penang.

Sun, L. (2020). Why is Corporate Governance Important? BusinessDictionary. Retrieved 20 April 2020, from http://www.businessdictionary.com/article/618/why-is-corporate-governance-important/

Sun, J., & Liu, G. (2011). Client-specific litigation risk and audit quality differentiation. *Managerial Auditing Journal*, *26*(4), 300–316. doi:10.1108/02686901111124639

Suntheim, F., & Sironi, A. (2012). CEO Overconfidence in Banking. Working Paper. https://ssrn.com/abstract=2250344

Susanto, Y. K., Pradipta, A., & Djashan, I. A. (2017). Free cash flow and earnings management: board of commissioner, board independence and audit quality. *Corporate Ownership and Control, 14*(4-1), 284-288.

Susanto, Y. K., & Pradipta, A. (2016). Corporate governance and real earnings management. *International Journal of Business. Economics and Law*, *9*(1), 17–23.

Tabachnick, B. G., & Fidell, L. S. (2001). *Using Multivariate Statistics*. Allyn and Bacon.

Tang, J., Crossan, M., & Rowe, W. G. (2011). Dominant CEO, deviant strategy, and extreme performance: The moderating role of a powerful board. *Journal of Management Studies*, *48*(7), 1479–1503. doi:10.1111/j.1467-6486.2010.00985.x

Tang, Y., Mack, D. Z., & Chen, G. (2018). The differential effects of CEO narcissism and hubris on corporate social responsibility. *Strategic Management Journal*, *39*(5), 1370–1387. doi:10.1002/smj.2761

Terjesen, S., & Singh, V. (2008). Female presence on corporate boards: A multi-country study of environmental context. *Journal of Business Ethics*, *83*(1), 55–63. doi:10.100710551-007-9656-1

Tharawat Magazine. (2014). *The Economic Impact of Family Business*. Author.

Tirdasari, N., & Dhewanto, W. (2012). Family business succession in Indonesia: A study of hospitality industry. *Social and Behavioral Sciences*, *57*, 69–74. doi:10.1016/j.sbspro.2012.09.1159

Torchia, M., Calabrò, A., & Huse, M. (2011). Women directors on corporate boards: From tokenism to critical mass. *Journal of Business Ethics*, *102*(2), 299–317. doi:10.100710551-011-0815-z

Tosi, H. L. Jr. (2008). Quo Vadis? Suggestions for future corporate governance research. *The Journal of Management and Governance*, *12*(2), 153–169. doi:10.1007/s10997-008-9054-9

Ulrich, D., & Barney, J. B. (1984). Perspectives in organizations: Resource dependence, efficiency, and population. *Academy of Management Review*, *9*(3), 471–481. doi:10.5465/amr.1984.4279680

University of Vermont. (2014). *Family Business Facts*. Available on line at: https:// www.uvm.edu/business/vfbi/?Page=facts.html

Useem, M. (1984). *The inner circle: Large corporations and the rise of business political activity in the U.S. and U.K.* New York: Oxford University Press.

Vafeas, N. (2000). On audit committee appointments. *Auditing: A Journal of Practice & Theory*, 197-207.

Vafeas, N. (2000). Board structure and the informativeness of earnings. *Journal of Accounting and Public Policy*, *19*(2), 139–160. doi:10.1016/S0278-4254(00)00006-5

Van den Berghe, L. A. A., & Baelden, T. (2005). The complex relation between director independence and board effectiveness. *Corporate Governance: The International Journal of Business in Society*.

Van Ees, H., Gabrielsson, J., & Huse, M. (2009). Toward a behavioral theory of boards and corporate governance. *Corporate Governance*, *17*(3), 307–319. doi:10.1111/j.1467-8683.2009.00741.x

van Essen, M., Van Oosterhout, J., & Heugens, P. P. (2013). Competition and cooperation in corporate governance: The effects of labor institutions on blockholder effectiveness in 23 European countries. *Organization Science*, *24*(2), 530–551. doi:10.1287/orsc.1120.0742

Van Knippenberg, D., De Dreu, C., & Homan, A. (2004). Work diversity and group performance: An Integrated model and research agenda. *The Journal of Applied Psychology*, *89*(6), 1008–1022. doi:10.1037/0021-9010.89.6.1008 PMID:15584838

Van Ness, R. K., Miesing, P., & Kang, J. (2009). Understanding governance and corporate boards: Is theory a problem. *European Journal of Management*, *7*(9), 186–199.

Vance, S. C. (1983). *Corporate leadership: Boards, directors, and strategy*. McGraw-Hill Book Co.

Venter, E., & Farrington, S. (2009). *The nature of family businesses and their importance for economic development*. Nelson Mandela Metropolitan University.

Vilanova, L. (2017). Does CEO Overconfidence Always Hurt Organizational Performance? A Social and Deception-Based Theory [Paper presentation]. *XXVIe Conference Internationale de Management Strategique*, Lyon.

Vincent, O., & Peter, O. (2011). Effects of selected corporate governance characteristics on firm performance: Empirical evidence from Kenya. *International Journal of Economics and Finance Issues*, *1*(3), 99–122.

Voser, P. (2012). *Sustainability Report 2012*. Retrieved from https://reports.shell.com/sustainability-report/2012/servicepages/welcome.html

Waddock, S. A., & Graves, S. B. (1997). The corporate social performance-financial performance link. *Strategic Management Journal*, *18*(4), 303–319. doi:10.1002/(SICI)1097-0266(199704)18:4<303::AID-SMJ869>3.0.CO;2-G

Wahab, E. A. A., Zain, M. M., & James, K. (2011). Political connections, corporate governance and audit fees in Malaysia. *Managerial Auditing Journal*, *26*(5), 393–418. doi:10.1108/02686901111129562

Wall Street Journal. (1986, Mar. 24). The board game: More women are becoming directors but it's still a token situation. *Wall Street Journal*, p. 29D.

Wallison, P. J. (2006). All the Rage: Will Independent Directors Produce Good. *Corporate Governance*.

Walsh, J. P., & Seward, J. K. (1990). On the efficiency of internal and external corporate control mechanisms. *Academy of Management Review*, *15*(3), 421–458. doi:10.5465/amr.1990.4308826

Walton, C. C. (1967). *Corporate social responsibilities*. Wadsworth.

Wang, J., Qin, S., & Cui, Y. (2010). Problems and Prospects of CSR System Development in China. *International Journal of Business and Management*, *5*(12), 128–134. doi:10.5539/ijbm.v5n12p128

Wang, Y. J., Tsai, Y. H., & Lin, C. P. (2013). Modeling the relationship between perceived corporate citizenship and organizational commitment considering organizational trust as a moderator. *Business Ethics (Oxford, England)*, *22*(2), 218–233. doi:10.1111/beer.12019

Wan-Jan, W. S. (2006). Defining Corporate Social Responsibility. *Journal of Public Affairs. Journal of Public Affairs*, *6*(3-4), 176–184. doi:10.1002/pa.227

Wartick, S. L., & Cochran, P. L. (1985). The evolution of the corporate social performance mode. *Academy of Management Review*, *10*(4), 758–769. doi:10.5465/amr.1985.4279099

Watson, J. (2002). Comparing the performance of Male and female controlled businesses: Relating outputs to inputs. *Entrepreneurship Theory and Practice*, *26*(3), 91–100. doi:10.1177/104225870202600306

Watts, R. L. (2003a). Conservatism in accounting part I: Explanations and Implications. *Accounting Horizons*, *17*(3), 207–221. doi:10.2308/acch.2003.17.3.207

Watts, R. L. (2003b). Conservatism in accounting part II: Evidence and Research Opportunities. *Accounting Horizons*, *17*(4), 287–301. doi:10.2308/acch.2003.17.4.287

Watts, R. L., & Zimmerman, J. L. (1983). Agency problems, auditing, and the theory of the firm: Some evidence. *The Journal of Law & Economics*, *26*(3), 613–633. doi:10.1086/467051

Watts, R. L., & Zimmerman, J. L. (1986). *Positive Accounting Theory*. Prentice-Hall Englewood Cliffs.

Wayne, C. D., Joseph, L. P., Joseph, R. S., Richard, D. T., Reich, T., Michael, V., & Marcus, E. R. (1997). Subgedual prefrontal cortex abnormalities in mood disorders. *Letters to Nature*, *386*(6627), 824–827. doi:10.1038/386824a0

WCED. (1987). *Our Common Future, World Commission on Environment and Development.* Oxford University Press.

WCED. (1987). *Report of the World Commission on Environment and Development: Our Common Future*. Retrieved from http://www.un-documents.net/wced-ocf.htm

Weber, J., Willenborg, M., & Zhang, J. (2008). Does auditor reputation matter? The case of KPMG Germany and ComROAD AG. *Journal of Accounting Research*, *46*(4), 941–972. doi:10.1111/j.1475-679X.2008.00298.x

Wei, X. (2007). Wage Compensation for job-related illness: Evidence from a matched employer and employee survey in the UK. *Journal of Risk and Uncertainty*, *34*(1), 85–99. doi:10.100711166-006-9000-7

Westphal, J., & Khanna, P. (2003). Keeping Directors in Line: Social Distancing as a Control Mechanism in the Corporate Elite. *Administrative Science Quarterly*, *48*(3), 361–398. doi:10.2307/3556678

Whisenant, S., Sankaraguruswamy, S., & Raghunandan, K. (2003). Evidence on the Joint Determination of Audit and Non-Audit Fees. *Journal of Accounting Research*, *41*(4), 721–744. doi:10.1111/1475-679X.00121

Wiersema, M., & Bantel, K. (1992). Top management team demography and corporate strategic change. *Academy of Management Journal*, *35*(1), 91–121.

Wilson, D., & Purushothaman, R. (2003). *Dreaming with BRICs: The path to 2050*. Goldman Sachs Global Economics Paper, 99.

Wilson, R. (2016). Does governance cause growth? Evidence from China. *World Development*, *79*, 138–151. doi:10.1016/j.worlddev.2015.11.015

Wistawan, M. A. P., Subroto, B., & Ghofar, A. (2015). The Characteristics Board of Directors, Family Ownership and Accounting Conservatism: Evidence from Family Public Firms in Indonesia. *Research Journal of Finance and Accounting*, *6*(22), 113–121. doi:10.21512/bbr.v9i3.4311

Wood, D. J. (1991). Corporate social performance revisited. *Academy of Management Review*, *16*(4), 691–718. doi:10.5465/amr.1991.4279616

Wood, D. J., & Logsdon, J. M. (2002, July). A Global Business Citizenship Process Model. In *Proceedings of the International Association for Business and Society* (Vol. 13, pp. 181-186). 10.5840/iabsproc20021325

World Bank. (2018). *World Development Indicators*. Retrieved from https://databank.worldbank.org/source/world-development-indicators

World Business Council for Sustainable Development (WBCSD). (2002). *Corporate Social Responsibility: The WBCSD's journey*. http://www.wbcsd.ch/

World Business Council for Sustainable Development. (1998). *Meeting Changing Expectations*. Corporate. www.wbcsd.org/work-program/business-role/previous-work/corporate-social-responsibility.aspx

Worthington, A. C., & West, T. (2001). Economic value-added: A review of the theoretical and empirical literature. *Asian Review of Accounting*, *9*(1), 67–86. doi:10.1108/eb060736

Wray, T. (2016). The role of leader hubris in the decline of RBS and Lehman Brothers. In G. Robinson & P. Garrard (Eds.), *The Intoxication of Power* (pp. 229–251). Palgrave Macmillan.

Wright, P., Kroll, M., & Elenkov, D. (2002). Acquisition Returns, Increase in Firm Size, and Chief Executive Officer Compensation: The Moderating Role of Monitoring. *Academy of Management Journal*, *45*(3), 599–608.

Wright, P., Kroll, M., Lado, A., & Van Ness, B. (2002). The Structure of Ownership and Corporate Acquisition Strategies. *Strategic Management Journal*, *23*(1), 41–53. doi:10.1002mj.208

Wu, C. -H., Wu, C., & Liu, V. W. (2008). The release timing of annual reports and board characteristics. *The International Journal of Business of Finance Research, 2*(1).

Wu, X. (2012). Corporate governance and audit fees: Evidence from companies listed on the Shanghai Stock Exchange. *China Journal of Accounting Research*, *5*(4), 321–342. doi:10.1016/j.cjar.2012.10.001

Yamahaki, C., & Frynas, J. G. (2016). Institutional determinants of private shareholder engagement in Brazil and South Africa: The role of regulation. *Corporate Governance*, *24*(5), 509–527. doi:10.1111/corg.12166

Yasser, Q. R. (2012). Affects of female directors on firms performance in Pakistan. *Modern Economy*, *3*(07), 817–825. doi:10.4236/me.2012.37104

Yermack, D. (1996). Higher market valuation of companies with a small board of directors. *Journal of Financial Economics*, *40*(2), 185–211. doi:10.1016/0304-405X(95)00844-5

Young, D. (1997). Economic value added: A primer for European managers. *European Management Journal*, *15*(4), 335–343. doi:10.1016/S0263-2373(97)00014-5

Yu, M., & Zhao, R. (2015). Sustainability and firm valuation: An international investigation. *International Journal of Accounting and Information Management*, *23*(3), 289–307. doi:10.1108/IJAIM-07-2014-0050

Yunos, R. M. (2011). *The effect of ownership concentration, board of directors, audit committee and ethnicity on conservative accounting: Malaysian evidence* (Doctoral thesis). School of Accounting, Finance and Economics Faculty of Business and Law, Australia.

Yusoff, W. F. W., & Alhaji, I. A. (2012). Insight of corporate governance theories. *Journal of Business and Management*, *1*(1), 52–63.

Zadek, S. (2001). The Civil Corporation: The new economy of corporate citizenship. *Earthscan, London, 2001*, 7.

Zahid, M., & Ghazali, Z. (2017). Corporate Sustainability Practices and Firm's Financial Performance: The Driving Force of Integrated Management System. *Global Business and Management Research*, 9.

Zajac, E. J., & Westphal, J. D. (1996). Director Reputation, CEO–Board Power, and the Dynamics of Board Interlocks. *Administrative Science Quarterly*, *41*(3), 507–529. doi:10.2307/2393940

Zajac, E., & Westphal, J. (1996). Director Reputation, CEO-Board Power, and the Dynamics of Board Interlocks. *Administrative Science Quarterly*, *41*(3), 507–529.

Zalata, A. M., Tauringana, V., & Tingbani, I. (2018). Audit committee financial expertise, gender, and earnings management: Does gender of the financial expert matter? *International Review of Financial Analysis*, *55*, 170–183. doi:10.1016/j.irfa.2017.11.002

Zald, M. N. (1969, July). The Power and Functions of Boards of Directors: A Theoretical Synthesis. *American Journal of Sociology*, *75*(1), 97–111. doi:10.1086/224747

Zapatero, M., Rodriguez, J. M., & Rodriguez Alcaide, J. (2012). El consejero en la empresa familiar: Teoria y praxis. *Revista de Empresa Familiar*, *2*(1), 45–54.

Zerban, A. M., Abdullah, M., & Abdullateef, M. (2017). Corporate Governance and Board of Directors Responsibilities: The Case of Saudi Arabia. *International Journal of Accounting Research.*, *5*(2), 1–5. doi:10.4172/2472-114X.1000171

Zhu, D. H., & Chen, G. (2015). CEO narcissism and the impact of prior board experience on corporate strategy. *Administrative Science Quarterly*, *60*(1), 31–65. doi:10.1177/0001839214554989

Zinkin, J. (2010). Independent directors must learn to ask CEOs the right questions. *The Star*.

About the Contributors

Qaiser Rafique Yasser has experience of more than 16 years working Pakistan and abroad with corporate sector, educational institutions and Government departments. Five book publications and 41 research papers in international renowned journals are under his name. He is an expert in corporate governance and corporate social responsibility. He holds a PhD (Financial Economics) degree from University Malaysia Sarawak (UNIMAS), Malaysia.

Abdullah Al-Mamun is a lecturer in the School of Accounting, Economics and Finance at the University of Wollongong, Australia. His research interests are corporate governance, corporate social responsibility, firm performance and emerging economies. Al-Mamun has completed his doctoral research degree from the University of Newcastle, Australia in 2018.

* * *

Reena Agrawal is an academician, consultant, researcher, and trainer with more than twenty years of experience in the field accounting and finance. She has contributed forty plus research articles in reputed refereed and Scopus indexed journals. Her academic research interests include: accounting, sustainability, design thinking, corporate social responsibility, entrepreneurship, financial inclusion and family businesses. She has conducted several training sessions for industry which include: 'Profitability Improvement Using Design Thinking Approach' for Indian Oil Corporation Limited; 'Analysis of Financial Statements' for Power Grid Corporation of India Limited; 'Financial and Cost Accounting' for the Board of Directors of Swayam Ksheer Producer Company Ltd, India; 'Entrepreneurship Opportunities' for Government Poly Techniques (India); 'Social Entrepreneurship' for Villgro a Social Entrepreneurship Incubator -Indian Institute of Technology Madras; 'Entrepreneurship & Design Thinking' for The Indus Entrepreneurs (TiE) Global; 'Hackathon on Road Safety' for Transport Department, Government of Uttar Pradesh (India); 'Improving Work Efficiency Using Design Thinking' for non-teaching staff of Jaipuria Schools (India); ' Financial Management' for National Thermal Power Corporation (India).

Sinem Ates has a PhD degree in Business Administration from Galatasaray University. She has been teaching accounting courses such as Introduction to Accounting, Financial Accounting, New Concepts in Accounting and Finance. Her main research interests include sustainability accounting, IFRS, value relevance, and accounting education.

Ganga Bhavani, Academician from last 17 years, which includes 11 years in UAE. She owns Ph.D. in commerce, CIMA & CGMA from U.K. and Forensic Accounting from Brentwood University, U.K. She has hands-on experience in organizing and conducting international conferences and workshops. She is an author for more than 15 publications including Scopus and ABDC journals and reviewer for many reputed journals. She is an active member in many international organization such as AAA, AOM, AIB, BAFA, EAA and CAAA. Her passion for research sprawls in the fields of Financial Accounting, Auditing and Forensic Accounting and Fraud Examination, Finance and General Management.

Ashok Chopra is a highly skilled, accomplished and experienced Senior Academician in Teaching, and Training & Development, with strong learning acumen. Demonstrated research success with multiple published articles; Expert in creating effective environments for applied learning which accommodates students'/trainees' diverse cultural and educational backgrounds, experiences, and individual learning styles. Have more than 24 years of international industry experience at senior and leadership positions; Entrepreneurial experience of more than 10 years and more than 10 years of experience in as academician and corporate trainer. A perfect blend of academia, industry and entrepreneurship. He has published two books, no. of book chapters, More than forty five papers in internal journal of repute, is on the editorial and advisory board of reputed journals, conferences and institutions. He has a PhD, MBA, Certified 6 Sigma Manager (Black Belt) Post Graduate in Business, Administrative, and Marketing & Sales Management, Chartered Fellow CILT UK & Full Member CIPS UK. Served as a consultant at FIAT/NAFLA (International Federation of Freight Forwarders Associations), Switzerland from Jan. 2014 to Dec. 2015. Currently Associate Professor (School of Management and Commerce0 and Program Leader PhD and MBA (Full Time & Working Professional) at Amity University Dubai. Have conducted more than Two Hundred Seventy Corporate Training Programs through an entrepreneurial venture – Provided Management Consultancy, to number of organizations, which are not started and managed by people having management qualification/background. His core skills as academician include ensuring program and course curricula are current, relevant and reflective of best practices within a professional/program discipline. Further defining, evaluating, and validating learning outcomes for courses and programs. Creating learning environments that accommodate students' diversity in cultures, education, experiences, and learning styles. Designing appropriate strategies and methods for facilitating and assessing student learning that are invitational and reflective of best practices in teaching. Developing methods to assess student performance consistent with the learning outcomes of the course, and metrics that address multiple learning styles. Producing multi-media materials, alternative delivery strategies, and incorporating a variety of educational technologies into the learning process. Communicating and ensuring that students are aware of course and program learning outcomes, learning strategies and evaluation techniques; providing individual tutoring and academic counselling as per student needs. He has won One Gold, Three Silver Medals and Two Cash Prizes for Topping among Twenty Six Centers in India in Post - Graduation in Business Management and Marketing & Sales Management.

Paola Ferretti, PhD, is Associate Professor of Financial Markets and Institutions at the Department of Economics and Management, University of Pisa, Italy, where she teaches "Risk management in financial institutions" and "Corporate and investment banking". She is also Director of the Master's Degree in "Consulting for business" at the Department of Economics and Management. Her main research interests are Basel III, risk management, corporate governance, and reputation management in banks.

Cristina Gonnella is a PhD student in Business Administration and Management, University of Pisa.

Satish R. Menon is a management professional with over twenty four years of industry experience, across diverse industry verticals. His various assignments has seen him in leadership positions with experience of managing many aspects of the human resources and management portfolios, ranging from Human Capital Management to Strategic Management. As an individual, he is someone who strongly believes in collaborative efforts to achieve organizational objectives. His ability to connect people and strategy has contributed towards building long term lasting relationships. In this context, Innovation has been close to his heart and have always looked at "what's next" and driven this thought process across teams that he has handled and respective executive management. In line with his academic pursuits, being a PH.D scholar, he is currently with Amity University, Dubai as an Assistant professor and Program Leader for BBA Specialization programs.

Thokozani Ian Nzimakwe is a senior lecturer in the School of Management, IT and Governance at the University of KwaZulu-Natal, South Africa. His research interests include governance, electronic governance and ICT applications in public sector settings.

Aarooj Kiran is a Visiting Lecturer at international Islamic University Islamabad. Principal at Dar.e.Arqam School Islamabad.

Sorbarikor Lebura holds a PhD in Strategic Management from De Montfort University, Leicester in the UK. He is currently a Lecturer at the Rivers State University, Port Harcourt, Nigeria where he teaches strategy, business policy and entrepreneurship at both the undergraduate and postgraduate levels. He has over 20 journal articles in local and foreign journals as well as book chapters on various topics in his areas of interests. His areas of interests are Business Policy, Strategy, Corporate Social Responsibility (CSR), Entrepreneurship and Qualitative Research Methods.

Igazeuma Adikema Okoroba is a Social Development Practitioner with over 16 years work experience in public, private sectors and civil society. Her research interests are corporate social responsibility, rural sustainability, gender and media for development. She looks forward to an enriching academic research experience that contributes to building African societies.

Index

D

E

F

G

H

I

L

O

P

R

S

V

W

Recommended Reference Books

IGI Global's reference books can now be purchased from three unique pricing formats:
Print Only, E-Book Only, or Print + E-Book.
Shipping fees may apply.

www.igi-global.com

ISBN: 978-1-7998-1048-3
EISBN: 978-1-7998-1049-0
© 2020; 605 pp.
List Price: US$ 285

ISBN: 978-1-5225-8933-4
EISBN: 978-1-5225-8934-1
© 2020; 667 pp.
List Price: US$ 295

ISBN: 978-1-7998-0357-7
EISBN: 978-1-7998-0359-1
© 2020; 451 pp.
List Price: US$ 235

ISBN: 978-1-7998-0070-5
EISBN: 978-1-7998-0071-2
© 2020; 144 pp.
List Price: US$ 175

ISBN: 978-1-5225-6980-0
EISBN: 978-1-5225-6981-7
© 2019; 339 pp.
List Price: US$ 235

ISBN: 978-1-5225-5390-8
EISBN: 978-1-5225-5391-5
© 2018; 125 pp.
List Price: US$ 165

Do you want to stay current on the latest research trends, product announcements, news, and special offers?
Join IGI Global's mailing list to receive customized recommendations, exclusive discounts, and more.
Sign up at: **www.igi-global.com/newsletters.**

Publisher of Peer-Reviewed, Timely, and Innovative Academic Research

IGI Global
PUBLISHER of TIMELY KNOWLEDGE

www.igi-global.com Sign up at www.igi-global.com/newsletters facebook.com/igiglobal twitter.com/igiglobal

Ensure Quality Research is Introduced to the Academic Community

Become an Evaluator for IGI Global Authored Book Projects

The overall success of an authored book project is dependent on quality and timely manuscript evaluations.

Applications and Inquiries may be sent to:
development@igi-global.com

Applicants must have a doctorate (or equivalent degree) as well as publishing, research, and reviewing experience. Authored Book Evaluators are appointed for one-year terms and are expected to complete at least three evaluations per term. Upon successful completion of this term, evaluators can be considered for an additional term.

If you have a colleague that may be interested in this opportunity, we encourage you to share this information with them.

IGI Global Author Services

Providing a high-quality, affordable, and expeditious service, IGI Global's Author Services enable authors to streamline their publishing process, increase chance of acceptance, and adhere to IGI Global's publication standards.

Benefits of Author Services:

- **Professional Service:** All our editors, designers, and translators are experts in their field with years of experience and professional certifications.
- **Quality Guarantee & Certificate:** Each order is returned with a quality guarantee and certificate of professional completion.
- **Timeliness:** All editorial orders have a guaranteed return timeframe of 3-5 business days and translation orders are guaranteed in 7-10 business days.
- **Affordable Pricing:** IGI Global Author Services are competitively priced compared to other industry service providers.
- **APC Reimbursement:** IGI Global authors publishing Open Access (OA) will be able to deduct the cost of editing and other IGI Global author services from their OA APC publishing fee.

Author Services Offered:

English Language Copy Editing
Professional, native English language copy editors improve your manuscript's grammar, spelling, punctuation, terminology, semantics, consistency, flow, formatting, and more.

Scientific & Scholarly Editing
A Ph.D. level review for qualities such as originality and significance, interest to researchers, level of methodology and analysis, coverage of literature, organization, quality of writing, and strengths and weaknesses.

Figure, Table, Chart & Equation Conversions
Work with IGI Global's graphic designers before submission to enhance and design all figures and charts to IGI Global's specific standards for clarity.

Translation
Providing 70 language options, including Simplified and Traditional Chinese, Spanish, Arabic, German, French, and more.

Hear What the Experts Are Saying About IGI Global's Author Services

*"Publishing with IGI Global has been **an amazing experience** for me for sharing my research. The **strong academic production** support ensures quality and timely completion."* – **Prof. Margaret Niess, Oregon State University, USA**

*"The service was **very fast, very thorough, and very helpful** in ensuring our chapter meets the criteria and requirements of the book's editors. I was **quite impressed and happy** with your service."* – **Prof. Tom Brinthaupt, Middle Tennessee State University, USA**

Learn More or Get Started Here:

For Questions, Contact IGI Global's Customer Service Team at cust@igi-global.com or 717-533-8845

IGI Global
PUBLISHER of TIMELY KNOWLEDGE
www.igi-global.com

IGI Global
PUBLISHER of TIMELY KNOWLEDGE
www.igi-global.com

Celebrating Over 30 Years of Scholarly Knowledge Creation & Dissemination

InfoSci®-Books

A Database of Nearly 6,000 Reference Books Containing Over 105,000+ Chapters Focusing on Emerging Research

InfoSci®-Books Database

The **InfoSci®-Books** is a database of nearly 6,000 IGI Global single and multi-volume reference books, handbooks of research, and encyclopedias, encompassing groundbreaking research from prominent experts worldwide that spans over 350+ topics in 11 core subject areas including business, computer science, education, science and engineering, social sciences, and more.

Open Access Fee Waiver (Read & Publish) Initiative

For any library that invests in IGI Global's InfoSci-Books and/or InfoSci-Journals (175+ scholarly journals) databases, IGI Global will match the library's investment with a fund of equal value to go toward **subsidizing the OA article processing charges (APCs) for their students, faculty, and staff** at that institution when their work is submitted and accepted under OA into an IGI Global journal.*

INFOSCI® PLATFORM FEATURES

- Unlimited Simultaneous Access
- No DRM
- No Set-Up or Maintenance Fees
- A Guarantee of No More Than a 5% Annual Increase for Subscriptions
- Full-Text HTML and PDF Viewing Options
- Downloadable MARC Records
- COUNTER 5 Compliant Reports
- Formatted Citations With Ability to Export to RefWorks and EasyBib
- No Embargo of Content (Research is Available Months in Advance of the Print Release)

**The fund will be offered on an annual basis and expire at the end of the subscription period. The fund would renew as the subscription is renewed for each year thereafter. The open access fees will be waived after the student, faculty, or staff's paper has been vetted and accepted into an IGI Global journal and the fund can only be used toward publishing OA in an IGI Global journal. Libraries in developing countries will have the match on their investment doubled.*

To Recommend or Request a Free Trial:
www.igi-global.com/infosci-books
eresources@igi-global.com • Toll Free: 1-866-342-6657 ext. 100 • Phone: 717-533-8845 x100

IGI Global
PUBLISHER of TIMELY KNOWLEDGE
www.igi-global.com

www.ingramcontent.com/pod-product-compliance
Lightning Source LLC
LaVergne TN
LVHW080558300926
849162LV00005B/990